p_0	Standard or reference value, central line	$\bar{s}$	Average sample standard deviation
$\bar{p}$	Average proportion or fraction nonconforming	U	Upper specification limit
		UCL	Upper control limit
		URL	Upper reject limit
$100p$	Percent nonconforming	u	Count of nonconformities per unit
$p_{0.95}$, $p_{0.05}$	Lot or process quality related to OC curves	u_0	Standard or reference value, central line
R	Range	$\bar{u}$	Average of non-conformities per unit
R_0	Standard or reference value, central line		
$\bar{R}$	Average of ranges	w	Weight
Q_u, Q_L	Quality indexes for U and L in variables sampling plan	X_i	Observed value
		$\underline{X}(\mu)$	Sample average or average (population mean)
q	Proportion or fraction conforming $(1 - p)$	$\bar{X}_0$	Standard or reference value, central line
SkSP	Skip-lot sampling plan	$\bar{\bar{X}}$	Average of averages or grand average
$s(\sigma)$	Sample standard deviation (population)	Z	Standardized normal value
$s^2(\sigma^2)$	Sample variance (population)	α	Producer's risk, Type I error
s_0	Standard or reference value, central line	β	Consumer's risk, Type II error
s_R	Sample standard deviation of ranges	λ	Failure rate
s_p	Sample standard deviation of proportions	μ	See $\bar{X}$
		Σ	"Sum of"
		σ	See s
$s_{\bar{x}}$	Sample standard deviation of averages	θ	Mean time to failure

THIRD EDITION

QUALITY CONTROL

DALE H. BESTERFIELD, PH.D., P.E.
Professor
Department of Technology
College of Engineering and Technology
Southern Illinois University

PRENTICE HALL
Englewood Cliffs, New Jersey 07632

Library of Congress Cataloging-in-Publication Data

Besterfield, Dale H.
    Quality control / Dale H. Besterfield. —3rd ed.
        p.   cm.
    Includes bibliographical references.
    ISBN 0-13-745100-8
    1. Quality control.   I. Title.
TS156.B   1990
658.5′62—dc20   89-26617
                                                  CIP

Editorial/production supervision: Cyndy Lyle Rymer
Cover design: Bruce Kenselaar
Cover Art: Slide Graphics of New England
Manufacturing buyer: Gina Chirco Brennan

 © 1990, 1986, 1976 by Prentice-Hall, Inc.
A Division of Simon & Schuster
Englewood Cliffs, New Jersey 07632

Printed in the United States of America
10   9   8   7   6   5   4

ISBN 0-13-745100-8

Prentice-Hall International (UK) Limited, *London*
Printice-Hall of Australia Pty. Limited, *Sydney*
Prentice-Hall Canada Inc., *Toronto*
Prentice-Hall Hispanoamericana, S.A., *Mexico*
Prentice-Hall of India Private Limited, *New Delhi*
Prentice-Hall of Japan, Inc., *Tokyo*
Simon & Schuster Asia Pte. Ltd., *Singapore*
Editora Prentice-Hall do Brasil, Ltda., *Rio de Janeiro*

CONTENTS

iii

13 QUALITY-IMPROVEMENT MANAGEMENT 405

APPENDIX 419

SELECTED BIBLIOGRAPHY 430

ANSWERS TO SELECTED PROBLEMS 432

INDEX 439

PREFACE

This book provides a fundamental, yet comprehensive, coverage of quality control concepts. A practical state-of-the-art approach is stressed throughout. Sufficient theory is presented to ensure that the reader has a sound understanding of the basic principles of quality control. The use of probability and statistical techniques is reduced to simple mathematics or is developed in the form of tables and charts.

The book has served the instructional needs of technology students in technical institutes, community colleges, and universities. It has also been used by undergraduate and graduate business students. Professional organizations and industrial corporations have found the book an excellent training manual for instruction of manufacturing, quality, inspection, marketing, purchasing, and product design personnel.

The book begins with an introductory chapter about quality responsibility. This is followed by a detailed description of the control chart method for variables and attributes. A subsequent group of chapters describes acceptance sampling and standard sampling plans. The final chapters cover the topics of reliability, quality costs, product liability, computer utilization, quality-improvement techniques, and quality-improvement management.

This third edition includes a complete updating of all material and an expanded treatment of topics.

More example problems and additional practical problems have been added. Throughout the book, the words defect and defective have been replaced by nonconformity and nonconforming unit.

The chapter on quality cost has been rewritten to include the latest information and provide a vehicle for quality improvement. Acceptance sampling has been revised to conform to the latest standards. Also, a section on the new skip-lot sampling plan has been added.

Two new chapters on quality improvement techniques and quality improvement management have been added. The chapter on quality improvement techniques has material on Pareto diagram, matrix analysis, Grier diagram, cause-and-effect diagram, check sheets, precontrol, scatter diagram, and flowchart.

I am indebted to the publishers and authors who have given permission to reproduce their charts, graphs, and tables. Professors, practitioners, and students throughout the world have been most helpful in pointing out the need for further clarification and additional material in the second edition. Finally, I am indebted to Mrs. Gayle George, who typed the two new chapters and retyped two of the original chapters.

Dale H. Besterfield

1

INTRODUCTION TO QUALITY

INTRODUCTION

Definitions

When the expression "quality" is used, we usually think in terms of an excellent product or service that fulfills or exceeds our expectations. These expectations are based on the intended use and the selling price. For example, a customer expects a different performance from a plain steel washer than from a chrome-plated steel washer because they are a different grade. When a product or service surpasses our expectations we consider that quality. Thus, it is somewhat of an intangible based on perception.

According to ANSI/ASQC Standard A3–1987, *quality* is the totality of features and characteristics of a product or service that bear on its ability to satisfy implied or stated needs. Stated needs are determined by the contract, whereas implied needs are a function of the market and must be identified and defined. These needs

1

involve safety, availability, maintainability, reliability, usability, economics (price), and environment. Price is easily defined by some monetary unit such as dollars. The other needs are defined by translating the features and characteristics for the manufacture of a product or the delivery of a service into specifications. Conformance of the product or service to these specifications is measurable and provides a quantifiable and operational definition of quality. If the specifications do not satisfy the customer needs (fitness for use), they should be changed. Needs usually change over time, thereby requiring a periodic reevaluation of specifications.

Quality control is the use of techniques and activities to achieve, sustain, and improve the quality of a product or service. It involves integrating the following related techniques and activities:

1. *Specifications* of what is needed
2. *Design* of the product or service to meet the specifications
3. *Production* or *installation* to meet the full intent of the specifications
4. *Inspection* to determine conformance to specifications
5. *Review of usage* to provide information for the revision of specifications if needed

Utilization of these activities provides the customer with the best product or service at the lowest cost. The aim should be continued quality improvement.

Statistical quality control (SQC) is a branch of quality control. It is the collection, analysis, and interpretation of data for use in quality control activities. While much of this book emphasizes the statistical approach to quality control, this is only a part of the total picture. Statistical process control (SPC) and acceptance sampling are the two major parts of SQC. A number of different techniques are needed.

All the planned or systematic actions necessary to provide adequate confidence that a product or service will satisfy given requirements for quality is called *quality assurance*. It involves making sure that quality is what it should be. This includes a continuing evaluation of adequacy and effectiveness with a view to having timely corrective measures and feedback initiated where necessary.

There is a distinct difference between quality control and quality assurance. Quality control is involved with the activities of specification, design, production or installation, inspection, and review of usage. These activities are the responsibility of the functional areas shown in Figure 1-1. Quality assurance is involved with these activities as well as the entire quality system. The generic elements of a quality system are given later in the chapter.

Historical Review

The history of quality control is undoubtedly as old as industry itself. During the Middle Ages the maintenance of quality was to a large extent controlled by the long periods of training required by the guilds. This training instilled in workers pride for quality of a product.

The concept of specialization of labor was introduced during the Industrial

Revolution. As a result, a worker no longer made the entire product, only a portion. This change brought about a decline in workmanship. Because most products manufactured during that early period were not complicated, quality was not greatly affected. As products became more complicated and jobs more specialized, it became necessary to inspect products after manufacture.

In 1924, W. A. Shewhart of Bell Telephone Laboratories developed a statistical chart for the control of product variables. This is considered to be the beginning of statistical quality control. Later in the same decade, H. F. Dodge and H. G. Romig, both of Bell Telephone Laboratories, developed the area of acceptance sampling as a substitute for 100% inspection. Recognition of the value of statistical quality control became apparent by 1942. Unfortunately, American managers failed to recognize its value.

In 1946, the American Society for Quality Control was formed. This organization, through its publications, conferences, and training sessions, has promoted the use of quality control for all types of production and service.

In 1950, W. Edwards Deming gave a series of lectures on statistical methods to Japanese engineers and on quality responsibility to top management. Joseph M. Juran made his first trip to Japan in 1954 and further emphasized management's responsibility to achieve quality. Using these concepts the Japanese set the quality standards for the rest of the world to follow.

In 1960 the first quality control circles were formed for the purpose of quality improvement. Simple statistical techniques were learned and applied by Japanese workers.

By the late 1970s and early 1980s, U.S. managers were making frequent trips to Japan to learn about the Japanese miracle. These trips were really not necessary—they could have read the writings of Deming and Juran. Nevertheless, a quality renaissance began to occur in U.S. products and services.

One U.S. company, American Telephone and Telegraph, continued to utilize the statistical quality control concepts that were developed in their laboratory. It is the author's opinion that prior to divestiture the outstanding quality of the U.S. telephone and telephone service is the result of statistical quality control. These are the concepts emphasized in this book.

In the late 1980s the automotive industry began to emphasize SPC. Suppliers and their suppliers were required to use these techniques. Other industries and the Department of Defense also implemented SPC. In addition a new concept of continuous quality improvement (CQI) emerged, which required total quality management (TQM).

Metric System

In 1960, the International Committee of Weights and Measures revised the metric system. This revision is the International System of Units (SI),[1] which has the following base units:

---

[1] Copies may be purchased from the Superintendent of Documents, Government Printing Office, Washington, D.C. 20402. (Order by SD Catalog No. C13.10: 330/3.)

Length—meter (m)

Mass—kilogram (kg)

Time—second (s)

Electrical current—ampere (A)

Thermodynamic temperature—kelvin (K)

Amount of matter—mole (mol)

Luminous intensity—candela (cd)

This book uses the metric system of units with U.S. units given in parentheses. Commonly used conversion factors are given in Table E of the Appendix.

RESPONSIBILITY FOR QUALITY

Departments Responsible

Quality is not the responsibility of any one person or department; it is everyone's job. It includes the assembly-line worker, the typist, the purchasing agent, and the president of the company. The responsibility for quality begins when marketing determines the customer's quality requirements and continues until the product is received by a satisfied customer.

The responsibility for quality is delegated to the various departments with the authority to make quality decisions. In addition, a method of accountability, such as cost, error rate, or nonconforming units, is included with that responsibility and authority. The departments responsible for quality control are shown in Figure 1-1. They are: marketing, product engineering, purchasing, manufacturing engineering, manufacturing, inspection and test, packaging and shipping, and product service. Figure 1-1 is a closed loop with the customer at the top and the departments in the proper sequence in the loop. Since quality assurance does not have direct responsibility for quality, it is not included in the closed loop of the figure.

The information in this section pertains to a manufactured item; however, the concepts can be adapted to a service.

Marketing

Marketing helps to evaluate the level of product quality that the customer wants, needs, and is willing to pay for. In addition, marketing provides the product-quality data and helps to determine quality requirements.

A certain amount of marketing information is readily available to perform this function. Information concerning customer dissatisfaction is provided by customer complaints, sales representative reports, product service, and product liability cases. The comparison of sales volume with the economy as a whole is a good predictor of customer opinion of product quality. A detailed analysis of spare-part sales can locate potential quality problems. Useful market quality information is also provided by government reports on consumer product safety and independent laboratory reports on quality.

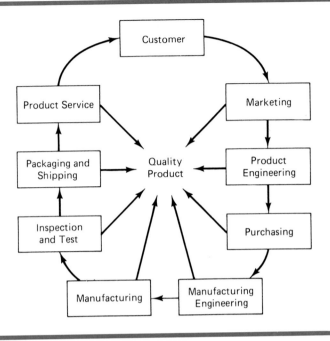

FIGURE 1-1 **Departments responsible for quality.**

When information is not readily available, there are four methods that can be developed to obtain the desired product quality data:

1. Visit or observe the customer to determine the conditions of product use and the problems of the user.
2. Establish a realistic testing laboratory such as an automotive test track.
3. Conduct a controlled market test.
4. Organize a dealer advisory or focus group.

Marketing evaluates all the data and determines the quality requirements for the product. An information-monitoring and feedback system on a continuing basis is essential to collect data in an effective manner.

Marketing provides the company with the product brief, which translates customer requirements into a preliminary set of specifications. Among the product brief elements are:

1. Performance characteristics, such as environmental, usage, and reliability considerations,
2. Sensory characteristics, such as style, color, taste, and smell,
3. Installation, configuration, or fit,
4. Applicable standards and statutory regulations,

5. Packaging, and

6. Quality verification.

Marketing is the liaison with the customer and as such is a vital link to the development of a product that surpasses customer expectations.

Product Engineering

Product engineering translates the customer's quality requirements into operating characteristics, exact specifications, and appropriate tolerances for a new product or revision of an established product. The simplest and least costly design that will meet the customer's requirements is the best design. As the complexity of the product increases, the quality and reliability decrease. Early involvement of marketing, manufacturing, quality, and purchasing are essential to prevent problems before they occur.

Whenever possible, product engineering should utilize proven designs and standard components. In this regard, industry and government standards are used when applicable.

Tolerance is the permissible variation in the size of the quality characteristic, and the selection of tolerances has a dual effect on quality. As tolerances are tightened, a better product results; however, the manufacturing and quality costs may increase. Ideally, tolerances should be determined scientifically by balancing the precision desired with the cost to achieve that precision. Since there are too many quality characteristics for scientific determination, many tolerances are set using standard dimensioning and tolerancing systems. Designed experiments are a very effective technique for determining which process and product characteristics are critical as well as their tolerances. Critical tolerances should be established in conjunction with the process capability.

The product designer determines the materials to be used in the product. Material quality is based on written specifications, which include physical characteristics, reliability, acceptance criteria, and packaging.

In addition to the functional aspect, a quality product is one that can be used safely. It is also one that can be repaired or maintained easily.

Design reviews are conducted at appropriate phases in the development of the product. These reviews should identify and anticipate problem areas and inadequacies, and initiate corrective action to ensure that the final design and supporting data meet customer requirements. After the design review team approves the product for manufacturing, the final quality requirements are distributed. Quality is designed into the product before it is released to manufacturing.

No design is perfect over time; therefore, provision must be made for design-change control. Also there should be a periodic reevaluation of the product in order to ensure that the design is still valid.

Purchasing

Using the quality requirements established by product engineering, purchasing has the responsibility of procuring quality materials and components. Purchases fall into four categories: standard materials, such as coiled steel and angle iron; standard hardware, such as fasteners and fittings; minor components, such as gears and diodes; and major components, which perform one of the primary functions of the product. The quality requirements will vary depending on the category of the purchase.

A particular raw material or component part may have a single vendor or multiple vendors. Single vendors as a source of supply are usually able to provide better quality at a lower price with better service. The concept of single vendor has been applied quite effectively in breweries, wherein the can or bottle manufacturer was located adjacent to the brewery. Multidivisional companies use the single-vendor technique and can control quality in a manner similar to the control between departments within a plant. The disadvantage of a single vendor is the potential for a material shortage that may result due to natural causes such as fire, earthquake, or flood or due to unnatural causes such as equipment breakdowns, labor problems, or financial difficulties.

To determine if a vendor is capable of supplying quality materials and components, a vendor quality survey is conducted by visiting the vendor's plant. The facilities are observed, the quality control procedures studied, and pertinent data collected. From this information a reasonable decision can be made regarding the ability of the vendor to provide quality materials and components. Once a vendor is a regular supplier, other techniques of evaluation are available.

There are a number of different methods used to obtain proof of conformance to quality standards. For small quantities, the purchasing department will frequently rely on the vendor. The inspection of incoming materials and components is one of the most common methods for proof of conformance. Source inspection is identical to incoming inspection except that the inspection is conducted in the vendor's plant. Statistical evidence of quality by means of process control, charts, and process capability is a very effective method. Proof of conformance can also be obtained by inspection of duplicate samples that are received by purchasing prior to the arrival of the shipment. Vendor surveillance is a method of controlling the quality in the vendor's plant by means of an acceptable plan, and proof, such as inspection records, that the plan is followed. Any combination of these methods can be used to achieve an effective and continuing evaluation of the product.

A vendor quality rating system can be used to evaluate performance. Factors such as rejected lots, scrap and rework costs, or complaint information are used for the evaluation. In addition, delivery performance and price are included.

To improve the quality of purchased materials and components, two-way communication between the vendor and purchasing is a necessity. Both positive and negative feedback should be given to the vendor.

Purchasing should be concerned with the total cost and not price. For example, vendor A has a lower price than vendor B; however, the cost to utilize vendor A's material is so much greater than vendor B's that the total cost is greater.

Manufacturing Engineering

Manufacturing engineering has the responsibility of developing processes and procedures that will produce a quality product. This responsibility is achieved by specific activities, which include process selection and development, production planning, and support activities.

A product design review is conducted in order to anticipate quality problems. Quality problems are frequently related to specifications. When process capability information indicates that a tolerance is too tight for satisfactory producibility, there are five options: purchase new equipment, revise the tolerance, improve the process, revise the design, or sort out the defective product during manufacturing.

Process selection and development is concerned with cost, quality, implementation time, and efficiency. One of the basic techniques of the manufacturing engineer is the process capability study, which determines the ability of a process to meet specifications. Process capability information provides data for make-or-buy decisions, equipment purchases, and selection of process routes.

The sequence of operations is developed to minimize quality difficulties such as the handling of fragile products and the location of precision operations in the sequence. Methods study is used to determine the best way of performing either a production operation or an inspection operation.

Additional manufacturing engineering responsibilities include the design of equipment, the design of inspection devices, and the maintenance of the production equipment.

Manufacturing

Manufacturing has the responsibility to produce quality products. Quality cannot be inspected into a product; it must be built into the product.

The first-line supervisor is the key to the manufacture of a quality product. Since the first-line supervisor is considered by operating personnel to represent management, his ability to convey quality expectations is critical for good employee relations. A first-line supervisor who is enthusiastic in his commitment to quality can motivate the employees to build quality into each and every part and, thus, into the final unit. It is the supervisor's responsibility to provide the employee with the proper tools for the job, to provide instructions in the method of performing the job and the quality expectations of the job, and to provide feedback on performance.

In order for the operator to know what is expected, training sessions on quality should be given periodically. These training sessions reinforce management's commitment to a quality product. During the training sessions, time can be allocated to presentations by field personnel, to discussions concerning the sources of quality variations, to methods of improving quality, and so on. The primary objective of the sessions is to develop an attitude of "quality mindedness" and an environment where two-way, nonpunitive communications can flourish.

According to Deming, only 15% of the quality problems can be attributed to operating personnel—the balance is due to the rest of the system. Statistical process control effectively controls quality and is an invaluable tool for quality improvement. Operating personnel should be trained to perform their own statistical process control.

Inspection and Test

Inspection and test has the responsibility to appraise the quality of purchased and manufactured items and to report the results. The reports are used by other departments to take corrective action when needed. Inspection and test may be a department by itself, part of the manufacturing department, or part of the quality assurance department. It might also be located in both manufacturing and quality assurance.

Although inspection is done by representatives of the inspection and test department, it does not relieve manufacturing of its responsibility to produce a quality product and make its own inspections. In fact, with automated production, workers frequently have time to perform 100% inspection before and after an operation. One of the major problems with the inspection activity is the tendency to view the inspector as a "police person" who has the quality responsibility. This attitude can lead to an ineffective inspection activity and a deterioration of quality.

In order to perform the inspection activity, accurate measuring equipment is needed. Normally, this equipment is purchased; however, it may be necessary to design and build it in cooperation with manufacturing engineering. In either case the equipment must be maintained in a constant state of repair and calibration.

It is necessary to continually monitor the performance of inspectors. Indications are that certain nonconformities are more difficult to find, that inspectors vary in their abilities, and that the quality level affects the number of nonconformities reported. Samples of known composition should be used to evaluate and improve the inspector's performance.

The efficiency of the appraisal activity is a function of the inspection methods and procedures (number inspected, type of sampling, and inspection location). Cooperation from manufacturing engineering, inspection and test, manufacturing, and quality assurance is necessary to maximize the inspector's performance.

Inspection and test should concentrate the majority of its efforts on statistical quality control which will lead to quality improvement. Passing the conforming items and discarding the nonconforming ones is *not* quality control. Quality cannot be inspected into a product or service. Dependency on mass inspection for quality control is in most cases a waste of effort, time, and money.

Packaging and Shipping

The packaging and shipping department has the responsibility to preserve and protect the quality of the product. Control of the product quality must extend beyond manufacturing to the distribution, installation, and use of the product. A dissatisfied customer is not concerned with where the nonconforming condition occurred.

Quality specifications are needed for the protection of the product during transit by all types of common carrier: truck, rail, boat, and air. These specifications are needed for vibration, shock, and environmental conditions such as temperature, moisture, and dust. Additional specifications are needed in regard to the handling of the product during loading, unloading, and warehousing. Occasionally, it is necessary to change the product or process design to correct quality difficulties that occur during transit. In some companies, the responsibility for the design of the package is vested in product engineering rather than packaging and shipping.

Product storage, while awaiting further processing, sale, or use, presents additional quality problems. Specifications and procedures are necessary to ensure that the product is properly stored and promptly used to minimize deterioration and degradation.

Product Service

Product service has the responsibility to provide the customer with the means for fully realizing the intended function of the product during its expected life. This responsibility includes erection, maintenance, repair, and replacement-parts service. Products should be serviced quickly whenever they are improperly installed or fail during the warranty period. Prompt service can change a dissatisfied customer into a satisfied one.

Product service and marketing work closely with each other to determine the quality the customer wants, needs, and obtains.

Quality Assurance

The quality assurance or quality control department (the name is not important) *does not* have direct responsibility for quality. Therefore, it is not shown in Figure 1-1. It assists or supports the other departments as they carry out their quality control responsibilities. Quality assurance *does* have the direct responsibility to continually evaluate the effectiveness of the total quality system. It determines the effectiveness of the quality system, appraises the current quality, determines quality problem areas or potential areas, and assists in the correction or minimization of these problem areas. The overall objective is the improvement of the product quality in cooperation with the responsible departments.

CHIEF EXECUTIVE OFFICER

The chief executive officer (CEO) of a plant has responsibility for each of the departments in the closed loop of Figure 1-1 and the quality assurance department. Therefore, the CEO has the ultimate responsibility for quality. The CEO must be involved directly in the quality effort. This activity requires a knowledge of quality and direct involvement with the quality improvement program. Merely stating that quality is important is not sufficient.

Direct involvement requires the creation of a quality council and chairing its activities. It also involves being a member of a quality improvement project team.

Perhaps the best way for the CEO to be involved is to have some measure of his or her quality performance. Financial information can provide a long-term measure of quality performance. However, in the short term, it is not too difficult to make the financial data look good when in reality the product quality is deteriorating. Quality improvement requires a long-term financial commitment to people, programs, and equipment.

The CEO's quality performance can be effectively measured by a proportion (percent nonconforming) chart that covers his or her area of responsibility, whether it be a plant or a corporation. If the percent nonconforming is increasing or is constant, then simply stated, the CEO's performance is poor. If the percent nonconforming is decreasing, the CEO's performance is good. This concept—measurement of quality performance—can be adapted for all managers, departments, and operating personnel. In conjunction with quality improvement, the proportion chart becomes a very effective technique for quality improvement.

2

FUNDAMENTALS
OF STATISTICS

INTRODUCTION

Definition of Statistics

The word *statistics* has two generally accepted meanings:

1. A collection of quantitative data pertaining to any subject or group, especially when the data are systematically gathered and collated. Examples of this meaning are blood pressure statistics, statistics of a football game, employment statistics, and accident statistics, to name a few.

2. The science that deals with the collection, tabulation, analysis, interpretation, and presentation of quantitative data.

It is noted that the second meaning is broader than the first, since it, too, is concerned with collection of data. The use of statistics in quality control deals with the second and broader meaning and involves the divisions of collection, tabulating, analyzing, interpreting, and presenting the quantitative data. Each division is dependent on the accuracy and completeness of the preceding one. Data may be collected by an inspector measuring the tensile strength of a plastic part or by a market researcher determining consumer color preferences. It may be tabulated by simple paper-and-pencil techniques or by the use of a computer. Analysis may involve a cursory visual examination or exhaustive calculations. The final results are interpreted and presented to assist in the making of decisions concerning quality.

There are two phases of statistics:

1. *Descriptive* or *deductive statistics,* which endeavors to describe and analyze a subject or group.

2. *Inductive statistics,* which endeavors to determine from a limited amount of data (sample) an important conclusion about a much larger amount of data (population). Since these conclusions or inferences cannot be stated with absolute certainty, the language of *probability* is often used.

This chapter covers the statistical fundamentals necessary to understand the subsequent quality control techniques. Fundamentals of probability are discussed in Chapter 4. An understanding of statistics is vital for an understanding of quality control and, for that matter, many other disciplines.

Collection of Data

Data may be collected by direct observation or indirectly through written or verbal questions. The latter technique is used extensively by market research personnel and public opinion pollsters. Data that are collected for quality control purposes are obtained by direct observation and are classified as either variables or attributes. *Variables* are those quality characteristics that are measurable, such as a weight measured in grams. *Attributes,* on the other hand, are those quality characteristics that are classified as either conforming or not conforming to specifications such as a "go/no go gage."

A variable that is capable of any degree of subdivision is referred to as *continuous.* The weight of a gray iron casting, which can be measured as 11 kg, 11.33 kg, or 11.3398 kg (25 lb), depending on the accuracy of the measuring instrument, is an example of a continuous variable. Measurements such as meters (feet), liters (gallons), and pascals (pounds per square inch) are examples of continuous data. Variables that exhibit gaps are called *discrete.* The number of nonconforming rivets in a travel trailer can be any whole number, such as 0, 3, 5, 10, 96, . . . ; however, there cannot be, say, 4.65 nonconforming rivets in a particular trailer. In general, continuous data are measurable, whereas discrete data are countable.

Sometimes it is convenient for verbal or nonnumerical data to assume the nature of a variable. For example, the quality of the surface finish of a piece of furniture can be classified as poor, average, or good. The poor, average, or good classification can be replaced by the numerical values of 1, 2, or 3, respectively. In a similar manner, educational institutions assign to the letter grades of A, B, C, D, and F the numerical values of 4, 3, 2, 1, and 0, respectively, and use those discrete numerical values as discrete variables for computational purposes.

While many quality characteristics are stated in terms of variables, there are many characteristics that must be stated as attributes. Frequently, those characteristics that are judged by visual observation are classified as attributes. The wire on an electric motor is either attached to the terminal or it is not; the words on this page are correctly spelled or they are incorrectly spelled; the switch is on or it is off; and the answer is right or it is wrong. The examples given in the previous sentence show conformance to a particular specification or nonconformance to that specification.

It is sometimes desirable for variables to be classified as attributes. Factory personnel are frequently interested in knowing if the product they are producing conforms to the specifications. For example, the numerical value for the weight of a package of sugar may not be as important as the information that the weight is within the prescribed limits. Therefore, the data, which are collected on the weight of the package of sugar, are reported as conforming or not conforming to specifications.

In collecting data the number of figures is a function of the intended use of the data. For example, in collecting data on the life of light bulbs, it is acceptable to record 995.6 h; however, recording a value of 995.632 h is too accurate and unnecessary. Similarly, if a keyway specification has a lower limit of 9.52 mm (0.375 in.) and an upper limit of 9.58 mm (0.377 in.), data would be collected to the nearest 0.001 mm and rounded to the nearest 0.01 mm. In general, the more figures to the right of the decimal point, the more sophisticated the measuring instrument.

Measuring instruments may not give a true reading because of problems due to accuracy and precision. Figure 2-1a shows an accurate series of repeated measurements because their average is close to the true value, which is at the center. In Figure 2-1b the repeated measurements in the series are very close together but are not close to the true value. Figure 2-1c shows the series of repeated measurements

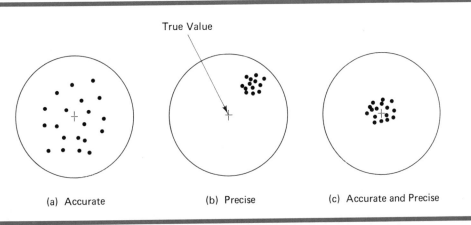

FIGURE 2-1 Difference between accuracy and precision.

tightly compacted around the true value and these measurements are both accurate and precise.

The rounding of data requires that certain conventions be followed. In rounding the numbers 0.9530, 0.9531, 0.9532, 0.9533, and 0.9534 to the nearest thousandth, the answer is 0.953, since all the numbers are closer to 0.953 than they are to 0.954. And in rounding the numbers 0.9535, 0.9536, 0.9537, 0.9538, and 0.9539, the answer is 0.954, since all the numbers are closer to 0.954 than to 0.953. In other words, if the next digit is 5 or greater, the number is rounded up.

In working with numerical data, *significant figures* are very important. The significant figures of a number are the digits exclusive of any leading zeros needed to locate the decimal point. For example, the number 3.69 has three significant figures; 36.900 has five significant figures; 2700 has four significant figures; 22.0365 has six significant figures; and 0.00270 has three significant figures. Trailing zeros are counted as being significant, while leading zeros are not. The rule gives some difficulty when working with whole numbers since the number 300 can have one, two, or three significant figures. This difficulty can be eliminated by the use of scientific notation. Therefore, 3×10^2 has one significant figure, 3.0×10^2 has two significant figures, and 3.00×10^2 has three significant figures. Numbers that are associated with counting have an unlimited number of significant figures, and the counting number 65 can be written as 65 or 65.000. . . .

When performing the mathematical operations of multiplication, division, and exponentiation, the answer has the same number of significant figures as the number with the fewest significant figures. The following examples will help to clarify this rule:

$$\sqrt{81.9} = 9.05$$

$$6.59 \times 2.3 = 15$$

$$32.65 \div 24 = 1.4 \qquad \text{(24 is not a counting number)}$$

$$32.65 \div 24 = 1.360 \qquad \text{(24 is a counting number with a value of 24.00 . . .)}$$

When performing the mathematical operations of addition and subtraction, the final answer can have no more significant figures after the decimal point than the number with the fewest significant figures after the decimal point. In cases involving numbers without decimal points, the final answer has no more significant figures than the number with the fewest significant figures. Examples to clarify this rule are as follows:

$$38.26 - 6 = 32 \qquad \text{(6 is not a counting number)}$$

$$38.26 - 6 = 32.26 \qquad \text{(6 is a counting number)}$$

$$38.26 - 6.1 = 32.2 \qquad \text{(answer was rounded from 32.16)}$$

$$8.1 \times 10^3 - 1232 = 6.9 \times 10^3 \qquad \text{(fewest significant figures are two)}$$

$$8.100 \times 10^3 - 1232 = 6868 \qquad \text{(fewest significant figures are four)}$$

Utilization of the rules above will avoid discrepancies in answers among quality control personnel; however, some judgment may sometimes be required. In any case, the final answer can be no more accurate than the incoming data.

Describing the Data

In industry, business, and government the mass of data that have been collected is voluminous. Even one item, such as the number of nonconforming smoke alarms in 35 lots of 1000 per lot, can represent such a mass of data that it can be more confusing than helpful. Consider the data shown in Table 2-1. Clearly these data, in this form, are difficult to use and are not effective in describing the data's characteristics. Some means of summarizing the data is needed to show what value or values the data tend to cluster about and how the data are dispersed or spread out. Two techniques are available to accomplish this summarization of data—graphical and analytical.

TABLE 2-1 **Number of Nonconforming Smoke Alarms in 35 Lots of 1000 per Lot**

0	1	3	0	0
0	5	4	1	2
1	0	2	0	0
2	1	1	1	2
0	4	0	3	1
0	3	4	0	0
1	3	0	1	2

The graphical technique is a plot or picture of a *frequency distribution*, which is a summarization of how the data points (observations) occur within each subdivision of observed values or groups of observed values. Analytical techniques summarize data by computing a *measure of central tendency* and a *measure of the dispersion*. Sometimes both the graphical and analytical techniques are used.

These techniques will be described in the subsequent sections of this chapter.

FREQUENCY DISTRIBUTION

Ungrouped Data

Ungrouped data comprise a listing of the observed values, while grouped data represent a lumping together of the observed values. The data can be discrete, as they are in this section, or continuous, as in the next section.

Because unorganized data are virtually meaningless, a method of processing the data is necessary. Table 2-1 will be used to illustrate the concept. An analyst reviewing the information as given in this table would have difficulty comprehending

TABLE 2-2   Tally of Number of Nonconforming Smoke Alarms

NUMBER NONCONFORMING	TABULATION	FREQUENCY
0	N̶J N̶J III	13
1	N̶J IIII	9
2	N̶J	5
3	IIII	4
4	III	3
5	I	1

the meaning of the data. A much better understanding can be obtained by tallying the frequency of each value, as shown in Table 2-2.

The first step is to establish an *array,* which is an arrangement of raw numerical data in ascending or descending order of magnitude. An array of ascending order from 0 to 5 is shown in the first column of Table 2-2. The next step is to tabulate the frequency of each value by placing a tally mark under the tabulation column and in the appropriate row of Table 2-2. Start with the numbers 0, 0, 1, 2, . . . of Table 2-1 and continue placing tally marks until all the data have been tabulated. The last column of Table 2-2 is the numerical value for the number of tallies and is called the *frequency.*

Analysis of Table 2-2 shows that one can visualize the distribution of the data. If the "Tabulation" column is eliminated, the resulting table is classified as a *frequency distribution,* which is an arrangement of data to show the frequency of values in each category.

The frequency distribution is a useful method of visualizing data and is a basic statistical concept. To think of a set of numbers as having some type of distribution is fundamental for solving quality control problems. There are different types of frequency distributions, and the type of distribution can indicate the problem-solving approach.

Frequency distributions are presented in graphical form when greater visual clarity is desired. There are a number of different ways to present the frequency distribution.

A *histogram* consists of a set of rectangles that represent the frequency in each category. It represents graphically the frequencies of the observed values. Figure 2-2a is a histogram for the data in Table 2-2. Since this is a discrete variable, a vertical line in place of a rectangle would have been theoretically correct (see Figure 2-5). However, the rectangle is commonly used.

Another type of graphic representation is the relative frequency distribution. Relative, in this sense, means the proportion or fraction of the total. Relative frequency is calculated by dividing the frequency for each data value (in this case, number nonconforming) by the total, which is the sum of the frequencies for each data value. These calculations are shown in the third column of Table 2-3. Graphical representation is shown in Figure 2-2b. Relative frequency has the advantage of a reference. For example, the proportion that is 2 nonconforming units is 0.14. Some practitioners prefer to use percents for the vertical scale rather than fractions.

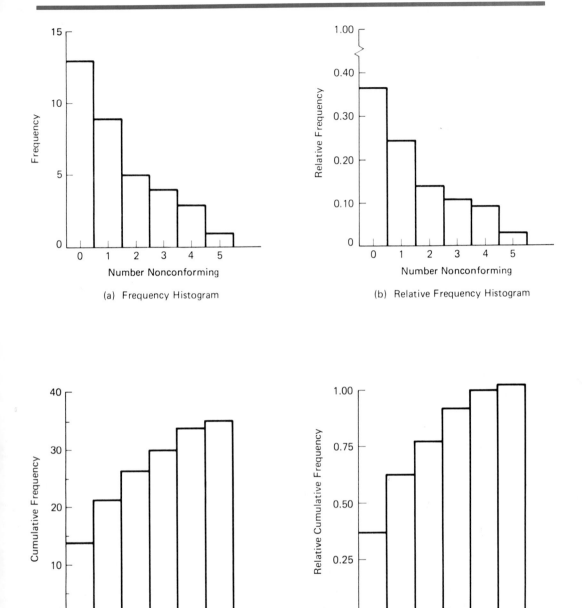

FIGURE 2-2 Graphic representation of data given in Table 2-2 and Table 2-3.

NUMBER NONCONFORMING	FREQUENCY	RELATIVE FREQUENCY	CUMULATIVE FREQUENCY	RELATIVE CUMULATIVE FREQUENCY
0	13	$13 \div 35 = 0.37$	13	$13 \div 35 = 0.37$
1	9	$9 \div 35 = 0.26$	$13 + 9 = 22$	$22 \div 35 = 0.63$
2	5	$5 \div 35 = 0.14$	$22 + 5 = 27$	$27 \div 35 = 0.77$
3	4	$4 \div 35 = 0.11$	$27 + 4 = 31$	$31 \div 35 = 0.89$
4	3	$3 \div 35 = 0.09$	$31 + 3 = 34$	$34 \div 35 = 0.97$
5	1	$1 \div 35 = 0.03$	$34 + 1 = 35$	$35 \div 35 = 1.00$
Total	35	1.00		

Cumulative frequency is calculated by adding the frequency of each data value to the sum of the frequencies for the previous data values. As shown in the fourth column of Table 2-3, the cumulative frequency for 0 nonconforming units is 13; for 1 nonconforming unit, $13 + 9 = 22$; for 2 nonconforming units, $22 + 5$; and so on. Cumulative frequency is the number of data points equal to or less than a data value. For example, the number of lots that have 2 or less nonconforming units is 27. Graphic representation is shown in Figure 2-2c.

Relative cumulative frequency is calculated by dividing the cumulative frequency for each data value by the total. These calculations are shown in the fifth column of Table 2-3, and the graphical representation is shown in Figure 2-2d. The graph shows that the proportion of the smoke alarm lots that have 2 or fewer non-conforming units is 0.77 or 77%.

The foregoing example is limited to a discrete variable with six values. Although this example is sufficient for a basic introduction to the frequency distribution concept, it does not provide a thorough knowledge of the subject.

Grouped Data

The construction of a frequency distribution for grouped data is more complicated because there is usually a larger number of categories. An example problem using a continuous variable illustrates the concept.

1. *Collect data and construct a tally sheet.* Data collected on the weights of 110 steel shafts are shown in Table 2-4. The first step is to make a tally of the values, as shown in Table 2-5. In order to be more efficient, the weights are coded from 2.500 kg, which is a technique used to simplify data. Therefore, a weight with a value of 31 is equivalent to 2.531 kg (2.500 + 0.031). Analysis of Table 2-5 shows that more information is conveyed to the analyst than from the data of Table 2-4; however, the general picture is still somewhat blurred.

In this problem there are 45 categories, which are too many and must be reduced by grouping into cells.[1] A cell is a grouping within specified boundaries of ob-

---

[1] The word "class" is sometimes used in place of the word "cell."

TABLE 2-4   Steel Shaft Weight (kilograms)

2.559	2.556	2.566	2.546	2.561
2.570	2.546	2.565	2.543	2.538
2.560	2.560	2.545	2.551	2.568
2.546	2.555	2.551	2.554	2.574
2.568	2.572	2.550	2.556	2.551
2.561	2.560	2.564	2.567	2.560
2.551	2.562	2.542	2.549	2.561
2.556	2.550	2.561	2.558	2.556
2.559	2.557	2.532	2.575	2.551
2.550	2.559	2.565	2.552	2.560
2.534	2.547	2.569	2.559	2.549
2.544	2.550	2.552	2.536	2.570
2.564	2.553	2.558	2.538	2.564
2.552	2.543	2.562	2.571	2.553
2.539	2.569	2.552	2.536	2.537
2.532	2.552	2.575 (H)	2.545	2.551
2.547	2.537	2.547	2.533	2.538
2.571	2.545	2.545	2.556	2.543
2.551	2.569	2.559	2.534	2.561
2.567	2.572	2.558	2.542	2.574
2.570	2.542	2.552	2.551	2.553
2.546	2.531 (L)	2.563	2.554	2.544

TABLE 2-5   Tally Sheet of Steel Shaft Weight (Coded from 2.500 kg)

WEIGHT	TABULATION	WEIGHT	TABULATION	WEIGHT	TABULATION
31	I	46	IIII	61	卌
32	II	47	III	62	II
33	I	48		63	I
34	II	49	II	64	III
35		50	IIII	65	II
36	II	51	卌 III	66	I
37	II	52	卌 I	67	II
38	III	53	III	68	II
39	I	54	II	69	III
40		55	I	70	III
41		56	卌	71	II
42	III	57	I	72	II
43	III	58	III	73	
44	II	59	卌	74	II
45	IIII	60	卌	75	II

served values along the abscissa (horizontal axis) of the histogram (see Figure 2-3). The grouping of data by cells simplifies the presentation of the distribution; however, some of the detail is lost. When the number of cells is large, the true picture of the distribution is distorted by cells having an insufficient number of items or none at all. Or, when the number of cells is small, too many items are concentrated in a few cells and the distribution is also distorted.

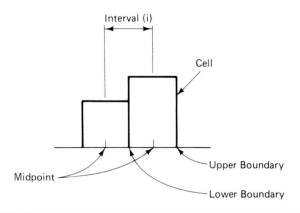

FIGURE 2-3 Cell nomenclature.

The number of cells or groups in a frequency distribution is largely a matter of judgment by the analyst. This judgment is based on the number of observations and can require trial and error to determine the optimum number of cells. In general, the number of cells should be between 5 and 20. Broad guidelines are as follows: use 5 to 9 cells when the number of observations is less than 100; use 8 to 17 cells when the number of observations is between 100 and 500; and use 15 to 20 cells when the number of observations is greater than 500. To provide flexibility, the number of cells in the guidelines are overlapping. It is emphasized that these guidelines are not rigid and can be adjusted when necessary to present an acceptable frequency distribution.

2. *Determine the range.* It is the difference between the highest observed value and the lowest observed value as shown by the formula

$$R = X_H - X_L$$

where R = range
X_H = highest number
X_L = lowest number

From Table 2-4 or Table 2-5 the highest number is 2.575 and the lowest number is 2.531. Thus

$$R = X_H - X_L$$

$$= 2.575 - 2.531$$

$$= 0.044$$

3. *Determine the cell interval.* The *cell interval* is the distance between adjacent cell midpoints as shown in Figure 2-3. Whenever possible, an odd interval such as 0.001, 0.07, 0.5, or 3 is recommended so that the midpoint values will be to the same number of decimal places as the data values. The cell interval (i) and the num-

FUNDAMENTALS OF STATISTICS

ber of cells (h) are interrelated by the formula, $h = R/i$. Since h and i are both unknown, a trial-and-error approach is used to find the interval that will meet the guidelines.

$$\text{Assume that } i = 0.003; \text{ then } h = \frac{R}{i} = \frac{0.044}{0.003} = 15$$

$$\text{Assume that } i = 0.005; \text{ then } h = \frac{R}{i} = \frac{0.044}{0.005} = 9$$

$$\text{Assume that } i = 0.007; \text{ then } h = \frac{R}{i} = \frac{0.044}{0.007} = 6$$

A cell interval of 0.005 with nine cells will give the best presentation of the data based on the guidelines for the number of cells given in step 1.

Another technique to obtain the cell interval is to use Sturgis' rule, which is

$$i = \frac{R}{1 + 3.322 \log n}$$

For the example problem the answer is

$$i = \frac{R}{1 + 3.322 \log n} = \frac{0.044}{1 + 3.322(2.041)} = 0.0057$$

and the closest odd interval for the data is 0.005. Both techniques give similar answers.

4. *Determine the cell midpoints.* The lowest cell midpoint must be located to include the lowest data value in its cell. The simplest technique is to select the lowest data point (2.531) as the midpoint value for the first cell. This technique is recommended for those readers who are just beginning their statistical career. Since the interval is 0.005, there are five data values in each cell; therefore, a midpoint value of 2.533 can be used for the first cell. This value will have the lowest data value (2.531) in the first cell, which will have data values of 2.531, 2.532, 2.533, 2.534, and 2.535.

Midpoint selection is a matter of judgment, and in this case a midpoint of 2.533 was selected so that the number of cells is 9. Selection of any other midpoint, although not incorrect, would have given 10 cells in the frequency distribution. Selection of different midpoint values will produce different frequency distributions—five are possible. The midpoints for the other eight cells are obtained by adding the cell interval to the previous midpoint: 2.533 + 0.005 = 2.538, 2.538 + 0.005 = 2.543, 2.543 + 0.005 = 2.548, . . . , 2.568 + 0.005 = 2.573. These midpoints are shown in Table 2-6.

The midpoint value is the most representative va.ue within a cell provided that the number of observations in a cell is large and the difference in boundaries is not too great. Even if this condition is not met, the number of observations above and below the midpoint of a cell will frequently be equal. And even if the number of observations above and below a cell midpoint is unbalanced in one direction, it will

TABLE 2-6 Frequency Distribution
of Steel Shaft Weight (kilograms)

CELL BOUNDARIES	CELL MIDPOINT	FREQUENCY
2.531–2.535	2.533	6
2.536–2.540	2.538	8
2.541–2.545	2.543	12
2.546–2.550	2.548	13
2.551–2.555	2.553	20
2.556–2.560	2.558	19
2.561–2.565	2.563	13
2.566–2.570	2.568	11
2.571–2.575	2.573	8
Total		110

probably be offset by an unbalance in the opposite direction of another cell. Midpoint values should be to the same degree of accuracy as the original observations.

5. *Determine the cell boundaries. Cell boundaries* are the extreme or limit values of a cell, referred to as the upper boundary and the lower boundary. All the observations that fall between the upper and lower boundaries are classified into that particular cell. Boundaries are established so there is no question as to the location of an observation. Therefore, the boundary values are an extra decimal place or significant figure in accuracy than the observed values. Since the interval is odd, there will be an equal number of data values on each side of the midpoint. For the first cell with a midpoint of 2.533 and an interval of 0.005, there will be two values on each side. Therefore, that cell will contain the values 2.531, 2.532, 2.533, 2.534, and 2.535. To prevent any gaps, the true boundaries are extended about halfway to the next number, which gives values of 2.5305 and 2.5355. The following number line illustrates this principle:

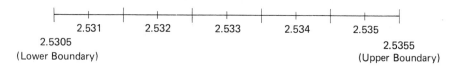

Some analysts prefer to leave the boundaries at the same number of decimal places as the data. No difficulty is encountered with this practice as long as the cell interval is odd and it is understood that the true boundaries are extended halfway to the next number. This practice is followed in this book. Therefore, the lower boundary for the first cell is 2.531.

Once the boundaries are established for one cell, the boundaries for the other cells are obtained by successive additions of the cell interval. Therefore, the lower boundaries are 2.531 + 0.005 = 2.536, 2.536 + 0.005 = 2.541, . . . , 2.566 + 0.005 = 2.571. The upper boundaries are obtained in a similar manner and are shown in the first column of Table 2-6.

FUNDAMENTALS OF STATISTICS

6. *Post the cell frequency.* The amount of numbers in each cell is posted to the frequency column of Table 2-6. An analysis of Table 2-5 shows that for the lowest cell there are: one 2.531, two 2.532, one 2.533, two 2.534, and zero 2.535. Therefore, there is a total of six values in the lowest cell, and the cell with a midpoint of 2.533 has a frequency of 6. The amounts are determined for the other cells in a similar manner.

The completed frequency distribution is shown in Table 2-6. This frequency distribution gives a better conception of the central value and how the data are dispersed about that value than the unorganized data or a tally sheet. The histogram is shown in Figure 2-4.

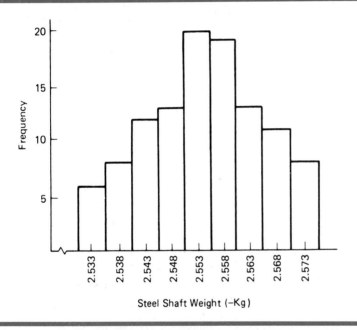

FIGURE 2-4   **Histogram of data given in Table 2-6.**

Information on the construction of the relative frequency, cumulative frequency, and relative cumulative frequency histograms for grouped data is the same as for ungrouped data but with one exception. With the two cumulative frequency histograms, the true upper cell boundary is the value labeled on the abscissa. Construction of these histograms for the example problem is left to the reader as an exercise.

The histogram describes the variation in the process. It is used to

1. Determine the process capability,
2. Compare with specifications,
3. Suggest the shape of the population, and
4. Indicate discrepancies in data such as gaps.

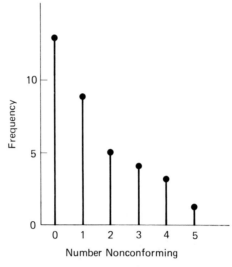

(a) Bar Graph of Data Given
in Table 2-1

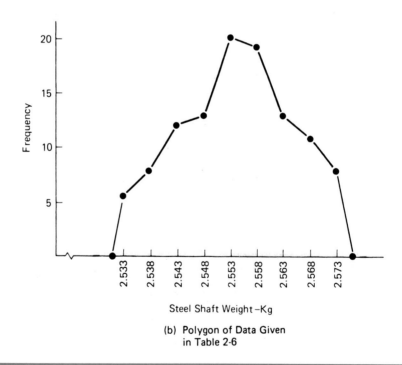

(b) Polygon of Data Given
in Table 2-6

FIGURE 2-5   **Other types of frequency distribution graphs.**

FUNDAMENTALS OF STATISTICS

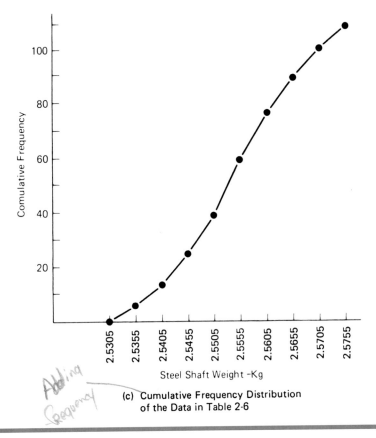

(c) Cumulative Frequency Distribution
of the Data in Table 2-6

FIGURE 2-5   (continued)

Other Types of Frequency Distribution Graphs

The bar chart can also represent frequency distributions, as shown in Figure 2-5a using the data of Table 2-1. As mentioned previously, the bar chart is theoretically correct for discrete data but is not commonly used.

The *polygon* or *frequency polygon* is another graphic way of presenting frequency distributions and is illustrated in Figure 2-5b using the data of Table 2-6. It is constructed by placing a dot over each cell midpoint at the height indicated for each frequency. The curve is extended at each end in order for the figure to be enclosed. Since the histogram shows the area in each cell, it is considered to present a better graphical picture than the polygon and is the one most commonly used.

The graph that is used to present the frequency of all values less than the upper cell boundary of a given cell is called a *cumulative frequency*, or *ogive*. Figure 2-5c shows a cumulative frequency distribution curve for the data in Table 2-6. The cumulative value for each cell is plotted on the graph and joined by a straight line. The true upper cell boundary is labeled on the abscissa.

Characteristics of Frequency Distribution Graphs

The graphs of Figure 2-6 use smooth curves rather than the rectangular associated with the histogram. A smooth curve represents a population frequency distribution, whereas the histogram represents a sample frequency distribution. The difference between a population and a sample is discussed in another section of this chapter.

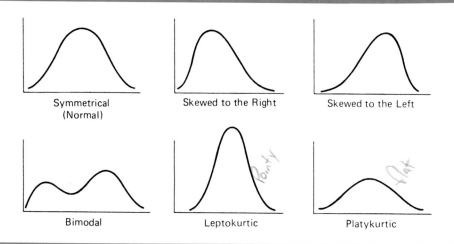

FIGURE 2-6   **Characteristics of frequency distributions.**

Frequency distribution curves have certain identifiable characteristics. One characteristic of the distribution concerns the symmetry or lack of symmetry of the data. Are the data equally distributed on each side of the central value, or are the data skewed to the right or to the left? Another characteristic concerns the number of modes or peaks to the data. There can be one mode, two modes (bimodal), or multiple modes. A final characteristic concerns the peakedness of the data. When the curve is quite peaked, it is referred to as *leptokurtic,* and when it is flatter, it is referred to as *platykurtic.*

Frequency distributions can give sufficient information about a quality control problem to provide a basis for decision making without further analysis. Distributions can also be compared in regard to location, spread, and shape as illustrated in Figure 2-7.

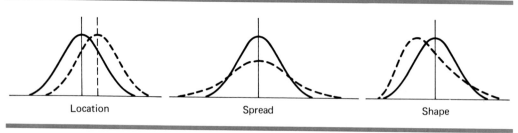

FIGURE 2-7   **Differences due to location, spread, and shape.**

Analysis of Histograms

Analysis of a histogram can provide information concerning specifications, the shape of the population frequency distribution, and a particular quality control problem. Figure 2-8 shows a histogram for the percentage of wash concentration in a steel tube cleaning operation prior to painting. The ideal concentration is between 1.45 and 1.74%, as shown by the crosshatched rectangle. Concentrations less than 1.45% produce poor quality; concentrations greater than 1.75%, while producing more than adequate quality, are costly and therefore reduce productivity. No complex statistics are needed to show that corrective measures are needed to bring the spread of the distribution closer to the ideal value of 1.6%.

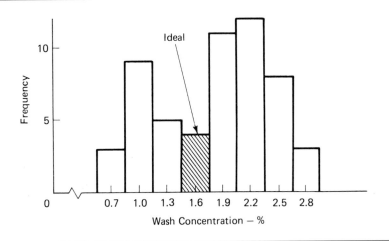

FIGURE 2-8   Histogram of wash concentration.

Final Comments

Another type of distribution that is similar to the histogram is the Pareto diagram. The reader is referred to Chapters 9 and 12 for a discussion of this type of distribution. A Pareto analysis is a very effective technique for determining the location of major quality problems. The differences between a Pareto diagram and a frequency distribution are twofold. Categories are used for the abscissa rather than data values and the categories are in descending order from the highest frequency to the lowest one rather than in numerical order.

One limitation of a frequency distribution is the fact that it does not show the order in which the data were produced. In other words, initial data could all be located on one side and later data on the other side. When this situation occurs, the interpretation of the frequency distribution will be different. A run chart, discussed at the end of Chapter 3, shows the order in which the data were produced and can aid in the analysis.

MEASURES OF CENTRAL TENDENCY

A frequency distribution is sufficient for many quality control problems. However, with a broad range of problems a graphical technique is either undesirable or needs the additional information provided by analytical techniques. Analytical methods of describing a collection of data have the advantage of occupying less space than a graph. They also have the advantage of allowing for comparisons between collections of data. And, they also allow for additional calculations and inferences. There are two principal analytical methods of describing a collection of data—measures of central tendency and measures of dispersion. The latter measure is described in the next section, while this section covers measures of central tendency.

A *measure of central tendency* of a distribution is a numerical value that describes the central position of the data or how the data tend to build up in the center. There are three measures in common use: (1) the average, (2) the median, and (3) the mode.

Average

The average is the sum of the observations divided by the number of observations. It is the most common measure of central tendency. There are three different techniques available for calculating the average: (1) ungrouped data, (2) grouped data, and (3) weighted average.

1. *Ungrouped data.* This technique is used when the data are unorganized. The average is represented by the notation $\overline{X}$, which is read as "X bar" and is given by the formula

$$\overline{X} = \frac{\sum\limits_{i=1}^{n} X_i}{n} = \frac{X_1 + X_2 + \cdots + X_n}{n}$$

where $\overline{X}$ = average
n = number of observed values
$X_1, X_2, \ldots, X_n$ = observed value identified by the subscript 1, 2, . . . , n or general subscript i
Σ = symbol meaning "sum of"

The first expression is a simplified method of writing the formula whereby $\sum_{i=1}^{n} X_i$ is read as "summation from 1 to n of X sub i" and means to add together the values of the observations.

EXAMPLE PROBLEM

An inspector checks the resistance value of five coils and records the values in ohms (Ω): $X_1 = 3.35$, $X_2 = 3.37$, $X_3 = 3.28$, $X_4 = 3.34$, and $X_5 = 3.30$. Determine the average.

$$\overline{X} = \frac{\sum\limits_{i=1}^{n} X_i}{n}$$

$$= \frac{3.35 + 3.37 + 3.28 + 3.34 + 3.30}{5}$$

$$= 3.33 \ \Omega$$

Most electronic hand calculators have the capability of automatically calculating the average after the data are entered.

2. *Grouped data*. When the data have been grouped into a frequency distribution, the following technique is applicable. The formula for the average of grouped data is

$$\overline{X} = \frac{\sum\limits_{i=1}^{h} f_i X_i}{n} = \frac{f_1 X_1 + f_2 X_2 + \cdots + f_h X_h}{f_1 + f_2 + \cdots + f_h}$$

where n = sum of the frequencies
$\quad\quad f_i$ = frequency in a cell or frequency of an observed value
$\quad\quad X_i$ = cell midpoint or an observed value
$\quad\quad h$ = number of cells or number of observed values

The formula is applicable when the grouping is by cells with more than one observed value per cell as illustrated by the steel shaft problem (Table 2-6). It is also applicable when each observed value, X_i, has its own frequency, f_i, as illustrated by the smoke alarm problem (Table 2-1). In this situation, h is the number of observed values.

In other words, if the frequency distribution has been grouped into cells, X_i is the cell midpoint and f_i is the number of observations in that cell. If the frequency distribution has been grouped by individual observed values, X_i is the observed value and f_i is the number of times that observed value occurs in the data. This practice holds for both discrete and continuous variables.

Each cell midpoint is used as the representative value of that cell. The midpoint is multiplied by its cell frequency; the products are summed; and they are divided by the total number of observations. In the example problem given below, the first three columns are those of a typical frequency distribution. The fourth column is derived from the product of the second column (midpoint) and third column (frequency) and is labeled "fX."

TABLE 2-7 Frequency Distributions of the Life of 320 Tires in 1000 km

BOUNDARIES	MIDPOINT, X_i	FREQUENCY f_i	COMPUTATION $f_i X_i$
23.6–26.5	25.0	4	100
26.6–29.5	28.0	36	1,008
29.6–32.5	31.0	51	1,581
32.6–35.5	34.0	63	2,142
35.6–38.5	37.0	58	2,146
38.6–41.5	40.0	52	2,080
41.6–44.5	43.0	34	1,462
44.6–47.5	46.0	16	736
47.6–50.5	49.0	6	294
Total		$n = 320$	$\Sigma f_i X_i = 11,549$

EXAMPLE PROBLEM

Given the frequency distribution of the life of 320 automotive tires in 1000 km (621.37 mi) as shown in Table 2-7, determine the average.

$$\bar{X} = \frac{\sum_{i=1}^{h} f_i X_i}{n}$$

$$= \frac{11,549}{320}$$

$$= 36.1 \quad \text{(which is in 1000 km)}$$

Therefore, $\bar{X} = 36.1 \times 10^3$ km.

When comparing an average calculated from this technique with one calculated using the ungrouped technique, there can be a slight difference. This difference is caused by the observations in each cell being unevenly distributed in the cell. In actual practice the difference will not be of sufficient magnitude to affect the accuracy of the problem.

3. *Weighted average.* When a number of averages are combined with different frequencies, a *weighted average* is computed. The formula for the weighted average is given by

$$\bar{X}_w = \frac{\sum_{i=1}^{n} w_i \bar{X}_i}{\sum_{i=1}^{n} w_i}$$

where $\bar{X}_w$ = weighted average
w_i = weight of the ith average

FUNDAMENTALS OF STATISTICS

EXAMPLE PROBLEM

Tensile tests on aluminum alloy rods are conducted at three different times, which results in three different average values in megapascals (MPa). On the first occasion five tests are conducted with a average of 207 MPa (30,000 psi); on the second occasion six tests, with a average of 203 MPa; and on the last occasion three tests, with a average of 206 MPa. Determine the weighted average.

$$\bar{X}_w = \frac{\sum\limits_{i=1}^{n} w_i \bar{X}_i}{\sum\limits_{i=1}^{n} w_i}$$

$$= \frac{(5)(207) + (6)(203) + (3)(206)}{5 + 6 + 3}$$

$$= 205 \text{ MPa}$$

The weighted average technique is a special case of the grouped data technique wherein the data are not organized into a frequency distribution. In the example above, the weights are whole numbers. Another method of solving the same problem is to use proportions. Thus,

$$w_1 = \frac{5}{5 + 6 + 3} = 0.36$$

$$w_2 = \frac{6}{5 + 6 + 3} = 0.43$$

$$w_3 = \frac{3}{5 + 6 + 3} = 0.21$$

and the sum of the weights equals 1.00. The latter technique would be necessary when the weights are given in percent or the decimal equivalent.

Unless otherwise noted, $\bar{X}$ stands for the average of observed values, $\bar{X}_x$. The same equation is used to find

$$\bar{X}_{\bar{x}} \text{ or } \bar{\bar{X}} \text{—average of averages}$$

$$\bar{R} \text{—average of ranges}$$

$$\bar{c} \text{—average of count of nonconformities}$$

$$\bar{s} \text{—average of sample standard deviations, etc.}$$

Median

Another measure of central tendency is the *median*, which is defined as the value which divides a series of ordered observations so that the number of items above it is equal to the number below it.

1. *Ungrouped technique.* Two situations are possible in determining the median of a series of ungrouped data—when the number in the series is odd and when the number in the series is even. When the number in the series is odd, the median is the midpoint of the values. Thus, the ordered set of numbers 3, 4, 5, 6, 8, 8, and 10 has a median of 6, and the ordered set of numbers 22, 24, 24, 24, and 30 has a median of 24. When the number in the series is even, the median is the average of the two middle numbers. Thus, the ordered set of numbers 3, 4, 5, 6, 8, and 8 has a median that is the average of 5 and 6, which is $(5 + 6)/2 = 5.5$. If both middle numbers are the same as in the ordered set of numbers 22, 24, 24, 24, 30, and 30, it is still computed as the average of the two middle numbers, since $(24 + 24)/2 = 24$. The reader is cautioned to be sure the numbers are ordered before computing the median.

2. *Grouped technique.* When data are grouped into a frequency distribution, the median is obtained by finding the cell that has the middle number and then interpolating within the cell. The interpolation formula for computing the median is given by

$$Md = L_m + \left(\frac{\frac{n}{2} - cf_m}{f_m} \right) i$$

where Md = median
L_m = lower boundary of the cell with the median
n = total number of observations
cf_m = cumulative frequency of all cells below L_m
f_m = frequency of median cell
i = cell interval

To illustrate the use of the formula, data from Table 2-7 will be used. By counting up from the lowest cell (midpoint 25.0), the halfway point ($320/2 = 160$) is reached in the cell with a midpoint value of 37.0 and a lower limit of 35.6. The cumulative frequency (cf_m) is 154, the cell interval is 3, and the frequency of the median cell is 58.

$$Md = L_m + \left(\frac{\frac{n}{2} - cf_m}{f_m} \right) i$$

$$= 35.6 + \left(\frac{\frac{320}{2} - 154}{58} \right) 3$$

$$= 35.9 \qquad \text{(which is in 1000 km)}$$

If the counting is begun at the top of the distribution, the cumulative frequency is counted to the cell upper limit and the interpolated quantity is subtracted from the upper limit. However, it is more common to start counting at the bottom of the distribution.

Mode

The *mode* (Mo) of a set of numbers is that value that occurs with the greatest frequency. It is possible for the mode to be nonexistent in a series of numbers or to have more than one value. To illustrate the series of numbers 3, 3, 4, 5, 5, 5, and 7 has a mode of 5; the series of numbers 22, 23, 25, 30, 32, and 36 does not have a mode; and the series of numbers 105, 105, 105, 107, 108, 109, 109, 109, 110, and 112 has two modes, 105 and 109. A series of numbers is referred to as *unimodal* if it has one mode, *bimodal* if it has two modes, and *multimodal* if there are more than two modes.

When data are grouped into a frequency distribution, the midpoint of the cell with the highest frequency is the mode, since this point represents the highest point (greatest frequency) of the histogram. It is possible to obtain a better estimate of the mode by interpolating in a manner similar to that used for the median. However, this is not necessary, since the mode is employed primarily as an inspection method for determining the central tendency, and greater accuracy than the cell midpoint is not required.

Relationship Among the Measures of Central Tendency

Differences among the three measures of central tendency are shown in the smooth polygons of Figure 2-9. When the distribution is symmetrical, the values for the average, median, and mode are identical; when the distribution is skewed, the values are different.

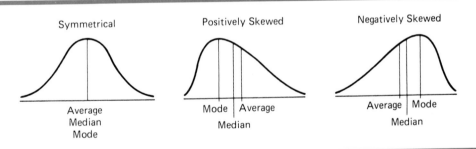

FIGURE 2-9   **Relationship among average, median, and mode.**

The average is the most commonly used measure of central tendency. It is used when the distribution is symmetrical or not appreciably skewed to the right or left; when additional statistics, such as measures of dispersion, control charts, and so on, are to be computed based on the average; and when a stable value is needed for inductive statistics.

The median becomes an effective measure of the central tendency when the distribution is positively (to the right) or negatively (to the left) skewed. It is used when an exact midpoint of a distribution is desired. When a distribution has extreme values, the average will be adversely affected while the median will remain unchanged. Thus, in a series of numbers such as 12, 13, 14, 15, 16, the median and average are identical and equal to 14. However, if the first value is changed to a 2, the median remains at 14, but the average becomes 12.

The mode is used when a quick and approximate measure of the central tendency is desired. Thus, the mode of a histogram is easily found by a visual examination. In addition, the mode is used to describe the most typical value of a distribution, such as the modal age of a particular group.

Other measures of central tendency are the geometric mean, harmonic mean, and quadratic mean. These measures are not used in quality control.

MEASURES OF DISPERSION

Introduction

In the preceding section, techniques for describing the central tendency of data were discussed. A second tool of statistics is composed of the *measures of dispersion*, which describe how the data are spread out or scattered on each side of the central value. Measures of dispersion and measures of central tendency are both needed to describe a collection of data. To illustrate, the employees of the plating and the assembly departments of a factory have identical average weekly wages of $225.36; however, the plating department has a high of $230.72 and a low of $219.43, while the assembly department has a high of $280.79 and a low of $173.54. The data for the assembly department are spread out or dispersed farther from the average than are those of the plating department.

Measures of dispersion discussed in this section are range, standard deviation, and variance. Other measures such as mean deviation and quartile deviation are not used in quality control.

Range

The *range* of a series of numbers is the difference between the largest and smallest values or observations. Symbolically, it is given by the formula

$$R = X_H - X_L$$

where R = range
X_H = highest observation in a series
X_L = lowest observation in a series

EXAMPLE PROBLEM

If the highest weekly wage in the assembly department is $280.79 and the lowest weekly wage is $173.54, determine the range.

$$R = X_H - X_L$$

$$= \$280.79 - \$173.54$$

$$= \$107.25$$

The range is the simplest and easiest to calculate of the measures of dispersion. A related measure, which is occasionally used, is the *midrange,* which is the range divided by 2, $R/2$.

Standard Deviation

The *standard deviation* is a numerical value in the units of the observed values that measures the spreading tendency of the data. A large standard deviation shows greater variability of the data than does a small standard deviation. In symbolic terms it is given by the formula

$$s = \sqrt{\frac{\sum\limits_{i=1}^{n} (X_i - \bar{X})^2}{n - 1}}$$

where s = sample standard deviation
X_i = observed value
$\bar{X}$ = average
n = number of observed values

Table 2-8 will be used to explain the standard deviation concept. The first column (X_i) gives six observed values in kilograms, and from these values the average, $\bar{X} = 3.0$, is obtained. The second column, $(X_i - \bar{X})$, is the deviation of the individual observed values from the average. If we sum the deviations, the answer will be 0, which is always the case; but it will not lead to a measure of dispersion. However, if the deviations are squared, they will all be positive and their sum will be greater than zero. Calculations are shown in the third column, $(X_i - \bar{X})^2$, with a resultant sum of 0.08, which will vary depending on the observed values. The average of the squared deviations can be found by dividing by n; however, for theoretical reasons we divide by $n - 1$.[2] Thus,

$$\frac{\sum (X_i - \bar{X})^2}{n - 1} = \frac{0.08}{6 - 1} = 0.016 \text{ kg}^2$$

which gives an answer that has the units squared. This result is not acceptable as a measure of the dispersion, but is valuable as a measure of variability for advanced

TABLE 2-8   Standard Deviation Analysis

X_i	$X_i - \bar{X}$	$(X_i - \bar{X})^2$
3.2	+0.2	0.04
2.9	−0.1	0.01
3.0	0.0	0.00
2.9	−0.1	0.01
3.1	+0.1	0.01
2.9	−0.1	0.01
$\bar{X} = 3.0$	$\Sigma = 0$	$\Sigma = 0.08$

[2] The reason for using $n - 1$ is because one degree of freedom is lost due to the use of the sample statistic, $\bar{X}$, rather than the population parameter, μ.

statistics. It is called the *variance* and is given the symbol s^2. If we take the square root, the answer will be in the same units as the observed values. Calculations are

$$s = \sqrt{\frac{\sum (X_i - \bar{X})^2}{n - 1}} = \sqrt{\frac{0.08}{6 - 1}} = 0.13 \text{ kg}$$

This formula is for explanation rather than for the purpose of calculation. Because the form of the data can be either grouped or ungrouped, there are different computing techniques.

1. *Ungrouped technique.* The formula used in the definition of standard deviation can be used for ungrouped data. However, an alternative formula is more convenient for computation purposes:

$$s = \sqrt{\frac{n \sum_{i=1}^{n} X_i^2 - \left(\sum_{i=1}^{n} X_i \right)^2}{n(n - 1)}}$$

EXAMPLE PROBLEM

Determine the standard deviation of the moisture content of a roll of kraft paper. The results of six readings across the paper web are 6.7, 6.0, 6.4, 6.4, 5.9, and 5.8%.

$$s = \sqrt{\frac{n \sum_{i=1}^{n} X_i^2 - \left(\sum_{i=1}^{n} X_i \right)^2}{n(n - 1)}}$$

$$= \sqrt{\frac{6(231.26) - (37.2)^2}{6(6 - 1)}}$$

$$= 0.35\%$$

After entry of the data, many hand calculators compute the standard deviation on command.

2. *Grouped technique.* When the data have been grouped into a frequency distribution, the following technique is applicable. The formula for the standard deviation of grouped data is

$$s = \sqrt{\frac{n \sum_{i=1}^{h} (f_i X_i^2) - \left(\sum_{i=1}^{h} f_i X_i \right)^2}{n(n - 1)}}$$

where the symbols f_i, X_i, n, and h have the same meaning as given for the average of grouped data.

To use this technique, two additional columns are added to the frequency distribution. These additional columns are labeled "fX" and "fX^2," as shown in Table 2-9. It will be recalled that the "fX" column is needed for the average computations; therefore, only one additional column is required to compute the standard deviation. The technique is shown by the following example problem.

TABLE 2-9 Passenger Car Speeds (in km/h) During a 15-Minute Interval on I-57 at Location 236

BOUNDARIES	MIDPOINT X_i	FREQUENCY f_i	COMPUTATIONS f_iX_i	$f_iX_i^2$
72.6–81.5	77.0	5	385	29,645
81.6–90.5	86.0	19	1634	140,524
90.6–99.5	95.0	31	2945	279,775
99.6–108.5	104.0	27	2808	292,032
108.6–117.5	113.0	14	1582	178,766
Total		$n = 96$	$\Sigma\ fX = 9354$	$\Sigma\ fX^2 = 920{,}742$

EXAMPLE PROBLEM

Given the frequency distribution of Table 2-9 for passenger car speeds during a 15-minute interval on I-57, determine the average and standard deviation.

$$\bar{x} = \frac{\sum\limits_{i=1}^{h} f_iX_i}{n} \qquad s = \sqrt{\frac{n\sum\limits_{i=1}^{h}(f_iX_i^2) - \left(\sum\limits_{i=1}^{h} f_iX_i\right)^2}{n(n-1)}}$$

$$= \frac{9354}{96} \qquad\qquad = \sqrt{\frac{96(920{,}742) - (9354)^2}{96(96-1)}}$$

$$= 97.4 \text{ km/h} \qquad = 9.9 \text{ km/h}$$

Do not round $\Sigma\ fX$ or $\Sigma\ fX^2$, as this action will affect accuracy. Most hand calculators have the capability to enter grouped data and calculate s on command.

Unless otherwise noted, s stands for s_X, the sample standard deviation of observed values. The same formula is used to find

$s_{\bar{x}}$—sample standard deviation of averages

s_p—sample standard deviation of proportions

s_R—sample standard deviation of ranges

s_s—sample standard deviation of standard deviations, etc.

The standard deviation is a reference value that measures the dispersion in the data. It is best viewed as an index that is defined by the formula. The smaller the value of the standard deviation the better the quality, since the distribution is more closely compacted around the central value. Also, the standard deviation helps to define populations.

Relationship Between the Measures of Dispersion

In quality control the range is a very common measure of the dispersion; it is used in one of the principal control charts. The primary advantage of the range is in providing a knowledge of the total spread of the data. It is also valuable when the amount of data is too small or too scattered to justify the calculation of a more precise measure of dispersion. The range is not a function of a measure of central tendency. As the number of observations increases, the accuracy of the range decreases, since it becomes easier for extremely high or low readings to occur. It is suggested that the use of the range be limited to a maximum of 10 observations.

The standard deviation is used when a more precise measure is desired. It is also the most common measure of the dispersion for quality control work and is used when subsequent statistics are to be calculated. When the data have an extreme value for the high or the low, the standard deviation is more desirable than the range.

OTHER MEASURES

There are two other measures that are frequently used to analyze a collection of data—skewness and kurtosis.

Skewness

As indicated previously, *skewness* is a lack of symmetry of the data. The formula is given by[3]

$$a_3 = \frac{\sum_{i=1}^{h} f_i(X_i - \overline{X})^3/n}{s^3}$$

where a_3 represents skewness.

Skewness is a number whose size tells us the extent of the departure from symmetry. If the value of a_3 is 0, the data are symmetrical; if greater than 0 (positive), the data are skewed to the right, which means that the long tail is to the right; and if less than 0 (negative), the data are skewed to the left, which means that the long tail is to the left. See Figure 2-9 for a graphical representation of skewness. Values of $+1$ or -1 imply a strong unsymmetrical distribution.

---

[3] This formula is an approximation that is good enough for most purposes.

TABLE 2-10 Data for Skewness and Kurtosis Example Problems

X_I	f_i	$X_i - \bar{X}$	$f_i(X_i - \bar{X})^3$	$f_i(X_i - \bar{X})^4$
1	1	$(1 - 7) = -6$	$1(-6)^3 = -216$	$1(-6)^4 = 1296$
4	6	$(4 - 7) = -3$	$6(-3)^3 = -162$	$6(-3)^4 = 486$
7	16	$(7 - 7) = 0$	$16(0)^3 = 0$	$16(0)^4 = 0$
10	8	$(10 - 7) = +3$	$8(+3)^3 = +216$	$8(+3)^4 = 648$
	$\Sigma = 31$		$\Sigma = -162$	$\Sigma = 2430$

EXAMPLE PROBLEM

Determine the skewness of the frequency distribution of Table 2-10. The average and sample standard deviation are calculated and are 7.0 and 2.32, respectively.

$$a_3 = \frac{\sum_{i=1}^{h} f_i(X_i - \bar{X})^3/n}{s^3}$$

$$= \frac{-162/31}{2.32^3}$$

$$= -0.42$$

The skewness value of -0.42 tells us that the data are quite skewed to the left. Visual examination of the X and f columns or a histogram would have indicated the same information.

In order to use the skewness value, the value of n must be large, say at least 100. Also, the distribution must be unimodal. The skewness value provides information concerning the shape of the population distribution. For example, a normal distribution has a skewness value of zero, $a_3 = 0$.

Kurtosis

As indicated previously, *kurtosis* is the peakedness of the data. The formula is given by[4]

$$a_4 = \frac{\sum_{i=1}^{h} f_i(X_i - \bar{X})^4/n}{s^4}$$

where a_4 represents kurtosis.

[4] This formula is an approximation that is good enough for most purposes.

Kurtosis is a dimensionless value that is used as a comparative measure of the height of the peak in two distributions. See Figure 2-6 and Figure 2-11 for a graphical representation of kurtosis.

EXAMPLE PROBLEM

Determine the kurtosis of the frequency distribution of Table 2-10, which has $\bar{X} = 7.0$ and $s = 2.32$.

$$a_4 = \frac{\sum\limits_{i=1}^{h} f_i(X_i - \bar{X})^4/n}{s^4}$$

$$= \frac{2430/31}{2.32^4}$$

$$= 2.70$$

The kurtosis value of 2.70 does not provide any information by itself—it must be compared to another distribution. Use of the kurtosis value is the same as skewness—large sample size, n, and unimodal distribution. It provides information concerning the shape of the population distribution. For example, a normal distribution, mesokurtic, has a kurtosis value of 3, $a_4 = 3$. If $a_4 > 3$, then the height of the distribution is more peaked than normal, leptokurtic, and if $a_4 < 3$, the height of the distribution is less peaked than normal, platykurtic.

The concepts of skewness and kurtosis are useful in that they provide some information about the shape of the distribution.

CONCEPT OF A POPULATION AND A SAMPLE

At this point, it is desirable to examine the concept of a population and a sample. In order to construct a frequency distribution of the weights of steel shafts, a small portion, or *sample,* is selected to represent all the steel shafts. Similarly, the data collected concerning the passenger car speeds represented only a small portion of all the passenger cars. The population is the whole collection of measurements, and in the examples above, the population would be all the steel shafts and all the passenger cars. When averages, standard deviations, and other measures are computed from samples, they are referred to as *statistics.* Since the composition of samples will fluctuate, the computed statistics will be larger or smaller than their true population values, or *parameters.* Parameters are considered to be fixed reference (standard) values or the best estimate of these values available at a particular time.

The population may have a finite number of items, such as a day's production of steel shafts. It may be infinite or almost infinite, such as the number of rivets in a year's production of jet airplanes. The population may be defined differently depending on the particular situation. Thus, a study of a product could involve the population of an hour's production, a week's production, 5000 pieces, and so on.

Since it is rarely possible to measure all of the population, a sample is selected. Sampling is necessary when it may be impossible to measure the entire population, when the expense to observe all the data is prohibitive; when the required inspection destroys the product; or when a test of the entire population may be too dangerous, as would be the case with a new medical drug. Actually, an analysis of the entire population may not be as accurate as sampling. It has been shown that 100% manual inspection is not as accurate as sampling. This is probably due to the fact that boredom and fatigue cause inspectors to prejudge each inspected item as being acceptable.

When designating a population, the corresponding Greek letter is used. Thus, the sample average has the symbol $\bar{X}$, and the population mean the symbol μ (mu). Note that the word "average" changes to "mean" when used for the population. The symbol $\bar{X}_0$ is the standard or reference value. Mathematical concepts are based on μ, which is the true value—$\bar{X}_0$ represents a practical equivalent in order to use the concepts. The sample standard deviation has the symbol s, and the population standard deviation the symbol σ (sigma). The symbol s_0 is the standard or reference value and has the same relationship to σ that $\bar{X}_0$ has to μ. The true population value may never be known; therefore, the symbols $\hat{\mu}$ and $\hat{\sigma}$ are sometimes used to indicate "estimate of." A comparison of sample and population is given in Table 2-11. Additional comparisons will be given as they occur.

TABLE 2-11   Comparison of Sample and Population

SAMPLE	POPULATION
Statistic	Parameter
$\bar{X}$—average	μ $(\bar{X}_0)$—mean
s—sample standard deviation	σ (s_0)—standard deviation

The primary objective in selecting a sample is to learn something about the population that will aid in making some type of decision. The sample selected must be of such a nature that it tends to resemble or represent the population. How successfully the sample represents the population is a function of the size of the sample, chance, sampling method, and whether the conditions change or not.

Table 2-12 shows the results of an experiment that illustrates the relationship between samples and the population. A container holds 800 blue and 200 green spheres 5 mm (approximately 3/16 in.) in diameter. The 1000 spheres are considered to be the population, with 20% being green. Samples of size 10 are selected and posted to the table and then replaced in the container. The table illustrates the differences between the sample results and what should be expected from the known population. Only in samples 2 and 7 are the sample statistics equal to the population parameter. There definitely is a chance factor that determines the composition of the sample. When the eight individual samples are combined into one large one, the

TABLE 2-12 Results of Eight Samples of Blue and Green Spheres from a Known Population

SAMPLE NUMBER	SAMPLE SIZE	NUMBER OF BLUE SPHERES	NUMBER OF GREEN SPHERES	PERCENTAGE OF GREEN SPHERES
1	10	9	1	10
2	10	8	2	20
3	10	5	5	50
4	10	9	1	10
5	10	7	3	30
6	10	10	0	0
7	10	8	2	20
8	10	9	1	10
Total	80	65	15	18.8

percentage of green spheres is 18.8, which is close to the population value of 20%.

While inferences are made about the population from samples, it is equally true that a knowledge of the population provides information for analysis of the sample. Thus, it is possible to determine whether a sample came from a particular population. This concept is necessary to understand control chart theory. A more detailed discussion is delayed until Chapter 3.

THE NORMAL CURVE

Description

Although there are as many different populations as there are conditions, they can be described by a few general types. One type of population that is quite common is called the *normal curve,* or *Gaussian distribution.* The normal curve is a symmetrical, unimodal, bell-shaped distribution with the mean, median, and mode having the same value.

A population curve or distribution is developed from a frequency histogram. As the sample size of a histogram gets larger and larger, the cell interval gets smaller and smaller. When the sample size is quite large and the cell interval is very small, the histogram will take on the appearance of a smooth polygon or a curve representing the population. A curve of the normal population of 1000 observations of the resistance in ohms of an electrical device with population mean, μ, of 90 Ω and population standard deviation, σ, of 2 Ω is shown in Figure 2-10.

Much of the variation in nature and in industry follows the frequency distribution of the normal curves. Thus, the variations in the weight of elephants, the speed of antelopes, and the height of human beings will follow a normal curve. Also, the variations found in industry, such as the weight of gray iron castings, the life of 60-W light bulbs, and the dimensions of a steel piston ring, will be expected to follow the normal curve. When considering the heights of human beings, we can expect a small percentage of them to be extremely tall and a small percentage to be extremely short, with the majority of human heights clustering about the average value. The normal curve is such a good description of the variations that occur to

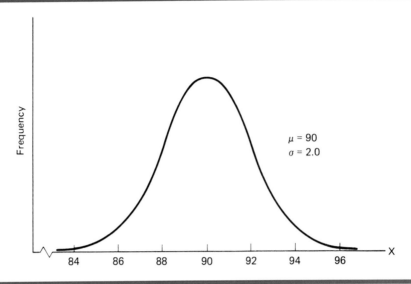

FIGURE 2-10 Normal distribution for resistance of an electrical device with μ = 90 ohms and σ = 2.0 ohms.

most quality characteristics in industry that it is the basis for many quality control techniques.

All normal distributions of continuous variables can be converted to the standardized normal distribution (see Figure 2-11) by using *the standardized normal value*, Z. For example, consider the value of 92 Ω in Figure 2-10, which is one standard deviation above the mean (μ + 1σ = 90 + 1(2) = 92). Conversion to the Z value is

$$Z = \frac{X_i - \mu}{\sigma} = \frac{92 - 90}{2} = +1$$

which is also 1σ above μ on the Z scale of Figure 2-11.

The formula for the standardized normal curve is

$$f(Z) = \frac{1}{\sqrt{2\pi}}e^{-Z^2/2} = 0.3989e^{-Z^2/2}$$

where π = 3.14159
e = 2.71828
$Z = \dfrac{X_i - \mu}{\sigma}$

Figure 2-11 shows the standardized curve with its mean of zero and standard deviation of 1. It is noted that the curve is asymptotic at Z = −3 and Z = +3.

The area under the curve is equal to 1.0000 or 100% and therefore can easily be used for probability calculations. Since the area under the curve between various points is a very useful statistic, a normal area table is provided as Table A in the appendix.

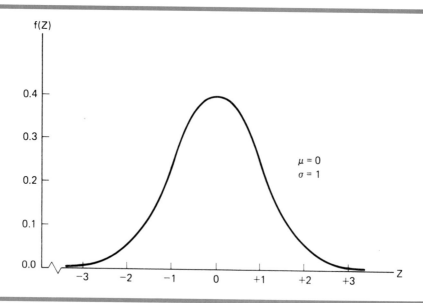

FIGURE 2-11   Standardized normal distribution with $\mu = 0$ and $\sigma = 1$.

The normal distribution can be referred to as a normal probability distribution. While it is the most important population distribution, there are a number of other ones for continuous variables. There are also a number of probability distributions for discrete variables. These distributions are discussed in Chapter 4.

Relationship to the Mean and Standard Deviation

As seen by the formula for the standardized normal curve, there is a definite relationship among the mean, the standard deviation, and the normal curve. Figure 2-12 shows three normal curves with different mean values; it is noted that the only change is in the location. Figure 2-13 shows three normal curves with the same mean but different standard deviations. The figure illustrates the principle that the

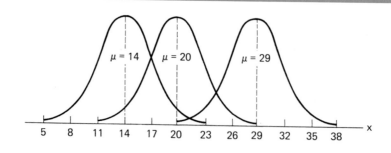

FIGURE 2-12   **Normal curve with different means but identical standard deviations.**

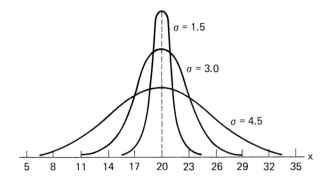

FIGURE 2-13 Normal curve with different standard deviations but identical means.

larger the standard deviation, the flatter the curve (data are widely dispersed), and the smaller the standard deviation, the more peaked the curve (data are narrowly dispersed). If the standard deviation is zero, all values are identical to the mean and there is no curve.

The normal distribution is fully defined by the population mean and population standard deviation. Also, as seen by Figures 2-12 and 2-13, these two parameters are independent. In other words, a change in one has no effect on the other.

A relationship exists between the standard deviation and the area under the normal curve as shown in Figure 2-14. The figure shows that in a normal distribution 68.26% of the items are included between the limits of $\mu + 1\sigma$ and $\mu - 1\sigma$, 95.46% of the items are included between the limits $\mu + 2\sigma$ and $\mu - 2\sigma$, and 99.73% of the items are included between $\mu + 3\sigma$ and $\mu - 3\sigma$. One hundred percent of the items are included between the limits $+\infty$ and $-\infty$. These percentages hold true regardless of the shape of the normal curve. The fact that 99.73% of the items are included between $\pm 3\sigma$ is the basis for control charts that are discussed in Chapter 3.

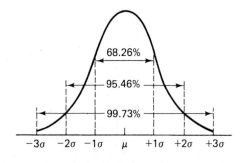

FIGURE 2-14 Percent of items included between certain values of the standard deviation.

Applications

The percentage of items included between any two values can be determined by calculus. However, this is not necessary, since the areas under the curve for various Z values are given in Table A in the appendix. Table A, "Areas Under the Normal Curve," is a left-reading table,[5] which means that the given areas are for that portion of the curve from $-\infty$ to a particular value, X_i.

The first step is to determine the Z value using the formula

$$Z = \frac{X_i - \mu}{\sigma}$$

where Z = standard normal value
$\quad\quad X_i$ = individual value
$\quad\quad \mu$ = mean
$\quad\quad \sigma$ = population standard deviation

Next, using the calculated Z value the area under the curve to the left of X_i is found in Table A. Thus, if a calculated Z value is -1.76, the value for the area is 0.0392. Since the total area under the curve is 1.0000, the 0.0392 value for the area can be changed to a percent of the items under the curve by moving the decimal point two places to the right. Therefore, 3.92% of the items are less than the particular X_i value.

Assuming that the data are normally distributed, it is possible to find the percent of the items in the data that are less than a particular value, greater than a particular value, or between two values. When the values are upper and/or lower specifications, a powerful statistical tool is available. The following example problems will illustrate the technique.

EXAMPLE PROBLEM

The mean value of the weight of a particular brand of cereal for the past year is 0.297 kg (10.5 oz) with a standard deviation of 0.024 kg. Assuming a normal distribution, find the percent of the data that falls below the lower specification limit of 0.274 kg. (*Note:* Since the mean and standard deviation were determined from a large number of tests during the year, they are considered to be valid estimates of the population values.)

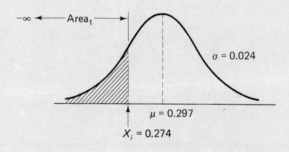

---

[5] In some texts the table for the areas under the normal curve is arranged in a different manner.

$$Z = \frac{X_i - \mu}{\sigma}$$

$$= \frac{0.274 - 0.297}{0.024}$$

$$= -0.96$$

From Table A it is found that for $Z = -0.96$,

$$\text{Area}_1 = 0.1685 \quad \text{or} \quad 16.85\%$$

Thus, 16.85% of the data are less than 0.274 kg.

EXAMPLE PROBLEM

Using the data from the preceding problem, determine the percentage of the data that fall above 0.347 kg.

Since Table A is a left-reading table, the solution to this problem requires the use of the relationship: $\text{Area}_1 + \text{Area}_2 = \text{Area}_T = 1.0000$. Therefore, Area_2 is determined and subtracted from 1.0000 to obtain Area_1.

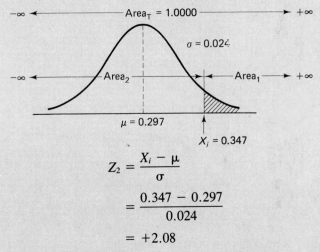

$$Z_2 = \frac{X_i - \mu}{\sigma}$$

$$= \frac{0.347 - 0.297}{0.024}$$

$$= +2.08$$

From Table A it is found that for $Z_2 = +2.08$,

$$\text{Area}_2 = 0.9812$$

$$\text{Area}_1 = \text{Area}_T - \text{Area}_2$$

$$= 1.0000 - 0.9812$$

$$= 0.0188 \text{ or } 1.88\%$$

Thus, 1.88% of the data are above 0.347 kg.

EXAMPLE PROBLEM

A large number of tests of line voltage to home residences show a mean of 118.5 V and a population standard deviation of 1.20 V. Determine the percentage of data between 116 and 120 V.

Since Table A is a left-reading table, the solution requires that the area to the left of 116 V be subtracted from the area to the left of 120 V. The graph and calculations show the technique.

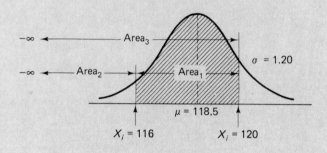

$$Z_2 = \frac{X_i - \mu}{\sigma} \qquad Z_3 = \frac{X_i - \mu}{\sigma}$$

$$= \frac{116 - 118.5}{1.20} \qquad = \frac{120 - 118.5}{1.20}$$

$$= -2.08 \qquad = +1.25$$

From Table A it is found that for $Z_2 = -2.08$, $\text{Area}_2 = 0.0188$; for $Z_3 = +1.25$, $\text{Area}_3 = 0.8944$.

$$\text{Area}_1 = \text{Area}_3 - \text{Area}_2$$

$$= 0.8944 - 0.0188$$

$$= 0.8756 \quad \text{or} \quad 87.56\%$$

Thus, 87.56% of the data are between 116 and 120 V.

EXAMPLE PROBLEM

If it is desired to have 12.1% of the line voltage below 115 V, how should the mean voltage be adjusted? The dispersion is $\sigma = 1.20$ V.

The solution to this type problem is the reverse of the other problems. First 12.1%, or 0.1210, is found in the body of Table A. This gives a Z value and using the formula for Z, we can solve for the mean voltage. From Table A with $\text{Area}_1 = 0.1210$, the Z value of -1.17 is obtained by interpolation.

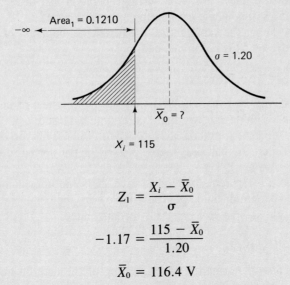

$$Z_1 = \frac{X_i - \overline{X}_0}{\sigma}$$

$$-1.17 = \frac{115 - \overline{X}_0}{1.20}$$

$$\overline{X}_0 = 116.4 \text{ V}$$

Thus, the mean voltage should be centered at 116.4 V for 12.1% of the values to be less than 115 V.

Note that $\overline{X}_0$ has been substituted in the equation. The normal curve concept is based on the values of μ and σ; however, $\overline{X}_0$ and s_σ can substitute provided there is some evidence that the distribution is normal. The last example problem illustrates the independence of μ and σ. A small change in the centering of the process does not affect the dispersion.

TESTS FOR NORMALITY

Because of the importance of the normal distribution, it is frequently necessary to determine if the data are normal. In using these techniques the reader is cautioned that none are 100% certain. The techniques of histogram, skewness and kurtosis, probability plots, and chi-square test are also applicable with some modification to other population distributions.

Histogram

Visual examination of a histogram developed from a large amount of data will give an indication of the underlying population distribution. If a histogram is unimodal, symmetrical, and tapers off at the tails, normality is a definite possibility and may be sufficient information in many practical situations. The histogram of Figure 2-4 of steel shaft weight is unimodal, tapers off at the tails, and is somewhat symmetrical except for the upper tail. If a sorting operation had discarded shafts with weights above 2.575, this would explain the upper tail cutoff.

The larger the sample size, the better the judgment of normality. A minimum sample size of 50 is recommended.

Skewness and Kurtosis

Skewness and kurtosis measurements are another test of normality. From the steel shaft data of Table 2-6, we find that $a_3 = -0.11$ and $a_4 = 2.19$. These values indicate that the data are moderately skewed to the left but are close to the normal value of 0; and that the data are not as peaked as the normal distribution, which would have an a_4 value of 3.0.

These measurements tend to give the same information as the histogram. As with the histogram, the larger the sample size, the better the judgment of normality. A minimum sample size of 100 is recommended.

Probability Plots

Another test of normality is the plotting of the data on normal probability paper. This type of paper is shown in Figure 2-15. Different probability papers are used for different distributions. To illustrate the procedure we will again use the steel shaft data in its coded form. The step-by-step procedure follows.

1. *Order the data.* The data from the first column of Table 2-4 are used to illustrate the concept. Each observation is recorded as shown in Table 2-13 from the smallest to the largest. Duplicate observations are recorded as shown by the value 46.

2. *Rank the observations.* Starting at 1 for the lowest observation, 2 for the next lowest observation, and so on, rank the observations. The ranks are shown in Column 2 of Table 2-13.

3. *Calculate the plotting position.* This step is accomplished using the formula

$$PP = \frac{100(i - 0.5)}{n}$$

where i = rank
PP = plotting position in percent
n = sample size

The first plotting position is $100(1 - 0.5)/22$, which is 2.3%; the others are calculated similarly and posted to Table 2-13.

4. *Label the data scale.* The coded values range from 32 to 71, so the vertical scale is labeled appropriately and is shown in Figure 2-15. The horizontal scale represents the normal curve and is preprinted on the paper.

5. *Plot the points.* The plotting position and the observation are plotted on the normal probability paper.

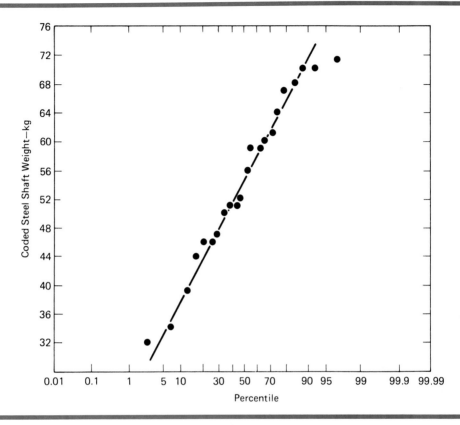

FIGURE 2-15   Probability plots of data from Table 2-13.

TABLE 2-13   Data on Steel Shaft Weight for Probability Plotting

OBSERVATION X_i	RANK i	PLOTTING POSITION	OBSERVATION X_i	RANK i	PLOTTING POSITION
32	1	2.3	56	12	52.3
34	2	6.8	59	13	56.8
39	3	11.4	59	14	61.4
44	4	15.9	60	15	65.9
46	5	20.5	61	16	70.5
46	6	25.0	64	17	75.0
47	7	29.5	67	18	79.5
50	8	34.1	68	19	84.1
51	9	38.6	70	20	88.6
51	10	43.2	70	21	93.2
52	11	47.7	71	22	97.7

6. *Attempt to fit by eye a "best" line.* A clear plastic straightedge will be most helpful in making this judgment. When fitting this line, greater weight should be given to the center values than to the extreme ones.

7. *Determine normality.* This decision is one of judgment as to how close the points are to the straight line. If we disregard the extreme points at each end of the line, we can reasonably assume that the data are normally distributed.

If normality appears reasonable, additional information can be obtained from the graph. The mean is located at the 50th percentile, which gives a value of approximately 55. Standard deviation is two-fifths the difference between the 90th percentile and the 10th percentile, which would be approximately $14[(2/5)(72 - 38)]$. We can also use the graph to determine the percent of data below, above, or between data values. For example, the percent less than 48 is approximately 31%. Even though the example problem used 22 data points with good results, a minimum sample size of 30 is recommended.

Chi-Square

The chi-square test is another technique of determining if the sample data fits a normal distribution or other distribution. This technique is beyond the scope of this book; however, it is available in most statistics textbooks. A minimum sample size of 125 is recommended.

It is important for the analyst to understand that none of these techniques prove that the data are normally distributed. We can only conclude that there is no evidence that the data cannot be treated as if they were normally distributed.

COMPUTER PROGRAM

Sample computer programs are given for this chapter and for Chapters 3, 4, 5, 6, and 7. These programs have been designed to run on microcomputers and have been written in Microsoft BASIC and tested on a Zenith Z-89. The programs are given in as simple a form as possible and follow the text so that the reader can understand the programming. Provision for storing input data and correcting input data errors is not included in the programs.

The sample program for this chapter computes the seven basic statistics and determines the frequency distribution. It is shown in Figure 2-16. If it is desired to print out the data, an LPRINT statement should be inserted after statement 110. Also, a coding statement can be used after statement 100. Provision is made in the program to change the frequency distribution by changing the cell interval and/or the lowest cell midpoint value. Data used for the program are given in Table 2-4.

The program can be enhanced by graphing the frequency distribution in the form of a histogram. This activity is a function of the graphical output device available. Also, relative frequency, cumulative frequency, and relative cumulative frequency can be developed with a few additional statements.

```
10 REM                        STAT-PACK
20 REM
30 REM          Average, Median, Range, Standard Deviation
40 REM                Variance, Kurtosis, Skewness,
50 REM                   Frequency Distribution
60 REM
70 DIM X(600), MP(20), LB(20), UB(20), F(600)
80 PRINT " Enter number of data points." : INPUT N
90 PRINT " Enter data."
100        FOR I = 1 TO N
110        INPUT X(I)
120        NEXT I
130 REM                        Average
140 SX = 0
150        FOR I=1 TO N
160        SX = SX + X(I)
170        NEXT I
180 AVG = SX / N
190 LPRINT TAB(5);" Average = ";AVG
200 REM                   Sample Standard Deviation, Variance,
210 REM                        Skewness, Kurtosis
220 S2 = 0 : S3 = 0 : S4 = 0
230        FOR I = 1 TO N
240        D = X(I) - AVG
250        S2 = S2 + D^2
260        S3 = S3 + D^3
270        S4 = S4 + D^4
280        NEXT I
290 SD = SQR(S2 / (N-1))
300 VA = SD^2
310 A3 = S3 / N / SD^3
320 A4 = S4 / N / SD^4
330 LPRINT TAB(5);" Sample Standard Deviation = ";SD
340 LPRINT TAB(5);" Variance = ";VA
350 LPRINT TAB(5);" Skewness = ";A3
360 LPRINT TAB(5);" Kurtosis = ";A4
370 REM                        Sort Routine
380        FOR J = 1 TO (N - 1)
390        K = N - J
400        FOR I = 1 TO K
410        Q = I + 1
420        IF X(I) < X(Q) GOTO 460
430        A = X(I)
440        X(I) = X(Q)
450        X(Q) = A
460        NEXT I
470        NEXT J
480 REM                        Range
490 R=X(N)-X(1)
500 LPRINT TAB(5);" Range = ";R
510 REM                        Median
520 J = (N + 1) / 2
530 K = (N + 1) / 2
540 MD = (X(J) + X(K)) / 2
550 LPRINT TAB(5);" Median = "; MD
560 REM                   Frequency Distribution
570 PRINT " Enter Interval---odd value preferred.
580 INPUT IN
590 PRINT " Enter 1 if lowest cell midpoint is lowest X(I) value."
600 PRINT " Enter 0 if another lowest cell midpoint is desired."
```

FIGURE 2-16 Computer program in BASIC to calculate the seven basic statistics and the frequency distribution.

```
610 INPUT M
620 IF M = 1 THEN MP(1) = X(1) : GOTO 650
630 PRINT " Enter midpoint value of lowest cell."
640 INPUT MP(1)
650 LB(1) = MP(1) - IN / 2
660 UB(1) = MP(1) + IN / 2
670 MPS = MP(1) : LBS = LB(1) : UBS = UB(1)
680        FOR K = 2 TO 20
690        MPS = MPS + IN
700        MP(K) = MPS
710        LBS = LBS + IN
720        LB(K) = LBS
730        UBS = UBS + IN
740        UB(K) = UBS
750        IF UB(K) >= X(N) GOTO 810
760        NEXT K
770 IF UB(K - 1) < X(N) GOTO 790
780 GOTO 810
790 PRINT " Cell interval too small select a larger one."
800 GOTO 570
810 H=K
820        FOR J=1 TO H
830        FS = 0
840        FOR I = 1 TO N
850        IF X(I) < LB(J) GOTO 890
860        IF X(I) > UB(J) GOTO 890
870        FS = FS + 1
880        F(J) = FS
890        NEXT I
900        NEXT J
910 LPRINT : LPRINT
920 LPRINT TAB(10);" BOUNDARIES";TAB(29);" MIDPOINT";TAB(45);" FREQUENCY"
930        FOR J = 1 TO H
940        LPRINT TAB(7); LB(J);"/";UB(J);TAB(31); MP(J);TAB(49); F(J)
950        NEXT J
960 PRINT " If the frequency distribution is satisfactory, Enter 1."
970 PRINT " If the frequency distribution is unsatisfactory, Enter 0."
980 PRINT "    and select another interval and/or midpoint."
990 INPUT M
1000 IF M = 1 GOTO 1020
1010 IF M = 0 GOTO 570
1020 END
```

```
Average =  2.554
Sample Standard Deviation =   .0111273
Variance =  1.23817E-04
Skewness = -.0837673
Kurtosis =  2.22477
Range =  .0440002
Median =  2.553
```

BOUNDARIES	MIDPOINT	FREQUENCY
2.5305 / 2.5355	2.533	6
2.5355 / 2.5405	2.538	8
2.5405 / 2.5455	2.543	12
2.5455 / 2.5505	2.548	13
2.5505 / 2.5555	2.553	20
2.5555 / 2.5605	2.558	19
2.5605 / 2.5655	2.563	13
2.5655 / 2.5705	2.568	11
2.5705 / 2.5755	2.573	8

FIGURE 2-16 (*cont.*)

PROBLEMS

1. Round the following numbers to two decimal places.
   (a) 0.862   (b) 0.625   (c) 0.149   (d) 0.475

2. Perform the operation indicated and leave the answer in the correct number of significant figures.
   (a) (34.6)(8.20)   (b) (0.035)(635)   (c) 3.8735/6.1   (d) 5.362/6 (6 is a counting number)   (e) 5.362/6 (6 is not a counting number)

3. Perform the operation indicated and leave the answer in the correct number of significant figures.
   (a) 64.3 + 2.05   (b) 381.0 − 1.95   (c) 8.652 − 4 (4 is not a counting number)   (d) 8.652 − 4 (4 is a counting number)   (e) 6.4 × 10² − 24.32

4. In his last 70 games a professional basketball player made the following scores:

10	17	9	17	18	20	16
7	17	19	13	15	14	13
12	13	15	14	13	10	14
11	15	14	11	15	15	16
9	18	15	12	14	13	14
13	14	16	15	16	15	15
14	15	15	16	13	12	16
10	16	14	13	16	14	15
6	15	13	16	15	16	16
12	14	16	15	16	13	15

   (a) Make a tally sheet in ascending order.
   (b) Using the data above, construct a histogram.

5. A company that fills bottles of shampoo tries to maintain a specific weight of the product. The table gives the weight of 110 bottles that were checked at random intervals. Make a tally of these weights and construct a frequency histogram. (Weight is in kilograms.)

6.00	5.98	6.01	6.01	5.97	5.99	5.98	6.01	5.99	5.98	5.96
5.98	5.99	5.99	6.03	5.99	6.01	5.98	5.99	5.97	6.01	5.98
5.97	6.01	6.00	5.96	6.00	5.97	5.95	5.99	5.99	6.01	6.00
6.01	6.03	6.01	5.99	5.99	6.02	6.00	5.98	6.01	5.98	5.99
6.00	5.98	6.05	6.00	6.00	5.98	5.99	6.00	5.97	6.00	6.00
6.00	5.98	6.00	5.94	5.99	6.02	6.00	5.98	6.02	6.01	6.00
5.97	6.01	6.04	6.02	6.01	5.97	5.99	6.02	5.99	6.02	5.99
6.02	5.99	6.01	5.98	5.99	6.00	6.02	5.99	6.02	5.95	6.02
5.96	5.99	6.00	6.00	6.01	5.99	5.96	6.01	6.00	6.01	5.98
6.00	5.99	5.98	5.99	6.03	5.99	6.02	5.98	6.02	6.02	5.97

6. Listed next are 125 readings obtained in a hospital by a motion-and-time-study analyst who took five readings each day for 25 days. Construct a tally sheet. Prepare a

table showing cell midpoints, cell boundaries, and observed frequencies. Plot a frequency histogram.

DAY	DURATION OF OPERATION TIME (MIN)				
1	1.90	1.93	1.95	2.05	2.20
2	1.76	1.81	1.81	1.83	2.01
3	1.80	1.87	1.95	1.97	2.07
4	1.77	1.83	1.87	1.90	1.93
5	1.93	1.95	2.03	2.05	2.14
6	1.76	1.88	1.95	1.97	2.00
7	1.87	2.00	2.00	2.03	2.10
8	1.91	1.92	1.94	1.97	2.05
9	1.90	1.91	1.95	2.01	2.05
10	1.79	1.91	1.93	1.94	2.10
11	1.90	1.97	2.00	2.06	2.28
12	1.80	1.82	1.89	1.91	1.99
13	1.75	1.83	1.92	1.95	2.04
14	1.87	1.90	1.98	2.00	2.08
15	1.90	1.95	1.95	1.97	2.03
16	1.82	1.99	2.01	2.06	2.06
17	1.90	1.95	1.95	2.00	2.10
18	1.81	1.90	1.94	1.97	1.99
19	1.87	1.89	1.98	2.01	2.15
20	1.72	1.78	1.96	2.00	2.05
21	1.87	1.89	1.91	1.91	2.00
22	1.76	1.80	1.91	2.06	2.12
23	1.95	1.96	1.97	2.00	2.00
24	1.92	1.94	1.97	1.99	2.00
25	1.85	1.90	1.90	1.92	1.92

7. The relative strength of 150 silver solder welds are tested, and the results are given in the table below. Tally these figures and arrange them in a frequency distribution. Determine the cell interval and the approximate number of cells. Make a table showing cell midpoints, cell boundaries, and observed frequencies. Plot a frequency histogram.

1.5	1.2	3.1	1.3	0.7	1.3
0.1	2.9	1.0	1.3	2.6	1.7
0.3	0.7	2.4	1.5	0.7	2.1
3.5	1.1	0.7	0.5	1.6	1.4
1.7	3.2	3.0	1.7	2.8	2.2
1.8	2.3	3.3	3.1	3.3	2.9
2.2	1.2	1.3	1.4	2.3	2.5
3.1	2.1	3.5	1.4	2.8	2.8
1.5	1.9	2.0	3.0	0.9	3.1
1.9	1.7	1.5	3.0	2.6	1.0
2.9	1.8	1.4	1.4	3.3	2.4
1.8	2.1	1.6	0.9	2.1	1.5

0.9	2.9	2.5	1.6	1.2	2.4
3.4	1.3	1.7	2.6	1.1	0.8
1.0	1.5	2.2	3.0	2.0	1.8
2.9	2.5	2.0	3.0	1.5	1.3
2.2	1.0	1.7	3.1	2.7	2.3
0.6	2.0	1.4	3.3	2.2	2.9
1.6	2.3	3.3	2.0	1.6	2.7
1.9	2.1	3.4	1.5	0.8	2.2
1.8	2.4	1.2	3.7	1.3	2.1
2.9	3.0	2.1	1.8	1.1	1.4
2.8	1.8	1.8	2.4	2.3	2.2
2.1	1.2	1.4	1.6	2.4	2.1
2.0	1.1	3.8	1.3	1.3	1.0

8. Using the data of Problem 4, construct:
  (a) A relative frequency histogram
  (b) A cumulative frequency histogram
  (c) A relative cumulative frequency histogram

9. Using the data of Problem 5, construct:
  (a) A relative frequency histogram
  (b) A cumulative frequency histogram
  (c) A relative cumulative frequency histogram

10. Using the data of Problem 6, construct:
  (a) A relative frequency histogram
  (b) A cumulative frequency histogram
  (c) A relative cumulative frequency histogram

11. Using the data of Problem 7, construct:
  (a) A relative frequency histogram
  (b) A cumulative frequency histogram
  (c) A relative cumulative frequency histogram

12. Construct a bar graph of the data in:
  (a) Problem 4
  (b) Problem 5

13. Using the data of Problem 6, construct:
  (a) A polygon
  (b) An ogive

14. Using the data of Problem 7, construct:
  (a) A polygon
  (b) An ogive

15. An electrician testing the incoming line voltage for a residential house obtains five readings: 115, 113, 121, 115, 116. What is the average?

16. An employee makes eight trips to load a trailer. If the trip distances in meters are 25.6, 24.8, 22.6, 21.3, 19.6, 18.5, 16.2, and 15.5, what is the average?

17. Tests of noise ratings at prescribed locations throughout a large stamping mill are given in the frequency distribution below. Noise is measured in decibels. Determine the average.

CELL MIDPOINT	FREQUENCY
148	2
139	3
130	8
121	11
112	27
103	35
94	43
85	33
76	20
67	12
58	6
49	4
40	2

18. The weight of 65 castings in kilograms is distributed as follows:

CELL MIDPOINT	FREQUENCY
3.5	6
3.8	9
4.1	18
4.4	14
4.7	13
5.0	5

Determine the average.

19. Destructive tests on the life of an electronic component were conducted on two different occasions. On the first occasion three tests had a mean of 3320 h; on the second occasion two tests had a mean of 3180 h. What is the weighted average?

20. The average height of 24 students in section 1 of a course in quality control is 1.75 m; the average height of 18 students in section 2 of quality control is 1.79 m; and the average height of 29 students in section 3 of quality control is 1.68 m. What is the average height of the students in the three sections of quality control?

21. Determine the median of the following numbers.
    (a) 22, 11, 15, 8, 18
    (b) 35, 28, 33, 38, 43, 36

22. Determine the median for the following:
    (a) The frequency distribution of Problem 17
    (b) The frequency distribution of Problem 18
    (c) The frequency distribution of Problem 28

(d) The frequency distribution of Problem 30

(e) The frequency distribution of Problem 6

(f) The frequency distribution of Problem 7

23. Given the following series of numbers, determine the mode.

(a) 50, 45, 55, 55, 45, 50, 55, 45, 55

(b) 89, 87, 88, 83, 86, 82, 84

(c) 11, 17, 14, 12, 12, 14, 14, 15, 17, 17

24. Determine the modal cell of the data in:

(a) Problem 4

(b) Problem 5

(c) Problem 6

(d) Problem 7

(e) Problem 17

(f) Problem 18

25. Determine the range for each set of numbers.

(a) 16, 25, 18, 17, 16, 21, 14

(b) 45, 39, 42, 42, 43

(c) The data in Problem 4

(d) The data in Problem 5

26. Frequency tests of a brass rod 145 cm long give values of 1200, 1190, 1205, 1185, and 1200 vibrations per second. What is the sample standard deviation?

27. Four readings of the thickness of the paper in this textbook are 0.076 mm, 0.082 mm, 0.073 mm, and 0.077 mm. Determine the sample standard deviation.

28. The frequency distribution given here shows the percent of organic sulfur in Illinois No. 5 coal. Determine the sample standard deviation.

CELL MIDPOINT (%)	FREQUENCY (NUMBER OF SAMPLES)
0.5	1
0.8	16
1.1	12
1.4	10
1.7	12
2.1	18
2.4	16
2.7	3

29. Determine the sample standard deviation for the following.

(a) The data of Problem 7

(b) The data of Problem 17

30. Determine the average and sample standard deviation for the frequency distribution of the number of inspections per day as follows:

CELL MIDPOINT	FREQUENCY
1000	6
1300	13
1600	22
1900	17
2200	11
2500	8

31. Using the data of Problem 17, construct:
(a) A polygon
(b) An ogive

32. Using the data of Problem 18, construct:
(a) A polygon
(b) An ogive

33. Using the data of Problem 28, construct:
(a) A polygon
(b) An ogive

34. Using the data of Problem 30, construct:
(a) A polygon
(b) An ogive

35. Using the data of Problem 17, construct:
(a) A histogram
(b) A relative frequency histogram
(c) A cumulative frequency histogram
(d) A relative cumulative frequency histogram

36. Using the data of Problem 18, construct:
(a) A histogram
(b) A relative frequency histogram
(c) A cumulative frequency histogram
(d) A relative cumulative frequency histogram

37. Using the data of Problem 28, construct:
(a) A histogram
(b) A relative frequency histogram
(c) A cumulative frequency histogram
(d) A relative cumulative frequency histogram

38. Using the data of Problem 30, construct:
(a) A histogram
(b) A relative frequency histogram
(c) A cumulative frequency histogram
(d) A relative cumulative frequency histogram

39. Determine the skewness and kurtosis of:
  (a) Problem 4
  (b) Problem 5
  (c) Problem 6
  (d) Problem 7
  (e) Problem 18
  (f) Problem 30

40. If the maximum allowable noise is 134.5 db, what percent of the data of Problem 17 is above that value?

41. Evaluate the histogram of Problem 18, where the specifications are 4.25 ± 0.60 kg.

42. A utility company will not use coal with a sulfur content of more than 2.25%. Based on the histogram of Problem 28, what percent of the coal is in that category?

43. The population mean of a company's racing bicycles is 9.07 kg (20.0 lb) with a population standard deviation of 0.40 kg. If the distribution is approximately normal, determine (a) the percentage of bicycles less than 8.30 kg, (b) the percentage of bicycles greater than 10.00 kg, and (c) the percentage of bicycles between 8.00 and 10.10 kg. $13-16 = -2$

44. If the mean time to clean a motel room is 16.0 min and the standard deviation is 1.5 min, what percentage of the rooms will take less than 13.0 min to complete? What percentage of the rooms will take more than 20.0 min to complete? What percentage of the rooms will take between 13.0 and 20.5 min to complete? The data are normally distributed.

45. A cold-cereal manufacturer wants 1.5% of the product to be below the weight specification of 0.567 kg (1.25 lb). If the data are normally distributed and the standard deviation of the cereal filling machine is 0.018 kg, what mean weight is required? $.606$ *working Backwards*

46. In the precision grinding of a complicated part, it is more economical to rework the part than to scrap it. Therefore, it is decided to establish the rework percentage at 12.5%. Assuming normal distribution of the data, a standard deviation of 0.01 mm, and an upper specification limit of 25.38 mm (0.99 in.), determine the process center. 25.37

47. Using the information of Problem 39, what is your judgment concerning the normality of the distribution?
  (a) Problem 4
  (b) Problem 5
  (c) Problem 6
  (d) Problem 7
  (e) Problem 18
  (f) Problem 30

48. Using normal probability paper, determine (judgment) the normality of the distribution of the following.
  (a) Second column of Table 2-4

(b) First three columns of Problem 5

(c) Second column of Problem 6

49. Test, and if necessary rewrite, the computer program for your computer.

50. Modify the computer program to output a histogram for your graphical output device.

51. Modify the computer program to output a relative frequency histogram, cumulative frequency histogram, and relative cumulative frequency histogram for your graphical output device.

3

CONTROL CHARTS FOR VARIABLES

INTRODUCTION

Variation

One of the axioms or truisms of manufacturing is that no two objects are ever made exactly alike. In fact, the variation concept is a law of nature in that no two natural items in any category are the same. The variation may be quite large and easily noticeable, such as the height of human beings, or the variation may be very small, such as the weight of fiber-tipped pens or the shape of snowflakes. When variations are very small, it may appear that items are identical; however, precision instruments will show differences. If two items appear to have the same measurement, it is due to the limits of our measuring instruments. As measuring instruments have become more refined, variation has continued to exist, only the increment of variation has changed. The ability to measure variation is necessary before it can be controlled.

There are three categories of variations in piece part production.

65

1. *Within-piece variation*. This type of variation is illustrated by the surface roughness of a piece wherein one portion of the surface is rougher than another portion; or the width of one end of a keyway varies from the other end.

2. *Piece-to-piece variation*. This type of variation occurs among pieces produced at the same time. Thus, the light intensity of four consecutive light bulbs produced from a machine will be different.

3. *Time-to-time variation*. This type of variation is illustrated by the difference in product produced at different times of the day. Thus, product produced in the early morning would be different from that produced later in the day; or as a cutting tool wears, the cutting characteristics change.

Categories of variation for other types of processes such as a continuous chemical process will not be exactly the same; however, the concept will be similar.

Variation is present in every process due to a combination of the equipment, materials, environment, and the operator. The first source of variation is the *equipment*. This source includes tool wear, machine vibration, workholding-device positioning, and hydraulic and electrical fluctuations. When all these variations are put together, there is a certain capability or precision within which the equipment operates. Even supposedly identical machines will have different capabilities, and this fact becomes a very important consideration when scheduling the manufacture of critical parts.

The second source of variation is the *material*. Since variation occurs in the finished product, it must also occur in the raw material (which was someone else's finished product). Such quality characteristics as tensile strength, ductility, thickness, porosity, and moisture content can be expected to contribute to the overall variation in the final product.

A third source of variation is the *environment*. Temperature, light, radiation, particle size, pressure and humidity can all contribute to variation in the product. In order to control this source, products are sometimes manufactured in white rooms. Experiments are conducted in outer space to learn more about the effect of the environment on product variation.

A fourth source is the *operator*. This source of variation includes the method by which the operator performs the operation. The operator's physical and emotional well-being also contribute to the variation. A cut finger, a twisted ankle, a personal problem, or a headache can make an operator's quality performance vary. An operator's lack of understanding of equipment and material variations due to lack of training may lead to frequent machine adjustments, thereby compounding the variability. As our equipment has become more automated, the operator's effect on variation has lessened.

The above four sources account for the true variation. There is also a reported variation, which is due to the *inspection* activity. Faulty inspection equipment, or the incorrect application of a quality standard, or too heavy a pressure on a micrometer, can be the cause of the incorrect reporting of variation. In general, variation due to inspection should be one-tenth of the four other sources of variations. It should be noted that three of these sources are present in the inspection activity—an inspector, inspection equipment, and the environment.

CONTROL CHARTS FOR VARIABLES

As long as these sources of variation fluctuate in a natural or expected manner, a stable pattern of many *chance causes* (random causes) of variation develops. Chance causes of variation are inevitable. Because they are numerous and individually of relatively small importance, they are difficult to detect or identify. Those causes of variation that are large in magnitude, and therefore readily identified, are classified as *assignable causes*.[1] When only chance causes are present in a process, the process is considered to be in a state of statistical control. It is stable and predictable. However, when an assignable cause of variation is also present, the variation will be excessive and the process is classified as out of control or beyond the expected natural variation.

The Control Chart Method

In order to indicate when observed variations in quality are greater than could be left to chance, the control chart method of analysis and presentation of data is used. The control chart method for variables is a means of visualizing the variations that occur in the central tendency and dispersion of a set of observations. It is a graphical record of the quality of a particular characteristic. It shows whether or not the process is in a stable state.

An example of a control chart is given in Figure 3-1. This particular chart is referred to as an $\bar{X}$ chart and is used to record the variation in the average value of samples. Another chart, such as the R chart (range), would have also served for explanation purposes. The horizontal axis is labeled "Subgroup Number," which

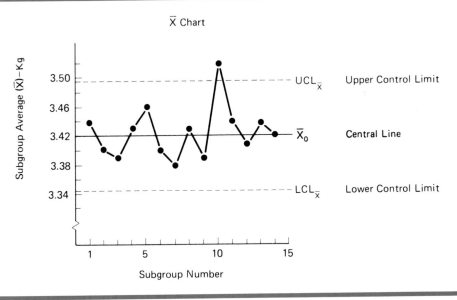

FIGURE 3-1   **Example of a control chart.**

[1] Deming uses the words common and special for chance and assignable.

identifies a particular sample consisting of a fixed number of observations. These subgroups are in order, with the first one inspected being 1 and the last one inspected being 14. The vertical axis of the graph is the variable, which in this particular case is weight measured in kilograms.

Each small solid circle represents the average value within a subgroup. Thus, subgroup number 5 consists of, say, four observations: 3.46, 3.49, 3.45, and 3.44, and their average is 3.46 kg. This value is the one posted on the chart for subgroup number 5. Averages are used on control charts rather than individual observations because average values will indicate a change in variation much faster.[2] Also, with two or more observations in a sample, a measure of the dispersion can be obtained for a particular subgroup.

The solid line in the center of the chart can have three different interpretations depending on the available data. First, it can be the average of the plotted points, which in the case of an $\overline{X}$ chart is the average of the averages or "X-double bar," $\overline{\overline{X}}$. Second, it can be a standard or reference value, $\overline{X}_0$, based on representative prior data, an economic value based on production costs or service needs, or an aimed-at value based on specifications. Third, it can be the population mean, μ, if that value is known.

The two dashed outer lines are the upper and lower control limits. These limits are established to assist in judging the significance of the variation in the quality of the product. Control limits are frequently confused with *specification limits,* which are the permissible limits of a quality characteristic of each *individual* unit of a product. However, *control limits* are used to evaluate the variations in quality from subgroup to subgroup. Therefore, for the $\overline{X}$ chart, the control limits are a function of the subgroup averages. A frequency distribution of the subgroup averages can be determined with its corresponding average and standard deviation. The control limits are then established at ± 3 standard deviations from the central line. One recalls, from the discussion of the normal curve, that the number of items between $+3\sigma$ and -3σ equals 99.73%. Therefore, it is expected that over 997 times out of a 1000, the subgroup values will fall between the upper and lower limits, and when this occurs, the process is considered to be in control. When a subgroup value falls outside the limits, the process is considered to be out of control and an assignable cause for the variation is present. Subgroup number 10 in Figure 3-1 is beyond the upper control limit; therefore, there has been a change in the stable nature of the process, causing the out-of-control point.

In practice, control charts are posted at individual machines or work centers to control a particular quality characteristic. Usually, an $\overline{X}$ chart for the central tendency and an R chart for the dispersion are used together. An example of this dual charting is illustrated in Figure 3-2, which shows a method of charting and reporting inspection results for a rubber durometer. At work center number 365-2 at 8:30 A.M., the operator selects four items for testing, and records the observations of 55, 52, 51, and 53 in the rows marked X_1, X_2, X_3, and X_4, respectively. A subgroup average value of 52.8 is obtained by summing the observations and dividing by 4, and

---

[2] For a proof of this statement, see J. M. Juran, ed., *Quality Control Handbook,* 4th ed. (New York: McGraw-Hill Book Company, 1988), Sec. 24, p. 10.

CONTROL CHARTS FOR VARIABLES

the range value of 4 is obtained by subtracting the low value, 51, from the high value, 55. The operator places a small solid circle at 52.8 on the $\bar{X}$ chart and a small solid circle at 4 on the R chart, and then proceeds with his other duties.

$\bar{X}$ AND R CHART

Work Center Number **365~2**
Quality Characteristic **Durometer**   Date **3/6/76**

Time	$8\frac{30}{AM}$	$9\frac{30}{AM}$	$10\frac{40}{AM}$	$11\frac{50}{AM}$	$1\frac{30}{PM}$									
Subgroup	1	2	3	4	5	6	7	8	9	10	11	12	13	14
X_1	55	51	48	45	53									
X_2	52	52	49	43	50									
X_3	51	57	50	45	48									
X_4	53	50	49	43	50									
Sum	211	210	196	176	201									
$\bar{X}$	52.8	52.5	49	44	50.2									
R	4	7	2	2	5									

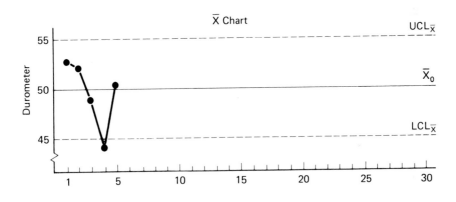

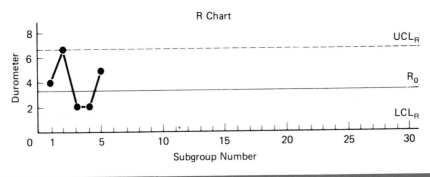

FIGURE 3-2   **Example of a method of reporting inspection results.**

The frequency with which the operator inspects a product at a particular machine or work center is determined by the quality of the product. When the process is in control and no difficulties are being encountered, fewer inspections may be required, and, conversely, when the process is out of control, or during start-up, more inspections may be needed. The inspection frequency at a machine or work center can also be determined by the amount of time that must be spent on noninspection activities. In the example problem, the inspection frequency appears to be every 60 or 65 minutes.

At 9:30 A.M. the operator performs the activities for subgroup 2 in the same manner as for subgroup 1. It is noted that the range value of 7 falls right on the upper control limit. Whether to consider this in control or out of control would be a matter of company policy. It is suggested that it be classified as in control, and a cursory examination for an assignable cause be conducted by the operator. A plotted point that falls on the control limit will be a rare occurrence.

The inspection results for subgroup 2 shows that the third observation, X_3, has a value of 57, which exceeds the upper control limit. The reader is cautioned to remember the earlier discussion on control limits and specifications. In other words, the 57 value is an individual observation and does not relate to the control limits. Therefore, the fact that an individual observation is greater than or less than a control limit is meaningless.

Subgroup 4 has an average value of 44, which is less than the lower control limit of 45. Therefore, subgroup 4 is out of control, and the operator will report this fact to the departmental supervisor. The operator and supervisor will then look for an assignable cause and, if possible, take corrective action. Whatever corrective action is taken will be noted by the inspector on the $\overline{X}$ and R chart or on a separate form. The control chart indicates when and where trouble has occurred; the identification and elimination of the difficulty is a production problem. Ideally, the control chart should be maintained by the operator provided time is available and proper training has been given. When the operator cannot maintain the chart then it is maintained by quality control.

A control chart is a statistical tool that distinguishes between natural and unnatural variation as shown in Figure 3-3. Unnatural variation is the result of assignable causes. It usually, but not always, requires corrective action by people close to the process such as operators, technicians, clerks, maintenance workers, and first-line supervisors.

Natural variation is the result of chance causes. It requires management intervention to achieve quality improvement. In this regard, between 80% and 85% of the quality problems are due to management or the system, and 15% to 20% due to operations.

The control chart is used to keep a continuing record of a particular quality characteristic. It is a picture of the process over time. When the chart is completed, it is replaced by a fresh chart, and the completed chart is stored in an office file. The chart is used to improve the process quality, to determine the process capability, to determine when to leave the process alone and when to make adjustments, and to investigate causes of unacceptable or marginal quality.

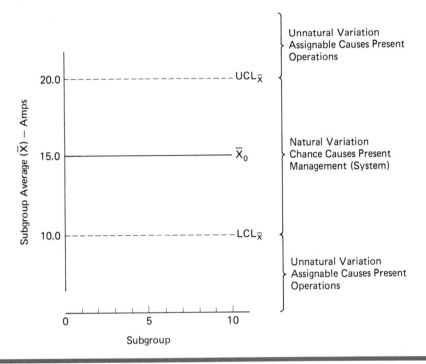

FIGURE 3-3   **Natural and unnatural causes of variation.**

Objectives of Variable Control Charts

Variable control charts provide information:

  1. For quality improvement. Having a variables control chart merely because it indicates that there is a quality control program is missing the point. A variable control chart is an excellent technique for achieving quality improvement.

  2. To determine the process capability. The true process capability can be achieved only after substantial quality improvement has been achieved. During the quality improvement cycle, the control chart will indicate that no further improvement is possible without a large dollar expenditure. At that point the true process capability is obtained.

  3. For decisions in regard to product specifications. Once the true process capability is obtained, effective specifications can be determined. If the process capability is ±0.003, then specifications of ±0.004 are realistically obtainable by operating personnel.

  4. For current decisions in regard to the production process. Thus, the control chart is used to decide when a natural pattern of variation occurs and the process

should be left alone, and when an unnatural pattern of variation is occurring which requires action to find and eliminate the disturbing or assignable causes.

In this regard, operating personnel are giving a quality performance as long as the plotted points are within the control limits. If this performance is not satisfactory, the solution is the responsibility of the system rather than the operator.

5. For current decisions in regard to recently produced items. Thus, the control chart is used as one source of information to help decide whether an item or items should be released to the next phase of the sequence or some alternative disposition made, such as sorting and repairing.

These purposes are frequently dependent on each other. For example, quality improvement is needed prior to determining the true process capability, which is needed prior to determining effective specifications. Control charts for variables should be established to achieve a particular purpose. Their use should be discontinued when the purpose has been achieved or their use continued with the inspection substantially reduced.

CONTROL CHART TECHNIQUES

Introduction

In order to establish a pair of control charts for the average ($\overline{X}$) and the range (R), it is desirable to follow a set procedure. The steps in this procedure are as follows:

1. Select the quality characteristic.
2. Choose the rational subgroup.
3. Collect the data.
4. Determine the trial central line and control limits.
5. Establish the revised central line and control limits.
6. Achieve the objective.

The procedure presented in this section relates to an $\overline{X}$ and R chart. Information on an s chart is also presented.

Select the Quality Characteristic

The variable that is chosen for an $\overline{X}$ and R chart must be a quality characteristic that is measurable and can be expressed in numbers. Quality characteristics that can be expressed in terms of the seven basic units: length, mass, time, electrical current, temperature, substance, or luminous intensity are appropriate as well as any of the derived units, such as power, velocity, force, energy, density, and pressure.

Those quality characteristics affecting the performance of the product would normally be given first attention. These may be a function of the raw materials, components parts, subassemblies, or finished parts. In other words, give high priority to the selection of those characteristics that are giving difficulty in terms of production problems and/or cost. An excellent opportunity for cost savings is frequently selected where spoilage and rework costs are high. A Pareto analysis[3] is also useful to establish priorities. Another possibility occurs where destructive testing is used to inspect a product.

In any manufacturing plant there are a large number of variables that make up a product. It is, therefore, impossible to place $\bar{X}$ and R charts on all variables, and a judicious selection of those quality characteristics is required. Since all variables can be treated as attributes, an attribute control chart (see Chapter 5) can also be used to achieve quality improvement.

Choose the Rational Subgroup

As previously mentioned, the data that are plotted on the control chart consist of groups of items that are called rational subgroups. It is important to understand that data collected in a random manner do *not* qualify as rational. A rational subgroup is one in which the variation within the group is due only to chance causes. This within-subgroup variation is used to determine the control limits. Variation between subgroups is used to evaluate long-term stability. There are two schemes for selecting the subgroup samples:

1. The first scheme is to select the subgroup samples from product produced at one instant of time or as close to that instant as possible. Four consecutive parts from a machine or four parts from a tray of recently produced parts would be an example of this subgrouping technique. The next subgroup sample would be similar but for product produced at a later time—say, 1 h later. This scheme is called the instant-time method.

2. The second scheme is to select product produced over a period of time so that it is representative of all the product. For example, an inspector makes a visit to a circuit breaker assembling process once every hour. The subgroup sample, of say four, is randomly selected from all the circuit breakers produced in the previous hour. On his next visit, the subgroup is selected from the product produced between visits and so forth. This scheme is called the period-of-time method.

In comparing the two schemes, the instant-time method will have a minimum variation *within* a subgroup and a maximum variation *among* subgroups. The period-of-time method will have a maximum variation *within* a subgroup and a minimum variation *among* subgroups. Some numerical values may help to illustrate this difference. Thus, for the instant-time method, subgroup average values ($\bar{X}$'s) could be from, say, 26 to 34 with subgroup range values (R's) from 0 to 4; whereas for the period-of-time method, the subgroup average values ($\bar{X}$'s) would vary from 28 to 32 with the subgroup range values (R's) from 0 to 8.

The instant-time method is the one most commonly used since it provides a particular time reference for determining assignable causes. It also provides a more

---

[3] An explanation of a Pareto analysis is given in Chapter 12.

sensitive measure of changes in the process average. Since all the values are close together, the variation will most likely be due to chance causes and thereby meet the rational subgroup criteria.

The advantage of the period-of-time method is that it provides better overall results and, therefore, quality reports will present a more accurate picture of the quality. It is also true that because of process limitations this method may be the only practical method of obtaining the subgroup samples. Assignable causes of variation *may* be present in the subgroup, which will make it difficult to ensure that a rational subgroup is present.

In rare situations, it may be desirable to use both subgrouping methods. When this occurs, two charts with different control limits are required.

Regardless of the scheme used to obtain the subgroup, the lots from which the subgroups are chosen must be homogeneous. By homogeneous is meant that the pieces in the lot are as alike as possible—same machine, same operator, same mold cavity, and so on. Similarly, a fixed quantity of material, such as that produced by one tool until it wears out and is replaced or resharpened, should be a homogeneous lot. Homogeneous lots can also be designated by equal time intervals, since this technique is easy to organize and administer. No matter how the lots are designated, the items in any one subgroup should have been produced under essentially the same conditions.

Decisions on the size of the sample or subgroup require a certain amount of empirical judgment; however, some helpful guidelines can be given:

1. As the subgroup size increases, the control limits become closer to the central value, which makes the control chart more sensitive to small variations in the process average.

2. As the subgroup size increases, the inspection cost per subgroup increases. Does the increased cost of larger subgroups justify the greater sensitivity?

3. When destructive testing is used and the item is expensive, a small subgroup size of 2 or 3 is necessary, since it will minimize the destruction of expensive product.

4. Because of the ease of computation a sample size of 5 is quite common in industry; however, when inexpensive electronic hand calculators are used this reason is no longer valid.

5. From a statistical basis a distribution of subgroup averages, $\overline{X}$'s, are nearly normal for subgroups of 4 or more even when the samples are taken from a nonnormal population. Proof of this statement is made later in the chapter.

6. When the subgroup size exceeds 10, the s chart should be used instead of the R chart for the control of the dispersion.

There is no rule for the frequency of taking subgroups, but the frequency should be often enough to detect process changes. The inconveniences of the factory or office layout and the cost of taking subgroups must be balanced with the value of the data obtained. In general, it is best to sample quite often at the beginning and reduce the sampling frequency when the data permit. The use of Table 3-1, which was

TABLE 3-1   Sample Sizes (From MIL-STD-414, Normal Inspection, Level IV)

LOT SIZE	SAMPLE SIZE
66–110	10
111–180	15
181–300	25
301–500	30
501–800	35
801–1,300	40
1,301–3,200	50
3,201–8,000	60
8,001–22,000	85

obtained from MIL-STD 414, can be a valuable aid in making judgments on the amount of sampling required. If a process is expected to produce 4000 pieces per day, then 60 total inspections are required. Therefore, with a subgroup size of four, 15 subgroups would be needed. The frequency of taking a subgroup is expressed in terms of the percent of items produced or in terms of a time interval.

In summary, the selection of the rational subgroup is made in such a manner that only chance causes are present in the subgroup.

Collect the Data

The next step is to collect the data. This step can be accomplished using the type form shown in Figure 3-2, wherein the data are recorded in a vertical fashion. By recording the measurements one below the other, the summing operation for each subgroup is somewhat easier. An alternative method of recording the data is shown in Table 3-2, wherein the data are recorded in a horizontal fashion. This method permits summing the $\bar{X}$ values in an easier fashion; however, the particular method makes no difference when an electronic hand calculator is available. For illustrative purposes, the latter method will be used.

Assuming that the quality characteristic and the plan for the rational subgroup have been selected, an inspector can be assigned the task of collecting the data as part of his or her normal duties. The first-line supervisor and the operator should be informed of the inspector's activities; however, no charts or data are posted at the work center at this time.

Because of difficulty in the assembly of a gear hub to a shaft using a key and keyway, the project team recommends using an $\bar{X}$ and R chart. The quality characteristic is the shaft keyway depth of 6.35 mm (0.250 in.). Using a rational subgroup of four, an inspector obtains five subgroups per day for 5 days using the instant-time method. The samples are measured, the subgroup average ($\bar{X}$) and range R are calculated, and the results are recorded on the form. Additional recorded information includes the date, time, and any comments pertaining to the process. For simplicity, individual measurements are coded from 6.00 mm.

It is necessary to collect a minimum of 20 subgroups of data. A fewer number of subgroups would not provide a sufficient amount of data for the accurate computa-

TABLE 3-2 Data on the Depth of the Keyway (millimeters)[a]

SUBGROUP NUMBER	DATE	TIME	X₁	X₂	X₃	X₄	AVERAGE $\overline{X}$	RANGE R	COMMENT
			MEASUREMENTS						
1	12/23	8:50	35	40	32	37	6.36	0.08	
2		11:30	46	37	36	41	6.40	0.10	
3		1:45	34	40	34	36	6.36	0.06	
4		3:45	69	64	68	59	6.65	0.10	New, temporary
5		4:20	38	34	44	40	6.39	0.10	operator
6	12/27	8:35	42	41	43	34	6.40	0.09	
7		9:00	44	41	41	46	6.43	0.05	
8		9:40	33	41	38	36	6.37	0.08	
9		1:30	48	44	47	45	6.46	0.04	
10		2:50	47	43	36	42	6.42	0.11	
11	12/28	8:30	38	41	39	38	6.39	0.03	
12		1:35	37	37	41	37	6.38	0.04	
13		2:25	40	38	47	35	6.40	0.12	
14		2:35	38	39	45	42	6.41	0.07	
15		3:55	50	42	43	45	6.45	0.08	
16	12/29	8:25	33	35	29	39	6.34	0.10	
17		9:25	41	40	29	34	6.36	0.12	
18		11:00	38	44	28	58	6.42	0.30	Damaged oil line
19		2:35	35	41	37	38	6.38	0.06	
20		3:15	56	55	45	48	6.51	0.11	Bad material
21	12/30	9:35	38	40	45	37	6.40	0.08	
22		10:20	39	42	35	40	6.39	0.07	
23		11:35	42	39	39	36	6.39	0.06	
24		2:00	43	36	35	38	6.38	0.08	
25		4:25	39	38	43	44	6.41	0.06	
Sum							160.25	2.19	

[a] For simplicity in recording, the individual measurements are coded from 6.00 mm.

tion of the control limits; and a larger number of subgroups would delay the introduction of the control chart.

Determine the Trial Control Limits

The central lines for the $\overline{X}$ and R charts are obtained using the formulas

$$\overline{\overline{X}} = \frac{\sum\limits_{i=1}^{g} \overline{X}_i}{g} \quad \text{and} \quad \overline{R} = \frac{\sum\limits_{i=1}^{g} R_i}{g}$$

where $\overline{\overline{X}}$ = average of the subgroup averages (read "X double bar")
$\overline{X}_i$ = average of the ith subgroup
g = number of subgroups
$\overline{R}$ = average of the subgroup ranges
R_i = range of the ith subgroup

CONTROL CHARTS FOR VARIABLES

Trial control limits for the charts are established at ± 3 standard deviations from the central value, as shown by the formulas

$$\text{UCL}_{\bar{X}} = \bar{\bar{X}} + 3\sigma_{\bar{X}} \qquad \text{UCL}_R = \bar{R} + 3\sigma_R$$

$$\text{LCL}_{\bar{X}} = \bar{\bar{X}} - 3\sigma_{\bar{X}} \qquad \text{LCL}_R = \bar{R} - 3\sigma_R$$

where UCL = upper control limit
     LCL = lower control limit
     $\sigma_{\bar{X}}$ = population standard deviation of the subgroup averages ($\bar{X}$'s)
     σ_R = population standard deviation of the range

In practice, the calculations are simplified by using the product of the range ($\bar{R}$) and a factor (A_2) to replace the three standard deviations ($A_2\bar{R} = 3\sigma_{\bar{X}}$)[4] in the formulas for the $\bar{X}$ chart. For the R chart, the range $\bar{R}$ is used to estimate the standard deviation of the range (σ_R).[5] Therefore, the derived formulas are

$$\text{UCL}_{\bar{X}} = \bar{\bar{X}} + A_2\bar{R} \qquad \text{UCL}_R = D_4\bar{R}$$

$$\text{LCL}_{\bar{X}} = \bar{\bar{X}} - A_2\bar{R} \qquad \text{LCL}_R = D_3\bar{R}$$

where A_2, D_3, and D_4 are factors that vary with the subgroup size and are found in Table B of the Appendix. For the $\bar{X}$ chart the upper and lower control limits are symmetrical about the central line. Theoretically, the control limits for an R chart should also be symmetrical about the central line. But, for this situation to occur, with subgroup sizes of 6 or less, the lower control limit would need to have a negative value. Since a negative range is impossible, the lower control limit is located at zero by assigning to D_3 the value of zero for subgroup sizes of 6 or less.

When the subgroup size is 7 or more, the lower control limit is greater than zero and symmetrical about the central line. However, when the R chart is posted at the work center, it may be more practical to keep the lower control limit at zero. This practice eliminates the difficulty of explaining to the operator that points below the lower control limit on the R chart are the result of exceptionally good performance rather than poor performance. However, quality personnel should keep their own charts with the lower control limit in its proper location, and any out-of-control low points investigated to determine the reason for the exceptionally good performance. Since subgroup sizes of seven or more are uncommon, the situation occurs infrequently.

---

[4] The derivation of $3\sigma_{\bar{X}} = A_2\bar{R}$ is based on the substitution of $\sigma_{\bar{X}} = \sigma/\sqrt{n}$ and an estimate of $\sigma = R/d_2$, where d_2 is a factor for the subgroup size.

$$3\sigma_{\bar{X}} = \frac{3\sigma}{\sqrt{n}} = \frac{3}{d_2\sqrt{n}}\bar{R}; \qquad \text{therefore, } A_2 = \frac{3}{d_2\sqrt{n}}$$

[5] The derivation of the simplified formula is based on the substitution of $d_3\sigma = \sigma_R$ and $\sigma = \bar{R}/d_2$, which gives

$$\left(1 + \frac{3d_3}{d_2}\right)\bar{R} \quad \text{and} \quad \left(1 - \frac{3d_3}{d_2}\right)\bar{R}$$

for the control limits. Thus, D_4 and D_3 are set equal to the coefficients of $\bar{R}$.

EXAMPLE PROBLEM

In order to illustrate the calculations necessary to obtain the trial control limits and the central line, the data in Table 3-2 concerning the depth of the shaft keyway will be used. From Table 3-2, the $\Sigma \bar{X} = 160.25$, $\Sigma R = 2.19$, and $g = 25$; thus, the central lines are

$$\bar{\bar{X}} = \frac{\sum_{i=1}^{g} \bar{X}_i}{g} \qquad \bar{R} = \frac{\sum_{i=1}^{g} R_i}{g}$$

$$= \frac{160.25}{25} \qquad = \frac{2.19}{25}$$

$$= 6.41 \text{ mm} \qquad = 0.0876 \text{ mm}$$

From Table B in the appendix, the values for the factors for a subgroup size (n) of four are $A_2 = 0.729$, $D_3 = 0$, and $D_4 = 2.282$. Trial control limits for the $\bar{X}$ chart are:

$$\text{UCL}_{\bar{x}} = \bar{\bar{X}} + A_2\bar{R} \qquad \text{LCL}_{\bar{x}} = \bar{\bar{X}} - A_2\bar{R}$$

$$= 6.41 + (0.729)(0.0876) \qquad = 6.41 - (0.729)(0.0876)$$

$$= 6.47 \text{ mm} \qquad = 6.35 \text{ mm}$$

Trial control limits for the R chart are

$$\text{UCL}_R = D_4\bar{R} \qquad \text{LCL}_R = D_3\bar{R}$$

$$= (2.282)(0.0876) \qquad = (0)(0.0876)$$

$$= 0.20 \text{ mm} \qquad = 0 \text{ mm}$$

Figure 3-4 shows the central lines and the trial control limits for the $\bar{X}$ and R charts for the preliminary data.

Establish the Revised Control Limits

The first step is to post the preliminary data to the chart along with the control limits and central lines. This has been accomplished and is shown in Figure 3-4.

The next step is to adopt standard values for the central lines, or, more appropriately stated, the best estimate of the standard values with the available data. If an analysis of the preliminary data shows good control, then $\bar{\bar{X}}$ and $\bar{R}$ can be considered as representative of the process and these become the standard values, $\bar{X}_0$ and R_0. Good control can be briefly described as that which has no out-of-control points, no long runs on either side of the central line, and no unusual patterns of variation. More information concerning in control and out of control is provided later in the chapter.

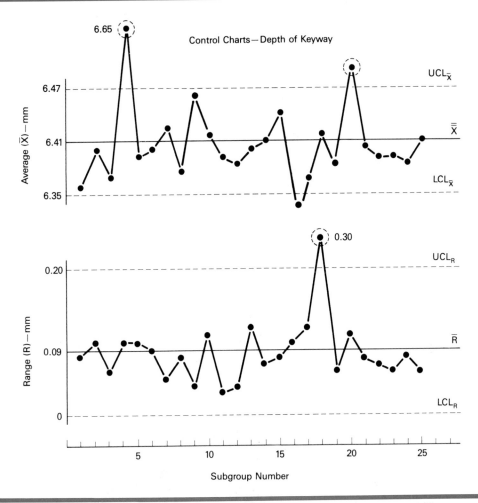

FIGURE 3-4 $\bar{X}$ and R chart for preliminary data with trial control limits.

Most industrial processes are not in control when first analyzed. An analysis of Figure 3-4 shows that there are out-of-control points on the $\bar{X}$ chart at subgroups 4, 16, and 20 and an out-of-control point on the R chart at subgroup 18. It also appears that there are a large number of points below the central line, which is no doubt due to the influence of the high points.

The R chart is analyzed first to determine if it is stable. Since the out-of-control point at subgroup 18 on the R chart has an assignable cause (damaged oil line), it can be discarded from the data. The remaining plotted points indicate a stable process.

The $\bar{X}$ chart can now be analyzed. Subgroups 4 and 20 had an assignable cause while the out-of-control condition for subgroup 16 does not. It is assumed that subgroup 16's out-of-control state is due to a chance cause and is part of the natural variation.

Subgroups 4, 18, and 20 are not part of the natural variation and are discarded from the data and new $\bar{X}$ and $\bar{R}$ values computed with the remaining data. The calculations are simplified by using the following formulas:

$$\bar{\bar{X}}_{new} = \frac{\Sigma \bar{X} - \bar{X}_d}{g - g_d} \qquad \bar{R}_{new} = \frac{\Sigma R - R_d}{g - g_d}$$

where $\bar{X}_d$ = discarded subgroup averages
g_d = number of discarded subgroups
R_d = discarded subgroup ranges

There are two techniques used to discard data. If either the $\bar{X}$ or the R value of a subgroup is out of control and has an assignable cause, both are discarded, or only the out-of-control value of a subgroup is discarded. In this book the latter technique is followed; thus, when an $\bar{X}$ value is discarded, its corresponding R value is not discarded and vice versa. Calculations for a new $\bar{X}$ are based on discarding the $\bar{X}$ values of 6.65 and 6.51 for subgroups 4 and 20, respectively. Calculations for a new $\bar{R}$ are based on discarding the R value of 0.30 for subgroup 18.

$$\bar{\bar{X}}_{new} = \frac{\Sigma \bar{X} - \bar{X}_d}{g - g_d} \qquad\qquad \bar{R}_{new} = \frac{\Sigma R - R_d}{g - g_d}$$

$$= \frac{160.25 - 6.65 - 6.51}{25 - 2} \qquad = \frac{2.19 - 0.30}{25 - 1}$$

$$= 6.40 \text{ mm} \qquad\qquad = 0.079 \text{ mm}$$

These new values of $\bar{\bar{X}}$ and $\bar{R}$ are used to establish the standard values of $\bar{X}_0$, R_0, and σ_0. Thus,

$$\bar{X}_0 = \bar{\bar{X}}_{new}, \qquad R_0 = \bar{R}_{new}, \quad \text{and} \quad \sigma_0 = \frac{R_0}{d_2}$$

where d_2 = a factor from Table B for estimating σ_0 from R_0. The standard or reference values can be considered to be the best estimate with the data available. As more data become available, better estimates or more confidence in the existing standard values are obtained.

Using the standard values, the central lines and the 3σ control limits for actual operations are obtained using the formulas

$$\text{UCL}_{\bar{X}} = \bar{X}_0 + A\sigma_0 \qquad \text{LCL}_{\bar{X}} = \bar{X}_0 - A\sigma_0$$

$$\text{UCL}_R = D_2\sigma_0 \qquad\qquad \text{LCL}_R = D_1\sigma_0$$

where A, D_1, and D_2 are factors from Table B for obtaining the 3σ control limits from $\bar{X}_0$ and σ_0. From Table B in the Appendix and for a subgroup size of 4, the factors are $A = 1.500$, $d_2 = 2.059$, $D_1 = 0$, and $D_2 = 4.698$. Calculations to determine $\bar{X}_0$ and σ_0 using the data previously given are:

$$\bar{X}_0 = \bar{\bar{X}}_{new} = 6.40 \text{ mm}$$

$$R_0 = \bar{R}_{new} = 0.079 = 0.08 \qquad \text{(for the chart)}$$

$$\sigma_0 = \frac{R_0}{d_2}$$

$$= \frac{0.079}{2.059}$$

$$= 0.038 \text{ mm}$$

[handwritten: 1.556, 1.543]

Thus, the control limits are:

$$\text{UCL}_{\bar{x}} = \bar{X}_0 + A\sigma_0 \qquad\qquad \text{LCL}_{\bar{x}} = \bar{X}_0 - A\sigma_0$$

$$= 6.40 + (1.500)(0.038) \qquad\qquad = 6.40 - (1.500)(0.038)$$

$$= 6.46 \text{ mm} \qquad\qquad\qquad = 6.34 \text{ mm}$$

$$\text{UCL}_R = D_2\sigma_0 \qquad\qquad\qquad \text{LCL}_R = D_1\sigma_0$$

$$= (4.698)(0.038) \qquad\qquad\qquad = (0)(0.038)$$

$$= 0.18 \text{ mm} \qquad\qquad\qquad = 0 \text{ mm}$$

The central lines and control limits are drawn on the $\bar{X}$ and R charts for the next period and are shown in Figure 3-5. For illustrative purposes the trial control limits and the revised control limits are shown on the same chart. The limits for both the $\bar{X}$ and R charts became narrower, as was expected. No change occurred in LCL_R because the subgroup size is less than 7. Figure 3-5 also illustrates a simpler charting technique in that lines are not drawn between the points.

The preliminary data for the initial 25 subgroups are not plotted with the revised control limits. These revised control limits are for reporting the results of future subgroups. To make effective use of the control chart during production, it should be displayed in a conspicuous place where it can be seen by operators and supervisors.

Before proceeding to the action step, some final comments are appropriate. First, many analysts eliminate this step in the procedure because it appears to be somewhat redundant. However, by discarding out-of-control points with assignable causes, the central line and control limits are more representative of the process.

Second, the formula for the control limits are mathematically equal. Thus, for the upper control limit, $\bar{X}_0 + A\sigma_0 = \bar{\bar{X}}_{new} + A_2\bar{R}_{new}$. Similar equivalences are true for the lower control limit and both control limits for the R chart.

Third, the parameter σ_0 is now available to obtain the initial estimate of the process capability, which is $6\sigma_0$. The true process capability is obtained in the next step.

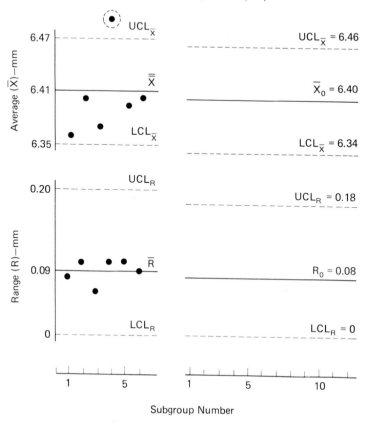

Control Charts—Depth of Keyway

FIGURE 3-5   Trial control limits and revised control limits for $\bar{X}$ and R charts.

Fourth, the central line $\bar{X}_0$ for the $\bar{X}$ chart is frequently based on the specifications. In such a case, the procedure is used only to obtain R_0 and σ_0. If in our example problem the nominal value of the characteristic is 6.38 mm, then $\bar{X}_0$ is set to that value and the upper and lower control limits are:

$$\text{UCL}_{\bar{x}} = \bar{X}_0 + A\sigma_0 \qquad\qquad \text{LCL}_{\bar{x}} = \bar{X}_0 - A\sigma_0$$
$$= 6.38 + (1.500)(0.038) \qquad = 6.38 - (1.500)(0.038)$$
$$= 6.44 \qquad\qquad\qquad\qquad = 6.32$$

The central line and control limits for the R chart do not change. This modification can be taken only if the process is adjustable. If the process is not adjustable then the original calculations must be used.

CONTROL CHARTS FOR VARIABLES

Fifth, it follows that adjustments to the process should be made while taking data. It is not necessary to run nonconforming material while collecting data, since we are primarily interested in obtaining R_0, which is not affected by the process setting. The independence of μ and σ provide the rationale for this concept.

Sixth, the process determines the central line and control limits. They are not established by design, manufacturing, marketing, or any other department, except for $\bar{X}_0$ when the process is adjustable.

Finally, when population values are known (μ and σ) the central lines and control limits may be calculated immediately, saving time and work. Thus $\bar{X}_0 = \mu$; $\sigma_0 = \sigma$; and $R_0 = d_2\sigma$ and the limits are obtained using the appropriate formulas.

Achieving the Objective

When control charts are first introduced at a work center, an improvement in the process performance usually occurs. This initial improvement is especially noticeable when the process is dependent on the skill of the operator. Posting a quality control chart appears to be a psychological signal to the operator to improve performance. Most workers want to produce a quality product; therefore, when management shows an interest in the quality, the operator responds.

Figure 3-6 illustrates the initial improvement that occurred after the introduction of the $\bar{X}$ and R charts in January. Owing to space limitations, only a representa-

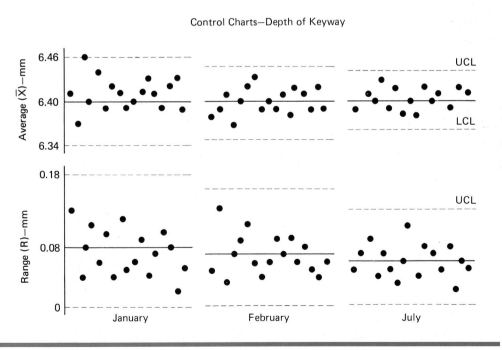

FIGURE 3-6 **Continuing use of control charts, showing improved quality.**

tive number of subgroups for each month are shown in the figure. During January the subgroup averages had less variation and tended to be centered at a slightly higher point. A reduction in the range variation occurred also.

Not all the improved performance in January was the result of operator effort. The first-line supervisor initiated a program of tool wear control, which was a contributing factor.

At the end of January new central lines and control limits were calculated using the data from subgroups obtained during the month. It is a good idea, especially when a chart is being initiated, to calculate standard values periodically to see if any changes have occurred. This reevaluation can be done for every 25 or more subgroups, and the results compared to the previous values.[6]

New central lines and control limits were established for the $\bar{X}$ and R chart for the month of February. During the ensuing months the maintenance department replaced a pair of worn gears; purchasing changed the material supplier; and tooling modified a workholding device. All these improvements were the result of investigations that tracked down the causes for out-of-control conditions or were ideas developed by a project team. The generation of ideas by many different personnel is the most essential ingredient for quality improvement. Ideas by the operator, first-line supervisor, quality assurance, maintenance, manufacturing engineering, and industrial engineering should be evaluated. This evaluation or testing of an idea requires 25 or more subgroups. The control chart will tell if the idea is good, poor, or has no effect on the process. Quality improvement occurs when the plotted points of the $\bar{X}$ chart converge on the central line, or when the plotted points of the R chart trend downward, or both actions occur. If a poor idea is tested then the reverse occurs. Of course, if the idea is neutral it will have no affect on the plotted point pattern.

In order to speed up the testing of ideas, the taking of subgroups can be compressed in time as long as the data represents the process by accounting for any hourly or day-to-day fluctuations. Only one idea should be tested at a time; otherwise, the results will be confounded.

At the end of June, the periodic evaluation of the past performance showed the need to revise the central lines and the control limits. The performance for the month of July and subsequent months showed a natural pattern of variation and no quality improvement. At this point no further quality improvement is possible without a substantial investment in new equipment or equipment modification.

W. Edward Deming has stated "that if he were a banker, he would not lend any money to a company unless statistical methods were used to prove that the money was necessary." This is precisely what the control chart can achieve, provided that all personnel use the chart as a method of quality improvement rather than a maintenance function.

When the objective for initiating the charts has been achieved, its use should be discontinued or the frequency of inspection be substantially reduced to a monitoring action by the operator. Efforts should then be directed toward the improvement of some other quality characteristic. If a project team was involved it should be congratulated for its performance and disbanded.

---

[6] These values are usually compared without the use of formal tests. An exact evaluation can be obtained by mathematically comparing the central lines to see if they are from the same population.

The Sample Standard Deviation Control Chart

While the $\bar{X}$ and R charts are the most common charts for variables, some companies prefer the sample standard deviation, s, as the measure of the subgroup dispersion. In comparing an R chart with an s chart, an R chart is easier to compute and easier to explain. On the other hand, the subgroup sample standard deviation for the s chart is calculated using all the data rather than just the high and the low value as done for the R chart. An s chart is therefore more accurate than an R chart. When subgroup sizes are less than 10, both charts will graphically portray the same variation;[7] however, as subgroups sizes increase to 10 or more, extreme values have an undue influence on the R chart. Therefore, at larger subgroup sizes the s chart is used.

The steps necessary to obtain the $\bar{X}$ and s trial control and revised control limits are the same as those used for the $\bar{X}$ and R chart except for different formulas. In order to illustrate the method, the same data will be used. They are reproduced in Table 3-3 with the addition of an s column and the elimination of the R column. The appropriate formulas used in the computation of the trial control limits are

$$\bar{s} = \frac{\sum_{i=1}^{g} s_i}{g} \qquad \bar{\bar{X}} = \frac{\sum_{i=1}^{g} \bar{X}_i}{g}$$

$$\text{UCL}_{\bar{x}} = \bar{\bar{X}} + A_3\bar{s} \qquad \text{UCL}_s = B_4\bar{s}$$

$$\text{LCL}_{\bar{x}} = \bar{\bar{X}} - A_3\bar{s} \qquad \text{LCL}_s = B_3\bar{s}$$

where
$\quad s_i$ = sample standard deviation of the subgroup values
$\quad \bar{s}$ = average of the subgroup sample standard deviations
A_3, B_3, B_4 = factors found in Table B of the Appendix for obtaining the 3σ control limits for $\bar{X}$ and s charts from $\bar{s}$

Formulas for the computation of the revised control limits using the standard values of $\bar{X}_0$ and σ_0 are

$$\bar{X}_0 = \bar{\bar{X}}_{\text{new}} = \frac{\sum \bar{X} - \bar{X}_d}{g - g_d}$$

$$s_0 = \bar{s}_{\text{new}} = \frac{\sum s - s_d}{g - g_d} \qquad \sigma_0 = \frac{s_0}{c_4}$$

$$\text{UCL}_{\bar{x}} = \bar{X}_0 + A\sigma_0 \qquad \text{UCL}_s = B_6\sigma_0$$

$$\text{LCL}_{\bar{x}} = \bar{X}_0 - A\sigma_0 \qquad \text{LCL}_s = B_5\sigma_0$$

where
$\quad s_d$ = sample standard deviation of the discarded subgroup
$\quad c_4$ = factor found in Table B for computing σ_0 from $\bar{s}$
A, B_5, B_6 = factors found in Table B for computing 3σ process control limits for $\bar{X}$ and s charts

[7] A proof of this statement can be observed by comparing the R chart of Figure 3-4 with the s chart of Figure 3-7.

TABLE 3-3   Data on the Depth of the Keyway (millimeters)[a]

SUBGROUP NUMBER	DATE	TIME	MEASUREMENTS X_1	X_2	X_3	X_4	AVERAGE $\overline{X}$	SAMPLE STANDARD DEVIATION, s	COMMENT
1	12/23	8:50	35	40	32	37	6.36	0.034	
2		11:30	46	37	36	41	6.40	0.045	
3		1:45	34	40	34	36	ʒ.36	0.028	
4		3:45	69	64	68	59	6.65	0.045	New, temporary
5		4:20	38	34	44	40	6.39	0.042	operator
6	12/27	8:35	42	41	43	34	6.40	0.040	
7		9:00	44	41	41	46	6.43	0.024	
8		9:40	33	41	38	36	6.37	0.034	
9		1:30	48	44	47	45	6.46	0.018	
10		2:50	47	43	36	42	6.42	0.045	
11	12/28	8:30	38	41	39	38	6.39	0.014	
12		1:35	37	37	41	37	6.38	0.020	
13		2:25	40	38	47	35	6.40	0.051	
14		2:35	38	39	45	42	6.41	0.032	
15		3:55	50	42	43	45	6.45	0.036	
16	12/29	8:25	33	35	29	39	6.34	0.042	
17		9:25	41	40	29	34	6.36	0.067	
18		11:00	38	44	28	58	6.42	0.125	Damaged oil line
19		2:35	35	41	37	38	6.38	0.025	
20		3:15	56	55	45	48	6.51	0.054	Bad material
21	12/30	9:35	38	40	45	37	6.40	0.036	
22		10:20	39	42	35	40	6.39	0.029	
23		11:35	42	39	39	36	6.39	0.024	
24		2:00	43	36	35	38	6.38	0.036	
25		4:25	39	38	43	44	6.41	0.029	
Sum							160.25	0.975	

[a] For simplicity in recording, the individual measurements are coded from 6.00 mm.

The first step is to determine the standard deviation for each subgroup from the preliminary data. For subgroup 1, with values of 6.35, 6.40, 6.32, and 6.37, the standard deviation is

$$s = \sqrt{\frac{n \sum_{i=1}^{n} X_i^2 - \left(\sum_{i=1}^{n} X_i\right)^2}{n(n-1)}}$$

$$= \sqrt{\frac{4(6.35^2 + 6.40^2 + 6.32^2 + 6.37^2) - (6.35 + 6.40 + 6.32 + 6.37)^2}{4(4-1)}}$$

$$= 0.034 \text{ mm}$$

The standard deviation for subgroup 1 is posted to the s column as shown in Table 3-3, and the process is repeated for the remaining 24 subgroups.

The next step is to obtain $\bar{s}$ and $\overline{\overline{X}}$, which are computed from Σs and $\Sigma \overline{X}$, whose values are found in Table 3-3.

$$\bar{s} = \frac{\sum\limits_{i=1}^{g} s}{g} \qquad\qquad \bar{\bar{X}} = \frac{\sum\limits_{i=1}^{g} \bar{X}_i}{g}$$

$$= \frac{0.975}{25} \qquad\qquad = \frac{160.25}{25}$$

$$= 0.039 \text{ mm} \qquad\qquad = 6.41 \text{ mm}$$

From Table B the values of the factors—$A_3 = 1.628$, $B_3 = 0$, and $B_4 = 2.266$—are obtained, and the trial control limits are

$$\text{UCL}_{\bar{x}} = \bar{\bar{X}} + A_3\bar{s} \qquad\qquad \text{LCL}_{\bar{x}} = \bar{\bar{X}} - A_3\bar{s}$$

$$= 6.41 + (1.628)(0.039) \qquad = 6.41 - (1.628)(0.039)$$

$$= 6.47 \text{ mm} \qquad\qquad = 6.35 \text{ mm}$$

$$\text{UCL}_s = B_4\bar{s} \qquad\qquad\qquad \text{LCL}_s = B_3\bar{s}$$

$$= (2.266)(0.039) \qquad\qquad = (0)(0.039)$$

$$= 0.088 \text{ mm} \qquad\qquad = 0 \text{ mm}$$

The next step is to plot the subgroup $\bar{X}$ and s on graph paper with the central lines and control limits. This step is shown in Figure 3-7. Subgroups 4, 16, and 20 are out of control on the $\bar{X}$ chart, and since subgroups 4 and 20 have assignable causes, they are discarded. Subgroup 18 is out of control on the s chart, and since it has an assignable cause, it is discarded. Computation to obtain the standard values of $\bar{X}_0$, s_0, and σ_0 are as follows:

$$\bar{\bar{X}}_{\text{new}} = \frac{\sum \bar{X} - \bar{X}_d}{g - g_d}$$

$$= \frac{160.25 - 6.65 - 6.51}{25 - 2}$$

$$= 6.40 \text{ mm}$$

$$\bar{X}_0 = \bar{\bar{X}}_{\text{new}} = 6.40 \text{ mm}$$

$$s_0 = \bar{s}_{\text{new}} = \frac{\sum s - s_d}{g - g_d}$$

$$= \frac{0.975 - 0.125}{25 - 1}$$

$$= 0.0354 \text{ mm}$$

$$\sigma_0 = \frac{s_0}{c_4} \qquad \text{from Table B,} \quad c_4 = 0.9213$$

$$= \frac{0.0354}{0.9213}$$

$$= 0.038 \text{ mm}$$

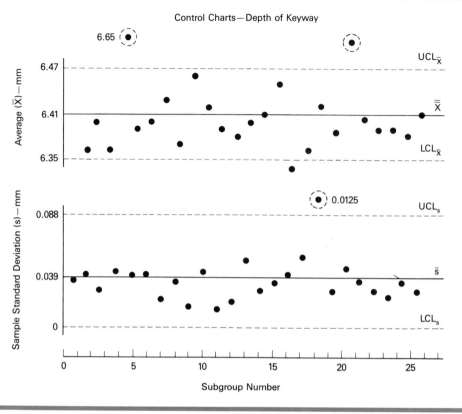

FIGURE 3-7 $\bar{X}$ and s chart for preliminary data with trial control limits.

The reader should note that the standard deviation, σ_0, is the same as the value obtained from the range in the preceding section. Using the standard values of $\bar{X}_0 = 6.40$ and $\sigma_0 = 0.038$, the revised control limits are computed.

$$\text{UCL}_{\bar{x}} = \bar{X}_0 + A\sigma_0 \qquad\qquad \text{LCL}_{\bar{x}} = \bar{X}_0 - A\sigma_0$$
$$= 6.40 + (1.500)(0.038) \qquad = 6.40 - (1.500)(0.038)$$
$$= 6.46 \text{ mm} \qquad\qquad\qquad = 6.34 \text{ mm}$$
$$\text{UCL}_s = B_6\sigma_0 \qquad\qquad\qquad \text{LCL}_s = B_5\sigma_0$$
$$= (2.088)(0.038) \qquad\qquad = (0)(0.038)$$
$$= 0.079 \text{ mm} \qquad\qquad\qquad = 0 \text{ mm}$$

Continuation of the $\bar{X}$ and s charts is accomplished in the same manner as the $\bar{X}$ and R charts.

STATE OF CONTROL

Process in Control

When the assignable causes have been eliminated from the process to the extent that the points plotted on the control chart remain within the control limits, the process is in a state of control. No higher degree of uniformity can be attained with the existing process. Greater uniformity can, however, be attained through a change in the basic process through quality improvement ideas.

When a process is in control, there occurs a natural pattern of variation, which is illustrated by the control chart in Figure 3-8. This natural pattern of variation has (1) about 68% of the plotted points within one standard deviation of the central line (34% each side), (2) about 13.5% of the plotted points in an imaginary band between one and two standard deviations on both sides of the central line, and (3) about 2.5% of the plotted points in an imaginary band between two and three standard deviations on both sides of the central line. The points are located back and forth across the central line in a random manner with no points beyond the control limits. The natural pattern of the points or subgroup values forms its own frequency distribution, which follows a normal curve. As the number of plotted points increases, the frequency distribution will take on the appearance of a smooth polygon. The dashed normal curve at the left end of Figure 3-10 represents the distribution of the points when a process is in control.

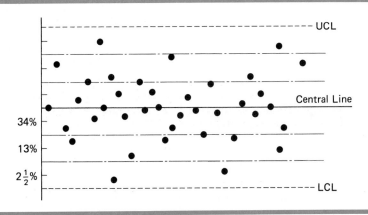

FIGURE 3-8 **Natural pattern of variation of a control chart.**

Control limits are usually established at three standard deviations from the central line. They are used as a basis to judge whether there is evidence of lack of control. The choice of 3σ limits is an economic one with respect to two types of errors that can occur. One error, called Type I by statisticians, occurs when looking for an assignable cause of variation when in reality a chance cause is present. When the limits are set at three standard deviations, a Type I error will occur 0.27% (3 out of 1000) of the time. In other words, when a point is outside the control limits, it is assumed to be due to an assignable cause even though it would be due to a chance cause 0.27% of the time. The other type error, called Type II, occurs when assuming that a chance cause of variation is present when in reality there is an assignable cause. In other words, when a point is inside the control limits, it is assumed to be due to a chance cause even though it might be due to an assignable cause. Abundant experience since 1930 in all types of industry indicates that 3σ limits provide an economic balance between the costs resulting from the two types of errors. Unless there are strong practical reasons for doing otherwise, the ±3 standard deviation limits should be used.

When a process is in control, only chance causes of variation are present. Small variations in machine performance, operator performance, and material characteristics are expected and are considered to be part of a stable process.

When a process is in control, certain practical advantages accrue to the producer and consumer.

1. Individual units of the product will be more uniform—or, stated another way, there will be less variation.

2. Since the product is more uniform, fewer samples are needed to judge the quality. Therefore, the cost of inspection can be reduced to a minimum. This advantage is extremely important when 100% conformance to specifications is not essential.

3. The process capability or spread of the process is easily attained from 6σ. With a knowledge of the process capability, a number of reliable decisions relative to specifications can be made, such as
 (a) To decide the product specifications,
 (b) To decide the amount of rework or scrap when there is insufficient tolerance, and
 (c) To decide whether to produce the product to tight specifications and permit interchangeability of components or to produce the product to loose specifications and use selective matching of components.

4. The percentage of product that falls within any pair of values may be predicted with the highest degree of assurance. For example, this advantage can be very important when adjusting filling machines to obtain different percentage of items below, between, or above particular values.

5. It permits the consumer to use the producer's data and, therefore, to test only a few subgroups as a check on the producer's records. The $\bar{X}$ and R charts are used as statistical evidence of process control.

6. The operator is performing satisfactorily from a quality viewpoint. Further improvement in the process can be achieved only by changing the input factors: materials, equipment, environment, and operators. These changes require action by management.

CONTROL CHARTS FOR VARIABLES

When only chance causes of variation are present, the process is stable and predictable over time, as shown in Figure 3-9a. We know that future variation as shown by the dotted curve will be the same unless there has been a change in the process due to an assignable cause.

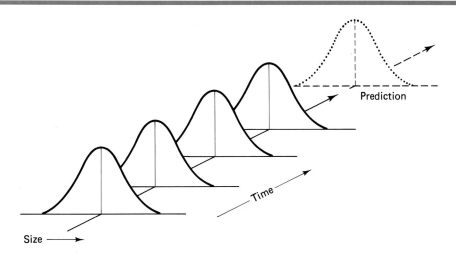

(a) Only Chance Causes of Variation Present

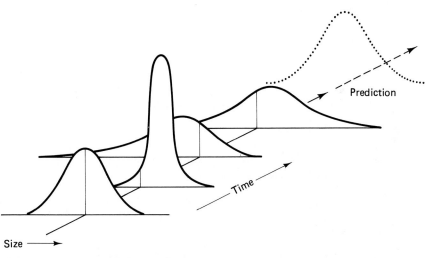

(b) Assignable Causes of Variation Present

FIGURE 3-9 **Stable and unstable variation.**

Process Out of Control

The term out of control is usually thought of as being undesirable; however, there are situations where this condition is desirable. It is best to think of the term out of control as a change in the process due to an assignable cause.

When a point (subgroup value) falls outside its control limits, the process is out of control. This means that an assignable cause of variation is present. Another way of viewing the out-of-control point is to think of the subgroup value as coming from a different population than the one from which the control limits were obtained. Figure 3-10 shows a frequency distribution of subgroup averages for cereal boxes, which was developed from a large number of subgroups and, therefore, represents the population mean, $\mu = 450$ g, and the population standard deviation for the averages, $\sigma_{\bar{x}} = 8$ g. The frequency distribution for subgroup averages is shown by a dashed line, which represents a smooth polygon. For instructional purposes the individual dots represent the number of subgroup averages at particular values. Future explanations will use only the dashed line to represent the frequency distribution of averages and will use a solid line for the frequency distribution of individual values. The out-of-control point has a value of 483 g. This point is so far away from the 3σ limits (99.73%) that it can only be considered to have come from another population. In other words, the process that produced the subgroup average of 483 g is a different process than the stable process from which the 3σ control limits were developed. Therefore, the process has changed; some assignable cause of variation is present.

Figure 3-9b illustrates the effect of assignable causes of variation over time. The unnatural, unstable nature of the variation makes it impossible to predict future

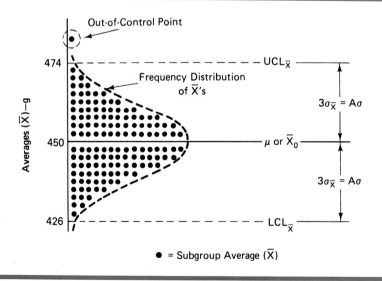

FIGURE 3-10 Frequency distribution of subgroup averages with control limits.

variation. This assignable cause must be found and corrected before a natural, stable process can continue.

A process can also be considered out of control even when the points fall inside the 3σ limits. This situation occurs when unnatural runs of variation are present in the process. First, let's divide the control chart into six equal standard deviation bands in the same manner as Figure 3-8. For identification purposes the bands are labeled A, B, and C zones as shown in Figure 3-11.

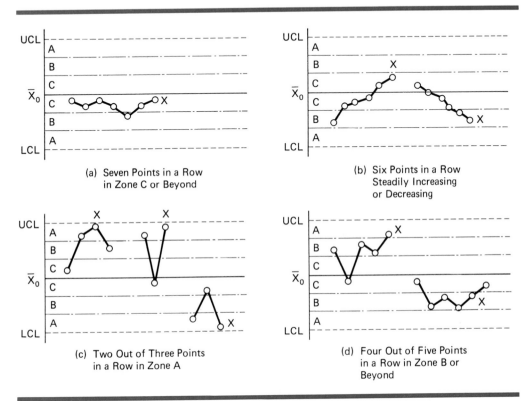

(a) Seven Points in a Row in Zone C or Beyond

(b) Six Points in a Row Steadily Increasing or Decreasing

(c) Two Out of Three Points in a Row in Zone A

(d) Four Out of Five Points in a Row in Zone B or Beyond

FIGURE 3-11 Some unnatural runs—process out of control.

It is not natural for seven or more consecutive points to be above or below the central line as shown in Figure 3-11a. Also when 10 out of 11 points or 12 out of 14 points, etc., are located on one side of the central line, it is unnatural. Another unnatural run occurs at (b), where six points in a row are steadily increasing or decreasing. In Figure 3-11c we have two out of three points in a row in zone A and at (d) four out of five points in a row in zone B and beyond. There are many statistical possibilities with the four common ones being shown in the figure. Actually, any significant divergence from the natural pattern as shown in Figure 3-8 would be unnatural and would be classified as an out-of-control condition. The chance that these unnatural runs will occur is the same chance that a point will fall outside the 3σ control limits.

Analysis of Out-of-Control Condition

When a process is out of control, the assignable cause responsible for the condition must be found. The detective work necessary to locate the cause of the out-of-control condition can be minimized by a knowledge of the types of out-of-control patterns and their assignable causes. Types of out-of-control $\bar{X}$ and R patterns are (1) change or jump in level, (2) trend or steady change in level, (3) recurring cycles, (4) two populations, and (5) mistakes.

1. *Change or jump in level.* This type is concerned with a sudden change in level to the $\bar{X}$ chart, to the R chart or to both charts. Figure 3-12 illustrates the change in level. For an $\bar{X}$ chart, the change in the process average can be due to
   (a) An intentional or unintentional change in the process setting
   (b) A new or inexperienced operator
   (c) A different raw material
   (d) A minor failure of a machine part

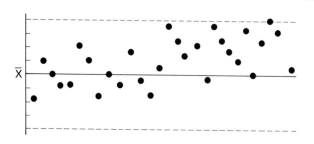

FIGURE 3-12   Out-of-control pattern: change or jump in level.

Some causes for a sudden change in the process spread or variability as shown on the R chart are
   (a) Inexperienced operator
   (b) Sudden increase in gear play
   (c) Greater variation in incoming material
Sudden changes in level can occur on both the $\bar{X}$ and the R charts. This situation is common during the beginning of control chart activity prior to the attainment of a state of control. There may be more than one assignable cause, or it may be a cause that could affect both charts, such as an inexperienced operator.

2. *Trend or steady change in level.* Steady changes in control chart level are a very common industrial phenomena. Figure 3-13 illustrates a trend or steady change that is occurring in the upward direction; the trend could have been illustrated in the downward direction. Some causes of steady progressive changes on an $\bar{X}$ chart are:
   (a) Tool or die wear
   (b) Gradual deterioration of equipment
   (c) Gradual change in temperature or humidity

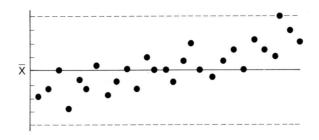

FIGURE 3-13   Out-of-control pattern: trend or steady change in level.

(d) Viscosity breakdown in a chemical process
(e) Buildup of chips in a work-holding device

A steady change in level or trend on the R chart is not as common as the $\bar{X}$ chart. It does, however, occur and some possible causes are:

(a) An improvement in worker skill (downward trend)
(b) A decrease in worker skill due to fatigue, boredom, inattention, and so on (upward trend)
(c) A gradual improvement in the homogeneity of incoming material

   3. *Recurring cycles.* When the plotted points on an $\bar{X}$ or R chart show a wave or periodic high and low points, it is called a *cycle*. A typical recurring out-of-control pattern is shown in Figure 3-14. For an $\bar{X}$ chart, some of the causes of recurring cycles are:

(a) The seasonal effects of incoming material
(b) The recurring effects of temperature and humidity (cold morning start-up)
(c) Any daily or weekly chemical, mechanical, or psychological event
(d) The periodic rotation of operators

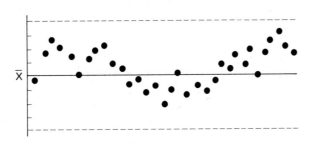

FIGURE 3-14   Out-of-control pattern: recurring cycles.

Periodic cycles on an R chart are not as common as for an $\bar{X}$ chart. Some affecting the R chart are due to:

(a) Operator fatigue and rejuvenation resulting from morning, noon, and afternoon breaks
(b) Lubrication cycles

The out-of-control pattern of a recurring cycle sometimes goes unreported because of the inspection cycle. Thus, a cyclic pattern of a variation that occurs approximately every 2 h could coincide with the inspection frequency. Therefore, only the low points on the cycle are reported, and there is no evidence that a cyclic event is present.

4. *Two populations* (*Also called mixture*). When there are a large number of points near or outside the control limits, a two-population situation may be present. This type of out-of-control pattern is illustrated in Figure 3-15. For an $\bar{X}$ chart the out-of-control pattern can be due to:
(a) Large differences in material quality
(b) Two or more machines on the same chart
(c) Large differences in test method or equipment
Some causes for an out-of-control pattern on an R chart are due to:
(a) Different workers using the same chart
(b) Materials from different suppliers

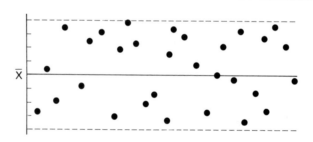

FIGURE 3-15   Out-of-control pattern: two populations.

5. *Mistakes*. Mistakes can be very embarrassing to quality assurance. Some causes of out-of-control patterns resulting from mistakes are:
(a) Measuring equipment out of calibration
(b) Errors in calculations
(c) Errors in using test equipment
(d) Taking samples from different populations
Many of the out-of-control patterns that have been described can also be attributed to inspection error or mistakes.

The causes given for the different types of out-of-control patterns are suggested possibilities and are not meant to be all-inclusive. These causes will give production and quality personnel ideas for the solution of problems. They can be a start toward the development of an assignable cause checklist, which is applicable to their particular manufacturing entity.

CONTROL CHARTS FOR VARIABLES

When out-of-control patterns occur in relation to the lower control limit of the *R* chart, it is the result of outstanding performance. The cause should be determined so that the outstanding performance can continue.

The preceding discussion has used the *R* chart as the measure of the dispersion. Information on patterns and causes also pertains to an *s* chart.

In the sixth step of the control chart method, it was stated that 25 subgroups were necessary to test an idea. The information given above on out of control can be used to make a decision with a fewer number of subgroups. For example, a run of six consecutive points in a downward trend on an *R* chart would indicate that the idea was a good one.

SPECIFICATIONS

Individual Values Compared to Averages

Before discussing specifications and their relationship with control charts, it appears desirable, at this time, to obtain a better understanding of individual values and average values. Figure 3-16 shows a tally of individual values (*X*'s) and a tally of the subgroup averages ($\bar{X}$'s) for the data on keyway depths given in Table 3-2. The four

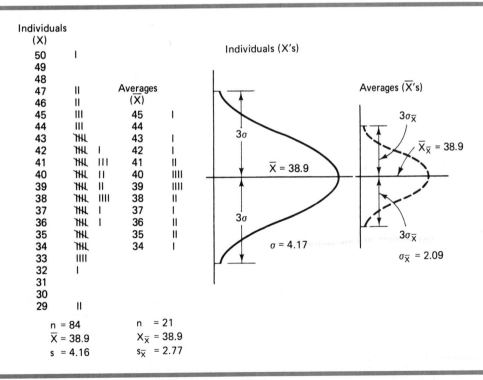

FIGURE 3-16   Comparison of individual values and averages using the same data.

out-of-control subgroups were not used in the two tallys; therefore, there are 84 individual values and 21 averages. It is observed that the averages are grouped much closer to the center than the individual values. When four values are averaged the effect of an extreme value is minimized because the chance of four extremely high or four extremely low values in one subgroup is slight.

Calculations of the average for both the individual values and for the subgroup averages are the same, $\overline{X} = 38.9$. However, the sample standard deviation of the individual values (s) is 4.16, while the sample standard deviation of the subgroup average $(s_{\overline{x}})$ is 2.77.

If there are a large number of individual values and subgroup averages, the smooth polygons of Figure 3-16 would represent their frequency distributions if the distribution is normal. The curve for the frequency distribution of the averages has a dashed line while the curve for the frequency distribution of individual values has a solid line; this convention will be followed throughout the book. In comparing the two distributions it is observed that both distributions are normal in shape; in fact, even if the curve for individual values was not quite normal, the curve for averages would be close to a normal shape. The base of the curve for individual values is about twice as large as the base of the curve for averages. When population values are available for the standard deviation of individual values (σ) and for the standard deviation of averages $(\sigma_{\overline{x}})$, there is a definite relationship between them, as given by the formula

$$\sigma_{\overline{x}} = \frac{\sigma}{\sqrt{n}}$$

where $\sigma_{\overline{x}}$ = population standard deviation of subgroup averages $(\overline{X}$'s)
σ = population standard deviation of individual values $(X$'s)
n = subgroup size

Thus, for a subgroup of size 5, $\sigma_{\overline{x}} = 0.45\sigma$, and for a subgroup of size 4, $\sigma_{\overline{x}} = 0.50\sigma$.

If we assume normality (which may or may not be true), the population standard deviation can be estimated from

$$\hat{\sigma} = \frac{s}{c_4}$$

where $\hat{\sigma}$ is the "estimate" of the population standard deviation[8] and c_4 is "approximately equal to ($\doteq$) 0.996997 for $n = 84$. Thus, $\sigma = s/c_4 = 4.16/0.996997 = 4.17$ and $\sigma_{\overline{x}} = \sigma/\sqrt{n} = 4.17/\sqrt{4} = 2.09$. Note that $s_{\overline{x}}$, which was calculated from sample data, and $\sigma_{\overline{x}}$, which was calculated above, are different. This difference is due to sample variation or the small number of samples, which was only 21, or some combination thereof. The difference would not be caused by a nonnormal population of X's.

----

[8] Values of c_4 are given in Table B of the Appendix up to $n = 20$. For values greater than 20,
$c_4 \doteq \dfrac{4(n-1)}{4n-3}$.

CONTROL CHARTS FOR VARIABLES

Since the height of the curve is a function of the frequency, the curve for individual values is higher. This is easily verified by comparing the tally sheet in Figure 3-16. However, if the curves represent relative or percentage frequency distributions, then the area under the curve must be equal to 100%. Therefore, the percentage frequency distribution curve for averages, with its smaller base, would need to be much higher to enclose the same area as the percentage frequency distribution curve for individual values.

Central Limit Theorem

Now that you are aware of the difference between the frequency distribution of individual values, X's, and the frequency distribution of averages, $\bar{X}$'s, the central limit theorem can be discussed. In simple terms it is:

> If the population from which samples are taken is *not* normal, the distribution of sample averages will tend toward normality provided that the sample size, n, is at least 4. This tendency gets better and better as the sample size gets larger. Furthermore, the standardized normal can be used for the distribution of averages with the modification,

$$Z = \frac{\bar{X} - \mu}{\sigma_{\bar{x}}} = \frac{\bar{X} - \mu}{\sigma/\sqrt{n}}$$

This theorem was illustrated by Shewhart[9] for a uniform population distribution and a triangular population distribution of individual values as shown in Figure 3-17.

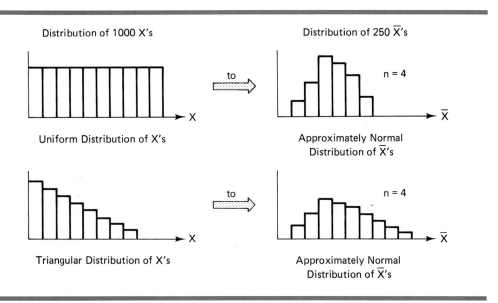

FIGURE 3-17   **Illustration of central limit theorem.**

[9] W. A. Shewhart, *Economic Control of Quality of Manufactured Product* (Princeton, N.J.: Van Nostrand Reinhold Company, Inc., 1931), pp. 180–186.

Obviously, the distribution of X's are considerably different than a normal distribution; however, the distribution of $\bar{X}$'s is approximately normal.

The central limit theorem is one of the reasons the $\bar{X}$ chart works, in that we do not need to be concerned if the distribution of X's is not normal provided that the sample size is 4 or more. Figure 3-18 shows the results of a dice experiment. At (a) is a distribution of individual rolls of a six-sided die; at (b) is a distribution of the average of rolls of two dice. The distribution of the averages ($\bar{X}$'s) is unimodal, symmetrical, and tapers off at the tails. This experiment provides practical evidence of the validity of the central limit theorem.

DICE EXPERIMENT

Results of X's

1	2	3	4	5	6
THL THL THL THL	THL THL THL THL	THL THL THL THL	THL THL THL THL	THL THL THL THL	THL THL THL THL

Results of $\bar{X}$'s, n = 2

1.0	1.5	2.0	2.5	3.0	3.5	4.0	4.5	5.0	5.5	6.0
IIII	THL III	THL THL II	THL THL THL I	THL THL THL	THL THL THL THL IIII	THL THL THL THL	THL THL THL I	THL THL II	THL III	IIII

FIGURE 3-18   Dice illustration of central limit theorem.

Control Limits and Specifications

Control limits are established as a function of the averages; in other words, control limits are for averages. Specifications, on the other hand, are the permissible variation in the size of the part and are, therefore, for individual values. The specification or tolerance limits are established by design engineers to meet a particular function. Figure 3-19 shows that the location of the specifications is optional and is not related to any of the other features in the figure. The control limits, process spread, distribution of averages, and distribution of individual values are interdependent. They are determined by the process, whereas the specifications have an optional location. Control charts cannot determine if the process is meeting specifications.

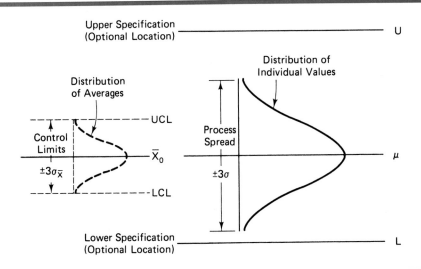

Upper Specification
(Optional Location) ————————————— U

Distribution of
Individual Values

Distribution
of Averages

—————— UCL

Process
Spread

Control
Limits

$\overline{X}_0$

$\pm 3\sigma_{\overline{X}}$

$\pm 3\sigma$

μ

—————— LCL

Lower Specification
(Optional Location) ————————————— L

FIGURE 3-19 **Relationship of limits, specifications, and distributions.**

Process Capability and Tolerance

While specifications can be established by the design engineer without regard for the spread of the process, hereafter referred to as the process capability (6σ), serious situations can result when this type of action is adopted. There are three situations: (1) when the process capability is less than the difference between specifications, hereafter referred to as the tolerance $(U - L)$, (2) when the process capability is equal to the tolerance, (3) and when the process capability is greater than the tolerance.

Case I: $6\sigma < U - L$. This situation, where the process capability (6σ) is less than the tolerance $(U - L)$, is the most desirable case. Figure 3-20a illustrates this ideal relationship by showing the distribution of individual values $(X$'s), the $\overline{X}$ control chart limits, and distribution of averages $(\overline{X}$'s). The process is in control. Since the tolerance is appreciably greater than the process capability, no difficulty is encountered even when there is a substantial shift in the process average, as shown at (b). This shift has resulted in an out-of-control condition as shown by the plotted points. However, no waste is produced because the distribution of individual values $(X$'s) has not exceeded the upper specification. Corrective action is required to bring the process into control.

Case II: $6\sigma = U - L$. Figure 3-21a illustrates this case where the process capability is equal to the tolerance. The frequency distribution s at (a) represents a natural pattern of variation. However, when there is a shift in the process average, as indicated at (b) the individual values $(X$'s) exceed the specifications. As long as the process remains in control, no nonconforming product is produced; however, when the process is out of control as indicated at (b), nonconforming product is produced. Therefore, assignable causes of variation must be corrected as soon as they occur.

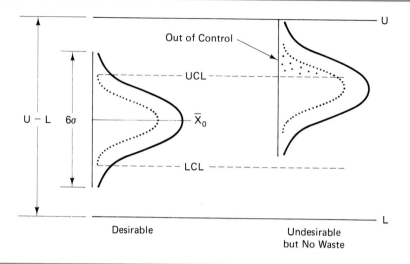

FIGURE 3-20   Case I $6\sigma < U - L$.

Case III: $6\sigma > U - L$. When the process capability is greater than the tolerance, an undesirable situation exists. Figure 3-22 illustrates this case. Even though a
natural pattern of variation is occurring, as shown by the frequency distribution of
X's at (a), some of the individual values are greater than the upper specification and
are less than the lower specification. This case presents the unique situation where
the process is in control as shown by the control limits and frequency distribution of
$\bar{X}$'s, but nonconforming product is produced. In other words, the process is not capable of manufacturing a product that will meet the specifications. When the process
changes as shown at (b), the problem is much worse.

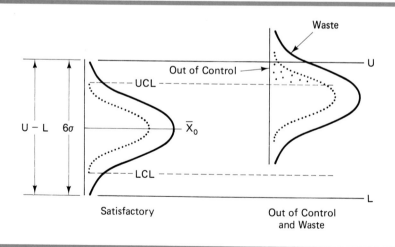

FIGURE 3-21   Case II $6\sigma = U - L$.

CONTROL CHARTS FOR VARIABLES

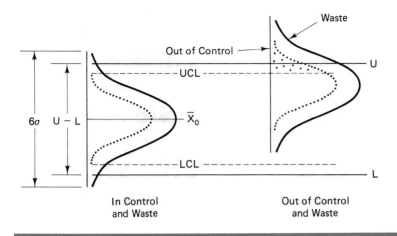

Waste

Out of Control

UCL

6σ $U - L$ $\bar{X}_0$

LCL

U

L

In Control
and Waste

Out of Control
and Waste

FIGURE 3-22   Case III $6\sigma > U - L$.

One solution is to discuss with the design engineer the possibility of increasing the tolerance. This solution may require reliability studies with mating parts to determine if the product can function with increased tolerance.

Another solution is to leave the process and the specifications alone and perform 100% inspection to eliminate the nonconforming parts. This is not an attractive solution, but it may be the most economical or only one.

A third possibility is to change the process dispersion so that a more peaked distribution occurs. To obtain a substantial reduction in the standard deviation might require new material, a more experienced operator, retraining, a new or overhauled machine, or possibly automatic in-process control.

Another solution is to shift the process average so that all of the nonconforming product occurs at one tail of the frequency distribution as indicated in Figure 3-22b. To illustrate this solution, assume that a shaft is being ground to tight specifications. If too much metal is removed, the part is scrapped; if too little is removed, the part must be reworked. By shifting the process average the amount of scrap is eliminated and the amount of rework is increased. A similar situation exists for an internal member such as a hole or keyway except that scrap occurs above the upper specification and rework occurs below the lower specification. This type of solution is feasible when the cost of the part is sufficient economically to justify the reworking operation.

EXAMPLE PROBLEM

Location pins for workholding devices are ground to a diameter of 12.50 mm (approximately $\frac{1}{2}$ in.), with a tolerance of 0.05 mm. If the process is centered at 12.50 mm (μ) and the dispersion is 0.02 mm (σ), what percent of the product must be scrapped and what percent can be reworked? How can the process center be changed to eliminate the scrap? What is the rework percentage?

The techniques for solving this problem were given in Chapter 2 and are shown below.

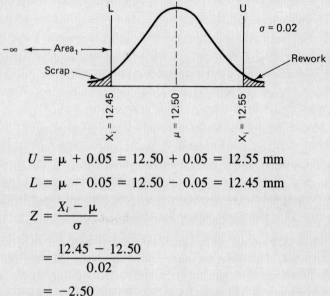

$$U = \mu + 0.05 = 12.50 + 0.05 = 12.55 \text{ mm}$$

$$L = \mu - 0.05 = 12.50 - 0.05 = 12.45 \text{ mm}$$

$$Z = \frac{X_i - \mu}{\sigma}$$

$$= \frac{12.45 - 12.50}{0.02}$$

$$= -2.50$$

From Table A of the appendix for a Z value of -2.50:

$$\text{Area}_1 = 0.0062 \text{ or } 0.62\% \text{ scrap}$$

Since the process is centered between the specifications and a symmetrical distribution is assumed, the rework percentage will be equal to the scrap percentage of 0.62%. The second part of the problem is solved using the following sketch:

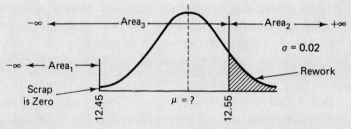

If the amount of scrap is to be zero, then $\text{Area}_1 = 0$. From Table A, the closest value to an Area_1 value of zero is 0.00017, which has a Z value of -3.59. Thus,

$$Z = \frac{X_i - \mu}{\sigma}$$

$$-3.59 = \frac{12.45 - \mu}{0.02}$$

$$\mu = 12.52 \text{ mm}$$

The percentage of rework is obtained by first determining Area$_3$.

$$Z = \frac{X_i - \mu}{\sigma}$$

$$= \frac{12.55 - 12.52}{0.02}$$

$$= +1.50$$

From Table A, Area$_3$ = 0.9332 and

$$\text{Area}_2 = \text{Area}_T - \text{Area}_3$$

$$= 1.0000 - 0.9332$$

$$= 0.0668, \quad \text{or} \quad 6.68\%$$

The amount of rework is 6.68%, which, incidentally, is considerably more than the combined rework and scrap percentage (1.24%) when the process is centered.

The preceding analysis of the process capability and the specifications was made utilizing an upper and a lower specification. Many times there is only one specification and it may be either the upper or lower. A similar and much simpler analysis would be for a single specification limit.

PROCESS CAPABILITY

The true process capability cannot be determined until the $\bar{X}$ and R charts have achieved the optimal quality improvement without a substantial investment for new equipment or equipment modification. Process capability is equal to $6\sigma_0$ when the process is in statistical control.

In the example problem for the $\bar{X}$ and R charts, the quality improvement process began in January with $\sigma_0 = 0.038$. The process capability is $6\sigma = (6)(0.038) = 0.228$ mm. By July, $\sigma_0 = 0.030$, which gives a process capability of 0.180 mm. This is a 20% improvement in the process capability, which in most situations would be sufficient to solve a quality problem.

It is frequently necessary to obtain the process capability by a quick method rather than by using the $\bar{X}$ and R charts. This method assumes the process is in statistical control, which may or may not be the case. The procedure is

1. Take 20 subgroups of size 4 for a total of 80 measurements.
2. Calculate the sample standard deviation, s, for each subgroup.
3. Calculate the average sample standard deviation, $\bar{s} = \Sigma\, s/g = \Sigma\, s/20$.

4. Calculate the estimate of the population standard deviation.

$$\hat{\sigma}_0 = \bar{s}/c_4$$

where c_4 is obtained from Table B and is 0.9213 for $n = 4$.

5. Process capability will equal $6\sigma_0$.

Remember that this technique does not give the true process capability and should be used only if circumstances require its use. Also, more than 20 subgroups can be used to improve accuracy.

EXAMPLE PROBLEM

A new process is started and the sum of the sample standard deviations for 20 subgroups of size 4 is 84. Determine the process capability.

$$\bar{s} = \frac{\Sigma s}{g} = \frac{84}{20} = 4.2$$

Subgroups

$$\sigma_0 = \frac{\bar{s}}{c_4} = \frac{4.2}{0.9213} = 4.56$$

$$6\sigma_0 = (6)(4.56) = 27.4$$

The process capability can also be obtained at the same time a histogram is constructed. Statistical control of the process is assumed. The procedure is

1. Take 10 subgroups of size 5 for a total of 50 measurements.
2. Calculate the range, R, for each subgroup.
3. Calculate the average range, $\bar{R} = \Sigma R/g = \Sigma R/10$.
4. Calculate the estimate of the population standard deviation

$$\hat{\sigma}_0 = \frac{\bar{R}}{d_2}$$

where d_2 is obtained from Table B and is 2.326 for $n = 5$.

5. Process capability will equal $6\sigma_0$.

More than 10 subgroups will improve the accuracy. A subgroup size of 4 could also be used. The advantage of this approach is the extra benefit of the histogram, which graphically presents the distribution of the process.

EXAMPLE PROBLEM

An existing process is not meeting the Rockwell-C specifications. Determine the process capability based on the range values for 10 subgroups of size 5. Data are 7, 5, 5, 3, 2, 4, 5, 9, 4, and 7.

CONTROL CHARTS FOR VARIABLES

$$\bar{R} = \frac{\Sigma R}{g} = \frac{51}{10} = 5.1$$

$$\sigma_0 = \frac{\bar{R}}{d_2} = \frac{5.1}{2.326} = 2.19$$

$$6\sigma_0 = (6)(2.19) = 13.2$$

Process capability and the tolerance are combined to form a *capability index*, defined as

$$C_p = \frac{U - L}{6\sigma_0}$$

where C_p = capability index
$U - L$ = upper specification $-$ lower specification, or tolerance
$6\sigma_0$ = process capability

If the capability index is 1.00, we have the case II situation discussed in the preceding section; if the ratio is greater than 1.00, we have the case I situation, which is desirable; and if the ratio is less than 1.00, we have the case III situation, which is undesirable. Figure 3-23 shows these three cases.

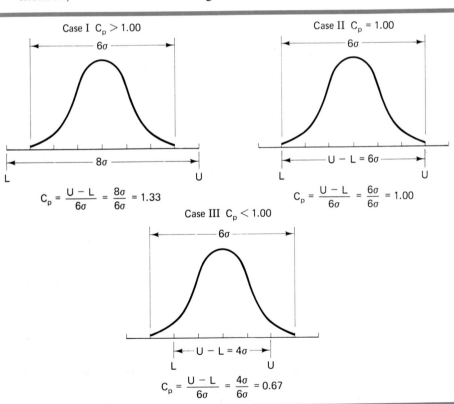

FIGURE 3-23 **Capability index and three cases.**

EXAMPLE PROBLEM

Assume that the specifications are 6.50 and 6.30 in the depth of keyway problem. Determine the capability index before ($\sigma_0 = 0.038$) and after ($\sigma_0 = 0.030$) improvement.

$$C_p = \frac{U - L}{6\sigma_0} = \frac{6.50 - 6.30}{6(0.038)} = 0.88$$

$$C_p = \frac{U - L}{6\sigma_0} = \frac{6.50 - 6.30}{6(0.030)} = 1.11$$

In the example problem the improvement in quality resulted in a desirable capability index (case I). The minimum capability index is frequently established at 1.33. Below this value, design engineers may be required to seek approval from manufacturing before the product can be released to production. A capability index of 1.33 is considered by most companies to be a de facto standard with even larger values desired.

Another measure of the capability is called the *capability ratio*, which is defined as

$$C_r = \frac{6\sigma_0}{U - L}$$

The only difference between the two measures is the change in the numerator and denominator. They are used for the same purpose; however, the interpretation is different. The de facto standard for a capability ratio is 0.75 with even smaller values desired. In both cases the de facto standard is established with the tolerance at $8\sigma_0$. To avoid misinterpretation between two parties, they should be sure which process capability measure is being used. In this book the capability index is used.

Using the capability index concept, we can measure quality provided the process is centered. The larger the capability index, the better the quality. We should strive to make the capability index as large as possible. This is accomplished by having realistic specifications and continual striving to improve the process capability.

The capability index does not measure process performance in terms of the nominal or target value. This measure is accomplished using C_{pk}, which is defined as

$$C_{pk} = \frac{Z(\text{Min})}{3\sigma}$$

where $Z(\text{Min})$ is the smaller of $Z(U) = (U - \bar{X})/\sigma$ or $Z(L) = (\bar{X} - L)/\sigma$.

EXAMPLE PROBLEM

Determine C_{pk} for the previous example problem ($U = 6.50$, $L = 6.30$, and $\sigma = 0.030$) when the average is 6.45.

$$Z(U) = \frac{U - \bar{X}}{\sigma} = \frac{6.50 - 6.45}{0.030} = 1.67$$

$$Z(L) = \frac{\bar{X} - L}{\sigma} = \frac{6.45 - 6.30}{0.030} = 5.00$$

1.33 · Cpk is desireed

$$C_{pk} = \frac{Z(\text{Min})}{3} = \frac{1.67}{3} = 0.56$$

Find C_{pk} when the average is 6.40.

$$Z(U) = \frac{U - \bar{X}}{\sigma} = \frac{6.50 - 6.40}{0.030} = 3.34$$

$$Z(L) = \frac{\bar{X} - L}{\sigma} = \frac{6.40 - 6.30}{0.030} = 3.34$$

$$C_{pk} = \frac{Z(\text{Min})}{3} = \frac{3.34}{3} = 1.11$$

Figure 3-24 illustrates C_p and C_{pk} values for a process that is centered and one that is off center by 1σ for the three cases. Comments concerning C_p and C_{pk} are as follows:

1. The C_p value does not change as the process center changes.
2. $C_p = C_{pk}$ when the process is centered.
3. C_{pk} is always equal to or less than C_p.
4. A C_{pk} value of 1.00 is a de facto standard. It indicates that the process is producing product that conforms to specifications.
5. A C_{pk} value less than 1.00 indicates that the process is producing product that does not conform to specifications. *U-L > 6σ*
6. A C_p value less than 1.00 indicates that the process is not capable. *U-L > 6σ*
7. A C_{pk} value of zero indicates the average is equal to one of the specification limits.
8. A negative C_{pk} value indicates that the average is outside the specifications.

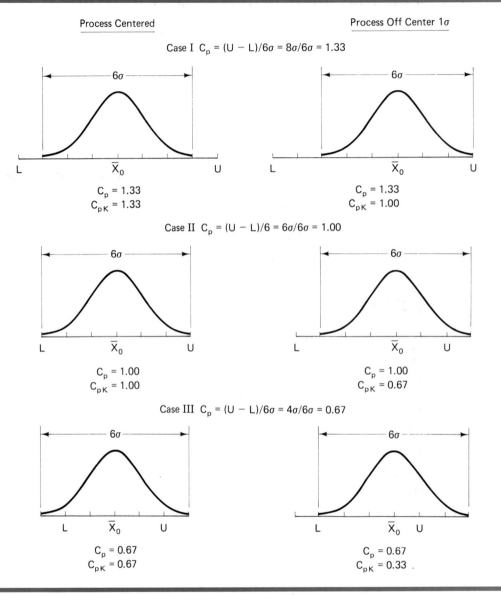

FIGURE 3-24 C_p and C_{pk} values for the three cases.

DIFFERENT CONTROL CHARTS

The basic control charts for variables were discussed in previous sections. While most of the quality control activity for variables is concerned with the $\overline{X}$ and R chart or the $\overline{X}$ and s chart, there are other charts which find application in some situations. These charts are discussed briefly in this section.

CONTROL CHARTS FOR VARIABLES

Charts for Better Operator Understanding

Since production personnel have difficulty understanding the relationships between averages, individual values, control limits, and specifications, various charts have been developed to overcome this difficulty.

1. *Placing individual values on the chart*. This technique plots both the individual values and the subgroup average and is illustrated in Figure 3-25. A small dot represents an individual value and a larger circle represents the subgroup average. In some cases, an individual value and a subgroup average are identical, in which case the small dot is located inside the circle. When two individual values are identical, the two dots are placed side by side. A further refinement of the chart can be made by the addition of upper and lower specification lines; however, this practice is not recommended.

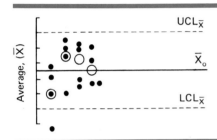

FIGURE 3-25   Chart showing a technique for plotting individual values and subgroup averages.

2. *Chart for subgroup sums*. This technique plots the subgroup sum, ΣX, rather than the subgroup average, $\overline{X}$. Since the values on the chart are of a different magnitude than the specifications, there is no chance for confusion. Figure 3-26 shows a subgroup sums chart, which is an $\overline{X}$ chart with the scale magnified by the subgroup size, n. The central line is $n\overline{X}_0$ and the control limits are obtained by the formulas

$$UCL_{\Sigma X} = n(UCL_{\bar{x}})$$

$$LCL_{\Sigma X} = n(LCL_{\bar{x}})$$

This chart is mathematically equal to the $\overline{X}$ chart and has the added advantage of simpler calculations. Only addition and subtraction are required.

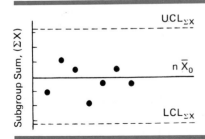

FIGURE 3-26   Subgroup sum chart.

Chart for Variable Subgroup Size

Every effort should be made to keep the subgroup size constant. Occasionally, however, because of lost material, laboratory tests, production problems, or inspection mistakes, the subgroup size varies. When this situation occurs, the control limits will vary with the subgroup size. As the subgroup size, n, increases, the control limits become narrower; as the subgroup size decreases, the control limits become wider apart (Figure 3-27). This fact is confirmed by an analysis of the control limit factors A, D_1, and D_2, which are a function of the subgroup size and which are part of the control limit formulas. Control limits will also vary for the R chart.

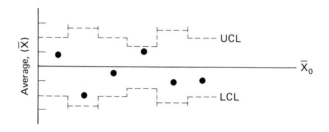

FIGURE 3-27   **Chart for variable subgroup size.**

One of the difficulties associated with a chart for variable subgroup size is the need to make a number of control limit calculations. A more serious difficulty involves the task of explaining to production people the reason for the different control limits. Therefore, this type of chart should be avoided.

Chart for Trends

When the plotted points of a chart have an upward or downward trend, it can be attributed to an unnatural pattern of variation or to a natural pattern of variation such as tool wear. In other words, as the tool wears, a gradual change in the average is expected and considered to be normal. Figure 3-28 illustrates a chart for a trend that reflects die wear. As the die wears, the measurement gradually increases until it reaches the upper reject limit. The die is then replaced or reworked.

Since the central line is on a slope, its equation must be determined. This is best accomplished using the least-squares method of fitting a line to a set of points. The equation for the trend line, using the slope-intercept form, is

$$\bar{X} = a + bW$$

where $\bar{X}$ = subgroup average and represents the vertical axis
W = subgroup number and represents the horizontal axis
a = point on the vertical axis where the line intercepts the vertical axis

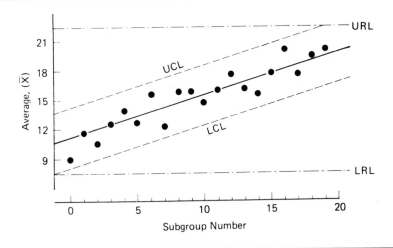

FIGURE 3-28   Chart for trend.

$$a = \frac{(\Sigma \bar{X})(\Sigma W^2) - (\Sigma W)(\Sigma W\bar{X})}{g \Sigma W^2 - (\Sigma W)^2}$$

b = the slope of the line

$$b = \frac{g \Sigma W\bar{X} - (\Sigma W)(\Sigma \bar{X})}{g \Sigma W^2 - (\Sigma W)^2}$$

g = number of subgroups

The coefficients of a and b are obtained by establishing columns for W, $\bar{X}$, $W\bar{X}$, and W^2, as illustrated in Table 3-4, determining their sums, and inserting the sums in the equation.

Once the trend-line equation is known, it can be plotted on the chart by assuming values of W and calculating $\bar{X}$. When two points are plotted, the trend line is

TABLE 3-4   Least-Squares Calculations for Trend Line

SUBGROUP NUMBER, W	SUBGROUP AVERAGE, $\bar{X}$	PRODUCT OF W AND $\bar{X}$, $W\bar{X}$	W^2
1	9	9	1
2	11	22	4
3	10	30	9
.	.	.	.
.	.	.	.
.	.	.	.
g	.	.	.
ΣW	$\Sigma \bar{X}$	$\Sigma W\bar{X}$	ΣW^2

drawn between them. The control limits are drawn on each side of the trend line a distance (in the perpendicular direction) equal to $A_2\bar{R}$ or $A\sigma_0$.

The R chart will generally have the typical appearance shown in Figure 3-6. However, the dispersion may also be increasing.

Chart for Moving Average and Moving Range

In some situations a chart is used to combine a number of individual values and plot them on a control chart. This type is referred to as a moving-average and moving-range chart and is quite common in the chemical industry, where only one reading is possible at a time. Table 3-5 illustrates the technique. In the development of Table 3-5, no calculations are made until the third day when the sum of the three values is posted to the three-period moving-sum column ($35 + 26 + 28 = 89$). The average and range are calculated ($\bar{X} = 89/3 = 29.6$)($R = 35 - 26 = 9$) and posted to the $\bar{X}$ and R columns. Subsequent calculations are accomplished by adding a new value and dropping the earliest one; therefore, 32 is added and 35 is dropped, making the sum $26 + 28 + 32 = 86$. The average and range calculations are $\bar{X} = 86/3 = 28.6$ and $R = 32 - 26 = 6$. Once the columns for $\bar{X}$ and R are completed, the charts are developed and used in the same manner as regular $\bar{X}$ and R charts.

TABLE 3-5   Calculations of Moving-Average and Moving-Range

VALUE	THREE-PERIOD MOVING SUM	$\bar{X}$	R
35	—	—	—
26	—	—	—
28	89	29.6	9
32	86	28.6	6
36	96	32.0	8
.	.	.	.
.	.	.	.
.	.	.	.
.	.	.	.
.	.	.	.
		$\sum \bar{X} =$	$\sum R =$

The discussion above used a time period of 3 h, the time period could have been 2 h, 5 days, 3 shifts, and so on.

In comparing the moving-average and moving-range charts with conventional charts, it is observed that an extreme reading has a greater effect on the former charts. This is true because an extreme value is used a number of times in the calculations.

Chart for Median and Range

A simplified variable control chart that minimizes calculations is the median and range. The data are collected in the conventional manner and the median, Md, and range, R, of each subgroup are found. These are arranged in ascending order and the median of the subgroup medians or grand median, Md_{Md}, and the median of the subgroup range, R_{Md}, are found by counting to the midpoint value. The median control limits are determined from the formulas

$$UCL_{Md} = Md_{Md} + A_5 R_{Md}$$

$$LCL_{Md} = Md_{Md} - A_5 R_{Md}$$

where Md_{Md} = grand median (median of the medians); Md_0 can be substituted in the formula

A_5 = factor for determining the 3σ control limits (see Table 3-6)

R_{Md} = median of subgroup ranges

TABLE 3-6   Factors for Computing 3σ Control Limits for Median and Range Charts from the Median Range

SUBGROUP SIZE	A_5	D_5	D_6	d_3
2	2.224	0	3.865	0.954
3	1.265	0	2.745	1.588
4	0.829	0	2.375	1.978
5	0.712	0	2.179	2.257
6	0.562	0	2.055	2.472
7	0.520	0.078	1.967	2.645
8	0.441	0.139	1.901	2.791
9	0.419	0.187	1.850	2.916
10	0.369	0.227	1.809	3.024

Source: Extracted by permission from P. C. Clifford, "Control Without Calculations," *Industrial Quality Control,* 15, No. 6 (May 1959), 44.

The range control limits are determined from the formulas

$$UCL_R = D_6 R_{Md}$$

$$LCL_R = D_5 R_{Md}$$

where D_5 and D_6 are factors for determining the 3σ control limits based on R_{Md} and are found in Table 3-6. An estimate of the population standard deviation can be obtained from $\sigma = R_{Md}/d_3$.

The principal benefits of the median chart are (1) less arithmetic, (2) easier to understand, and (3) can be maintained by the operators. However, the median chart fails to grant any weight to extreme values in a subgroup.

When these charts are maintained by operating personnel a subgroup size of 3 is recommended. For example, consider the three values 36, 39, and 35. The Md is 36 and R is 4—all three values are used. Figure 3-29 is an example of a median chart. Subgroup sizes of 5 give a better chart; however, the operator will have to order the data before determining the median. While these charts are not as sensitive to variation as the $\overline{X}$ and R, they can be quite effective, especially after quality improvement has been obtained and the process is in a monitoring phase.

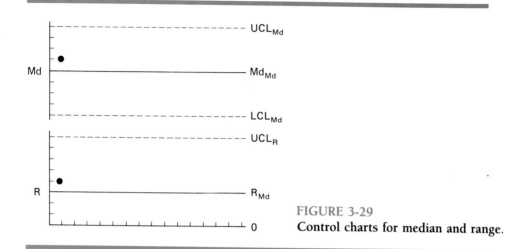

FIGURE 3-29
Control charts for median and range.

Chart for Individual Values

In many situations only one measurement is taken on a quality characteristic. This may be due to the fact that it is too expensive, too time consuming, or there are few items to inspect. In such cases an X chart will provide some information from limited data, whereas an $\bar{X}$ chart would provide no information or information only after considerable delay to obtain sufficient data. Figure 3-30 illustrates an X chart.

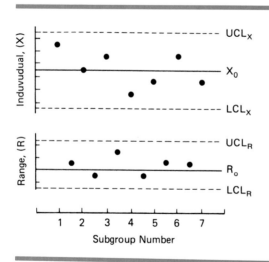

FIGURE 3-30   Control charts for individual values and moving range.

Formulas for the trial central line and control limits are

$$\bar{X} = \frac{\Sigma X}{g} \qquad\qquad \bar{R} = \frac{\Sigma R}{g}$$

$$\text{UCL}_x = \bar{X} + 2.660\bar{R} \qquad \text{UCL}_R = 3.276\bar{R}$$

$$\text{LCL}_x = \bar{X} - 2.660\bar{R} \qquad \text{LCL}_R = (0)\bar{R}$$

These formulas require the moving range technique with a subgroup size of 2.[10] To obtain the first range point, the value of X_1 is subtracted from X_2; to obtain the second point, X_2 is subtracted from X_3; and so forth. Each individual value is used for two different points except for the first and last: therefore, the name "moving" range. The range points are placed between the subgroup number on the R chart since they are obtained from both values.

These range points are averaged to obtain $\bar{R}$. Note that g for obtaining $\bar{R}$ will be one less than g for obtaining $\bar{X}$.

Formulas for the revised central line and control limits are

$$X_0 = \bar{X}_{\text{new}} \qquad\qquad R_0 = \bar{R}_{\text{new}}$$

$$\text{UCL}_x = X_0 + 3\sigma_0 \qquad \text{UCL}_R = (3.686)\sigma_0$$

$$\text{LCL}_x = X_0 - 3\sigma_0 \qquad \text{LCL}_R = (0)\sigma_0$$

where $\sigma_0 = 0.8865 R_0$.

The X chart has the advantage of being easier for production personnel to understand and of providing a direct comparison with specifications. It does have the disadvantages of (1) requiring too many subgroups to indicate an out-of-control condition, (2) not summarizing the data as well as $\bar{X}$, and (3) distorting the control limits when the distribution is not normal. To correct for the last disadvantage, tests for normality should be used since the central limit theorem will not be applicable. Unless there is an insufficient amount of data, the $\bar{X}$ chart is recommended.

OTHER CHARTS

There are other charts that may assist quality personnel in the attainment of quality improvement.

Charts with Reject Limits

Reject limits have the same relationship to averages as specifications have to individual values. Figure 3-31 shows the relationship of reject limits, control limits, and specifications for the three cases discussed in the section on specifications. The up-

---

[10] This technique is the simplest approach to X and R charts. Other techniques are given on pages 23–15 to 23–17 of Juran, *Quality Control Handbook,* 3d ed.

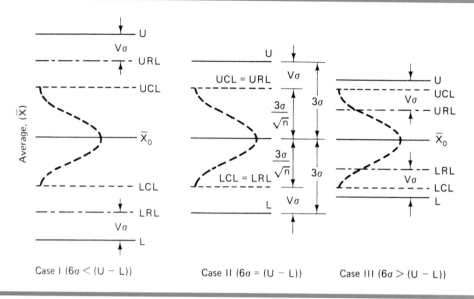

Case I ($6\sigma < (U - L)$) Case II ($6\sigma = (U - L)$) Case III ($6\sigma > (U - L)$)

FIGURE 3-31 Relationship of reject limits, control limits, and specifications.

per, U, and lower, L, specifications are shown in Figure 3-31 to illustrate the technique and are not included in actual practice.

In case I the reject limits are greater than the control limits, which is a desirable situation, since an out-of-control condition will not result in nonconforming product. Case II shows the situation where the reject limits are equal to the control limits; therefore, any out-of-control situations will result in nonconforming product being manufactured. Case III illustrates the situation where the reject limits are inside the control limits, and therefore some nonconforming product will be manufactured even when the process is in control.

The figure shows that the reject limits are a prescribed distance from the specifications. This distance is equal to $V\sigma$, where V varies with the subgroup size and is equal to the value $3 - 3/\sqrt{n}$. The formula for V was derived from case II, because in that situation the control limits are equal to the reject limits.

Control limits tell what the process is capable of doing and reject limits tell when the product is conforming to specifications. This can be a valuable tool for the quality professional and perhaps the first-line supervisor. Posting of reject limits for operating personnel should be avoided since they will be confusing and may lead to unnecessary adjustment. Also, the operator is only responsible to maintain the process between the control limits.

Chart for Short Production Runs

Short production runs present a problem in that the run may be completed before the control chart can be implemented. For this situation a chart can be designed that will give some measure of control and a method for quality improvement. The central line and the control limits for this type of chart are established using the specifications.

Assume that the specifications call for 25.00 ± 0.12 mm. Then the central line, $\bar{X}_0, = 25.00$. The difference between the upper specification and the lower specification $(U - L)$ is 0.24 mm, which is the spread of the process under the case II situation. Therefore, $6\sigma = U - L = 0.24$ and $\sigma = 0.04$. It follows that $\sigma_{\bar{x}} = \sigma/\sqrt{n}$ and for a subgroup size of 4, $\sigma_{\bar{x}} = 0.04/\sqrt{4} = 0.02$. Thus,

$$\text{URL}_{\bar{x}} = \bar{X}_0 + 3\sigma_{\bar{x}} \qquad\qquad \text{LRL}_{\bar{x}} = \bar{X} - 3\sigma_{\bar{x}}$$

$$= 25.00 + 3(0.02) \qquad\qquad = 25.00 - 3(0.02)$$

$$= 25.06 \qquad\qquad\qquad = 24.94$$

$$\text{URL}_R = D_2\sigma_0 \qquad\qquad\qquad \text{LRL}_R = D_1\sigma_0$$

$$= (4.698)(0.04) \qquad\qquad = (0)(0.04)$$

$$= 0.19 \qquad\qquad\qquad\quad = 0$$

These limits represent what we would like the process to do (as a maximum condition) rather than what it is capable of doing. Actually these limits are reject limits as discussed in the previous section. The method of calculation is slightly different.

Run Chart

A run chart does not have control limits but can be used to analyze the data especially in the development stage of a product or prior to a state of statistical control. The data points are plotted by order of production, as shown in Figure 3-32. It is obvious from the chart that the hardness resulting from a heat-treating operation is declining. Plotting the data points is a very effective way of finding out about the process. This should be done as the first step in data analysis. Without a run chart other data analysis tools, such as the average, sample standard deviation, and histogram, can lead to erroneous conclusions.

Many chemical processing plants are designed to produce a few basic products to customer specifications. While the ingredients and process are essentially the same, the specifications will change with each customer's batch. Figure 3-33 shows a run chart for batch viscosity. The solid point represents the viscosity value and the vertical line represents the specification range. A cursory analysis of the batches shows that eight of the 10 plotted points are on the high end of the specification. This information may lead to a minor adjustment so that the viscosity of future batches will be closer to the center of each batch specification. Run charts such as this for the other quality characteristics can be an effective technique for quality improvement.

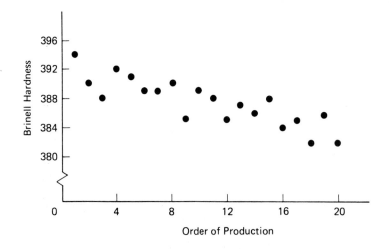

FIGURE 3-32   **Run chart for heat treatment operation.**

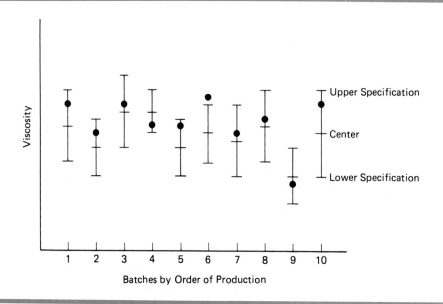

FIGURE 3-33   **Run chart for different batches with different specifications.**

COMPUTER PROGRAM

The computer program given in Figure 3-34 computes the central line and control limits for the $\bar{X}$ and R charts. If it is desired to print out the incoming data, an LPRINT statement can be added after statement 170. Also, additional LPRINT

120

statements can be added to print out the subgroup values that are discarded. Data used for the program are the same as the example problem. By using the coding statement $X(I) = 6.00 + X(I)/100$ after statement 300, coded data using the last two digits was entered.

The program can be enhanced by graphing the chart and plotting the actual points. This activity is a function of the available graphical output device.

```
10  REM                        XBAR and R CHARTS
20  REM
30  REM                    N = Subgroup Size
40  REM                    G = Number of Subgroups
50  REM                 X(I) = Observed Values
60  REM            A(J)/R(J) = Subgroups Average/Range
70  REM          ABAR/RBAR = Average of Averages/Ranges
80  REM            UCL/LCL = Central Limits(A & R)
90  REM              AO/RO = Standard Value and Central Line
100 REM                      of Average/Range
110 REM                 SO = Standard value of Standard
120 REM                      Deviation
130 REM    A2,D,D1,D2,D3,D4 = Control Chart Factors
140 REM             Note:  A = 3 / SQR(N)
150 REM
155 DIM X(25), A(30), R(30)
160 PRINT " Enter subgroup size." : INPUT N : LPRINT " n = ";N
170 PRINT " Enter control chart factors A2, d2, D1, D2, D3, D4."
180 INPUT A2, D, D1, D2, D3, D4
190 LPRINT
200 LPRINT " A2 = ";A2," d2 = ";D," D1 = ";D1
210 LPRINT " D2 = ";D2," D3 = ";D3," D4 = ";D4
220 LPRINT
230 PRINT " Enter number of subgroups. " : INPUT G : LPRINT " g = ";G
240 LPRINT
250 J = 0
260 SX = 0
270 J = J + 1
280 PRINT " Enter subgroup values. "
290       FOR I = 1 TO N
300       INPUT X(I)
310       SX = SX + X(I)
320       NEXT I
330 REM                      Sort Routine
340       FOR K = 1 TO (N - 1)
350       L = N - K
360           FOR M = 1 TO L
370           Q = M + 1
380           IF X(M) < X(Q) GOTO 420
390           A = X(M)
```

FIGURE 3-34 Computer program in BASIC to calculate the central line and control limits for $\overline{X}$ and R charts.

FIGURE 3-34 (continued)

```
400                 X(M) = X(Q)
410                 X(Q) = A
420                 NEXT M
430         NEXT K
440 REM             Subgroup Average & Range
450 R(J) = X(N) - X(1)
460 A(J) = SX / N
480 IF J < G GOTO 260
490 REM                       Trial Central Lines(A Bar & R Bar)
500 SA = 0 : SR = 0
510       FOR K = 1 TO G
520       SA = SA + A(K)
530       SR = SR + R(K)
540       NEXT K
550 ABAR = SA / G
560 RBAR = SR / G
580 REM                       Trial Control Limits
590 UCLA = ABAR + A2 * RBAR
600 LCLA = ABAR - A2 * RBAR
610 UCLR = D4 * RBAR
620 LCLR = D3 * RBAR
630 REM                       Discard Out-of-Control
640 DA = G : DR = G
650       FOR J = 1 TO G
660       IF A(J) < LCLA GOTO 710
670       IF A(J) > UCLA GOTO 770
680       IF R(J) < LCLR GOTO 800
690       IF R(J) > UCLR GOTO 860
700       GOTO 890
710       PRINT " Subgroup number = ";J
720       PRINT " A < LCL; Enter 0 to discard, else 1."
730       INPUT K
740       IF K = 1 GOTO 890
750       IF K = 0 THEN SA = SA - A(J) : DA = DA - 1
760       GOTO 890
770       PRINT " Subgroup number = ";J
780       PRINT " A > UCL; Enter 0 to discard, else 1."
790       INPUT K : GOTO 740
800       PRINT " Subgroup number = ";J
810       PRINT " R < LCL; Enter 0 to discard, else 1."
820       INPUT L
830       IF L = 1 GOTO 890
840       IF L = 0 THEN SR = SR - R(J) : DR = DR - 1
850       GOTO 890
860       PRINT " Subgroup number = ";J
870       PRINT " R > UCL; Enter 0 to discard, else 1."
880       INPUT L : GOTO 830
890       NEXT J
900 REM                       Standard Values and Central Line
910 XO = SA / DA
920 RO = SR / DR
930 SO = RO / D
940 REM                Control Limits
950 UCLA = XO + (3 / SQR(N)) * SO
960 LCLA = XO - (3 / SQR(N)) * SO
```

```
970 UCLR = D2 * SO
980 LCLR = D1 * SO
990 LPRINT " XO = ";XO," RO = ";RO," SO = ";SO
1000 LPRINT " UCLA = ";UCLA,"   LCLA = ";LCLA
1010 LPRINT " UCLR = ";UCLR,"   LCLR = ";LCLR
1020 END

n = 4

A2 = .729      d2 = 2.059      D1 = 0
D2 = 4.698     D3 = 0          D4 = 2.282

g = 25

XO = 6.39522        RO = .0787499        SO = .0382467
UCLA = 6.45259      LCLA = 6.33785
UCLR = .179683      LCLR = 0
```

PROBLEMS

1. Control charts for $\bar{X}$ and R are to be established on a certain dimension part, measured in millimeters. Data were collected in subgroup sizes of 6 and are given below. Determine the trial central line and control limits. Assume assignable causes and revise the central line and limits.

Calculate $\bar{X}$ $\bar{R}$ Trial Control limits

SUBGROUP NUMBER	$\bar{X}$	R	SUBGROUP NUMBER	$\bar{X}$	R
1	20.35	0.34	14	20.41	0.36
2	20.40	0.36	15	20.45	0.34
3	20.36	0.32	16	20.34	0.36
4	20.65	0.36	17	20.36	0.37
5	20.20	0.36	18	20.42	0.73
6	20.40	0.35	19	20.50	0.38
7	20.43	0.31	20	20.31	0.35
8	20.37	0.34	21	20.39	0.38
9	20.48	0.30	22	20.39	0.33
10	20.42	0.37	23	20.40	0.32
11	20.39	0.29	24	20.41	0.34
12	20.38	0.30	25	20.40	0.30
13	20.40	0.33			

2. The table following gives the average and range in kilograms for tensile tests on an improved plastic cord. The subgroup size is 4. Determine the trial central line and control limits. If any points are out of control, assume assignable causes and calculate revised limits and central line.

SUBGROUP NUMBER	$\bar{X}$	R	SUBGROUP NUMBER	$\bar{X}$	R
1	476	32	14	482	22
2	466	24	15	506	23
3	484	32	16	496	23
4	466	26	17	478	25
5	470	24	18	484	24
6	494	24	19	506	23
7	486	28	20	476	25
8	496	23	21	485	29
9	488	24	22	490	25
10	482	26	23	463	22
11	498	25	24	469	27
12	464	24	25	474	22
13	484	24			

3. Rework Problem 1 assuming a subgroup size of 3.

4. Rework Problem 2 assuming a subgroup size of 5.

5. Control charts for $\bar{X}$ and R are kept on the weight in kilograms of a color pigment for a batch process. After 25 subgroups with a subgroup size of 4, $\Sigma \bar{X} = 52.08$ kg (114.8 lb), $\Sigma R = 11.82$ kg (26.1 lb). Assuming the process is in a state of control, compute the $\bar{X}$ and R chart central line and control limits for the next production period.

6. On page 125 is a typical $\bar{X}$ and R chart form with information on acid content in milliliters. Complete all calculations, plot the points, and draw the trial central line and limits. Analyze the plotted points to determine if the process is stable.

7. For the next production period, it is decided to use a subgroup size of 4 for the data of Problem 1. What are the new control limits? How do they compare with the limits for a subgroup size of 6?

SUBGROUP NUMBER	$\bar{X}$	s	SUBGROUP NUMBER	$\bar{X}$	s
1	540	26	14	551	24
2	534	23	15	522	29
3	545	24	16	579	26
4	561	27	17	549	28
5	576	25	18	508	23
6	523	50	19	569	22
7	571	29	20	574	28
8	547	29	21	563	33
9	584	23	22	561	23
10	552	24	23	548	25
11	541	28	24	556	27
12	545	25	25	553	23
13	546	26			

VARIABLES CONTROL CHART

PART ID: OPERATION ID: DEPT/AREA: CHART ID: Problem 6

CHECK METHOD: NOMINAL VALUE: 0.70 ml   CHARACTERISTIC: Acid Content   TOLERANCE: ± 0.20

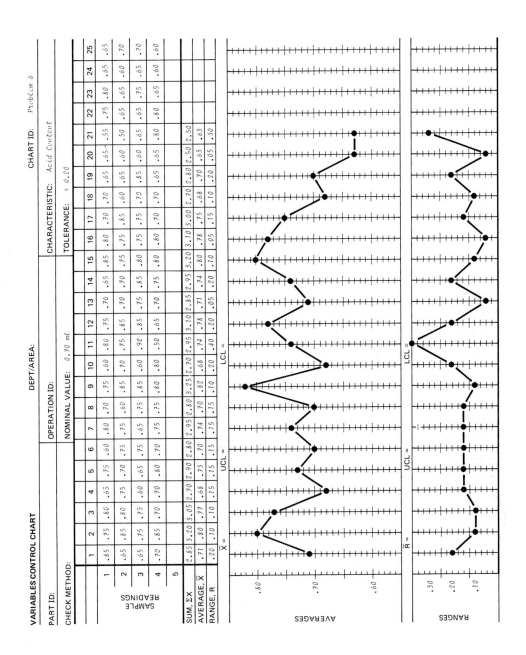

SAMPLE READINGS	1	2	3	4	5	6	7	8	9	10	11	12	13	14	15	16	17	18	19	20	21	22	23	24	25
1	.85	.75	.80	.65	.75	.60	.80	.70	.75	.60	.80	.75	.70	.65	.85	.80	.70	.70	.65	.65	.55	.75	.80	.65	.65
2	.65	.85	.80	.75	.70	.75	.75	.60	.85	.70	.75	.85	.70	.70	.75	.75	.85	.60	.65	.60	.50	.65	.65	.60	.70
3	.65	.75	.75	.60	.65	.75	.65	.75	.85	.60	.90	.85	.75	.85	.80	.75	.75	.79	.85	.60	.65	.65	.75	.65	.70
4	.70	.85	.70	.70	.80	.70	.75	.75	.80	.80	.50	.65	.70	.75	.80	.80	.70	.70	.65	.65	.80	.80	.65	.60	.60
5																									

	1	2	3	4	5	6	7	8	9	10	11	12	13	14	15	16	17	18	19	20	21	22	23	24	25
SUM, ΣX	2.85	3.20	3.05	2.70	2.90	2.80	2.95	2.80	3.25	2.70	2.95	3.10	2.85	2.95	3.20	3.10	3.00	2.70	2.80	2.50	2.50				
AVERAGE, X̄	.71	.80	.77	.68	.73	.70	.74	.70	.82	.68	.74	.78	.71	.74	.80	.78	.75	.68	.70	.63	.63				
RANGE, R	.20	.10	.10	.15	.15	.15	.15	.15	.10	.20	.40	.20	.05	.20	.10	.05	.15	.10	.20	.05	.30				

$\bar{X} =$

$\bar{R} =$

UCL =   LCL =

AVERAGES

RANGES

8. Control charts for $\bar{X}$ and s are to be established on the Brinell hardness of hardened tool steel in kilograms per square millimeter. Data for subgroup sizes of 8 are shown on page 124. Determine the trial central line and control limits for the $\bar{X}$ and s charts. Assume that the out-of-control points have assignable causes. Calculate the revised limits and central line.

9. Control charts for $\bar{X}$ and s are maintained on the resistance in ohms of an electrical part. The subgroup size is 6. After 25 subgroups, $\Sigma \bar{X} = 2046.5$ and $\Sigma s = 17.4$. If the process is in statistical control, what are the control limits and central line?

10. Rework Problem 8 assuming a subgroup size of 3.

11. Copy the s chart of Figure 3-7 on transparent paper. Place this copy on top of the R chart of Figure 3-4 and compare the pattern of variation.

12. In filling bags of nitrogen fertilizer, it is desired to hold the average overfill to as low a value as possible. The lower specification limit is 22.00 kg (48.50 lb), the population mean weight of the bags is 22.73 kg (50.11 lb), and the population standard deviation is 0.80 kg (1.76 lb). What percent of the bags contain less than 22 kg? If it is permissible for 5% of the bags to be below 22 kg, what would be the average weight? Assume a normal distribution.

13. Plastic strips that are used in a sensitive electronic device are manufactured to a maximum specification of 305.70 mm (approximately 12 in.) and a minimum specification of 304.55 mm. If the strips are less than the minimum specification, they are scrapped; if greater than the maximum specification, they are reworked. The part dimensions are normally distributed with a population mean of 305.20 mm and a population standard deviation of 0.25 mm. What percentage of the product is scrap? What percentage is rework? How can the process be centered to eliminate all but 0.1% of the scrap? What is the rework percentage now?

14. A company that manufactures oil seals found the population mean to be 49.15 mm (1.935 in.), the population standard deviation to be 0.51 mm (0.020 in.), and the data to be normally distributed. If the ID of the seal is below the lower specification limit of 47.80 mm, the part is reworked. However, if above the upper specification limit of 49.80 mm, the seal is scrapped. (a) What percentage of the seals are reworked? What percentage are scrapped? (b) For various reasons the process average is changed to 48.50 mm. With this new mean or process center, what percentage of the seals is reworked? What percentage is scrapped? If rework is economically feasible, is the change in the process center a wise decision?

15. Determine the process capability of the data on Table 3-3. Use the first 20 subgroups.

16. Repeat Problem 15 using the last 20 subgroups and compare the results.

17. Determine the process capability of the case-hardening process of Problem 8.

18. Determine the process capability of the tensile tests of the improved plastic cord of Problem 2.

19. What is the process capability of:
    (a) Problem 1
    (b) Problem 5

20. Determine the capability index before ($\sigma_0 = 0.038$) and after ($\sigma_0 = 0.030$) improvement for the chapter example problem using specifications of 6.40 ± 0.15 mm.

21. A new process is started and the sum of the sample standard deviations for 20 subgroups of size 4 is 600. If the specifications are 700 ± 80, what is the process capability index? What action would you recommend?

22. What is the C_{pk} value after improvement for Problem 20 when the process center is 6.40? When the process center is 6.30? Explain.

23. What is the C_{pk} value for the information in Problem 21 when the process average is 700, 740, 780, and 820? Explain.

24. Determine the revised central line and control limits for a subgroup sum chart using the data of:
    (a) Problem 1
    (b) Problem 2

25. Determine the trial central line and control limits for moving-average and moving-range chart using a time period of 3. Data in liters are as follows: 4.56, 4.65, 4.66, 4.34, 4.65, 4.40, 4.50, 4.55, 4.69, 4.29, 4.58, 4.71, 4.61, 4.66, 4.46, 4.70, 4.65, 4.61, 4.54, 4.55, 4.54, 4.54, 4.47, 4.64, 4.72, 4.47, 4.66, 4.51, 4.43, 4.34. Are there any out-of-control points?

26. Repeat Problem 25 using a time period of 4. What is the difference in the central line and control limits? Are there any out-of-control points?

27. The Get-Well Hospital has completed a quality improvement project on the time to admit a patient using $\overline{X}$ and R charts. They now wish to monitor the activity using median and range charts. Determine the central line and control limits with the latest data in minutes as given below.

SUBGROUP NUMBER	OBSERVATION			SUBGROUP NUMBER	OBSERVATION		
	X_1	X_2	X_3		X_1	X_2	X_3
1	6.0	5.8	6.1	13	6.1	6.9	7.4
2	5.2	6.4	6.9	14	6.2	5.2	6.8
3	5.5	5.8	5.2	15	4.9	6.6	6.6
4	5.0	5.7	6.5	16	7.0	6.4	6.1
5	6.7	6.5	5.5	17	5.4	6.5	6.7
6	5.8	5.2	5.0	18	6.6	7.0	6.8
7	5.6	5.1	5.2	19	4.7	6.2	7.1
8	6.0	5.8	6.0	20	6.7	5.4	6.7
9	5.5	4.9	5.7	21	6.8	6.5	5.2
10	4.3	6.4	6.3	22	5.9	6.4	6.0
11	6.2	6.9	5.0	23	6.7	6.3	4.6
12	6.7	7.1	6.2	24	7.4	6.8	6.3

28. Determine the trial central line and control limits for median and range charts for the data of Table 3-2. Assume assignable causes for any out-of-control points and

determine the revised central line and control limits. Compare the pattern of variation with the $\bar{X}$ and R charts in Figure 3-4.

29. An X and R chart is to be maintained on the pH value for the swimming pool water of a leading motel. One reading is taken each day for 30 days. Data are: 7.8, 7.9, 7.7, 7.6, 7.4, 7.2, 6.9, 7.5, 7.8, 7.7, 7.5, 7.8, 8.0, 8.1, 8.0, 7.9, 8.2, 7.3, 7.8, 7.4, 7.2, 7.5, 6.8, 7.3, 7.4, 8.1, 7.6, 8.0, 7.4, and 7.0. Plot the data on graph paper, determine the trial central line and limits, and evaluate the variation.

30. Determine upper and lower reject limits for the $\bar{X}$ chart of Problem 1. The specifications are 20.40 ± 0.25. Compare these limits to the revised control limits.

31. Determine the central line and control limits for a short production run that will be completed in 3 h. The specifications are 25.0 ± 0.3 Ω. Use n = 4.

32. A new process is starting and there is the possibility that the process temperature will give problems. Eight readings are taken each day at 8:00 A.M., 10:00 A.M., 12:00 noon, 2:00 P.M., 4:00 P.M., 6:00 P.M., 8:00 P.M., and 10:00 P.M. Prepare a run chart and evaluate the results.

DAY	TEMPERATURE (0°C)							
Monday	78.9	80.0	79.6	79.9	78.6	80.2	78.9	78.5
Tuesday	80.7	80.5	79.6	80.2	79.2	79.3	79.7	80.3
Wednesday	79.0	80.6	79.9	79.6	80.0	80.0	78.6	79.3
Thursday	79.7	79.9	80.2	79.2	79.5	80.3	79.0	79.4
Friday	79.3	80.2	79.1	79.5	78.8	78.9	80.0	78.8

33. The viscosity of a liquid is checked every half-hour during one three-shift day. Prepare a histogram with five cells and the midpoint value of the first cell equal to 29 and evaluate the distribution. Prepare a run chart and evaluate the distribution again. What does the run chart indicate? Data are: 39, 42, 38, 37, 41, 40, 38, 36, 40, 36, 35, 38, 34, 35, 37, 36, 39, 34, 38, 36, 32, 37, 35, 34, 33, 35, 32, 32, 38, 34, 37, 35, 35, 34, 31, 33, 35, 32, 36, 31, 29, 33, 32, 31, 30, 32, 32, and 29.

34. Test, and if necessary rewrite, the computer program for the $\bar{X}$ and R charts for your computer.

35. Modify the computer program to output the central line and control limits for your graphical output device. Also, write the program to plot the subgroup $\bar{X}$ and R values.

36. Write a computer program for:
    (a) $\bar{X}$ and s charts
    (b) Short production run chart
    (c) Moving average and moving range charts
    (d) Median and range charts
    (e) Upper and lower reject limits
    (f) Process capability (quick method)
    (g) C_p and C_{pk}

4

FUNDAMENTALS
OF PROBABILITY

BASIC CONCEPTS

Definition of Probability

The term *probability* has a number of synonyms, such as likelihood, chance, tendency, and trend. To the layperson, probability is a well-known term that refers to the chance that something will happen. "I will probably play golf tomorrow" or "I will probably receive an A in this course" are typical examples. When the commentator on the evening news states that, "The probability of rain tomorrow is 25%," the definition has been quantified. It is possible to define probability with extreme mathematical rigor; however, in this text we will define probability from a practical viewpoint as it applies to quality control.

If a nickel is tossed, the probability of a head is $\frac{1}{2}$ and the probability of a tail is $\frac{1}{2}$. A die, which is used in games of chance, is a cube with six sides and spots on each side from one to six. When the die is tossed on the table, the likelihood or probability of one spot is $\frac{1}{6}$, the probability of two spots is $\frac{1}{6}$, . . . , the probability of six spots is $\frac{1}{6}$. Another example of probability is illustrated by the drawing of a card from a deck of cards. The probability of a spade is $\frac{13}{52}$, since there are 13 spades in a deck of cards that contains 52 total cards. For hearts, diamonds, and clubs, the other three suits in the deck, the probability is also $\frac{13}{52}$.

Figure 4-1 shows the probability distributions for the examples above. It is noted that the area of each distribution is equal to 1.000 ($\frac{1}{2} + \frac{1}{2} = 1.000$; $\frac{1}{6} + \frac{1}{6} + \frac{1}{6} + \frac{1}{6} + \frac{1}{6} + \frac{1}{6} = 1.000$; and $\frac{13}{52} + \frac{13}{52} + \frac{13}{52} + \frac{13}{52} = 1.000$). It is recalled that the area under the normal distribution curve, which is a probability distribution, is also equal to 1.000. Therefore, the total probability of any situation will be equal to 1.000. The probability is expressed as a decimal such as (1) the probability of heads is 0.500 which is expressed in symbols as [$P(h) = 0.500$], (2) the probability of a 3 on a die is 0.167[$P(3) = 0.167$], and (3) the probability of a spade is 0.250[$P(s) = 0.250$].

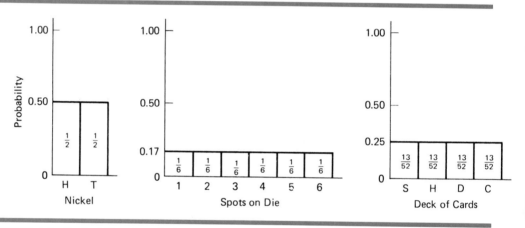

FIGURE 4-1   **Probability distributions.**

The probabilities given in the preceding examples will occur provided sufficient trials are made and provided there is an equal likelihood of the events occurring. In other words, the probability of a head (the event) will be 0.500 provided that the chance of a head or a tail is equal (equally likely). In most coins the equally likely condition is met; however, the addition of a little extra metal on one side would produce a biased coin and the equally likely condition could not be met. Similarly, an unscrupulous person might fix a die so that a three appears more often than one out of six times, or he might stack a deck of cards so that all the aces were at the top.

Returning to the example of a six-sided die, there are six possible outcomes (1, 2, 3, 4, 5, and 6). An *event* is a collection of outcomes. Thus, the event of a 2 or 4 occurring on a throw of the die has two outcomes and the total number of outcomes is 6. The probability is obviously $\frac{2}{6}$, or 0.333.

From the discussion above, a definition based on a frequency interpretation can be given. If an event A can occur in N_A outcomes out of a total of N possible and equally likely outcomes, then the probability that the event will occur is

$$P(A) = \frac{N_A}{N}$$

where $P(A)$ = probability of an event A occurring
$\quad\quad N_A$ = number of successful outcomes of event A
$\quad\quad N$ = total number of possible outcomes

This definition can be used when the number of outcomes is known or when the number of outcomes is found by experimentation.

EXAMPLE PROBLEM

A part is selected at random from a container of 50 parts that are known to have 10 nonconforming units. The part is returned to the container and a record of the number of trials and the number nonconforming is maintained. After 90 trials, 16 nonconforming units were recorded. What is the probability based on known outcomes and on experimental outcomes?

Known outcomes:

$$P(A) = \frac{N_A}{N} = \frac{10}{50} = 0.200$$

Experimental outcomes:

$$P(A) = \frac{N_A}{N} = \frac{16}{90} = 0.178$$

The probability calculated using known outcomes is the true probability and the one calculated using experimental outcomes is different due to the chance factor. If, say, 900 trials were taken, the probability using experimental outcomes would be much closer since the chance factor would be minimized.

In most cases, the number nonconforming in the container would not be known; therefore, the probability with known outcomes cannot be determined. If we consider the probability using experimental outcomes to represent the sample and known outcomes to represent the population, there is the same relationship between sample and population that was discussed in Chapter 2.

The definition above is useful for finite situations where N_A, the number of successful outcomes, and N, total number of outcomes, are known or must be found experimentally. For an infinite situation, where $N = \infty$, the definition would always lead to a probability of zero. Therefore, in the infinite situation the probability of an event occurring is proportional to the population distribution. A discussion of this situation is given under the discussion of continuous and discrete probability distributions.

Theorems of Probability

Theorem 1. Probability is expressed as a number between 1.000 and 0, where a value of 1.000 is a certainty that an event will occur and a value of 0 is a certainty that an event will not occur.

Theorem 2. If $P(A)$ is the probability that event A will occur, then the probability that A will not occur, $P(\cancel{A})$, is $1.000 - P(A)$.

EXAMPLE PROBLEM

If the probability of finding an error on an income tax return is 0.04, what is the probability of finding an acceptable return?

$$P(\cancel{A}) = 1.000 - P(A)$$
$$= 1.000 - 0.040$$
$$= 0.960$$

Therefore, the probability of finding an acceptable income tax return is 0.960.

Before proceeding to the other theorems, it is appropriate to learn where they are applicable. In Figure 4-2, we see that if the probability of only one event is desired, then Theorem 3 or 4 is used, depending on whether the event is mutually exclusive or not. If the probability of two or more events are desired, then Theorem 6 or 7 is used, depending on whether the events are independent or not. Theorem 5 is not included in the figure, since it pertains to a different concept.

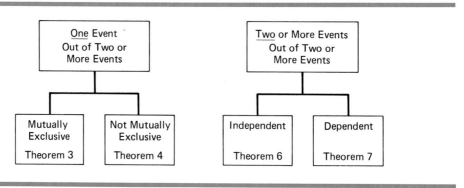

FIGURE 4-2   **When to use theorems 3, 4, 6, and 7.**

If one event happens the other can not

Theorem 3. If A and B are two mutually exclusive events, then the probability that either event A or event B will occur is the sum of their respective probabilities.

$$P(A \text{ or } B) = P(A) + P(B)$$

Mutually exclusive means that the occurrence of one event makes the other event impossible. Thus, if on one throw of a die a 3 occurred (event A), then event B, say a 5, could not possibly occur.

Whenever an "or" is verbalized, the mathematical operation is addition, or as we shall see in Theorem 4, it can be subtraction. Theorem 3 was illustrated with two events—it is equally applicable for more than two [$P(A$ or B or $\dots$ or $F) = P(A) + P(B) + \dots + P(F)$].

TABLE 4-1   Inspection Results by Supplier

SUPPLIER	NUMBER ACCEPTABLE	NUMBER NONCONFORMING	TOTAL
X	50	3	53
Y	125	6	131
Z	75	2	77
Total	250	11	261

EXAMPLE PROBLEM

If the 261 parts described in Table 4-1 are contained in a box, what is the probability of selecting a random part produced by supplier X or by supplier Z?

$$P(X \text{ or } Z) = P(X) + P(Z)$$

$$= \frac{53}{261} + \frac{77}{261} \qquad 0.203$$

$$= 0.498$$

What is the probability of selecting a nonconforming part from supplier X or an acceptable part from supplier Z?

$$P(\text{nc. } X \text{ or ac. } Z) = P(\text{nc. } X) + P(\text{ac. } Z)$$

$$= \frac{3}{261} + \frac{75}{261}$$

$$= 0.299$$

Add Probabilities

If the 261 parts described in Table 4-1 are contained in a box, what is the probability that a randomly selected part will be from supplier Z, a nonconforming unit from supplier X, or an acceptable from supplier Y?

$$P(Z \text{ or nc. } X \text{ or ac. } Y) = P(Z) + P(\text{nc. } X) + P(\text{ac. } Y)$$

$$= \frac{77}{261} + \frac{3}{261} + \frac{125}{261}$$

$$= 0.785$$

Theorem 3 is frequently referred to as the *additive law of probability*.

Theorem 4. If event A and event B are not mutually exclusive events, then the probability of either event A or event B or both is given by

$$P(A \text{ or } B \text{ or both}) = P(A) + P(B) - P(\text{both})$$

Events that are not mutually exclusive have some outcomes in common.

If the 261 parts described in Table 4-1 are contained in a box, what is the probability that a randomly selected part will be from supplier X or a nonconforming unit?

$$P(X \text{ or nc. or both}) = P(X) + P(\text{nc.}) - P(X \text{ and nc.})$$

$$= \frac{53}{261} + \frac{11}{261} - \frac{3}{261}$$

$$= 0.234$$

In the example problem, there are three outcomes common to both events. The 3 nonconforming units of supplier X are counted twice as outcomes of $P(X)$ and of $P(\text{nc.})$; therefore, one set of three is subtracted out. This theorem is also applicable to more than two events. A Venn diagram is sometimes used to describe the not mutually exclusive concept as shown in Figure 4-3. The circle on the left contains 53 units from supplier X and the circle on the right contains 11 nonconforming units. The 3 nonconforming units from supplier X are found where the two circles intersect.

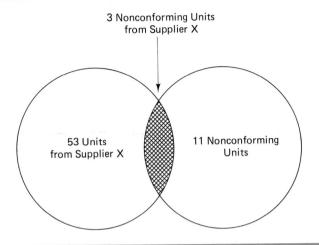

3 Nonconforming Units
from Supplier X

53 Units
from Supplier X

11 Nonconforming
Units

FIGURE 4-3   **Venn diagram for theorem 4 example problem.**

Theorem 5. The sum of the probabilities of the events of a situation is equal to 1.000.

$$P(A) + P(B) + \cdots + P(N) = 1.000$$

This theorem was illustrated in Figure 4-1 for the coin-tossing, die-rolling, and card-drawing situations wherein the sum of the events equaled 1.000.

EXAMPLE PROBLEM

A health inspector examines three products in a subgroup to determine if they are acceptable. From past experience it is known that the probability of finding no nonconforming units in the sample of 3 is 0.990, the probability of 1 non-conforming unit in the sample of 3 is 0.006, and the probability of finding 2 nonconforming units in the sample of 3 is 0.003. What is the probability of finding 3 nonconforming units in the sample of 3?

There are four, and only four, events to this situation: 0 nonconforming units, 1 nonconforming unit, 2 nonconforming units, and 3 nonconforming units.

$$P(0) + P(1) + P(2) + P(3) = 1.000$$

$$0.990 + 0.006 + 0.003 + P(3) = 1.000$$

$$P(3) = 0.001$$

Thus, the probability of 3 nonconforming units in the sample of 3 is 0.001.

Theorem 6. If A and B are independent events, then the probability of both A and B occurring is the product of their respective probabilities.

$$P(A \text{ and } B) = P(A) \times P(B)$$

An independent event is one where its occurrence has no influence on the probability of the other event or events. This theorem is referred to as the *multiplicative law of probabilities*. Whenever an "and" is verbalized, the mathematical operation is multiplication.

EXAMPLE PROBLEM

If the 261 parts described in Table 4-1 are contained in a box, what is the probability that two randomly selected parts will be from supplier X and supplier Y? Assume that the first part is returned to the box before the second part is selected (called with replacement).

$$P(X \text{ and } Y) = P(X) \times P(Y)$$

$$= \left(\frac{53}{261}\right)\left(\frac{131}{261}\right)$$

$$= 0.102$$

At first thought, the result of the example problem seems too low, but there are five other possibilities: XX, YY, ZZ, XZ, and YZ. This theorem is applicable to more than two events.

Theorem 7. If A and B are *dependent* events, the probability of both A and B occurring is the product of the probability of A and the probability that if A occurred, then B will occur also.

$$P(A \text{ and } B) = P(A) \times P(B|A)$$

The symbol $P(B|A)$ is defined as the probability of event B provided that event A has occurred. A dependent event is one whose occurrence influences the probability of the other event or events. This theorem is sometimes referred to as the *conditional theorem,* since the probability of the second event depends on the result of the first event. It is applicable to more than two events.

EXAMPLE PROBLEM

Assume that in the preceding example problem the first part was not returned to the box before the second part is selected. What is the probability?

$$P(X \text{ and } Y) = P(X) \times P(Y \mid X)$$

$$= \left(\frac{53}{261}\right)\left(\frac{131}{260}\right)$$

$$= 0.102$$

Since the first part was not returned to the box, there was a total of only 260 parts in the box.

What is the probability of both parts from supplier Z?

$$P(Z \text{ and } Z) = P(Z) \times P(Z \mid Z)$$

$$= \left(\frac{77}{261}\right)\left(\frac{76}{260}\right)$$

$$= 0.086$$

Since the first part was from supplier Z, there are only 76 from supplier Z of the new total of 260 in the box.

To solve many probability problems it is necessary to use several theorems as shown by the example below, which uses theorems 3 and 6.

EXAMPLE PROBLEM

If the 261 parts described in Table 4-1 are contained in a box, what is the probability that two randomly selected parts (with replacement) will have one acceptable from supplier X and one acceptable from supplier Y or supplier Z?

$$P[\text{ac. } X \text{ and } (\text{ac. } Y \text{ or ac. } Z)] = P(\text{ac. } X)[P(\text{ac. } Y) + P(\text{ac. } Z)]$$

$$= \left(\frac{50}{261}\right)\left(\frac{125}{261} + \frac{75}{261}\right)$$

$$= 0.147$$

Counting of Events

Many probability problems, such as those where the events are uniform probability distributions, can be solved using counting techniques. There are three counting techniques which are quite often used in the computation of probabilities.

1. *Simple multiplication.* If an event A can happen in any of *a* ways or outcomes, and after it has occurred another, event B can happen in *b* ways or outcomes, the number of ways that both events can happen is *ab*.

A witness to a hit-and-run accident remembered the first three digits of the license plate out of five and noted the fact that the last two were numerals. How many owners of automobiles would the police have to investigate?

$$ab = (10)(10)$$

$$= 100$$

If the last two were letters, how many would need to be investigated?

$$ab = (26)(26)$$

$$= 676$$

2. *Permutations.* A *permutation* is an ordered arrangement of a set of objects. The permutations of the word *cup* are cup, cpu, upc, ucp, puc, and pcu. In this case there are 3 objects in the set and we arranged them in groups of 3 to obtain six permutations. This is referred to as a permutation of *n* objects taking *r* at a time where $n = 3$ and $r = 3$. How many permutations would there be for 4 objects taken 2 at a time? Using the word *fork* to represent the four objects, the permutations are fo, of, fr, rf, fk, kf, or, ro, ok, ko, rk, and kr. As the number of objects, *n*, and the number that are taken at one time, *r* become larger, it becomes a tedious task to list all the permutations. The formula to find the number of permutations more easily is

$$P_r^n = \frac{n!}{(n - r)!}$$

where P_r^n = number of permutations of *n* objects taken *r* of them at a time (the symbol is sometimes written as $_nP_r$)

n = total number of objects

r = number of objects selected out of the total number

The expression *n*! is read "*n* factorial" and means $n(n - 1)(n - 2) \cdots (1)$. Thus, $6! = 6 \cdot 5 \cdot 4 \cdot 3 \cdot 2 \cdot 1 = 720$. By definition, $0! = 1$.

How many permutations are there of 5 objects taken 3 at a time?

$$P_r^n = \frac{n!}{(n - r)!}$$

$$P_3^5 = \frac{5!}{(5 - 3)!} = \frac{5 \cdot 4 \cdot 3 \cdot 2 \cdot 1}{2 \cdot 1}$$

$$= 60$$

EXAMPLE PROBLEM

In the license plate example, suppose the witness further remembers that the numerals were not the same.

$$P_r^n = \frac{n!}{(n - r)!}$$

$$P_2^{10} = \frac{10!}{(10 - 2)!} = \frac{10 \cdot 9 \cdot 8 \cdot 7 \cdots 1}{8 \cdot 7 \cdots 1}$$

$$= 90$$

This problem could also have been solved by simple multiplication where $a = 10$ and $b = 9$. In other words, there are 10 ways for the first digit but only 9 ways for the second since duplicates are not permitted.

The symbol P is used for both permutation and probability. No confusion should result from this dual usage, since for permutations the superscript n and subscript r are used.

3. *Combinations.* If the way the objects are ordered is unimportant, then we have a *combination*. The word *cup* has *six* permutations when the 3 objects are taken 3 at a time. However, there is only *one* combination, since the same three letters are in a different order. The word *fork* has 12 permutations when the 4 letters are taken 2 at a time; but the number of combinations is fo, fr, fk, or, ok, and rk, which gives a total of six. The formula for the number of combinations is

$$C_r^n = \frac{n!}{r!(n - r)!}$$

where C_r^n = number of combinations of n objects taken r at a time (the symbol is

sometimes written $_nC_r$ or $\binom{n}{r}$)

n = total number of objects

r = number of objects selected out of the total number

EXAMPLE PROBLEM

An interior designer has five different colored chairs and will use three in a living room arrangement. How many different combinations are possible?

$$C_r^n = \frac{n!}{r!(n - r)!}$$

$$C_3^5 = \frac{5!}{3!(5 - 3)!} = \frac{5 \cdot 4 \cdot 3 \cdot 2 \cdot 1}{3 \cdot 2 \cdot 1 \cdot 2 \cdot 1}$$

$$= 10$$

There is a symmetry associated with combinations such that $C_3^5 = C_2^5$, $C_1^4 = C_3^4$, $C_2^{10} = C_8^{10}$, and so on. Proof of this symmetry is left as an exercise.

The probability definition, the seven theorems, and the three counting techniques are all used to solve probability problems. Many hand calculators have permutation and combination functional keys which eliminate calculation errors provided that the correct keys are punched.

DISCRETE PROBABILITY DISTRIBUTIONS

When specific values such as the integers 0, 1, 2, 3 are used, then the probability distribution is discrete. Typical discrete probability distributions are hypergeometric, binomial, and Poisson.

Hypergeometric Probability Distribution

The *hypergeometric* probability distribution occurs when the population is finite and the random sample is taken without replacement. The formula for the hypergeometric is constructed of three combinations (total combinations, nonconforming combinations, and acceptable combinations) and is given by

$$P(d) = \frac{C_d^D C_{n-d}^{N-D}}{C_n^N}$$

where $P(d)$ = probability of d nonconforming units in a sample of size n
C_n^N = combinations of all units
C_d^D = combinations of nonconforming units
C_{n-d}^{N-D} = combinations of acceptable units
N = number of units in the lot (population)
n = number of units in the sample
$N - D$ = number of acceptable units in the lot
$n - d$ = number of acceptable units in the sample
D = number of nonconforming units in the lot
d = number of nonconforming units in the sample

The formula is obtained from the application of the probability definition, simple multiplication, and combinations. In other words, the numerator is the ways or outcomes of obtaining nonconforming units times the ways or outcomes of obtaining acceptable units and the denominator is the total possible ways or outcomes. Note that symbols in the combination formula have been changed to make them more appropriate for quality control.

An example will make the application of this distribution more meaningful.

EXAMPLE PROBLEM

A lot of 9 thermostats located in a container has 3 nonconforming units. What is the probability of drawing one nonconforming unit in a random sample of 4? For instructional purposes a graphical illustration of the problem is shown below.

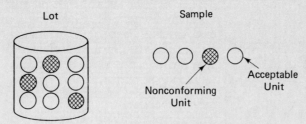

Lot　　　　　　　Sample

Nonconforming Unit

Acceptable Unit

From the picture or from the statement of the problem, $N = 9$, $D = 3$, $n = 4$, and $d = 1$.

$$P(d) = \frac{C_d^D C_{n-d}^{N-D}}{C_n^N}$$

$$P(1) = \frac{C_1^3 C_{4-1}^{9-3}}{C_4^9}$$

$$= \frac{\dfrac{3!}{1!(3-1)!} \cdot \dfrac{6!}{3!(6-3)!}}{\dfrac{9!}{4!(9-4)!}}$$

$$= 0.476$$

Similarly, $P(0) = 0.119$, $P(2) = 0.357$, and $P(3) = 0.048$. Since there are only 3 nonconforming units in the lot, $P(4)$ is impossible. The sum of the probabilities must equal 1.000, and this is verified as follows:

$$P(T) = P(0) + P(1) + P(2) + P(3)$$

$$= 0.119 + 0.476 + 0.357 + 0.048$$

$$= 1.000$$

The complete probability distribution is given in Figure 4-4 on page 142. As the parameters of the hypergeometric distribution change, the shape of the distribution changes as illustrated by Figure 4-5 on page 142. Therefore, each hypergeometric distribution has a unique shape based on N, n, and D. Hypergeometric tables are available; however, since four variables (including d) are involved, they are quite large. With hand calculators and microcomputers, these tables are no longer necessary for the efficient calculation of the distribution.

Some solutions require an "or less" probability. In such cases the method is to add up the respective probabilities. Thus,

$$P(2 \text{ or less}) = P(2) + P(1) + P(0)$$

Similarly, some solutions require an "or more" probability and use the formulas

$$P(2 \text{ or more}) = P(T) - P(1 \text{ or less})$$

$$= P(2) + P(3) + \cdots$$

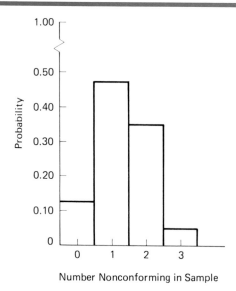

Number Nonconforming in Sample

FIGURE 4-4 Hypergeometric distribution for $N = 9$, $n = 4$, and $D = 3$.

In the latter series, the number of terms to calculate is determined by the sample size, the number nonconforming in the lot, or when the value is less than 0.001.

Binomial Probability Distribution

The *binomial* probability distribution is applicable to discrete probability problems that have an infinite number of items or that have a steady stream of items coming from a work center. The binomial is applied to problems that have attributes, such as

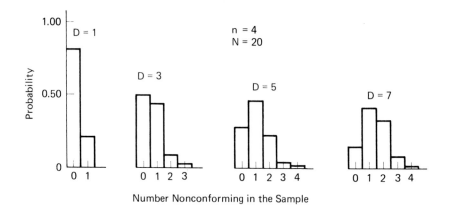

Number Nonconforming in the Sample

FIGURE 4-5 Comparison of hypergeometric distributions with different fraction defective in lot.

conforming or nonconforming, success or failure, pass or fail, and heads or tails. It corresponds to successive terms in the binomial expansion, which is

$$(p + q)^n = p^n + np^{n-1}q + \frac{n(n - 1)}{2}p^{n-2}q^2 + \cdots + q^n$$

where p = probability of an event such as a nonconforming unit (the probability of a single article being nonconforming is the same as the proportion nonconforming)

$q = 1 - p$ = probability of a nonevent such as a conforming unit (proportion conforming)

n = number of trials or the sample size

Applying the expansions to the distribution of tails ($p = \frac{1}{2}, q = \frac{1}{2}$) resulting from an infinite number of throws of 11 coins at once, the expansion is

$$(\tfrac{1}{2} + \tfrac{1}{2})^{11} = (\tfrac{1}{2})^{11} + 11(\tfrac{1}{2})^{10}(\tfrac{1}{2}) + 55(\tfrac{1}{2})^9(\tfrac{1}{2})^2 + \cdots + (\tfrac{1}{2})^{11}$$

$$= 0.001 + 0.005 + 0.027 + 0.080 + 0.161 + \cdots + 0.001$$

The probability distribution of the number of tails is shown in Figure 4-6. Since $p = q$, the distribution is symmetrical regardless of the value of n; however, when $p \neq q$, the distribution is asymmetrical. In quality control work p is the proportion or fraction nonconforming and is usually less than 0.15. Figure 4-7 on page 144 illustrates the change in the distribution as the sample size increases for the fraction nonconforming of $p = 0.10$, and Figure 4-8 illustrates the change for $p = 0.05$. As the sample size gets larger, the shape of the curve will become symmetrical even though $p \neq q$. Comparing the distribution for $p = 0.10$ and $n = 15$ in Figure 4-7 with the distribution of $p = 0.05$, $n = 15$ in Figure 4-8, it is noted that for the same value of n, the larger the value of the proportion nonconforming p, the greater the symmetry of the distribution.

The shape of the distribution is always a function of the sample size, n, and the proportion nonconforming, p. Change either of these values and a different distribution results.

In most cases in quality control work, we are not interested in the entire distri-

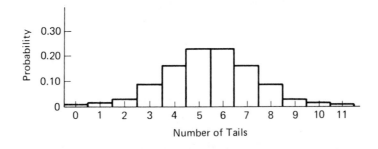

FIGURE 4-6 Distribution of the number of tails for an infinite number of tosses of 11 coins.

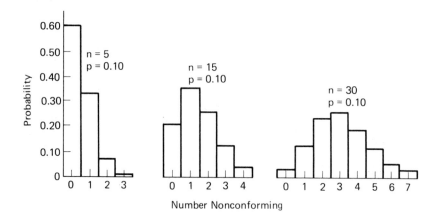

FIGURE 4-7   Binomial distribution for various sample sizes when $p = 0.10$.

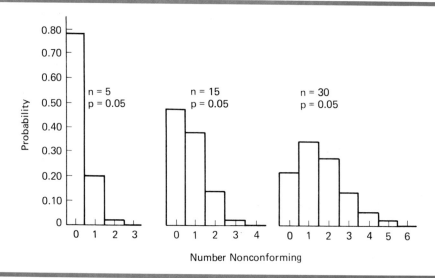

FIGURE 4-8   Binomial distributions for various sample sizes when $p = 0.05$.

bution, only in one or two terms of the binomial expansion. The binomial formula for a single term is

$$P(d) = \frac{n!}{d!(n - d)!} p_0^d q_0^{n-d}$$

where $P(d)$ = probability of d nonconforming units

n = number in the sample

d = number nonconforming in the sample

p_0 = proportion (fraction) nonconforming in the population[1]

[1] Also standard or reference value; see Chapter 5.

144   FUNDAMENTALS OF PROBABILITY

q_0 = proportion (fraction) conforming $(1 - p_0)$ in the population

Since the binomial is for the infinite situation, there is no lot size, N, in the formula.

EXAMPLE PROBLEM

A random sample of 5 hinges is selected from a steady stream of product from a punch press and the proportion nonconforming is 0.10. What is the probability of 1 nonconforming unit in the sample? What is the probability of 1 or less? What is the probability of 2 or more?

$$q_0 = 1 - p_0 = 1.00 - 0.10 = 0.90$$

$$P(d) = \frac{n!}{d!(n-d)!} p_0^d q_0^{n-d}$$

$$P(1) = \frac{5!}{1!(5-1)!} (0.10^1)(0.90^{5-1})$$

$$= 0.328$$

What is the probability of 1 or less nonconforming units? To solve, we need to use the addition theorem and add $P(1)$ and $P(0)$.

$$P(d) = \frac{n!}{d!(n-d)!} p_0^d q_0^{n-d}$$

$$P(0) = \frac{5!}{0!(5-0)!} (0.10^0)(0.90^{5-0})$$

$$= 0.590 \,49$$

Thus,

$$P(1 \text{ or less}) = P(0) + P(1)$$

$$= 0.590 + 0.328$$

$$= 0.918$$

What is the probability of 2 or more nonconforming units? Solution can be accomplished using the addition theorem and adding the probabilities of 2, 3, 4, and 5 nonconforming units.

$$P(2 \text{ or more}) = P(2) + P(3) + P(4) + P(5)$$

Or it can be accomplished by using the theorem that the sum of the probabilities is 1.

$$P(2 \text{ or more}) = P(T) - P(1 \text{ or less})$$

$$= 1.000 - 0.918$$

$$= 0.082$$

Calculations for two nonconforming units and three nonconforming units for the data in the example problem give $P(2) = 0.073$ and $P(3) = 0.008$. The complete distribution is shown as the graph on the left of Figure 4-7. Calculations for $P(4)$ and $P(5)$ give values less than 0.001 so they are not included in the graph.

Tables are available for the binomial distribution. However, since three variables (n, p, and d) are needed, they require a considerable amount of space. The hand calculator and microcomputer can make the required calculations quite efficiently; therefore, there is no longer any need for the tables.

The binomial is used for the infinite situation but will approximate the hypergeometric under certain conditions that are discussed later in the chapter. It requires that there be two and only two possible outcomes (a nonconforming or a conforming unit), and that the probability of each outcome does not change. In addition, the use of the binomial requires that the trials are independent; that is, if a nonconforming unit occurs, then the chance of the next one being nonconforming neither increases nor decreases.

In addition, the binomial distribution is the basis for one of the control chart groups discussed in Chapter 5.

Poisson Probability Distribution

A third discrete probability distribution is referred to as the Poisson, named after Simeon Poisson, who described it in 1837. The distribution is applicable to many situations that involve observations per unit of time. For example, the count of cars arriving at a highway toll booth in 1-min intervals, the count of machine breakdowns in 1 day, and the count of shoppers entering a grocery store in 5-min intervals. The distribution is also applicable to situations involving observations per unit of amount. For example, the count of weaving nonconformities in 1000 m^2 of cloth, the count of nonconformities per lot of product, and the count of rivet nonconformities in a mobile home.

In each of the preceding situations, there are many equal opportunities for the occurrence of an event. Each rivet in a recreational vehicle has an equal opportunity to be a nonconformity; however, there will only be a few nonconformities out of the hundreds of rivets. The Poisson is applicable when n is quite large and p_0 is small. The formula for the Poisson distribution is

$$P(c) = \frac{(np_0)^c}{c!} e^{-np_0}$$

where c = count, or number, of events of a given classification occurring in a sample, such as count of nonconformities, cars, customers, or machine breakdowns

np_0 = average count, or average number, of events of a given classification occuring in a sample

e = 2.718281

When the Poisson is used as an approximation to the binomial (to be discussed later in the chapter), the symbol c has the same meaning as d has in the binomial and hypergeometric formulas. Since c and np_0 have similar definitions, there is some confusion, which can be corrected by thinking of c as an individual value and np_0 as an average or population value.

Using the formula, a probability distribution can be determined. Suppose that the average count of cars which arrive at a highway toll booth in a 1-min interval is 2, then the calculations are

$$P(c) = \frac{(np_0)^c}{c!} e^{-np_0}$$

$$P(0) = \frac{(2)^0}{0!} e^{-2} = 0.135$$

$$P(1) = \frac{(2)^1}{1!} e^{-2} = 0.271$$

$$P(2) = \frac{(2)^2}{2!} e^{-2} = 0.271$$

$$P(3) = \frac{(2)^3}{3!} e^{-2} = 0.180$$

$$P(4) = \frac{(2)^4}{4!} e^{-2} = 0.090$$

$$P(5) = \frac{(2)^5}{5!} e^{-2} = 0.036$$

$$P(6) = \frac{(2)^6}{6!} e^{-2} = 0.012$$

$$P(7) = \frac{(2)^7}{7!} e^{-2} = 0.003$$

The resulting probability distribution is the one on the right in Figure 4-9. This distribution indicates the probability that a certain count of cars will arrive in any

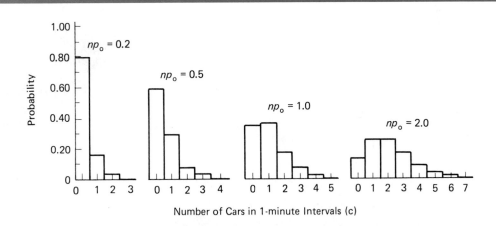

FIGURE 4-9 Poisson probability distributions for various np_0 values.

1-min time interval. Thus, the probability of zero cars in any 1-min interval is 0.135, the probability of one car in any 1-min interval is 0.271, . . . , and the probability of seven cars in any 1-min interval is 0.003.

Figure 4-9 also illustrates the property that as np_0 gets larger, the distribution approaches symmetry. Other properties of the Poisson distribution are that the mean equals np_0, and the standard deviation equals $\sqrt{np_0}$.

Probabilities for the Poisson distribution for np_0 values of from 0.1 to 5.0 in intervals of 0.1 and from 6.0 to 15.0 in intervals of 1.0 are given in Table C. Values in parentheses in the table are cumulative probabilities for obtaining "or less" answers. The use of this table simplifies the calculations as illustrated in the following problem.

EXAMPLE PROBLEM

The average count of billing errors at a local bank per 8-h shift is 1.0. What is the probability of two billing errors? The probability of one or less? The probability of two or more?

From Table C for an np_0 value of 1.0:

$$P(2) = 0.184$$

$$P(1 \text{ or less}) = 0.736$$

$$P(2 \text{ or more}) = 1.000 - P(1 \text{ or less})$$

$$= 1.000 - 0.736$$

$$= 0.264$$

The Poisson distribution can be used as an approximation to the binomial in some situations. Given below is an example problem that illustrates this concept.

EXAMPLE PROBLEM

If the probability that a heat-treating batch will be defective is 0.01, what is the probability of two bad batches out of 250? What is the probability of 2 or less?

$$np_0 = (250)(0.01) = 2.5$$

From Table C, the intersection of the column with an np_0 value of 2.5 and the row with a c value of 2 gives

$$P(2) = 0.256 \qquad P(2 \text{ or less}) = 0.543$$

The answers using the binomial are

$$P(2) = 0.257 \qquad P(2 \text{ or less}) = 0.543$$

The Poisson probability distribution is the basis for attribute control charts and for acceptance sampling, which are discussed in subsequent chapters. In addition to the quality control applications, the Poisson distribution is used in other industrial situations, such as accident frequencies, computer simulation, operations research, and work sampling.

From a theoretical viewpoint a discrete probability distribution should use a bar graph. However, it is a common practice (and the one followed for the figures in this book) to use the histogram.

Other discrete probability distributions are the uniform, geometric, and negative binomial. The uniform distribution was illustrated in Figure 4-1. From an application viewpoint it is the one used to generate a random number table. The geometric and negative binomial are used in reliability studies for discrete data.

CONTINUOUS PROBABILITY DISTRIBUTIONS

When measurable data such as meters, kilograms, and ohms are used, the probability distribution is continuous. While there are many continuous probability distributions, only the normal is of sufficient importance in quality control to warrant a detailed discussion in an introductory text.

Normal Probability Distribution

The *normal curve* is a continuous probability distribution. Solutions to probability problems that involve continuous data can be solved using the normal probability distribution. In Chapter 2, techniques were learned to determine the percentage of the data that were above a certain value, below a certain value, or between two values. These same techniques are applicable to probability problems, as illustrated in the following example problem.

EXAMPLE PROBLEM

If the operating life of an electric mixer, which is normally distributed, has a mean of 2200 h and standard deviation of 120 h, what is the probability that a single electric mixer will fail to operate at 1900 h or less?

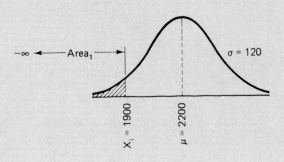

$$Z = \frac{X_i - \mu}{\sigma}$$

$$= \frac{1900 - 2200}{120}$$

$$= -2.5$$

From Table A of the appendix, for a Z value of -2.5, $area_1 = 0.0062$. Therefore, the probability of an electric mixer failing is

$$P\text{(failure at 1900 h or less)} = 0.0062$$

The answer in the problem could have been stated as "The percent of items less than 1900 h is 0.62%." Therefore, the areas under the normal curve can be treated as either a probability value or a relative frequency value.

Under certain conditions the normal probability distribution will approximate the binomial probability distribution. These conditions will be discussed later in the chapter. For the present, we are concerned with the problem-solving technique which is illustrated in the next example problem.

EXAMPLE PROBLEM

Find the probability of getting 2, 3, or 4 tails in 12 tosses of a coin by the normal approximation to the binomial. The problem is shown graphically below. The required probability area is crosshatched and can be approximated by the normal curve, which is shown as a dashed line. Since the data must be continuous for the normal curve, the probability of obtaining 2 to 4 tails is considered to be from 1.5 to 4.5.

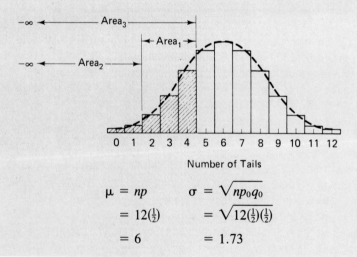

$$\mu = np \qquad \sigma = \sqrt{np_0 q_0}$$

$$= 12(\tfrac{1}{2}) \qquad = \sqrt{12(\tfrac{1}{2})(\tfrac{1}{2})}$$

$$= 6 \qquad = 1.73$$

$$Z_2 = \frac{X_i - \mu}{\sigma} \quad Z_3 = \frac{X_i - \mu}{\sigma}$$

$$= \frac{1.5 - 6}{1.73} \quad = \frac{4.5 - 6}{1.73}$$

$$= -2.60 \quad = -0.87$$

From Table A, for $Z_2 = -2.60$, area$_2$ = 0.0047, and for $Z_3 = -0.87$, area$_3$ = 0.1922.

$$\text{Area}_1 = \text{Area}_3 - \text{Area}_2$$

$$= 0.1922 - 0.0047$$

$$= 0.1875$$

Thus, the required probability is

$$P(2, 3, \text{ or } 4 \text{ tails}) = 0.1875$$

Other Continuous Probability Distributions

Of the many other continuous probability distributions only two are of significant importance to mention their practical applications. The exponential probability distribution is used in reliability studies when there is a constant failure rate and the Weibull is used when the time to failure is not constant. These two distributions are discussed in Chapter 8.

DISTRIBUTION INTERRELATIONSHIP

With so many distributions, it is sometimes difficult to know when they are applicable. Certainly, since the Poisson can be easily calculated using Table C, it should be used whenever appropriate. Figures 4-5, 4-8, and 4-9 show a similarity among the hypergeometric, binomial, and Poisson distributions.

The hypergeometric is used for finite lots of stated size N. It can be approximated by the binomial when $n/N \leqq 0.10$; or by the Poisson when $n/N \leqq 0.10$, $p_0 \leqq 0.10$, and $np_0 \leqq 5$; or by the normal when $n/N \leqq 0.10$ and the normal approximates the binomial.

The binomial is used for infinite situations or when there is a steady stream of product so that an infinite situation is assumed. It can be approximated by the Poisson when $p_0 \leqq 0.10$ and $np_0 \leqq 5$. The normal curve is an excellent approximation when p_0 is close to 0.5 and $n \geqq 10$. As np_0 deviates from 0.5, the approximation is still good as long as $np_0 \geqq 5$ and n increases to 50 or more for values of p_0 as low as 0.10 and as high as 0.90. Since the binomial calculation time is not too much different than the normal calculation time, there is little advantage to using the normal as an approximation.

```
10 REM                    Hypergeometric Distribution
20 REM
30 REM              NL = Lot Size(N)
40 REM              NS = Sample Size(n)
50 REM              DL = Number Nonconforming in Lot(D)
60 REM              DS = Number Nonconforming in Sample(d)
70 REM              P  = Probability
80 REM              C  = Combination
90 REM              CG = Combinations Conforming
100 REM             CD = Combinations Nonconforming
110 REM             CT = Combinations Total
120 REM
130 REM DIM P(100)
140 PRINT " Enter the Lot Size." : INPUT NL
150 LPRINT TAB(5);" N = ";NL
160 PRINT " Enter the Number Nonconforming in the Lot." INPUT DL
170 LPRINT TAB(5);" D = ";DL
180 PRINT " Enter the Sample Size." : INPUT NS
190 LPRINT TAB(5):" n = ";NS : LPRINT
200 LPRINT TAB(5);" Number Nonconforming";TAB(30);" Probability"
210 DS = 0
220 K = 0
230 K = K + 1
240 IF K = 1 GOTO 270
250 IF K = 2 GOTO 280
260 N = NL : R = NS : GOTO 300
270 N = NL - DL : R = NS - DS : GOTO 300
280 N = DL : R = DS
290 REM                    COMBINATION ROUTINE
300 IF R = 0 THEN C = 1
310 IF R = 1 THEN C = N
320 IF R < 2 GOTO 400
330 CS = 1
340       FOR I = N TO (N - R + 1) STEP -1
350       J = I - (R - N)
360       CS = SC * (I / J)
370       NEXT I
380 C = CS
390 REM                    HYPERGEOMETRIC CALCULATION
400 IF K = 1 THEN CG = C
410 IF K = 2 THEN CD = C
420 IF K < 3 GOTO 230
430 CT = C
440 P(DS) = CG * (CD / CT)
450 LPRINT TAB (12); DS; TAB (32) ; P(DS)
460 IF DS = NS GOTO 510
470 IF DS = DL GOTO 510
480 IF P(DS) < .005 GOTO 510
490 DS = DS + 1
500 GOTO 220
510 SP = 0
520       FOR I = 0 TO DS
530       SP = SP + P(I)
540       NEXT I
550 LPRINT
560 LPRINT TAB(5);" Sum of Probabilities = ";SP
570 END


        N = 20
        D = 5
        n = 4


    Number Nonconformimg                Probability
            0                            .281734
            1                            .469556
            2                            .216718
            3                            .0309598
            4                           1.03199E-03
```

FIGURE 4-10   Computer program in BASIC to calculate the hypergeometric distribution.

The information given above can be considered to provide approximation guidelines rather than absolute laws. Approximations are better the farther the data are from the limiting values. For the most part the efficiency of the calculator and microcomputer have made the use of approximations obsolete.

COMPUTER PROGRAM

The computer program given in Figure 4-10 calculates the hypergeometric probability distribution for a lot of size, N, number nonconforming in the lot, D, and sample size, n. Since three combinations must be calculated, a combination routine is established in the program. Provision is made for 0! and the special cases where $r = 0$ and $r = 1$. Also, the combination numerator and denominator operate together to eliminate the possibility of any overflow problems. The probability is limited by D, n, and the lowest probability, 0.001. The answer is the same as shown in Figure 4-4.

PROBLEMS

1. If an event is certain to occur, what is its probability? If an event will not occur, what is its probability?

2. What is the probability that you will live forever? What is the probability that an octopus will fly?

3. If the probability of obtaining a 3 on a 6-sided die is 0.167, what is the probability of obtaining any number but a 3?

4. Determine an event that has a probability of 1.000.

5. The probability of drawing a pink chip from a bowl of different-colored chips is 0.35, the probability of a blue chip is 0.46, the probability of a green chip is 0.15, and the probability of a purple chip is 0.04. What is the probability of a blue or a purple chip? What is the probability of a pink or a blue chip?

6. At any hour in a hospital intensive care unit the probability of an emergency is 0.247. What is the probability that there will be tranquility for the staff?

7. If a hotel has 20 king-size beds, 50 queen-size beds, 100 double beds, and 30 twin beds available, what is the probability that you will be given a queen-size or a twin bed when you register?

8. A ball is drawn at random from a container that holds 8 yellow balls numbered 1 to 8, 6 orange balls numbered 1 to 6, and 10 gray balls numbered 1 to 10. What is the probability of obtaining an orange ball or a ball numbered 5 or an orange ball numbered 5 in a draw of one ball? What is the probability of a gray ball or a ball numbered 8 or a gray ball numbered 8 in a draw of one ball?

9. If the probability of obtaining 1 nonconforming unit in a sample of 2 from a large lot of neoprene gaskets is 0.18 and the probability of 2 nonconforming units 0.25, what is the probability of 0 nonconforming units?

10. Using the information of Problem 9, find the probability of obtaining 2 nonconforming units on the first sample of 2 and 1 nonconforming unit on the second sample of 2. What is the probability of 0 nonconforming units on the first sample and 2 nonconforming units on the second? The first gasket selected is returned to the lot before the second one is selected.

11. A basket contains 34 heads of lettuce, 5 of which are spoiled. If a sample of 2 is drawn and not replaced, what is the probability that both will be spoiled?

12. If a sample of 1 can be drawn from an automatic storage and retrieval rack with three different storage racks and 6 different trays in each rack, what is the number of different ways of obtaining the sample of one?

13. A small model-airplane motor has four starting components: key, battery, wire, and glow plug. What is the probability that the system will work if the probability that each component will work is as follows: key (0.998), battery (0.997), wire (0.999), and plug (0.995)?

14. An inspector has to inspect products from three machines in one department, five machines in another, and two machines in a third. The quality manager wants to vary the inspector's route. How many different ways are possible?

15. If in the example problem with the hit-and-run driver, there were one numeral and one letter, how many automobiles would need to be investigated?

16. A sample of 3 is selected from 10 people on a Caribbean cruise. How many permutations are possible?

17. From a lot of 90 airline tickets a sample of 8 is selected. How many permutations are possible?

18. A sample of 4 is selected from a lot of 20 piston rings. How many different sample combinations are possible?

19. From a lot of 100 hotel rooms, a sample of 3 is selected for audit. How many different sample combinations are possible?

20. A sample of 2 is selected from a tray of 20 bolts. How many different sample combinations are possible?

21. In the Illinois lottery, the numbers available are 1 to 54. On Saturday night 6 numbers are selected. How many different combinations are possible?

22. In the Illinois lottery each participant selects two sets of 6 numbers. What is the probability of having all 6 numbers?

23. The game of KENO has 80 numbers and you select 15. What is the probability of having all 15 numbers and winning the jackpot?

24. An automatic garage-door opener has 12 switches that can be set on or off. Both the transmitter and receiver are set the same and the owner has the option of setting 1 to 12 switches. What is the probability that another person with the same model transmitter could open the door?

25. Compare the answers of C_3^5 with C_2^5, C_1^4 with C_3^4, and C_2^{10} with C_8^{10}. What conclusion can you draw? Cabinations

26. Calculate C_0^6, C_0^{10}, and C_0^{25}. What conclusion can you draw?

27. Calculate C_3^3, C_9^9, and C_{35}^{35}. What conclusion can you draw?

28. Calculate C_1^7, C_1^{12}, and C_1^{18}. What conclusion can you draw?

29. A random sample of 4 insurance claims is selected from a lot of 12 that has 3 nonconforming units. Using the hypergeometric distribution, what is the probability that the sample will contain exactly 0 nonconforming units? 1 nonconforming unit? 2 nonconforming units? 3 nonconforming units? 4 nonconforming units?

30. A finite lot of 20 digital watches is 20% nonconforming. Using the hypergeometric distribution, what is the probability that a sample of 3 will contain 2 nonconforming watches?

31. In Problem 30 what is the probability of obtaining 2 or more nonconforming units? What is the probability of 2 or less nonconforming units?

32. A steady stream of income tax returns has a proportion nonconforming of 0.03. What is the probability of obtaining 2 nonconforming units from a sample of 20? Use the binomial distribution.

33. Find the probability, using the binomial distribution, of obtaining 2 or more nonconforming units when sampling 5 typewriters from a batch known to be 6% nonconforming.

34. Using the binomial distribution, find the probability of obtaining 2 or less nonconforming restaurants in a sample of 9 when the lot is 15% nonconforming.

35. What is the probability of guessing correctly exactly 4 answers on a true-false examination that has 9 questions? Use the binomial distribution.

36. An injection molder produces golf tees that are 15.0% nonconforming. Using the normal distribution as an approximation to the binomial, find the probability that, in a random sample of 300 golf tees, 34 or less are nonconforming.

37. A random sample of 10 automotive bumpers is taken from a stream of product that is 5% nonconforming. Using the Poisson as an approximation to the binomial distribution, determine the probability of 2 nonconforming automotive bumpers. Compare the result with the binomial distribution.

38. If the probability is 0.08 that a single article is nonconforming, what is the probability that a sample of 20 will contain 2 or less nonconforming units? Use the Poisson as an approximation to the binomial distribution.

39. Using the data from Problem 38, determine the probability of 2 or more nonconforming units.

40. A sample of 10 washing machines is selected from a finite lot of 100. If $p_0 = 0.08$, what is the probability of 1 nonconforming washing machine in the sample? Is the Poisson a good approximation?

41. A lot of 15 has 3 nonconforming units. What is the probability that a sample of 3 will have 1 nonconforming unit? Would the Poisson be a good approximation?

42. A sample of 3 medicine bottles is taken from a tray of 30 bottles. If the tray is 10% nonconforming, what is the probability of 1 nonconforming medicine bottle in the sample? Is the binomial a good approximation?

43. A steady stream of light bulbs has a fraction nonconforming of 0.09. If 67 are sam-

pled, what is the probability of 3 nonconforming units? Is the Poisson a good approximation?

44. Test and, if necessary, rewrite the computer program for your computer.

45. Modify the computer program to output the information for your graphical output device.

46. Write a computer program for:
    (a) The binomial probability distribution
    (b) The Poisson probability distribution

5

CONTROL CHARTS
FOR ATTRIBUTES

Attribute

An attribute was defined in Chapter 2 and is repeated to refresh the reader's memory. The term *attribute,* as used in quality control, refers to those quality characteristics that conform to specifications or do not conform to specifications.

There are two types of attributes:

1. Where measurements are not possible—for example, visually inspected items such as color, missing parts, scratches, and damage.

2. Where measurements can be made but are not made because of time, cost, or need. In other words, while the diameter of a hole can be measured with an inside micrometer, it may be more convenient to use a "go–no go" gage and determine if it conforms or does not conform to specifications.

157

Where an attribute does not conform to specifications, various descriptive terms are used. A *nonconformity* is a departure of a quality characteristic from its intended level or state that occurs with a severity sufficient to cause an associated product or service not to meet a specification requirement. The definition of a *defect* is similar, except it is concerned with satisfying intended normal, or reasonably foreseeable, usage requirements. Defect is appropriate for use when evaluation is in terms of usage, and nonconformity is appropriate for conformance to specifications.

The term *nonconforming unit* is used to describe a unit of product or service containing at least one nonconformity. *Defective* is analogous to defect and is appropriate for use when a unit of product or service is evaluated in terms of usage rather than conformance to specifications.

In this book we are using the terms conformity and nonconforming unit. This practice avoids the confusion and misunderstanding that occurs with defect and defective in product-liability lawsuits.

Limitations of Variable Charts

Variable control charts are excellent means for controlling quality and subsequently improving it; however, they do have limitations. One obvious limitation is that these charts cannot be used for quality characteristics which are attributes. The converse is not true, since a variable can be changed to an attribute by stating that it conforms or does not conform to specifications. In other words, defects such as missing parts, incorrect color, and so on, are not measureable and a variable control chart is not applicable.

Another limitation concerns the fact that there are many variables in a manufacturing entity. Even a small manufacturing plant could have as many as 10,000 variable quality characteristics. Since an $\bar{X}$ and R chart is needed for each characteristic, 10,000 charts would be required. Clearly, this would be too expensive and impractical. A control chart for attributes can minimize this limitation by providing overall quality information at a fraction of the cost.

Types of Attribute Charts

There are two different groups of control charts for attributes. One group of charts is for nonconforming units. It is based on the binomial distribution. A proportion, p, chart shows the proportion nonconforming in a sample or subgroup. The proportion is expressed as a fraction or a percent. Similarly we could have charts for proportion conforming and they too could be expressed as a fraction or a percent. Another chart in the group is for the number nonconforming, an np chart, and it too could also be expressed as number conforming.

Another group of charts is for nonconformities. It is based on the Poisson distribution. A c chart shows the count of nonconformities in an inspected unit such as an automobile, bolt of cloth, or roll of paper. Another closely related chart is the u chart, which is for the count of nonconformities per unit.

Much of the information on control charts for attributes is similar to that given in Chapter 3. The reader is referred to the sections on "State of Control" and "Analysis of Out-of-Control Condition."

CONTROL CHARTS FOR NONCONFORMING UNITS

Introduction

The p chart is used for data that consist of the proportion of the number of occurrences of an event to the total number of occurrences. It is used in quality control to report the fraction nonconforming in a product, quality characteristic, or group of quality characteristics. As such, the *fraction* nonconforming is the proportion of the number nonconforming in a sample or subgroup to the total number in the sample or subgroup. In symbolic terms the formula is

$$p = \frac{np}{n}$$

where p = proportion or fraction nonconforming in the sample or subgroup
    n = number in the sample or subgroup
    np = number nonconforming in the sample or subgroup

EXAMPLE PROBLEM

During the first shift, 450 inspections are made of book-of-the-month shipments and 5 nonconforming units are found. Production during the shift was 15,000 units. What is the fraction nonconforming?

$$p = \frac{np}{n} = \frac{5}{450} = 0.011$$

The fraction nonconforming, p, is usually quite small, say 0.15 or less. Except in unusual circumstances values greater than 0.15 would indicate that the company is in serious difficulty and that measures more drastic than a control chart are required. Since the fraction nonconforming is very small, the subgroup sizes must be quite large to produce a meaningful chart.

The p chart is an extremely versatile control chart. It can be used to control one quality characteristic, as is done with the $\bar{X}$ and R chart; to control a group of quality characteristics of the same type or of the same part; or to control the entire product. The p chart can be established to measure the quality produced by a work center, by a department, by a shift, or by an entire plant. It is frequently used to report the performance of an operator, group of operators, or management as a means of evaluating their quality performance.

The subgroup size of the p chart can be either variable or constant. A constant subgroup size is preferred; however, there may 100 percent automated inspection, where the subgroup size changes.

Objectives

The objectives of nonconforming charts are to:

1. Determine the average quality level. Knowledge of the quality average is essential as a benchmark. This information provides the process capability in terms of attributes.

2. Bring to the attention of management any changes in the average. Once the average quality (proportion nonconforming) is known, changes, either increasing or decreasing, become significant.

3. Improve the product quality. In this regard a p chart can motivate operating and management personnel to initiate ideas for quality improvement. The chart will tell whether the idea is an appropriate or inappropriate one. A continual and relentless effort must be made to improve the quality.

4. Evaluate the quality performance of operating and management personnel. Supervisors of manufacturing activities and especially the chief executive officer (CEO) should be evaluated by a chart for nonconforming units. Other functional areas, such as engineering, sales, finance, and so on, may find a chart for nonconformities more applicable for evaluation purposes.

5. Suggest places to use $\bar{X}$ and R charts. Even though the cost of computing and charting $\bar{X}$ and R charts is more than the chart for nonconforming units, the $\bar{X}$ and R charts are much more sensitive to variations and are more helpful in diagnosing causes. In other words, the chart for nonconforming units suggests the source of difficulty and the $\bar{X}$ and R chart finds the cause.

6. Determine acceptance criteria of a product before shipment to the customer. Knowledge of the proportion nonconforming provides management with information on whether or not to release an order.

These objectives indicate the scope and value of a nonconforming chart.

p-Chart Construction for Constant Subgroup Size

The general procedures that apply to variable control charts also apply to the p chart.

1. *Select the quality characteristic(s).* The first step in the procedure is to determine the use of the control chart. A p chart can be established to control the proportion nonconforming of (a) a single quality characteristic, (b) a group of quality characteristics, (c) a part, (d) an entire product, or (e) a number of products. This establishes a hierarchy of utilization so that any inspections applicable for a single quality characteristic also provide data for other p charts, which represent larger groups of characteristics, parts, or products.

A p chart can also be established for performance control of an (a) operator, (b) work center, (c) department, (d) shift, (e) plant, or (f) corporation. Using the chart in this manner, comparisons may be made between like units. It is also possible to evaluate the quality performance of a unit. A hierarchy of utilization exists so that data collected for one chart can also be used on a more all-inclusive chart.

The use for the chart or charts will be based on securing the greatest benefit for a minimum of cost. One chart should measure the CEO's quality performance.

2. *Determine the subgroup size and method.* The size of the subgroup is a function of the proportion nonconforming. If a part has a proportion nonconforming, p, of 0.001 and a subgroup size, n, of 1000, then the average number nonconforming, np, would be one per subgroup. This would *not* make a good chart, since a large number of values, posted to the chart, would be zero. If a part has a proportion nonconforming of 0.15 and a subgroup size of 50, the average number nonconforming would be 7.5, which would make a good chart.

Therefore, the selection of the subgroup size requires some preliminary observations to obtain a rough idea of the proportion nonconforming and some judgment as to the average number of nonconforming units that will make an adequate graphical chart. A minimum size of 50 is suggested as a starting point. Inspection can either be by audit or on-line. Audits are usually done in a laboratory under optimal conditions. On-line provides immediate feedback for corrective action; however, a policeperson mentality is created.

3. *Collect the data.* The quality technician will need to collect sufficient data for at least 25 subgroups, or the data may be obtained from historical records. Table 5-1 on page 162 gives the inspection results for the blower motor in an electric hair dryer for the motor department. For each subgroup the proportion nonconforming is calculated by the formula $p = np/n$. The quality technician reported that subgroup 19 had an abnormally large number of nonconforming units, owing to faulty contacts.

4. *Calculate the trial central line and control limits.* The formula for the trial control limits is given by

$$UCL = \bar{p} + 3\sqrt{\frac{\bar{p}(1 - \bar{p})}{n}}$$

$$LCL = \bar{p} - 3\sqrt{\frac{\bar{p}(1 - \bar{p})}{n}}$$

where $\bar{p}$ = average proportion nonconforming for many subgroups
$\qquad n$ = number inspected in a subgroup

The average proportion nonconforming, $\bar{p}$, is the central line and is obtained by the formula $\bar{p} = \Sigma\, np/\Sigma\, n$. Calculations for the 3σ trial control limits using the data on the electric hair dryer are as follows:

$$\bar{p} = \frac{\Sigma\, np}{\Sigma\, n} = \frac{138}{7500} = 0.018$$

$$\text{UCL} = \bar{p} + 3\,\sqrt{\frac{\bar{p}(1 - \bar{p})}{n}} \qquad\qquad \text{LCL} = \bar{p} - 3\,\sqrt{\frac{\bar{p}(1 - \bar{p})}{n}}$$

$$= 0.018 + 3\,\sqrt{\frac{0.018(1 - 0.018)}{300}} \qquad\qquad = 0.018 - 3\,\sqrt{\frac{0.018(1 - 0.018)}{300}}$$

$$= 0.041 \qquad\qquad\qquad\qquad\qquad\qquad = -0.005 \text{ or } 0.0$$

Calculations for the lower control limit resulted in a *negative* value, which is a theoretical result. In practice, a negative proportion nonconforming would be impossible. Therefore, the lower control limit value of -0.005 is changed to zero.

When the lower control limit is positive, it may in some cases be changed to zero. If the p chart is to be viewed by operating personnel, it would be difficult to explain why a proportion nonconforming that is below the lower control limit is out of control. In other words, performance of exceptionally good quality would be

TABLE 5-1 Inspection Results of Hair Dryer Blower Motor, Motor Department, May

SUBGROUP NUMBER	NUMBER INSPECTED n	NUMBER NONCONFORMING np	PROPORTION NONCONFORMING p
1	300	12	0.040
2	300	3	0.010
3	300	9	0.030
4	300	4	0.013
5	300	0	0.0
6	300	6	0.020
7	300	6	0.020
8	300	1	0.003
9	300	8	0.027
10	300	11	0.037
11	300	2	0.007
12	300	10	0.033
13	300	9	0.030
14	300	3	0.010
15	300	0	0.0
16	300	5	0.017
17	300	7	0.023
18	300	8	0.027
19	300	16	0.053
20	300	2	0.007
21	300	5	0.017
22	300	6	0.020
23	300	0	0.0
24	300	3	0.010
25	300	2	0.007
Total	7500	138	

classified as out of control. To avoid the need to explain this situation to operating personnel, the lower control limit is changed from a positive value to zero. When the *p* chart is to be used by quality control personnel and by management, a positive lower control limit is left unchanged. In this manner exceptionally good performance (below the lower control limit) will be treated as an out-of-control situation and investigated for an assignable cause. It is hoped that the assignable cause will indicate how the situation can be repeated.

The central line, $\bar{p}$, and the control limits are shown in Figure 5-1; the proportion nonconforming, *p*, from Table 5-1 is also posted to that chart. This chart is used to determine if the process is stable. It is important to recognize that the central line and control limits were determined from the data.

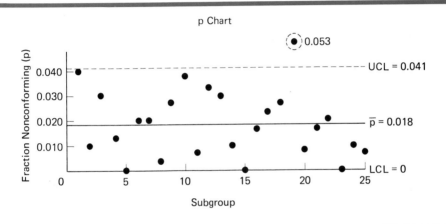

FIGURE 5-1 *p* Chart to illustrate the trial central line and control limits using the data from Table 5-1.

5. *Establish the revised central line and control limits.* In order to determine the revised 3σ control limits, the standard or reference value for the proportion nonconforming, p_0, needs to be determined. If an analysis of the chart of step 4 above shows good control (a stable process), then $\bar{p}$ can be considered to be representative of that process. Therefore, the best estimate of p_0 at this time, is $\bar{p}$, and $p_0 = \bar{p}$.

Most industrial processes, however, are not in control when first analyzed, and this fact is illustrated in Figure 5-1 by subgroup 19, which is above the upper control limit and, therefore, out of control. Since subgroup 19 has an assignable cause, it can be discarded from the data and a new $\bar{p}$ computed with all of the subgroups except 19. The calculations can be simplified by using the formula

$$\bar{p}_{new} = \frac{\Sigma np - np_d}{\Sigma n - n_d}$$

where np_d = number nonconforming in the discarded subgroups
n_d = number inspected in the discarded subgroups

In discarding data it must be remembered that only those subgroups with assignable causes are discarded. Those subgroups without assignable causes are left in the data. Also, out-of-control points below the lower control limit are not discarded, since they represent exceptionally good quality. If the out-of-control point on the low side is due to an inspection error, it should be discarded.

With an adopted standard or reference value for the proportion nonconforming, p_0, the revised control limits are given by

$$p_0 = \bar{p}_{new}$$

$$UCL = p_0 + 3\sqrt{\frac{p_0(1 - p_0)}{n}}$$

$$LCL = p_0 - 3\sqrt{\frac{p_0(1 - p_0)}{n}}$$

where p_0, the central line, represents the reference or standard value for the fraction nonconforming. These formulas are for the control limits for three standard deviations from the central line p_0.

Thus, for the preliminary data in Table 5-1, a new $\bar{p}$ is obtained by discarding subgroup 19.

$$\bar{p}_{new} = \frac{\Sigma\, np - np_d}{\Sigma\, n - n_d}$$

$$= \frac{138 - 16}{7500 - 300}$$

$$= 0.017$$

Since $\bar{p}_{new}$ is the best estimate of the standard or reference value, $p_0 = 0.017$. The revised control limits for the p chart are obtained as follows:

$$UCL = p_0 + 3\sqrt{\frac{p_0(1 - p_0)}{n}} \qquad LCL = p_0 - 3\sqrt{\frac{p_0(1 - p_0)}{n}}$$

$$= 0.017 + 3\sqrt{\frac{0.017(1 - 0.017)}{300}} \qquad = 0.017 - 3\sqrt{\frac{0.017(1 - 0.017)}{300}}$$

$$= 0.039 \qquad\qquad = -0.005 \text{ or } 0.0$$

The revised control limits and the central line, p_0, are shown in Figure 5-2. This chart, without the plotted points, is posted in an appropriate place.

6. *Achieve the objective.* The first five steps are planning. The last step involves action and leads to the achievement of the objective.

The revised control limits were based on data collected in May. Some representative values of inspection results for the month of June are shown in Figure 5-2. Analysis of the June results shows that the quality improved. This improvement is expected, since the posting of a quality control chart usually results in improved

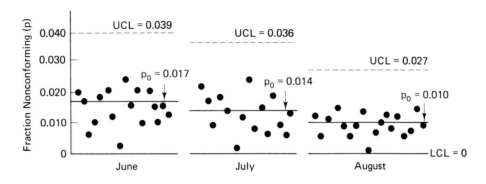

FIGURE 5-2   Continuing use of the *p* chart for representative values of the proportion nonconforming, *p*.

quality. Using the June data, a better estimate of the proportion nonconforming is obtained. The new value ($p_0 = 0.014$) is used to obtain the UCL of 0.036.

During the latter part of June and the entire month of July, various quality improvement ideas generated by a project team are tested. These ideas are new shellac, change in wire size, stronger spring, $\overline{X}$ and R charts on the armature, and so on. In testing ideas there are three criteria: a minimum of 25 subgroups are required, the 25 subgroups can be compressed in time as long as no sampling bias occurs, and only one idea can be tested at one time. Sample sizes can be reduced, which will speed up the testing process, because more subgroups will occur per day. The control chart will tell whether the idea improves the quality, reduces the quality, or has no effect on the quality. The control chart should be located in a conspicuous place so operating personnel can view it.

Data from July are used to determine the central line and control limits for August. The pattern of variation for August indicates that no further improvement resulted. However, a 41% improvement occurred from June (0.017) to August (0.010). At this point, we have obtained considerable improvement testing the ideas of the project team. While this improvement is very good, we must continue our relentless pursuit of quality improvement—1 out of every 100 is still nonconforming. Perhaps a detailed failure analysis or technical assistance from product engineering will lead to additional ideas that can be evaluated. A new project team may help.

Quality improvement is never terminated. Efforts may be redirected to other areas based on need and/or resources available.

Some Comments on *p* Charts

Like the $\overline{X}$ and R chart, the p chart is most effective if it is posted where operating and quality control personnel can view it. Also, like the $\overline{X}$ and R chart, the control limits are three standard deviations from the central value. Therefore, approximately 99% of the plotted points, p, will fall between the upper and lower control limits.

A state of control for a p chart is treated in a manner similar to that described in Chapter 3. The reader may wish to briefly review that section. A control chart for subgroup values of p will aid in disclosing the occasional presence of assignable causes of variation in the manufacturing process. The elimination of these assignable causes will lower p_0 and, therefore, have a positive effect on spoilage, production efficiency, and cost per unit. A p chart will also indicate long-range trends in the quality, which will help to evaluate changes in personnel, methods, equipment, tooling, materials, and inspection techniques.

If the population fraction nonconforming, ϕ, is known, it is not necessary to calculate the trial control limits. This is a considerable time saver, since $p_0 = \phi$, which allows the p chart to be introduced immediately. Also, p_0 may be assigned a desired value—in which case the trial control limits are not necessary.

Since the p chart is based on the binomial distribution, there must be a constant chance of selecting a nonconforming product. In some manufacturing operations, if one nonconforming unit occurs, all product that follows will be nonconforming until the condition is corrected. This type of condition also occurs in batch processes where the entire batch is nonconforming or when an error is made in dimensions, color, and so on. In such cases a constant chance of obtaining a nonconforming unit does not occur, and therefore the p chart is not suitable.

Presentation Techniques

The information in the preceding example is presented as a fraction nonconforming. It could also be presented in percent nonconforming, fraction conforming, or percent conforming. All four techniques convey the same information, as shown by Figure 5-3. The two lower figures show opposite information from the respective upper figures.

Table 5-2 shows the equations for calculating the central line and control limits for the three techniques as a function of p_0.

Many companies are taking the positive approach and using either of the two conforming presentation techniques. The use of the chart and the results will be the same no matter which chart is used.

p-Chart Construction for Variable Subgroup Size

Whenever possible, p charts should be developed and used with a constant subgroup size. This situation is not possible when the p chart is used for 100% inspection of output that varies from day to day. Also, data for p-chart use from sampling inspection might vary for a variety of reasons. Since the control limits are a function of the subgroup size, n, the control limits will vary with the subgroup size. Therefore, they need to be calculated for each subgroup.

While a variable subgroup size is undesirable, it does exist and must be handled. The procedures of data collection, trial central line and control limits, and revised central line and control limits are the same as that used for a p chart with constant subgroup size. An example without steps 1 and 2 will be used to illustrate the procedure.

Step 3. Collect the data. A computer modem manufacturer has collected data from the final test of the product for the end of March and all of April. Subgroup

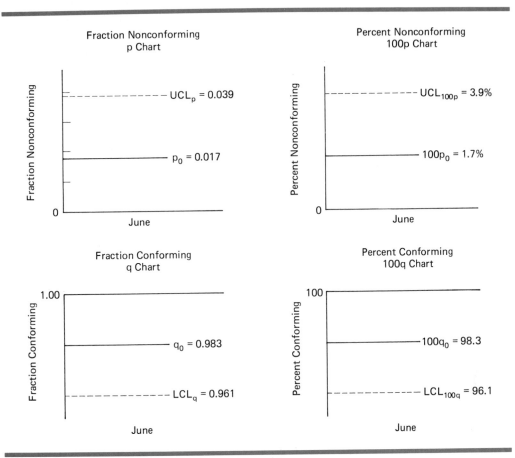

FIGURE 5-3   Different techniques for presenting p chart information.

size was one day's inspection results. The inspection results for 25 subgroups are shown in the first three columns of Table 5-3 on page 168: subgroup designation, number inspected, and number nonconforming. A fourth column for the fraction nonconforming is calculated by the inspector using the formula $p = np/n$. The last two columns are for the upper and lower control limit calculations, which are discussed in the next section.

TABLE 5-2   Calculating Central Line and Limits for the Different Presentation Techniques

	FRACTION NONCONFORMING	PERCENT NONCONFORMING	FRACTION CONFORMING	PERCENT CONFORMING
Central line	p_0	$100p_0$	$q_0 = 1 - p_0$	$100q_0 = 100(1 - p_0)$
Upper control limit	UCL_p	$100(UCL_p)$	$UCL_q = 1 - UCL_p$	$100(UCL_q)$
Lower control limit	LCL_p	$100(LCL_p)$	$LCL_q = 1 - LCL_p$	$100(LCL_q)$

TABLE 5-3   Preliminary Data of Computer Modem Final Test and Control Limits for Each Subgroup

SUBGROUP	NUMBER INSPECTED n	NUMBER NONCONFORMING np	FRACTION NONCONFORMING p	LIMIT	
				UCL	LCL
March 29	2,385	55	0.023	0.029	0.011
30	1,451	18	0.012	0.031	0.009
31	1,935	50	0.026	0.030	0.010
April 1	2,450	42	0.017	0.028	0.012
2	1,997	39	0.020	0.029	0.011
5	2,168	52	0.024	0.029	0.011
6	1,941	47	0.024	0.030	0.010
7	1,962	34	0.017	0.030	0.010
8	2,244	29	0.013	0.029	0.011
9	1,238	53	0.043	0.032	0.008
12	2,289	45	0.020	0.029	0.011
13	1,464	26	0.018	0.031	0.009
14	2,061	47	0.023	0.029	0.011
15	1,667	34	0.020	0.030	0.010
16	2,350	31	0.013	0.029	0.011
19	2,354	38	0.016	0.029	0.011
20	1,509	28	0.018	0.031	0.009
21	2,190	30	0.014	0.029	0.011
22	2,678	113	0.042	0.028	0.012
23	2,252	58	0.026	0.029	0.011
26	1,641	34	0.021	0.030	0.010
27	1,782	19	0.011	0.030	0.010
28	1,993	30	0.015	0.030	0.010
29	2,382	17	0.007	0.029	0.011
30	2,132	46	0.022	0.029	0.011
	50,515	1,015			

The variation in the number inspected per day can be due to a number of reasons. Machines may have breakdowns or not be scheduled. Product models may have different production requirements, which will cause day-to-day variations. For the data in Table 5-3, there was a low on April 9 of 1238 inspections because the second shift did not work, and a high on April 22 of 2678 inspections because of overtime in one work center.

Step 4. *Determine the trial central line and control limits.* Control limits are calculated using the same procedures and formulas as for a constant subgroup. However, since the subgroup size changes each day, limits must be calculated for each day. First the average fraction nonconforming, which is the central line, must be determined, and it is

$$\bar{p} = \frac{\Sigma\, np}{\Sigma\, n} = \frac{1015}{50,515} = 0.020$$

Using $\bar{p}$, the control limits for each day can be obtained; for March 29 the limits are

$$UCL_{29} = \bar{p} + 3\sqrt{\frac{\bar{p}(1-\bar{p})}{n_{29}}} \qquad\qquad LCL_{29} = \bar{p} - 3\sqrt{\frac{\bar{p}(1-\bar{p})}{n_{29}}}$$

$$= 0.020 + 3\sqrt{\frac{0.020(1-0.020)}{2385}} \qquad\qquad = 0.020 - 3\sqrt{\frac{0.020(1-0.020)}{2385}}$$

$$= 0.029 \qquad\qquad\qquad\qquad\qquad = 0.011$$

For March 30 the control limits are

$$UCL_{30} = \bar{p} + 3\sqrt{\frac{\bar{p}(1-\bar{p})}{n_{30}}} \qquad\qquad LCL_{30} = \bar{p} - 3\sqrt{\frac{\bar{p}(1-\bar{p})}{n_{30}}}$$

$$= 0.020 + 3\sqrt{\frac{0.020(1-0.020)}{1451}} \qquad\qquad = 0.020 - 3\sqrt{\frac{0.020(1-0.020)}{1451}}$$

$$= 0.031 \qquad\qquad\qquad\qquad\qquad = 0.009$$

The control limit calculations above are repeated for the remaining 23 subgroups. Since n is the only variable that is changing, it is possible to simplify the calculations as follows:

$$CL\text{'s} = \bar{p} \pm \frac{3\sqrt{\bar{p}(1-\bar{p})}}{\sqrt{n}}$$

$$= 0.020 \pm \frac{3\sqrt{0.020(1-0.020)}}{\sqrt{n}}$$

$$= 0.020 \pm \frac{0.42}{\sqrt{n}}$$

Using this technique the calculations are much quicker. The control limits for all 25 subgroups are shown in columns four and five of Table 5-3. A graphical illustration of the trial control limits, central line, and subgroup values are shown in Figure 5-4 on page 170.

Note that as the subgroup size gets larger, the control limits are closer together; as the subgroup size gets smaller, the control limits become wider apart. This fact is apparent from the formula and by comparing the subgroup size, n, with its UCL and LCL.

Step 5. *Establish revised central line and control limits*. A review of Figure 5-4 shows that an out-of-control situation is present on April 9, April 22, and April 29. There was a problem with the wave solder on April 9 and April 22. Also, it was found that on April 29 the testing instrument was out of calibration. Since all these

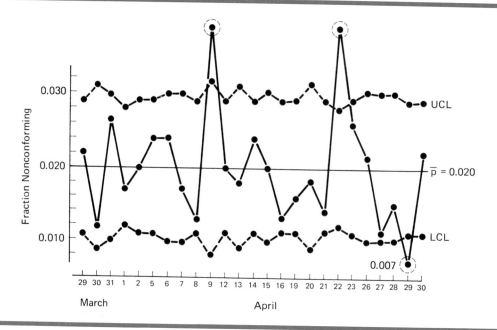

FIGURE 5-4 **Preliminary data, central line, and trial control limits.**

out-of-control points have assignable causes, they are discarded. A new $\bar{p}$ is obtained as follows:

$$\bar{p}_{new} = \frac{\Sigma\, np - np_d}{\Sigma\, n - n_d}$$

$$= \frac{1015 - 53 - 113 - 17}{50{,}515 - 1238 - 2678 - 2382}$$

$$= 0.019$$

Since this value represents the best estimate of the standard or reference value of the fraction nonconforming, $p_0 = 0.019$.

The fraction nonconforming, p_0, is used to calculate upper and lower control limits for the next period, which is the month of May. However, the limits cannot be calculated until the end of each day, when the subgroup size, n, is known. This means that the control limits are never known ahead of time. Table 5-4 shows the inspection results for the first three working days in May. Control limits and the fraction nonconforming for May 3 are as follows:

$$p_{May\,3} = \frac{np}{n} = \frac{31}{1535} = 0.020$$

$$UCL_{May\,3} = p_0 + 3\sqrt{\frac{p_0(1 - p_0)}{n_{May\,3}}}$$

$$= 0.019 + 3\sqrt{\frac{0.019(1 - 0.019)}{1535}}$$

$$= 0.029$$

$$LCL_{May\ 3} = p_0 - 3\sqrt{\frac{p_0(1 - p_0)}{n_{May\ 3}}}$$

$$= 0.019 - 3\sqrt{\frac{0.019(1 - 0.019)}{1535}}$$

$$= 0.009$$

TABLE 5-4   Inspection Results for May 3, 4, and 5

SUBGROUP	NUMBER INSPECTED	NUMBER NONCONFORMING
May 3	1535	31
4	2262	28
5	1872	45

The upper and lower control limits and the fraction nonconforming for May 3 are posted to the p chart as illustrated in Figure 5-5. In a similar manner, calculations are made for May 4 and 5 and the results posted to the chart.

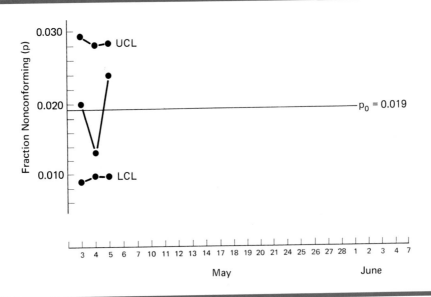

FIGURE 5-5   Control limits and fraction nonconforming for first three working days in May.

The chart is continued until the end of May, using $p_0 = 0.019$. Since an improvement usually occurs after introduction of a chart, a better estimate of p_0 will probably be obtained at the end of May using that month's data. In the future the value of p_0 should be evaluated periodically.

If p_0 is known, the process of data collection and trial control limits is not necessary. This saves considerable time and effort.

Since some confusion occurs among p_0, $\bar{p}$, and p, their definitions will be repeated:

1. p is the fraction nonconforming in a single subgroup. It is posted to the chart but is *not* used to calculate the control limits.

2. $\bar{p}$ is the average fraction nonconforming of many subgroups. It is the sum of the number nonconforming divided by the sum of the number inspected and is used to calculate the trial control limits.

3. p_0 is the standard or reference value of the fraction nonconforming based on the best estimate of $\bar{p}$. It is used to calculate the revised control limits. It can be specified as a desired value.

4. ϕ is the population fraction nonconforming. When this value is known, it can be used to calculate the limits, since $p_0 = \phi$.

Minimizing the Effect of Variable Subgroup Size

When the control limits vary from subgroup to subgroup, it presents an unattractive chart that is difficult to explain to operating personnel. It is also difficult to explain that control limits are calculated at the end of each day or time period rather than ahead of time. There are two techniques that minimize the effect of the variable subgroup size.

1. *Control limits for an average subgroup size.* By using an average subgroup size, one limit can be calculated and placed on the control chart. The average group size can be based on the anticipated production for the month or the previous month's inspections. As an example, the average number inspected for the preliminary data in Table 5-3 would be

$$n_{av} = \frac{\Sigma n}{g} = \frac{50,515}{25} = 2020.6, \qquad \text{say } 2000$$

Using a value of 2000 for the subgroup size, n, and $p_0 = 0.019$, the upper and lower control limits become

$$\text{UCL} = p_0 + 3\sqrt{\frac{p_0(1 - p_0)}{n_{av}}} \qquad\qquad \text{LCL} = p_0 - 3\sqrt{\frac{p_0(1 - p_0)}{n_{av}}}$$

$$= 0.019 + 3\sqrt{\frac{0.019(1 - 0.019)}{2000}} \qquad = 0.019 - 3\sqrt{\frac{0.019(1 - 0.019)}{2000}}$$

$$= 0.028 \qquad\qquad\qquad\qquad\qquad = 0.010$$

These control limits are shown in the p chart of Figure 5-6 along with the fraction nonconforming, p, for each day in May.

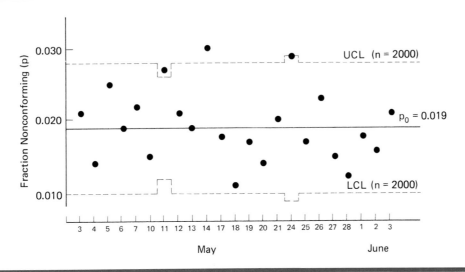

FIGURE 5-6   Chart for May data illustrating use of an average subgroup size.

When an average subgroup size is used, there are four situations that occur between the control limits and the individual fraction nonconforming values.

Case I. This case occurs when a point (subgroup fraction nonconforming) falls inside the limits and its subgroup size is smaller than the average subgroup size. The data for May 6, $p = 0.011$ and $n = 1828$, represent this case. Since the May 6 subgroup size (1828) is less than the average of 2000, the control limits for May 6 will be wider apart than the control limits for the average subgroup size. Therefore, in this case individual control limits are not needed. If p is in control when $n = 2000$, it must also be in control when $n = 1828$.

Case II. This case occurs when a point (subgroup fraction nonconforming) falls inside the average limits and its subgroup size is larger than the average subgroup size. The data for May 11, $p = 0.027$ and $n = 2900$, illustrate this case. Since the May 11 subgroup size is greater than the average subgroup size, the control limits for May 11 will be closer together than the control limits for the average subgroup size. Therefore, when there is a substantial difference in the subgroup size, individual control limits are calculated. For May 11 the values for the upper and lower control limits are 0.026 and 0.012, respectively. These individual control limits are shown in Figure 5-6. It is seen that the point is beyond the individual control limit and so we have an out-of-control situation.

Case III. This case occurs when a point (subgroup fraction nonconforming) falls outside the limits and its subgroup size is larger than the average subgroup size. The data for May 14, $p = 0.030$ and $n = 2365$, illustrate this case. Since the May 14 subgroup size (2365) is greater than the average of 2000, the control limits for May 14 will be narrower than the control limits for the average sub-

CONTROL CHARTS FOR NONCONFORMING UNITS   173

group size. Therefore, in this case individual control limits are not needed. If p is out of control when $n = 2000$, it must also be out of control when $n = 2365$.

Case IV. This case occurs when a point (subgroup fraction nonconforming) falls outside the limits and its subgroup size is less than the average subgroup size. The data for May 24, $p = 0.029$ and $n = 1590$, illustrate this case. Since the May 24 subgroup size (1590) is less than the average of 2000, the control limits for May 24 will be wider apart than the control limits for the average subgroup size. Therefore, when there is a substantial difference in the subgroup size, individual control limits are calculated. For May 24 the values for the upper and lower control limits are 0.029 and 0.009, respectively. These individual control limits are shown in Figure 5-6. It is seen that the point is on the individual control limit and is assumed to be in control.

It is not always necessary to calculate the individual control limits in cases II and IV. Only when the value of p is close to the control limits is it necessary to determine the individual limits. For this example problem p values within, say, ± 0.002 of the original limits should be checked. Since approximately 5% of the p values will be close to the control limits, few p values will need to be evaluated.

In addition, it is not necessary to calculate individual control limits as long as the subgroup size does not deviate substantially from the average, say 15%. For this example, subgroup sizes of from 1700 to 2300 would be satisfactory and not need to have individual limit calculations.

Actually, when the average subgroup size is used, individual control limits are determined infrequently—about once every 3 months.

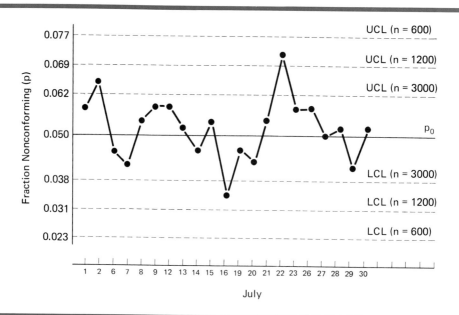

FIGURE 5-7 *p* **Chart illustrating central line and control limits for different subgroup sizes.**

2. *Control limits for different subgroup sizes.* Another technique, which has been found to be effective, is to establish control limits for different subgroup sizes. Figure 5-7 illustrates such a chart. Using the different control limits and the four cases described previously, the need to calculate individual control limits would be rare. For example, the subgroup for July 16 with 1150 inspections is in control, and the subgroup for July 22 with 3500 inspections is out of control.

An analysis of Figure 5-7 shows that the relationship of the control limits to the subgroup size, n, is exponential rather than linear. In other words, the control limit lines are not equally spaced for equal subdivisions of the subgroup size, n.

Number Nonconforming Chart

The number nonconforming chart (np chart) is almost the same as the p chart. In fact, however, you would not use both for the same objective.

The np chart is easier for operating personnel to understand than the p chart. Also, inspection results are posted directly to the chart without any calculations.

If the subgroup size is allowed to vary, the central line and the control limits will vary, which presents a chart that is almost meaningless. Therefore, one limitation of an np chart is the requirement that the subgroup size be constant. The sample size should be shown on the chart so viewers have a reference point.

Since the number nonconforming chart is mathematically equivalent to the proportion nonconforming chart, the central line and control limits are changed by a factor of n. Formulas are

$$\text{Central line} = np_0$$

$$\text{Control limits} = np_0 \pm 3\sqrt{np_0(1 - p_0)}$$

If the fraction nonconforming p_0 is unknown, then it must be determined by collecting data, calculating trial control limits, and obtaining the best estimate of p_0. The trial control limit formulas are obtained by substituting $\bar{p}$ for p_0 in the formulas above.

EXAMPLE PROBLEM

An example problem will illustrate the technique. A government agency samples 200 documents per day from a daily lot of 6000. From past records the standard or reference value for the fraction nonconforming, p_0, is 0.075.

Central line and control limit calculations are:

$$np_0 = 200(0.075) = 15.0$$

$$\text{UCL} = np_0 + 3\sqrt{np_0(1 - p_0)} \qquad \text{LCL} = np_0 - 3\sqrt{np_0(1 - p_0)}$$
$$= 15 + 3\sqrt{15(1 - 0.075)} \qquad = 15 - 3\sqrt{15(1 - 0.075)}$$
$$= 26.2 \qquad = 3.8$$

Since the number nonconforming is a whole number, the limit values should be whole numbers; however, they can be left as fractions. This practice prevents a plotted point from falling on a control limit. Of course the central line is a fraction. The control chart is shown in Figure 5-8 for four weeks in October.

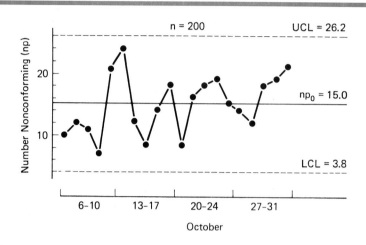

FIGURE 5-8 **Number nonconforming chart (*np* chart).**

Run Chart

A run chart for variables was described in Chapter 3. The same type of chart can be used for attributes. Figure 5-9 shows a run chart for percent nonconforming covering a 5-week period. The results of each day's inspections are posted to the chart.

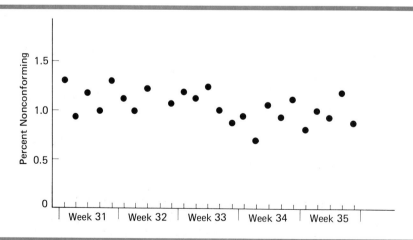

FIGURE 5-9 **Run chart for percent nonconforming.**

This type of chart is very effective during the start-up phase of a new item or process when the process is very erratic. Also, many companies prefer to use this type of chart to measure quality performance rather than a control chart. Since zero percent nonconforming is the goal, the central line and control limits may convey to operating personnel that a percentage less than zero is acceptable. This type of approach is satisfactory as long as management recognizes that system constraints may be limiting the quality rather than operating personnel. An analysis of Figure 5-9 indicates that the process is relatively stable; therefore, better quality can only result in improvements to the system.

Since the run chart does not have limits, it is not a control chart. This fact does not limit its effectiveness in many situations.

Process Capability

The process capability of a variable was described in Chapter 3. For an attribute this process is much simpler. In fact, the process capability is the central line of the control chart.

Figure 5-10 shows a percent nonconforming chart for first-run automobile water leaks with a central line of 5.0%. The 5.0% value is the process capability and the plotted points vary from the capability within the control limits. This variation occurs in a random manner but follows the binomial distribution.

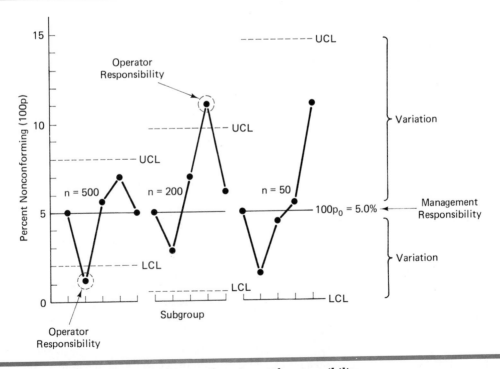

FIGURE 5-10 Process capability explanation and responsibility.

While the control limits show the limits of the variation of the capability, it should be understood that the limits are a function of the subgroup size. This fact is shown in Figure 5-10 for subgroup sizes of 500, 200, and 50. As the subgroup size increases, the control limits become closer to the central line.

Management is responsible for the capability. If the 5% value is not satisfactory, then management must initiate the procedures and provide the resources to take the necessary corrective action. As long as operating personnel (operators, first-line supervisors, maintenance workers, and inspectors) are maintaining the plotted points within the control limits, they are doing what the process is capable of doing. When the plotted point is outside the control limit, operating personnel are usually responsible. A plotted point below the lower control limit is due to exceptionally good quality. It should be investigated to determine the assignable cause so that if it is not due to an inspection error, it can be repeated.

CONTROL CHARTS FOR COUNT OF NONCONFORMITIES

Introduction

The other group of attribute charts is the nonconformity charts. While a p chart controls the proportion nonconforming in the product, the nonconformities chart controls the count of nonconformities in the product. Remember an item is classified as a nonconforming unit whether it has one or many nonconformities. There are two types of charts: count of nonconformities (c) chart and count of nonconformities per unit (u) chart.

Since these charts are based on the Poisson distribution, two conditions must be met. First, the average count of nonconformities must be much less than the total possible count of nonconformities. In other words, the opportunity for nonconformities is large, whereas the chance of a nonconformity at any one location is very small. This situation is typified by the rivets on a commercial airplane, where there are a large number of rivets but a small chance of any one rivet being a nonconformity. The second condition specifies that the occurrences are independent. In other words, the occurrence of one nonconformity does not increase or decrease the chance of the next occurrence being a nonconformity. For example, if a typist types an incorrect letter there is an equal likelihood of the next letter being incorrect. Any beginning typist knows that this is not always the case because if the hands are not on the home keys, the chance of the second letter being incorrect is almost a certainty.

Other places where a chart of nonconformities meets the two conditions are: imperfections in a large roll of paper, typographical errors on a printed page, rust spots on steel sheets, seeds or air pockets in glassware, adhesion nonconformities per 1000 square feet of corrugated board, mold marks on fiberglass canoes, billing errors, and errors on forms.

Like nonconforming unit charts, the control limits for charts for nonconformities are based on three standard deviations from the central line. Therefore, approximately 99% of the subgroup values will fall within the limits. It is suggested that the reader review the section "State of Control" in Chapter 3, since much of that information is applicable to the defect charts.

Objectives

While the charts for count of nonconformities are not as inclusive as the $\bar{X}$ and R charts or the p charts, they still have a number of applications, some of which have been mentioned.

The objectives of charts for count of nonconformities are to:

1. Determine the average quality level as a benchmark or starting point. This information gives the process capability.

2. Bring to the attention of management any changes in the average. Once the average quality is known, any change becomes significant.

3. Improve the product quality. In this regard a chart for count of nonconformities can motivate operating and management personnel to initiate ideas for quality improvement. The chart will tell whether the idea is an appropriate or inappropriate one. A continual and relentless effort must be made to improve the quality.

4. Evaluate the quality performance of operating and management personnel. As long as the chart is in control operating personnel are performing satisfactorily. Since the charts for count of nonconformities are usually applicable to errors, they are very effective in quality evaluation of the functional areas of finance, sales, customer service, and so on.

5. Suggest places to use the $\bar{X}$ and R charts. Some applications of the charts for count of nonconformities lend themselves to more detailed analysis by $\bar{X}$ and R charts.

6. Provide information concerning the acceptability of the product prior to shipment.

These objectives are almost identical to those for nonconforming charts. Therefore, the reader is cautioned to be sure that the appropriate group of charts is being used.

Because of the limitations of the charts for count of nonconformities, many plants and industries do not have occasion for their use.

c-Chart Construction

The procedures for the construction of a c chart are the same as those for the p chart. If the count of nonconformities, c_0, is unknown, it must be found by collecting data, calculating trial control limits, and obtaining the best estimate.

1. *Select the quality characteristic(s).* The first step in the procedure is to determine the use of the control chart. Like the p chart, it can be established to control (a) a single quality characteristic, (b) a group of quality characteristics, (c) a

part, (d) an entire product, or (e) a number of products. It can also be established for performance control of (a) an operator, (b) a work center, (c) a department, (d) a shift, (e) a plant, or (f) a corporation. The use for the chart or charts will be based on securing the greatest benefit for a minimum of cost.

2. *Determine the subgroup size and method.* The size of a c chart is one inspected unit. An inspected unit could be one airplane, one case of soda cans, one gross of pencils, one bundle of Medicare applications, one stack of labels, and so forth. The method of obtaining the sample can either be by audit or on-line.

3. *Collect the data.* Data were collected on the count of nonconformities of a blemish nature for plastic canoes. These data were collected during the first and second weeks of May by inspecting random production samples. Data are shown in Table 5-5 for 25 canoes, which is the minimum number of subgroups needed for trial control limit calculations. Note that canoes MY132 and MY278 both had production difficulties.

TABLE 5-5   Count of Blemish Nonconformities (c) by Canoe Serial Number

SERIAL NUMBER	COUNT OF NONCONFORMITIES	COMMENT	SERIAL NUMBER	COUNT OF NONCONFORMITIES	COMMENT
MY102	7		MY198	3	
MY113	6		MY208	2	
MY121	6		MY222	7	
MY125	3		MY235	5	
MY132	20	Mold Sticking	MY241	7	
MY143	8		MY258	2	
MY150	6		MY259	8	
MY152	1		MY264	0	
MY164	0		MY267	4	
MY166	5		MY278	14	Fell off skid
MY172	14		MY281	4	
MY184	3		MY288	5	
MY185	1				
			Total	$\Sigma c = 141$	

4. *Calculate the trial central line and control limits.* The formulas for the trial control limits are

$$UCL = \bar{c} + 3\sqrt{\bar{c}}$$
$$LCL = \bar{c} - 3\sqrt{\bar{c}}$$

where $\bar{c}$ is the average count of nonconformities for a number of subgroups. The value of $\bar{c}$ is obtained from the formula $\bar{c} = \Sigma c/g$, where g is the number of subgroups and c is the count of nonconformities. For the data in Table 5-5, the calculations are:

$$\bar{c} = \frac{\Sigma c}{g} = \frac{141}{25} = 5.64$$

$$\text{UCL} = \bar{c} + 3\sqrt{\bar{c}} \qquad\qquad \text{LCL} = \bar{c} - 3\sqrt{\bar{c}}$$

$$= 5.64 + 3\sqrt{5.64} \qquad\qquad = 5.64 - 3\sqrt{5.64}$$

$$= 12.76 \qquad\qquad\qquad = -1.48, \quad \text{or} \quad 0$$

Since a lower control limit of a -1.48 is impossible, it is changed to zero. The upper control limit of 12.76 is left as a fraction so that a plotted point that is a whole number cannot lie on the control limit. Figure 5-11 illustrates the central line, $\bar{c}$, the control limits, and the count of nonconformities, c, for each canoe of the preliminary data.

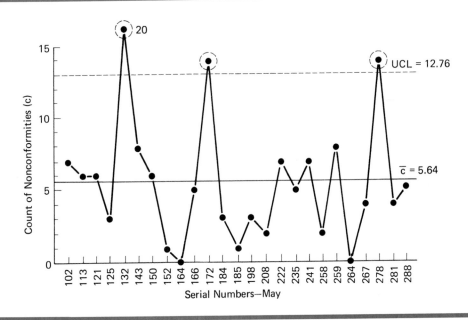

FIGURE 5-11. **Control chart for count of nonconformities (c chart), using preliminary data.**

5. *Establish the revised central line and control limits.* In order to determine the revised 3σ control limits, the standard or reference value for the count of defects, c_0, is needed. If an analysis of the preliminary data shows good control, then $\bar{c}$ can be considered to be representative of that process $c_0 = \bar{c}$. Usually, however, an analysis of the preliminary data does not show good control, as illustrated in Figure 5-11. A better estimate of $\bar{c}$ (one that can be adopted for c_0) can be obtained by discarding out-of-control values with assignable causes. Low values that do not have an assignable cause represent exceptionally good quality. The calculations can be simplified by using the formula

$$\bar{c}_{\text{new}} = \frac{\Sigma c - c_d}{g - g_d}$$

where c_d = count of nonconformities in the discarded subgroups
g_d = number of discarded subgroups

Once an adopted standard or reference value is obtained, the revised 3σ control limits are found using the formulas

$$UCL = c_0 + 3\sqrt{c_0}$$
$$LCL = c_0 - 3\sqrt{c_0}$$

where c_0 is the reference or standard value for the count of nonconformities. The count of nonconformities, c_0, is the central line of the chart; it is the best estimate using the available data and equals $\bar{c}_{new}$.

Using the information from Figure 5-11 and Table 5-5, revised limits can be obtained. An analysis of Figure 5-11 shows that canoe numbers 132, 172, and 278 are out of control. Since canoes 132 and 278 have an assignable cause (see Table 5-5), they are discarded; however, canoe 172 may be due to a chance cause and is not discarded. Therefore, $\bar{c}_{new}$ is obtained as follows:

$$\bar{c}_{new} = \frac{\Sigma c - c_d}{g - g_d}$$

$$= \frac{141 - 20 - 14}{25 - 2}$$

$$= 4.65$$

Since $\bar{c}_{new}$ is the best estimate of the central line, $c_0 = 4.65$. The revised control limits for the c chart are:

$$UCL = c_0 + 3\sqrt{c_0} \qquad LCL = c_0 - 3\sqrt{c_0}$$
$$= 4.65 + 3\sqrt{4.65} \qquad = 4.65 - 3\sqrt{4.65}$$
$$= 11.1 \qquad = -1.82, \quad \text{or} \quad 0$$

These control limits are used to start the chart beginning with canoes produced during the third week of May and are shown in Figure 5-12. It is noted that the lower control limit will be negative as long as c_0 is less than 9; therefore, it can be given the value of zero without the necessity of performing the calculations.

If c_0 had been known, the data collection and trial control limit phase would have been unnecessary.

6. *Achieve the objective.* The reason for the control chart is to achieve one or more of the previously stated objectives. Once the objective is reached, the chart is discontinued or inspection activity is reduced and resources are allocated to another quality problem. Some of the objectives, however, such as the first one, can be on-going.

As with the other types of control charts, an improvement in the quality is expected after the introduction of a chart. At the end of the initial period, a better estimate of the number of nonconformities can be obtained. Figure 5-12 illustrates the change in c_0 and in the control limits for August as the chart is continued in use.

Chart for Canoe Blemish Nonconformities
Model—17S

Type of Nonconformity																													
Scratches	1		2		2		3			1			2							1	2	1					1	1	
Paint Imperfections						1	2	1							1	3				1				1					3
Indentations	1		2						2						1			1		1	2			1					
Scuff Marks	1	1	5		3	4	3	5	2	2			4	1	2		1	2		1	3	1	5	2	1	2	2		3
Total	3	1	9	0	5	5	8	6	4	3		0	6	1	4	3	1	3	0	4	7	2	5	4	1	2	3	1	6
Serial Number	305	310	321	354	373	409	441	469	485	487		129	150	178	185	209	230	260	283	303	321	347	359	407	471	485	493	564	589

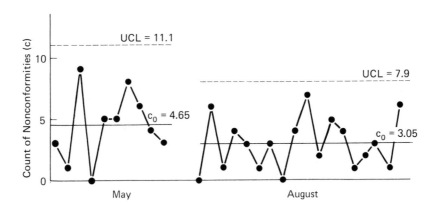

FIGURE 5-12   *c* Chart for canoe blemish nonconformities.

Quality improvement resulted from the evaluation of ideas generated by the project team such as attaching small pieces of carpet to the skids, faster drying ink, worker training programs, and so on. The control chart shows whether the idea improves the quality, reduces the quality, or does not change the quality. A minimum of 25 subgroups is needed to evaluate each idea. The subgroups can be taken as often as practical as long as they are representative of the process. Only one idea should be evaluated at a time.

Figure 5-12 also illustrates a technique for reporting the number of nonconformities of individual quality characteristics, while the graph reports the total. This is an excellent technique for presenting the total picture and one that is accomplished with little additional time or cost. It is interesting to note that the serial numbers of the canoes that were selected for inspection were obtained from a random-number table.

The control chart should be placed in a conspicuous place where it can be viewed by operating personnel.

Chart for Count of Nonconformities/Unit (u Chart)

The c chart is applicable where the subgroup size is an inspected unit of one such as a canoe, an airplane, 1000 square feet of cloth, a ream of paper, 100 income tax forms, and a keg of nails. The inspected unit can be any size that meets the objective; however, it must be constant. Recall that the subgroup size, n, is not in the calculations because its value is one. When situations arise where the subgroup size varies, then the u chart (count of nonconformities/unit) is the appropriate chart. The u chart can also be used when the subgroup size is constant.

The u chart is mathematically equivalent to the c chart.

The u chart is developed in the same manner as the c chart, with the collection of 25 subgroups, calculation of trial central line and control limits, obtaining an estimate of the standard or reference count of nonconformities per unit, and calculation of the revised limits. Formulas used for the procedure are:

$$u = \frac{c}{n} \qquad \bar{u} = \frac{\Sigma c}{\Sigma n}$$

$$\text{UCL} = \bar{u} + 3\sqrt{\frac{\bar{u}}{n}} \qquad \text{LCL} = \bar{u} - 3\sqrt{\frac{\bar{u}}{n}}$$

where c = count of nonconformities in a subgroup
$\quad n$ = number inspected in a subgroup
$\quad u$ = count of nonconformities/unit in a subgroup
$\quad \bar{u}$ = average count of nonconformities/unit for many subgroups

Revised control limits are obtained by substituting u_0 in the trial-control limit formula. The u chart will be illustrated by an example.

Each day a clerk inspects the waybills of a small overnight air freight company for errors. Because the number of waybills varies from day to day, a u chart is the appropriate technique. Data are collected as shown in Table 5-6. The date, number inspected, and count of nonconformities are obtained and posted to the table. The count of nonconformities per unit, u, is calculated and posted. Also, because the subgroup size varies, the control limits are calculated for each subgroup. Data for 5 weeks at 6 days per week are collected for a total of 30 subgroups. Although only 25 subgroups are required, this approach eliminates any bias that could occur from the low activity that occurs on Saturday. The calculation for the trial central line is

$$\bar{u} = \frac{\Sigma c}{\Sigma n} = \frac{3389}{2823} = 1.20$$

Calculations for the trial control limits and the plotted point, u, must be made for each subgroup. For January 30 they are

$$\text{UCL}_{\text{Jan 30}} = \bar{u} + 3\sqrt{\frac{\bar{u}}{n}} \qquad \text{LCL}_{\text{Jan 30}} = \bar{u} - 3\sqrt{\frac{\bar{u}}{n}}$$

$$= 1.20 + 3\sqrt{\frac{1.20}{110}} \qquad\qquad = 1.20 - 3\sqrt{\frac{1.20}{110}}$$

$$= 1.51 \qquad\qquad\qquad\qquad = 0.89$$

$$u_{\text{Jan 30}} = \frac{c}{n} = \frac{120}{110} = 1.09$$

TABLE 5-6   Count of Nonconformities per Unit for Waybills

DATE		NUMBER INSPECTED n	COUNT OF NONCONFORMITIES c	NONCONFORMITIES PER UNIT u	UCL	LCL
Jan.	30	110	120	1.09	1.51	0.89
	31	82	94	1.15	1.56	0.84
Feb.	1	96	89	.93	1.53	0.87
	2	115	162	1.41	1.50	0.90
	3	108	150	1.39	1.51	0.89
	4	56	82	1.46	1.64	0.76
	6	120	143	1.19	1.50	0.90
	7	98	134	1.37	1.53	0.87
	8	102	97	.95	1.53	0.87
	9	115	145	1.26	1.50	0.90
	10	88	128	1.45	1.55	0.85
	11	71	83	1.16	1.59	0.81
	13	95	120	1.26	1.54	0.86
	14	103	116	1.13	1.52	0.88
	15	113	127	1.12	1.51	0.89
	16	85	92	1.08	1.56	0.84
	17	101	140	1.39	1.53	0.87
	18	42	60	1.19	1.70	0.70
	20	97	121	1.25	1.53	0.87
	21	92	108	1.17	1.54	0.86
	22	100	131	1.31	1.53	0.87
	23	115	119	1.03	1.50	0.90
	24	99	93	.94	1.53	0.87
	25	57	88	1.54	1.64	0.76
	27	89	107	1.20	1.55	0.85
	28	101	105	1.04	1.53	0.87
Mar.	1	122	143	1.17	1.49	0.91
	2	105	132	1.26	1.52	0.88
	3	98	100	1.02	1.53	0.87
	4	48	60	1.25	1.67	0.73
	Total	2823	3389			

These calculations must be repeated for 29 subgroups and and the values posted to the table.

A comparison of the plotted points with the upper and lower control limits in Figure 5-13 shows that there are no out-of-control values. Therefore, $\bar{u}$ can be considered the best estimate of u_0 and $u_0 = 1.20$. There are no out-of-control points,

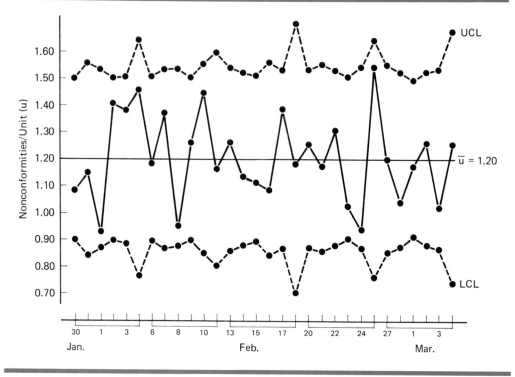

FIGURE 5-13　*u* Chart for errors on waybills.

and a visual inspection of the plotted points indicates a stable process. This situation is somewhat unusual at the beginning of control-charting activities.

To determine control limits for the next 5-week period, we can use an average subgroup size in the same manner as the variable subgroup size of the *p* chart. A review of the chart shows that the control limits for Saturday are much wider apart than for the rest of the week. This condition is due to the smaller subgroup size. Therefore, it appears appropriate to establish separate control limits for Saturday. Calculations are as follows:

$$n_{\text{Sat. avg.}} = \frac{\Sigma n}{g} = \frac{(56 + 71 + 42 + 57 + 48)}{5} = 55$$

$$\text{UCL} = u_0 + 3\sqrt{\frac{u_0}{n}} \qquad \text{LCL} = u_0 - 3\sqrt{\frac{u_0}{n}}$$

$$= 1.20 + 3\sqrt{\frac{1.20}{55}} \qquad = 1.20 - 3\sqrt{\frac{1.20}{55}}$$

$$= 1.64 \qquad = 0.76$$

$$n_{\text{daily avg.}} = \frac{\Sigma n}{g} = \frac{2823 - 274}{25} = 102, \quad \text{say } 100$$

$$\text{UCL} = u_0 + 3\sqrt{\frac{u_0}{n}} \qquad \text{LCL} = u_0 + 3\sqrt{\frac{u_0}{n}}$$

$$= 1.20 + 3\sqrt{\frac{1.20}{100}} \qquad = 1.20 + 3\sqrt{\frac{1.20}{100}}$$

$$= 1.53 \qquad\qquad\qquad = 0.87$$

The control chart for the next period is shown in Figure 5-14. When the subgroup is a day's inspections, the true control limits will need to be calculated about once every 3 months.

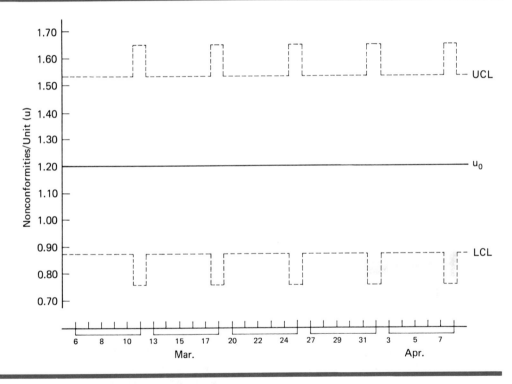

FIGURE 5-14   *u* Chart for next period.

The control chart can now be used to achieve the objective. If a project team is involved, it can test ideas for quality improvement.

The *u* chart is identical to the *c* chart in all aspects except two. One difference is the scale, which is continuous for a *u* chart but discrete for the *c* chart. This difference provides more flexibility for the *u* chart since the subgroup size can vary. The other difference is the subgroup size which is one for the *c* chart.

The *u* chart is limited in that we do not know the location of the nonconformities. For example, in Table 5-6, February 4 has 82 nonconformities out of 56 inspected for a value of 1.46. All 82 nonconformities could have been counted on one unit or it is possible that 56 units had one nonconformity each.

Final Comments

Process capability for nonconfomities is treated in a manner similar to nonconforming units. The reader is referred to Figure 5-10.

Figure 5-15 shows when to use the various attribute charts. First you need to decide whether to chart nonconformities or nonconforming units. Next you need to determine whether the subgroup size will be constant or will vary. These two decisions give the appropriate chart.

		Attribute Chart	
		Nonconforming Units	Nonconformities
Sample Size	Constant	np	c (n = 1)
	Constant or Varies	p	u

FIGURE 5-15 **When to use the various attribute charts.**

A QUALITY RATING SYSTEM

Introduction

In the attribute charts of the preceding section, all nonconformities and nonconforming units had the same weight, regardless of their seriousness. For example, in the inspection of desk chairs, one chair might have 5 nonconformities, all related to the surface finish, while another chair might have 1 nonconformity, a broken leg. The usable chair with 5 trivial nonconformities has five times the influence on the attribute chart as the unusable chair with 1 serious nonconformity. This situation presents an incorrect evaluation of the product quality. A quality rating system will correct this deficiency.

There are industrial and nonindustrial situations where it is desirable to compare the performance of operators, shifts, plants, or vendors. In order to compare quality performance, a quality rating system is needed to classify, weigh, and evaluate nonconformities.

Nonconformity Classification

Nonconformities, and for that matter, nonconforming units, are classified according to their severity. MIL-STD-105D groups nonconformities into three classes:

1. *Critical nonconformities.* A critical nonconformity is a nonconformity that judgment and experience indicate is likely to result in hazardous or unsafe conditions for individuals using, maintaining, or depending upon the product; or a nonconformity that judgment and experience indicate is likely to prevent performance of the function of the product.

2. *Major nonconformities.* A major nonconformity is a nonconformity, other than critical, that is likely to result in failure, or to reduce materially the usability of the product for its intended purpose.

3. *Minor nonconformities.* A minor nonconformity is a nonconformity that is not likely to reduce materially the usability of the product for its intended purpose. Minor nonconformities are usually associated with appearance.

To summarize, a critical nonconformity *will* affect usability; a major nonconformity *might* affect usability; and a minor nonconformity *will not* affect usability of the unit.

Other classification systems use four classes or two classes, depending on the complexity of the product. A catastrophic class is sometimes used.

Once the classifications are determined, the weights to assign to each class can be established. While any weights can be assigned to the classifications, 9 points for a critical, 3 points for a major, and 1 point for a minor are usually considered to be satisfactory since a major is three times as important as a minor and a critical is three times as important as a major.

Control Chart

Control charts are established and plotted for count of demerits per unit. A demerit per unit is given by the formula

$$D = w_c u_c + w_{ma} u_{ma} + w_{mi} u_{mi}$$

where D = demerits per unit

w_c, w_{ma}, w_{mi} = weights for the three classes—critical, major, and minor

u_c, u_{ma}, u_{mi} = count of nonconformities per unit in each of the three classes—critical, major, minor

When w_c, w_{ma}, and w_{mi} are 9, 3 and 1, respectively, the formula is

$$D = 9u_c + 3u_{ma} + 1u_{mi}$$

The D values calculated from the formula are posted to the chart for each subgroup. The central line and the 3σ control limits are obtained from the formulas

$$D_0 = 9u_{0c} + 3u_{0ma} + 1u_{0mi}$$

$$\sigma_{0u} = \sqrt{\frac{9^2 u_{0c} + 3^2 u_{0ma} + 1^2 u_{0mi}}{n}}$$

$$\text{UCL} = D_0 + 3\sigma_{0u} \qquad \text{LCL} = D_0 - 3\sigma_{0u}$$

where u_{0c}, u_{0ma}, and u_{0mi} represent the standard nonconformities per unit for the critical, major, and minor classifications, respectively. The nonconformities per unit for the critical, major, and minor classifications are obtained by separating the nonconformities into the three classifications and treating each as a separate u chart.

EXAMPLE PROBLEM

Assuming that a 9:3:1 three-class weighting system is used, determine the central line and control limits when $u_{0c} = 0.08$, $u_{0ma} = 0.5$, $u_{0mi} = 3.0$, and $n = 40$. Also calculate the demerits per unit for May 25 when critical nonconformities are 2, major nonconformities are 26, and minor nonconformities are 160 for the 40 units inspected on that day. Is the May 25 subgroup in control or out of control?

$$D_0 = 9u_{0c} + 3u_{0ma} + 1u_{0mi}$$

$$= 9(0.08) + 3(0.5) + 1(3.0)$$

$$= 5.2$$

$$\sigma_{0u} = \sqrt{\frac{9^2 u_{0c} + 3^2 u_{0ma} + 1^2 u_{0mi}}{n}}$$

$$= \sqrt{\frac{81(0.08) + 9(0.5) + 1(3.0)}{40}}$$

$$= 0.59$$

$$\text{UCL} = D_0 + 3\sigma_{0u} \qquad\qquad \text{LCL} = D_0 - 3\sigma_{0u}$$

$$= 5.2 + 3(0.59) \qquad\qquad = 5.2 - 3(0.59)$$

$$= 7.0 \qquad\qquad\qquad = 3.4$$

The central line and control limits are illustrated in Figure 5-16. Calculations for the May 25 subgroup are

$$D_{\text{May 25}} = 9u_c + 3u_{ma} + 1u_{mi}$$

$$= 9\left(\frac{2}{40}\right) + 3\left(\frac{26}{40}\right) + 1\left(\frac{160}{40}\right)$$

$$= 6.4 \quad \text{(in control)}$$

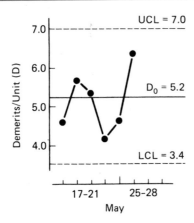

FIGURE 5-16   Demerit-per-unit chart (*D* chart).

Quality rating systems based on demerits per unit are useful for performance control and can be an important feature of a total quality control system.

COMPUTER PROGRAM

The computer program given in Figure 5-17 on page 192 computes the central line and control limits for a fraction defective chart for a fixed subgroup size. If it is desired to print out the incoming data, an LPRINT statement can be added after statement 210. Data used for the program are from Problem 2 at the end of the chapter. The program can be enhanced by graphing the chart and plotting the actual points. This activity is a function of the available graphical output device.

PROBLEMS

1. Determine the trial central line and control limits for a *p* chart using the following data, which are for the payment of dental insurance claims. Plot the values on graph paper and determine if the process is stable. If there are any out-of-control points, assume an assignable cause and determine the revised central line and control limits.

```
10 REM                        p   CHART
20 REM                   Fixed Subgroup Size
30 REM
40 REM              N = Sample Size(n)
50 REM              P = Fraction Nonconforming(p)
60 REM             NP = Number Nonconforming(np)
70 REM              G = Number of Subgroups(g)
80 REM           PBAR = Average Fraction Nonconforming(p bar)
90 REM            UCL = Upper Control Limit
100 REM           LCL = Lower Control Limit
110 REM            PO = Standard Value or Central Line
120 REM
130 DIM NP(30), P(30)
140 PRINT " Enter Subgroup Size.": INPUT N
150 LPRINT TAB(5); " n = ";N : LPRINT
160 PRINT " Enter Number of Subgroups." : INPUT G
170 REM               TRIAL CENTRAL LINE AND CONTROL LIMITS
180 NPS = 0
190 PRINT " Enter Data (np)."
200        FOR I = 1 TO G
210        INPUT NP(I)
220        NPS = NPS + NP(I)
230        NEXT I
240 PBAR = NPS / (N * G)
250 UCLT = PBAR + 3 * SQR(PBAR * (1 - PBAR) / N)
260 LCLT = PBAR - 3 * SQR(PBAR * (1 - PBAR) / N)
270 REM               DISCARD OUT-OF-CONTROL POINTS
280 D = G
290        FOR I = 1 TO G
300        P(I) = NP(I) / N
310        IF P(I) < LCLT GOTO 340
320        IF P(I) > UCLT GOTO 400
330        GOTO 430
340        PRINT " Subgroup Number = ";I
350        PRINT "p < LCL ; Enter 0 to discard, else 1."
360        INPUT K
370        IF K = 1 GOTO 430
380        IF K = 0 THEN NPS = NPS - NP(I)
390        D = D - 1 : GOTO 430
400        PRINT "Subgroup number = ";I
410        PRINT "p > UCL ; Enter 0 to discard, else 1."
420        INPUT K: GOTO 370
430        NEXT I
440 REM               REVISED CENTRAL LINE AND CONTROL LIMITS
450 PO = NPS / (N * D)
460 UCL = PO + 3 * SQR(PO * (1 - PO) / N)
470 LCL = PO + 3 * SQR(PO * (1 - PO) / N)
480 PRINT TAB(5); "Standard Value and Central Line = ";PO
490 PRINT TAB(5); "Upper Control Limit = ";UCL
500 PRINT TAB(5); "Lower Control Limit = ";LCL
510 END


n = 1750

Standard Value and Central Line =  .0261863
Upper Control Limit =   .0376382
Lower Control Limit =   .0147344
```

FIGURE 5-17   Computer program in BASIC to calculate the central line and control limits for a *p* chart.

SUBGROUP NUMBER	NUMBER INSPECTED	NUMBER NONCONFORMING	p	SUBGROUP NUMBER	NUMBER INSPECTED	NUMBER NONCONFORMING	p
1	300	3	.01	14	300	6	.023
2	300	6	.02	15	300	7	.013
3	300	4	.013	16	300	4	.016
4	300	6	.02	17	300	5	.023
5	300	20	.067	18	300	7	.016
6	300	2	.006	19	300	5	
7	300	6	.02	20	300	0	
8	300	7	.03	21	300	2	.006
9	300	3	.01	22	300	3	.01
10	300	0		23	300	6	.02
11	300	6	.02	24	300	1	.003
12	300	9	.03	25	300	8	.026
13	300	5	.016				

2. The supervisor is not sure about the best way to display the quality performance determined in Problem 1. Calculate the central line and limits for the other methods of presentation.

3. After achieving the objective in the example problem concerning the hair dryer motor, it is decided to reduce the sample size to 80. What are the central line and control limits?

4. Fifty motor generators are inspected per day from a stable process. The best estimate of the fraction nonconforming is 0.076. Determine the central line and control limits. On a particular day 5 nonconforming generators were discovered. Is this in control or out of control?

5. Inspection results of video-of-the-month shipments to customers for 25 consecutive days are given in the table. What central line and control limits should be established and posted if it is assumed that any out-of-control points have assigned causes? The number of inspections each day is constant and equals 1750.

DATE	NUMBER NONCONFORMING	DATE	NUMBER NONCONFORMING
July 6	47	July 23	37
7	42	26	39
8	48	27	51
9	58	28	44
12	32	29	61
13	38	30	48
14	53	Aug. 2	56
15	68	3	48
16	45	4	40
19	37	5	47
20	57	6	25
21	38	9	35
22	53		

6. The performance of the first shift is reflected in the inspection results of electric carving knives. Determine the trial central line and control limits for each subgroup. Assume that any out-of-control points have assignable causes and determine the standard value for the fraction nonconforming for the next production period.

DATE	NUMBER INSPECTED	NUMBER NONCONFORMING	DATE	NUMBER INSPECTED	NUMBER NONCONFORMING
Sept. 6	500	5	Sept. 23	525	10
7	550	6	24	650	3
8	700	8	27	675	8
9	625	9	28	450	23
10	700	7	29	500	2
13	550	8	30	375	3
14	450	16	Oct. 1	550	8
15	600	6	4	600	7
16	475	9	5	700	4
17	650	6	6	600	9
20	650	7	7	450	8
21	550	8	8	500	6
22	525	7	11	525	1

7. Daily inspection results for the model 305 electric range assembly line are given in the table. Determine trial control limits for each subgroup. Assume that any out-of-control points have assignable causes and determine the standard value for the fraction nonconforming for December.

DATE AND SHIFT	NUMBER INSPECTED	NUMBER NONCONFORMING	DATE AND SHIFT	NUMBER INSPECTED	NUMBER NONCONFORMING
Nov. 8 I	171	31	Nov. 17 I	165	16
II	167	6	II	170	35
9 I	170	8	18 I	175	12
II	135	13	II	167	6
10 I	137	26	19 I	141	50
II	170	30	II	159	26
11 I	45	3	22 I	181	16
II	155	11	II	195	38
12 I	195	30	23 I	165	33
II	180	36	II	140	21
15 I	181	38	24 I	162	18
II	115	33	II	191	22
16 I	165	26	25 I	139	16
II	189	15	II	181	27

8. Control limits are to be established based on the average number inspected from the information of Problem 7. What are these control limits and the central line? Describe the cases where individual control limits will need to be calculated.

9. Control charts are to be established on the manufacture of backpack frames. The revised fraction nonconforming is 0.08. Determine control limit lines for inspection rates of 1000 per day, 1500 per day, and 2000 per day. Draw the control chart. Why are the control limits unequally spaced?

10. Determine the revised central line and control limits for a percent nonconforming chart for the information in:
    (a) Problem 1
    (b) Problem 5

    Plot these.   graph

11. From the information of Problem 1, determine the revised central line and control limits for an *np* chart.

12. From the information of Problem 5, determine the revised central line and control limits for an *np* chart. Which chart is more meaningful to operating personnel?

13. An *np* chart is to be established on a painting process that is in statistical control. If 35 pieces are to be inspected every 4 hours and the fraction nonconforming is 0.06, determine the central line and control limits.

14 Determine the revised central line and control limits for *fraction conforming, percent conforming,* and *number conforming* charts for the information in:
    (a) Problem 1
    (b) Problem 5

15. On page 197 is a typical attribute chart form with information concerning 2-L soda bottles. Complete all calculations, plot the points, and draw the trial central line and control limits.

16. Find the process capability for:
    (a) Problem 5
    (b) Problem 6
    (c) Problem 9
    (d) Problem 15

17. Using the data in Figure 5-9, construct a run chart for *percent conforming*.

18. The count of surface nonconformities in 1000 square meters of 20-kg kraft paper is given in the table. Determine the trial central line and control limits and the revised central line and control limits assuming that out-of-control points have assignable causes.

LOT NUMBER	COUNT OF NONCONFORMITIES	LOT NUMBER	COUNT OF NONCONFORMITIES
20	10	35	30
21	8	36	2
22	6	37	12
23	6	38	0
24	2	39	6
25	10	40	14
26	8	41	10
27	10	42	8
28	0	43	6

LOT NUMBER	COUNT OF NONCONFORMITIES	LOT NUMBER	COUNT OF NONCONFORMITIES
29	2	44	2
30	8	45	14
31	2	46	16
32	20	47	10
33	10	48	2
34	6	49	5
		50	3

19. A leading bank has compiled the data in the table showing the count of nonconformities for 1000 accounting transactions per day during December and January. What control limits and central line are recommended for the control chart for February? Assume any out-of-control points have assignable causes.

COUNT OF NONCONFORMITIES	COUNT OF NONCONFORMITIES
8	17
19	14
14	9
18	7
11	15
16	22
8	19
15	38
21	12
8	13
23	5
10	2
9	16

20. An inspector has collected data on the count of rivet nonconformities in 4-m travel trailers. After 30 trailers, the total count of nonconformities is 316. Trial control limits have been determined and a comparison with the data shows no out-of-control points. What is the recommendation for the central line and the revised control limits for a count of nonconformities chart?

21. One hundred product labels are inspected every day for surface nonconformities. Results for the past 25 days are 22, 29, 25, 17, 20, 16, 34, 11, 31, 29, 15, 10, 33, 23, 27, 15, 17, 17, 19, 22, 23, 27, 29, 33, and 21. Plot the points on graph paper and determine if the process is stable. Determine trial central line and control limits.

22. Determine the trial control limits and revised control limits for a u chart using the data in the table for the surface finish of rolls of white paper. Assume any out-of-control points have assignable causes.

ATTRIBUTES CONTROL CHART

PART ID: 2 LITER-BOTTLE

CHECK METHOD: VISUAL

p ☒ np ☐ u ☐ c ☐

OPERATION ID: NEW PACKAGING LINE

CHARACTERISTIC: CASE PACKING DEFECTS

DEPT/AREA: PACKAGING

CHART ID:

DAY:	1	2	3	4	5	6	7	8	9	10	11	12	13	14	15	16	17	18	19	20	21	22	23	24	25
SAMPLE (n)	400	400	400	400	400	400	400	400	400	400	400	400	400	400	400	400	400	400	400	400	400	400	400	400	400
NUMBER (np, c)	43	21	14	20	15	16	8	12	18	4	6	12	5	4	3	8	7	31	8	6	4	7	9	6	10
PROPORTION (p, u)	.108	.053	.035	.050	.038	.040	.020	.030	.045	.010	.015	.030	.013	.010	.008	.020	.018	.078	.020	.015					

AVG =   UCL =   LCL =

197

LOT NUMBER	SAMPLE SIZE	TOTAL NONCONFORMITIES	LOT NUMBER	SAMPLE SIZE	TOTAL NONCONFORMITIES
1	10	45 *4.5*	15	10	48
2	10	51	16	11	35
3	10	36	17	10	39
4	9	48	18	10	29
5	10	42	19	10	37
6	10	5	20	10	33
7	10	33	21	10	15
8	8	27	22	10	33
9	8	31	23	11	27
10	8	22	24	10	23
11	12	25	25	10	25
12	12	35	26	10	41
13	12	32	27	9	37
14	10	43	28	10	28

23. A warehouse distribution activity has been in statistical control and control limits are needed for the next period. If the subgroup size is 100, the total count of non-conformities is 835, and the number of subgroups is 22, what are the new control limits and central line?

24. Construct a control chart for the data in the table for empty bottle inspections of a soft-drink manufacturer. Assume assignable causes for any points that are out of control.

C Chart

NUMBER OF BOTTLES	CHIPS, SCRATCHES, OTHER	FOREIGN MATERIAL ON SIDES	FOREIGN MATERIAL ON BOTTOM	TOTAL NONCONFORMITIES
40	9	9	27	45
40	10	1	29	40
40	8	0	25	33
40	8	2	33	43
40	10	6	46	62
52	12	16	51	79
52	15	2	43	60
52	13	2	35	50
52	12	2	59	73
52	11	1	42	54
52	15	15	25	55
52	12	5	57	74
52	14	2	27	43
52	12	7	42	61
40	11	2	30	43
40	9	4	19	32
40	5	6	34	45
40	8	11	14	33

NUMBER OF BOTTLES	CHIPS, SCRATCHES, OTHER	FOREIGN MATERIAL ON SIDES	FOREIGN MATERIAL ON BOTTOM	TOTAL NONCONFORMITIES
40	3	9	38	50
40	9	9	10	28
52	13	8	37	58
52	11	5	30	46
52	14	10	47	71
52	12	3	41	56
52	12	2	28	42

25. Assuming that a 10:5:1 demerit weighting system is used, determine the central line and control limits when $u_c = 0.11$, $u_{ma} = 0.70$, $u_{mi} = 4.00$, and $n = 50$. If the subgroup inspection results for a particular day are 1 critical, 35 major, and 110 minor nonconformities, determine if the results are in control or out of control.

26. Test, and if necessary rewrite, the computer program for your computer.

27. Modify the computer program to output the central line and control limits for your graphical output device. Also, write the program to plot the subgroup values.

28. Write a computer program for:
    (a) c and u charts
    (b) D chart
    (c) p chart for a variable subgroup size
    (e) np chart

6

LOT-BY-LOT ACCEPTANCE SAMPLING BY ATTRIBUTES

FUNDAMENTAL CONCEPTS

Description

Lot-by-lot acceptance sampling by attributes is the most common type of sampling. With this type of sampling, a predetermined number of units (sample) from each lot is inspected by attributes. If the number of nonconforming units is less than the prescribed minimum, the lot is accepted; if not, the lot is rejected as being below standard. Acceptance sampling can be used either for the number of nonconforming units or for nonconformities per unit. To simplify the presentation in this chapter, the number of nonconforming units is used; however, it is understood that the information is also applicable to nonconformities per unit. Sampling plans are established by severity (critical, major, minor) or on a demerit-per-unit basis.

A single sampling plan is defined by the lot size, N, the sample size, n, and the acceptance number, c. Thus, the plan

life threatening   fitness   more Demerits
                   for use.   " severe

$$N = 9000$$

$$n = 300$$

$$c = 2$$

means that a lot of 9000 units has 300 units inspected. And if two or fewer nonconforming units are found in the 300-unit sample, the lot is accepted. If three or more nonconforming units are found in the 300-unit sample, the lot is rejected.

Acceptance sampling can be performed in a number of different situations where there is a consumer-producer relationship. The consumer and producer can be from two different companies, two plants within the same company, or two departments within the same plant. In any case, there is always the problem of deciding whether to accept or reject the product.

Acceptance sampling of the product is most likely to be used in one of five situations.

1. When the test is destructive (such as a test on an electrical fuse or a tensile test), sampling is necessary; otherwise, all of the product will be destroyed by testing.

2. When the cost of 100% inspection is high in relation to the cost of passing a nonconforming unit.

3. When there are many similar units to be inspected, sampling will produce as good, if not better, results than 100% inspection. This is true because with manual inspection, fatigue and boredom cause a higher percentage of nonconforming material to be passed than would occur on the average using a sampling plan.

4. When information concerning producer's quality, such as $\bar{X}$ and R, p or c charts, is not available.

5. When automated inspection is not available.

Advantages and Disadvantages of Sampling

When sampling is compared with 100% inspection, it has the following advantages:

1. Places responsibility for quality in the appropriate place rather than inspection, thereby encouraging rapid improvement in the product.

2. More economical owing to fewer inspections (fewer inspectors) and less handling damage during inspection.

3. Upgrading the inspection job from monotonous piece-by-piece decisions to lot-by-lot decisions.

4. Applicable to destructive testing.

5. Rejection of entire lots rather than the return of nonconforming units, thereby providing stronger motivation for improvement.

Inherent disadvantages of acceptance sampling are:

1. There are certain risks of rejecting acceptable lots and accepting unacceptable lots.

2. More time and effort is devoted to planning and documentation.

3. Less information is provided about the product, although there is usually enough.

4. It will not give assurance that the entire lot conforms to specifications.

Types of Sampling Plans

There are three types of sampling plans: single, double, and multiple. In the single sampling plan, one sample is taken from the lot and a decision to reject or accept the lot is made based on the inspection results of that sample. This type of sampling plan was described earlier in the chapter.

Double sampling plans are somewhat more complicated. On the initial sample a decision, based on the inspection results, is made whether (1) to accept the lot, (2) to reject the lot, or (3) to take another sample. If the quality is very good the lot is accepted on the first sample and a second sample is not taken; if the quality is very poor the lot is rejected on the first sample and a second sample is not taken. Only when the quality level is neither very good nor very bad is a second sample taken.

If a second sample is required, the results of that inspection and the first inspection are used to reject or accept the lot. A double sampling plan is defined by

N = lot size

n_1 = sample size on the first sample

c_1 = acceptance number on the first sample

(sometimes the symbol Ac is used)

r_1 = rejection number on the first sample

(sometimes the symbol Re is used)

n_2 = sample size on the second sample

c_2 = acceptance number for *both* samples

r_2 = rejection number for *both* samples

If values are not given for r_1 and r_2, they are equal to $c_2 + 1$.

An illustrative example will help to clarify the double sampling plan: $N = 9000$, $n_1 = 60$, $c_1 = 1$, $r_1 = 5$, $n_2 = 150$, $c_2 = 6$, and $r_2 = 7$. An initial sample (n_1) of 60 is selected from the lot (N) of 9000 and inspected. One of the following judgments is made:

1. If there are 1 or fewer nonconforming units (c_1), the lot is accepted.

2. If there are 5 or more nonconforming units (r_1), the lot is rejected.

3. If there are 2, 3, or 4 nonconforming units no decision is made and a second sample is taken.

A second sample of 150 (n_2) from the lot (N) is inspected, and one of the following judgments is made:

1. If there are 6 or fewer nonconforming units (c_2) in both samples, the lot is accepted. This number (6 or fewer) is obtained by 2 in the first sample and 4 or fewer in the second sample, by 3 in the first sample and 3 or fewer in the second sample, or by 4 in the first sample and 2 or fewer in the second sample.

2. If there are 7 or more nonconforming units (r_2) in both samples, the lot is rejected. This number (7 or more) is obtained by 2 in the first sample and 5 or more in the second sample, by 3 in the first sample and 4 or more in the second sample, or by 4 in the first sample and 3 or more in the second sample.

A multiple sampling plan is a continuation of double sampling in that three, four, five, or as many samples as desired can be established. Sample sizes are much smaller. The technique is the same as that described for double sampling; therefore, a detailed description is not given. Multiple sampling plans can be truncated after any specific number of samples or can continue until the lot is exhausted or a decision made. Examples of multiple sampling plans are illustrated later in the chapter.

All three types of sampling plans can give the same results; therefore, the chance of a lot being accepted under a single sampling plan is the same under the appropriate double or multiple sampling plan. Thus, the type of plan for a particular unit is based on factors other than effectiveness. These factors are simplicity, administrative costs, quality information, number of units inspected, and psychological impact.

Perhaps the most important factor is simplicity. In this regard, single sampling is the best and multiple sampling the poorest.

Administrative costs for training, inspection, record keeping, and so on, are least for single sampling, greater for double sampling, and greatest for multiple sampling.

Single sampling provides more information concerning the quality level in each lot than double sampling and much more than multiple sampling.

In general, the number of units inspected is more under single sampling than double sampling provided the lot quality is such that second samples are needed only occasionally. Multiple sampling generally requires fewer units inspected than double sampling provided that the decision to accept or reject the lot is made at an early stage in the sampling process.

A fifth factor concerns the psychological impact of the three types of sampling plans. Under single sampling there is no second chance; however, in double sampling, if the first sample is borderline, a second chance is possible by taking another sample. Many producers like the second-chance psychology provided by the double sample. In multiple sampling there are a number of "second chances"; therefore, the psychological impact is less than with double sampling.

Careful consideration of the five factors is necessary to select a type of sampling plan that will be best for the particular situation.

Formation of Lots

Lot formation can influence the effectiveness of the sampling plan. Guidelines are as follows:

1. Lots should be homogeneous, which means that all product in the lot is produced by the same machine, same operator, same input material, and so on. When product from different sources is mixed, the sampling plan does not function properly. Also, it is difficult to take corrective action to eliminate the source of nonconforming product.

2. Lots should be as large as possible. Since sample sizes do not increase as rapidly as lot sizes, a lower inspection cost results with larger lot sizes. For example, a lot of 2000 would have a sample size of 125 (6.25%), while an equally effective sampling plan for a lot of 4000 would have a sample size of 200 (5.00%). When an organization starts a just-in-time procurement philosophy, the lot sizes are usually reduced to a 2- or 3-day supply. Thus, the relative amount inspected and the inspection costs will increase. The benefits to just-in-time are far greater than the increase in inspection costs; therefore, smaller lot sizes are to be expected.

The reader is cautioned not to confuse the packaging requirements for shipment and materials handling with the concept of a homogeneous lot. In other words, a lot may consist of a number of packages and may also consist of a number of shipments. If two different machines and/or two different operators are included in a shipment, they are separate lots and should be so identified. The reader should also be aware that partial shipments of a homogeneous lot, can be treated as if they are homogeneous lots.

Sample Selection

The sample units selected for inspection should be representative of the entire lot. All sampling plans are based on the premise that each unit in the lot has an equal likelihood of being selected. This is referred to as *random sampling*.

The basic technique of random sampling is to assign a number to each unit in the lot. Then a series of random numbers is generated that tells which of the numbered units are to be sampled and inspected. Random numbers can be generated from a computer, electronic hand calculator, 20-sided random-number die, numbered chips in a bowl, and so on. They may be used to select the sample or to develop a table of random numbers.

A random-number table is shown in Table D of the appendix. A portion of Table D is reproduced here as Table 6-1. To use the table it is entered at random and numbers selected sequentially from one direction, such as up, down, left, or right. Any number that is not appropriate is discarded. For locating convenience, this table is established with 5 digits per column. It could have been established with 2, 3, 6, or any number per column. In fact, the digits could have run across the page with no

TABLE 6-1 Random Numbers

74972	38712	36401	45525	40640	16281	13554	79945
75906	91807	56827	30825	40113	08243	08459	28364
29002	46453	25653	06543	27340	10493	60147	15702
80033	69828	88215	27191	23756	54935	13385	22782
25348	04332	18873	96927	64953	99337	68689	03263

spaces, but that format would make the table difficult to read. Any number of digits can be used for a random number.

An example will help to illustrate the technique. Assume that a lot of 90 units has been assigned numbers from 1 to 90 and it is desired to select a sample of 8. A two-digit number is selected at random, as indicated by the number 53. Numbers are selected downward and the first three numbers are 53, 15, and 73. Starting at the top of the next column the numbers 45, 30, 06, 27, and 96 are obtained. The number 96 is too high and is discarded. The next numbers are 52 and 82. Units with the numbers 53, 15, 73, 45, 30, 06, 52, and 82 comprise the sample.

Many products have serial numbers that can be used as the assigned number. This practice avoids the difficult process of assigning numbers to each unit. In many situations, units are systematically packed in a container and the assigned number can be designated by the location. A three-digit number would represent the width, height and depth in a container as shown in Figure 6-1. Thus, the random number 328 could specify the unit located at the third row, second level, and eighth unit from the front. For fluid or other well-mixed products, the sample can be taken from any location, since the product is presumed to be homogeneous.

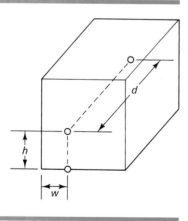

FIGURE 6-1 **Location and random numbers.**

It is not always practical to assign a number to each unit, utilize a serial number, or utilize a locational number. Stratification of the lot or package with samples drawn from each stratum can be an effective substitute for random sampling. The technique is to divide the lot or package into strata or layers as shown in Figure 6-2.

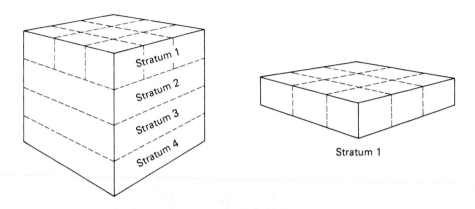

FIGURE 6-2   Dividing a lot for stratified sampling.

Each stratum is further subdivided into cubes, as illustrated by stratum 1. Within each cube, samples are drawn from the entire volume. The dividing of the lot or package into strata and cubes within each stratum is an imaginary process done by the inspector. By this technique pieces are selected from all locations in the lot or package.

Unless an adequate sampling method is used, a variety of biases can occur. An example of a biased sample occurs when the operator makes sure that units on the top of a lot are the best quality, and the inspector selects his or her sample from the same location. Adequate supervision of operators and inspectors is necessary to ensure that no bias occurs.

Rejected Lots

Once a lot has been rejected, there are a number of courses of action that can be taken.

1. The rejected lot can be passed to the production facilities and the nonconforming units sorted by production personnel. This action is not a satisfactory alternative since it defeats the purpose of sampling inspection and slows production. However, if the units are badly needed, there may be no other choice.

2. The rejected lot can be rectified at the consumer's plant by personnel from either the producer's or the consumer's plant. While shipping costs are saved, there is a psychological disadvantage, since all the consumer's personnel are aware that producer X had product rejected. This fact may be used as a crutch to explain poor performance when using producer X's material at a future time. In addition, space at the consumer's plant must be provided for personnel to perform the sorting operation.

3. The rejected lot can be returned to the producer for rectification. This is the only appropriate course of action, since it results in long-run improvement in the

quality. Since shipping costs are paid in both directions for a rejected lot, cost becomes a motivating factor to improve the quality. Also, when the lot is sorted in the producer's plant, all the employees are aware that consumer Y expects to receive a quality product. This, too, is a motivating factor for quality improvement the next time an order is run for consumer Y. This course of action may require the production line to be shut down, which would be a loud and clear signal to the supplier and operating personnel that quality is important.

It is assumed that rejected lots will receive 100% inspection and the nonconforming units discarded. A resubmitted lot is not normally reinspected, but if it is, the inspection should be confined to the original nonconformity. Since the nonconforming units are discarded, a resubmitted lot will have fewer units than the original.

STATISTICAL ASPECTS

OC Curve for Single Sampling Plans

An excellent evaluation technique is an *operating characteristic* (OC) *curve*. In judging a particular sampling plan, it is desirable to know the probability that a lot submitted with a certain percent nonconforming, $100p_0$, will be accepted or rejected. The OC curve will provide this information, and a typical OC curve is shown in Fig-

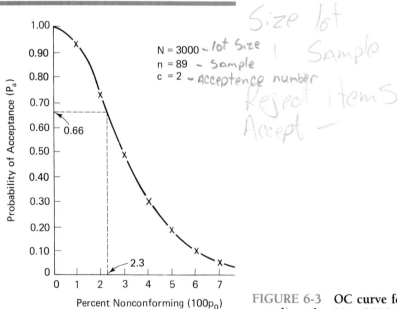

FIGURE 6-3 OC curve for the single sampling plan $N = 3000$, $n = 89$, and $c = 2$.

ure 6-3. When the percent nonconforming is low, the probability of the lot being accepted is large and decreases as the percent nonconforming increases.

The construction of an OC curve can be illustrated by a concrete example. A single sampling plan has a lot of size $N = 3000$, a sample size $n = 89$, and an acceptance number $c = 2$. It is assumed that the lots are from a steady stream of product that can be considered infinite, and therefore the binomial probability distribution can be used for the calculations. Fortunately, the Poisson is an excellent approximation to the binomial for almost all sampling plans; therefore, the Poisson is used for determining the probability of the acceptance of a lot.

In graphing the curve with the variables P_a (probability of acceptance) and $100p_0$ (percent nonconforming), one value $100p_0$ will be assumed and the other calculated. For illustrative purposes we will assume a $100p_0$ value of 2%, which gives an np_0 value of

$$p_0 = 0.02$$

$$np_0 = (89)(0.02) = 1.8$$

Acceptance of the lot is based on the acceptance number $c = 2$ and is possible when there are 0 nonconforming units in the sample, 1 nonconforming unit in the sample, or 2 nonconforming units in the sample. Thus

$$P_a = P_0 + P_1 + P_2$$

$$= P_2 \text{ or less}$$

$$= 0.731$$

The P_a value is obtained from Table C for $c = 2$ and $np_0 = 1.8$.

A table can be used to assist with the calculations, as shown in Table 6-2. The curve is terminated when the P_a value is close to 0.05. Since $P_a = 0.055$ for $100p_0 = 7\%$, it is not necessary to make any calculations for values greater than 7%. Approximately seven points are needed to describe the curve with a greater concentration of points where the curve changes direction.

Information from the table is plotted to obtain the OC curve shown in Figure 6-3. The steps are: (1) assume p_0 value, (2) calculate np_0 value, (3) attain P_a values

TABLE 6-2   Probabilities of Acceptance for the Single Sampling Plan: $n = 89$, $c = 2$

ASSUMED PROCESS QUALITY		SAMPLE		PROBABILITY OF ACCEPTANCE,
p_0	$100p_0$	SIZE, n	np_0	P_a
0.01	1.0	89	0.9	0.938
0.02	2.0	89	1.8	0.731
0.03	3.0	89	2.7	0.494
0.04	4.0	89	3.6	0.302
0.05	5.0	89	4.5	0.174
0.06	6.0	89	5.3	0.106
0.07	7.0	89	6.2	0.055*

*By interpolation.

from the Poisson table using the applicable c and np_0 values, (4) plot point $(100p_0, P_a)$, and (5) repeat 1, 2, 3, and 4 until a smooth curve is obtained.

Once the curve is constructed, it shows the chance of a lot being accepted for a particular incoming quality. Thus, if the incoming process quality is 2.3% nonconforming, the probability of the lot being accepted is 0.66. Similarly, if 55 lots, from a process that is 2.3% nonconforming, are inspected using this sampling plan, 36 $[(55)(0.66) = 36.3]$ will be accepted and 19 $[55 - 36 = 19]$ will be rejected.

This OC curve is unique to the sampling plan defined by $N = 3000$, $n = 89$, and $c = 2$. If this sampling plan does not give the desired effectiveness, then the sampling plan should be changed and a new OC curve constructed and evaluated.

OC Curve for Double Sampling Plans

The construction of an OC curve for double sampling plans is somewhat more involved since two curves must be determined. One curve is for the probability of acceptance on the first sample; the second curve is the probability of acceptance on the combined samples.

A typical OC curve is shown in Figure 6-4 for the double sampling plan $N = 2400$, $n_1 = 150$, $c_1 = 1$, $r_1 = 4$, $n_2 = 200$, $c_2 = 5$, and $r_2 = 6$. The first step in the construction of the OC curve is to determine the equations. If there is one or fewer nonconforming units on the first sample, the lot is accepted. Symbolically, the

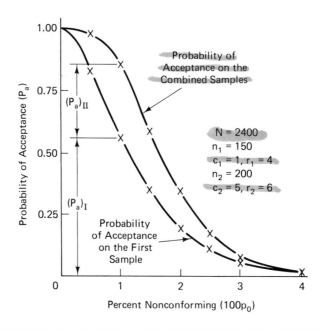

FIGURE 6-4   OC curve for double sampling plan.

equation is

$$(P_a)_\text{I} = (P_\text{1 or less})_\text{I}$$

To obtain the equation for the second sample, the number of different ways in which the lot can be accepted is determined. A second sample is taken only if there are two or three nonconforming units on the first sample. If there is one or less, the lot is accepted; if there are four or more, the lot is rejected. Therefore, the lot can be accepted by obtaining:

1. two nonconforming units on the first sample *and* three or less nonconforming units on the second sample,
2. *or* three nonconforming units on the first sample *and* two or less nonconforming units on the second sample.

The and's and or's are emphasized above to illustrate the use of the additive and multiplicative theorems, which were discussed in Chapter 4. Where an "and" occurs, multiply, and where an "or" occurs, add and the equation becomes

$$(P_a)_\text{II} = (P_2)_\text{I}(P_\text{3 or less})_\text{II} + (P_3)_\text{I}(P_\text{2 or less})_\text{II}$$

Roman numerals are used as a subscript for the sample number. The equations derived above are applicable only to this double sampling plan; another plan will require a different set of equations. Figure 6-5 graphically illustrates the technique. Note that the number of nonconforming units in each term in the second equation is equal to or less than the acceptance number, c_2. By combining the equations, the probability of acceptance for the combined samples is obtained:

$$(P_a)_\text{combined} = (P_a)_\text{I} + (P_a)_\text{II}$$

Once the equations are obtained, the OC curves are found by assuming various p_0 values and calculating the respective first and second sample P_a values. For example, using Table C of the appendix and assuming a p_0 value of 0.01 ($100p_0 = 1.0$),

$$(np_0)_\text{I} = (150)(0.01) = 1.5$$

$$(P_a)_\text{I} = (P_\text{1 or less})_\text{I} = 0.558$$

$$(np_0)_\text{II} = (200)(0.01) = 2.0$$

$$(P_a)_\text{II} = (P_2)_\text{I}(P_\text{3 or less})_\text{II} + (P_3)_\text{I}(P_\text{2 or less})_\text{II}$$

$$(P_a)_\text{II} = (0.251)(0.857) + (0.126)(0.677)$$

$$(P_a)_\text{II} = 0.300$$

$$(P_a)_\text{combined} = (P_a)_\text{I} + (P_a)_\text{II}$$

$$(P_a)_\text{combined} = 0.558 + 0.300$$

$$(P_a)_\text{combined} = 0.858$$

These results are illustrated in Figure 6-4. When the two sample sizes are different, the np_0 values are different, which can cause a calculating error. Another source of

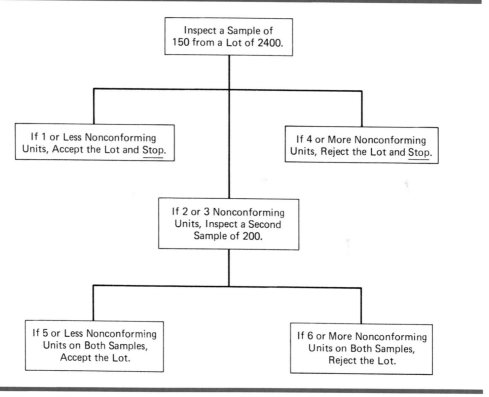

FIGURE 6-5 Graphical description of the double sampling plan: $N = 2400$, $n_1 = 150$, $c_1 = 1$, $r_1 = 4$, $n_2 = 200$, $c_2 = 5$, and $r_2 = 6$.

error is neglecting to use the "or less" probabilities. Calculations are usually to three decimal places. The remaining calculations for other points on the curve are:

For $p_0 = 0.005$ ($100p_0 = 0.5$),

$$(np_0)_\mathrm{I} = (150)(0.005) = 0.75 \qquad (np_0)_\mathrm{II} = (200)(0.005) = 1.00$$

$$(P_a)_\mathrm{I} = 0.826$$

$$(P_a)_\mathrm{II} = (0.133)(0.981) + (0.034)(0.920) = 0.162$$

$$(P_a)_\mathrm{combined} = 0.988$$

For $p_0 = 0.015$ ($100p_0 = 1.5$),

$$(np_0)_\mathrm{I} = (150)(0.015) = 2.25 \qquad (np_0)_\mathrm{II} = (200)(0.015) = 3.00$$

$$(P_a)_\mathrm{I} = 0.343$$

$$(P_a)_\mathrm{II} = (0.266)(0.647) + (0.200)(0.423) = 0.257$$

$$(P_a)_\mathrm{combined} = 0.600$$

For $p_0 = 0.020$ ($100p_0 = 2.0$),

$$(np_0)_I = (150)(0.020) = 3.00 \qquad (np_0)_{II} = (200)(0.020) = 4.00$$

$$(P_a)_I = 0.199$$

$$(P_a)_{II} = (0.224)(0.433) + (0.224)(0.238) = 0.150$$

$$(P_a)_{combined} = 0.349$$

For $p_0 = 0.025$ ($100p_0 = 2.5$),

$$(np_0)_I = (150)(0.025) = 3.75 \qquad (np_0)_{II} = (200)(0.025) = 5.00$$

$$(P_a)_I = 0.112$$

$$(P_a)_{II} = (0.165)(0.265) + (0.207)(0.125) = 0.070$$

$$(P_a)_{combined} = 0.182$$

For $p_0 = 0.030$ ($100p_0 = 3.0$),

$$(np_0)_I = (150)(0.030) = 4.5 \qquad (np_0)_{II} = (200)(0.030) = 6.0$$

$$(P_a)_I = 0.061$$

$$(P_a)_{II} = (0.113)(0.151) + (0.169)(0.062) = 0.028$$

$$(P_a)_{combined} = 0.089$$

For $p_0 = 0.040$ ($100p_0 = 4.0$),

$$(np_0)_I = (150)(0.040) = 6.0 \qquad (np_0)_{II} = (200)(0.040) = 8.0$$

$$(P_a)_I = 0.017$$

$$(P_a)_{II} = (0.045)(0.043) + (0.089)(0.014) = 0.003$$

$$(P_a)_{combined} = 0.020$$

Similar to the construction of the OC curve for single sampling, points are plotted as they are calculated, with the last few calculations used for locations where the curve changes direction. Whenever possible, both sample sizes should be the same value to simplify the calculations and the inspector's job. Also, if r_1 and r_2 are not given, they are equal to $c_2 + 1$.

The steps are: (1) assume p_0 value, (2) calculate $(np_0)_I$ and $(np_0)_{II}$ values, (3) determine P_a value using the three equations and Table C, (4) plot points, and repeat steps 1, 2, 3, and 4 until a smooth curve is obtained.

OC Curve for Multiple Sampling Plans

The construction of an OC curve for multiple sampling plans is more involved than double or single sampling plans; however, the technique is the same. A multiple sampling plan with four levels is illustrated in Figure 6-6 and is specified as:

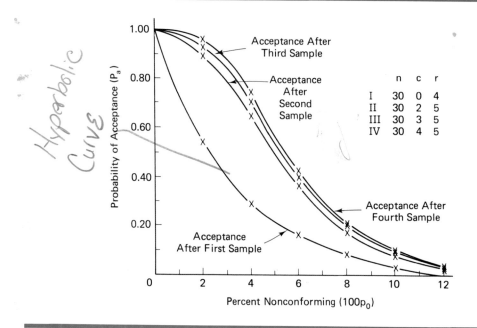

Hyperbolic Curve (handwritten annotation)

FIGURE 6-6　OC curve for multiple sampling plan.

$$N = 3000$$　*reject* (handwritten)

$$n_1 = 30 \qquad c_1 = 0 \qquad r_1 = 4$$

$$n_2 = 30 \qquad c_2 = 2 \qquad r_2 = 5$$

$$n_3 = 30 \qquad c_3 = 3 \qquad r_3 = 5$$

$$n_4 = 30 \qquad c_4 = 4 \qquad r_4 = 5$$

Equations for this multiple sampling plan are: *Number of N.C. that ARE Acceptable* (handwritten)

$$(P_a)_{\mathrm{I}} = (P_0)_{\mathrm{I}}$$

$$(P_a)_{\mathrm{II}} = (P_1)_{\mathrm{I}}(P_{1\,\mathrm{or\,less}})_{\mathrm{II}} + (P_2)_{\mathrm{I}}(P_0)_{\mathrm{II}}$$

$$(P_a)_{\mathrm{III}} = (P_1)_{\mathrm{I}}(P_2)_{\mathrm{II}}(P_0)_{\mathrm{III}} + (P_2)_{\mathrm{I}}(P_1)_{\mathrm{II}}(P_0)_{\mathrm{III}} + (P_3)_{\mathrm{I}}(P_0)_{\mathrm{II}}(P_0)_{\mathrm{III}}$$

$$(P_a)_{\mathrm{IV}} = (P_2)_{\mathrm{I}}(P_2)_{\mathrm{II}}(P_1)_{\mathrm{III}}(P_0)_{\mathrm{IV}} + (P_1)_{\mathrm{I}}(P_3)_{\mathrm{II}}(P_0)_{\mathrm{III}}(P_0)_{\mathrm{IV}}$$

$$+ (P_2)_{\mathrm{I}}(P_1)_{\mathrm{II}}(P_1)_{\mathrm{III}}(P_0)_{\mathrm{IV}} + (P_2)_{\mathrm{I}}(P_2)_{\mathrm{II}}(P_0)_{\mathrm{III}}(P_0)_{\mathrm{IV}}$$

$$+ (P_3)_{\mathrm{I}}(P_0)_{\mathrm{II}}(P_1)_{\mathrm{III}}(P_0)_{\mathrm{IV}} + (P_3)_{\mathrm{I}}(P_1)_{\mathrm{II}}(P_0)_{\mathrm{III}}(P_0)_{\mathrm{IV}}$$

Using the equations above and varying the fraction nonconforming p_0, the OC curve of Figure 6-6 is constructed. This is a tedious task and one that is ideally suited for the computer.

Comment

An operating characteristic curve evaluates the effectiveness of a particular sampling plan. If that sampling plan is not satisfactory, as shown by the OC curve, another one should be selected and its OC curve constructed.

Since the process quality or lot quality is usually not known, the OC curve (as well as other curves in this chapter) are "what if" curves. In other words, if the quality is a particular percent nonconforming, its probability of acceptance can be obtained from the curve.

O.C.

Difference Between Type A and Type B OC Curves

The OC curves that were constructed in the previous sections are type B curves. It was assumed that the lots came from a continuous stream of product, and therefore the calculations are based on an infinite lot size. The binomial is the exact distribution for calculating the acceptance probabilities; however, the Poisson was used, since it is a good approximation. Type B curves are continuous.

Type A OC curves give the probability of accepting an isolated finite lot. With a finite situation the hypergeometric is used to calculate the acceptance probabilities. As the lot size of a type A curve increases, it approaches the type B curve and will become almost identical when the lot size is at least 10 times the sample size ($n/N \leq 0.10$). A type A curve is shown in Figure 6-7, with the small circles representing the discrete data and a discontinuous curve; however, the curve is drawn as a continuous one. Thus, a 4% value is impossible, since it represents 2.6 nonconforming units in the lot of 65 [$(0.04)(65) = 2.6$], but 4.6% nonconforming units are possible, as it represents 3 nonconforming units in the lot of 65 [$(0.046)(65) = 3.0$]. Therefore, the "curve" only exists where the small circles are located.

In comparing the type A and type B curves of Figure 6-7, the type A curve is always lower than the type B curve. When the lot size is small in relation to the sample size, the difference between the curves is significant enough to construct the type A curve.

Unless otherwise stated, all discussion of OC curves will be in terms of type B curves.

OC Curve Properties

Acceptance sampling plans with similar properties can give different OC curves. Four of these properties and the OC curve information are given in the information that follows.

1. *Sample size as a fixed percentage of lot size.* Prior to the use of statistical concepts for acceptance sampling, inspectors were frequently instructed to sample a fixed percentage of the lot. If this value is, say, 10% of the lot size, plans for lot

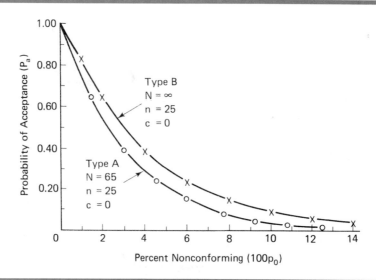

FIGURE 6-7　**Types A and B OC curves.**

sizes of 900, 300, and 90 are:

$$N = 900 \qquad n = 90 \qquad c = 0$$
$$N = 300 \qquad n = 30 \qquad c = 0$$
$$N = 90 \qquad n = 9 \qquad c = 0$$

Figure 6-8 shows the OC curves for the three plans, and it is evident that they offer different levels of protection. For example, for a process that is 5% nonconforming, $P_a = 0.02$ for lot sizes of 900, $P_a = 0.22$ for lot sizes of 300, and $P_a = 0.63$ for lot sizes of 90.

2. *Fixed sample size.* When a fixed or constant sample size is used, the OC curves are very similar. Figure 6-9 illustrates this property for the type A situation were $n \geqq 10\%$ of N. Naturally, for type B curves or when $n < 10\%$ of N, the curves are identical. The sample size has more to do with the shape of the OC curve and the resulting quality protection than does the lot size.

3. *As sample size increases, the curve becomes steeper.* Figure 6-10 illustrates the change in the shape of the OC curve. As the sample size increases, the slope of the curve becomes steeper and approaches a straight vertical line. Sampling plans with large sample sizes are better able to discriminate between acceptable and unacceptable quality. Therefore, the consumer has fewer lots of unacceptable quality accepted and the producer fewer lots of acceptable quality rejected.

4. *As the acceptance number decreases, the curve becomes steeper.* The change in the shape of the OC curve as the acceptance number changes is shown in

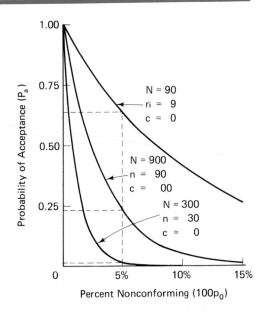

FIGURE 6-8 OC curves for sample sizes that are 10% of the lot size.

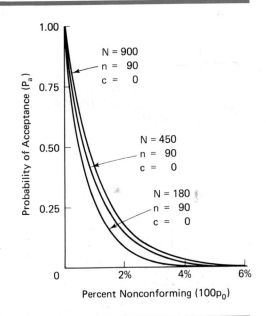

FIGURE 6-9 OC curves for constant sample size (type A).

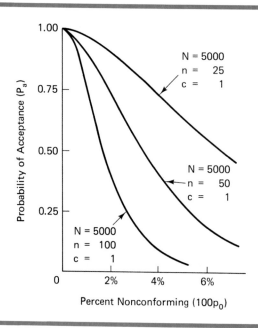

FIGURE 6-10 OC curves illustrating change in sample size.

Figure 6-11. As the acceptance number decreases, the curve becomes steeper. This fact has frequently been used to justify the use of sampling plans with acceptance numbers of zero. However, the OC curve for $N = 2000$, $n = 300$, and $c = 2$, which is shown by the dashed line, is steeper than the plan with $c = 0$. A disadvantage of sampling plans with $c = 0$ is the fact that their curves drop sharply down rather than have a horizontal plateau before descending.

Since this is the area of the producer's risk (discussed in the next section) sampling plans with $c = 0$ are more demanding of the producer. Sampling plans with acceptance numbers greater than zero can actually be superior to those with zero; however, these require a larger sample size which is more costly. In addition, many producers have a psychological aversion to plans that reject lots when only one nonconforming unit is found in the sample. The primary advantage of sampling plans with $c = 0$ is the perception that nonconforming product will not be tolerated.

Consumer-Producer Relationship

When acceptance sampling is used, there is a conflicting interest between the consumer and the producer. The producer wants all acceptable lots accepted and the consumer wants all unacceptable lots rejected. Only an ideal sampling plan that has an OC curve that is a vertical line can satisfy both the producer and consumer. An "ideal" OC curve, as shown in Figure 6-12, can only be achieved with 100% inspection, and the pitfalls of this type of inspection were mentioned earlier in the chapter.

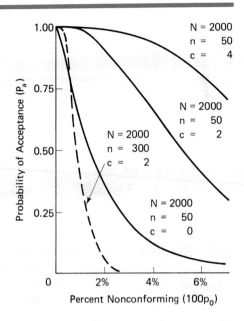

FIGURE 6-11   OC curves illustrating change in acceptance number.

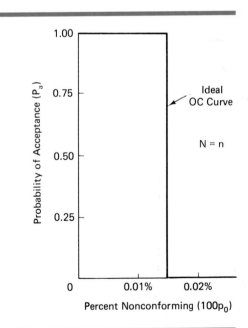

FIGURE 6-12   Ideal OC curve.

Therefore, sampling carries risks of rejecting lots that are acceptable and of accepting lots that are unacceptable. Because of the seriousness of these risks, various terms and concepts have been standardized.

The *producer's risk*, which is represented by the symbol α, is the probability of rejection of a lot that is acceptable. This risk is frequently given as 0.05, but it can range from 0.001 to 0.10 or more. Since α is expressed in terms of the probability of rejection, it cannot be located on an OC curve unless specified in terms of the probability of acceptance. This conversion is accomplished by subtracting from 1. Thus, $P_a = 1 - \alpha$, and for $\alpha = 0.05$, $P_a = 1 - 0.05 = 0.95$. Figure 6-13 shows the producer's risk, α, or 0.05 on an imaginary axis labeled probability of rejection.

Associated with the producer's risk is a numerical definition of an acceptable lot, which is called *acceptable quality level* (AQL). The AQL is the maximum percent nonconforming that can be considered satisfactory for the purposes of acceptance sampling. It is a reference point on the OC curve and is not meant to convey to the producer that any percent nonconforming is acceptable. The only way the producer can be guaranteed that a lot will be accepted is to have zero percent nonconforming or to have the number nonconforming in the lot less than or equal to the acceptance number. In other words, the producer's quality goal is to meet or exceed the specifications so that no nonconforming units are present in the lot.

For the sampling plan $N = 4000$, $n = 300$, and $c = 4$, the AQL = 0.7% for $\alpha = 0.05$, as shown in Figure 6-13. In other words, product that is 0.7% noncon-

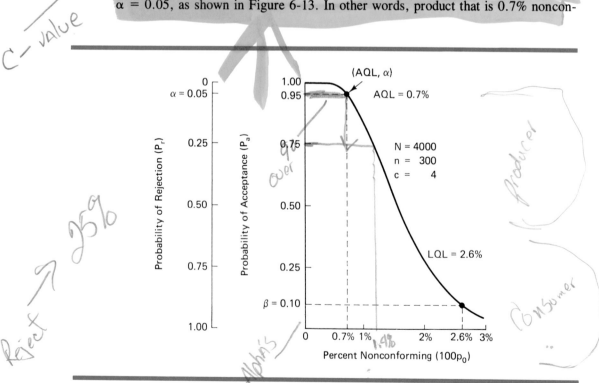

FIGURE 6-13   Consumer-producer relationship.

forming will have a rejection probability of 0.05, or 5%. Or, stated another way, 1 out of 20 lots that are 0.7% nonconforming will be rejected by the sampling plan.

The *consumer's risk*, represented by the symbol β, is the probability of acceptance of an unacceptable lot. This risk is frequently given as 0.10. Since β is expressed in terms of probability of acceptance, no conversion is necessary.

Associated with the consumer's risk is a numerical definition of an unacceptable lot, called *limiting quality level* (LQL). The LQL is the percent nonconforming in a lot or batch for which, for acceptance sampling purposes, the consumer wishes the probability of acceptance to be low. For the sampling plan in Figure 6-13, the LQL = 2.6% for β = 0.10. In other words, lots that are 2.6% nonconforming will have an acceptance probability of 0.10, or 10%. Or, stated another way, 1 out of 10 lots that are 2.6% nonconforming will be accepted by this sampling plan.

Average Outgoing Quality

The *average outgoing quality* (AOQ) is another technique for the evaluation of a sampling plan. Figure 6-14 shows an AOQ curve for the sampling plan N = 3000, n = 89, and c = 2. This is the same plan as the one for the OC curve shown in Figure 6-3.

The information for the construction of an average outgoing quality curve is obtained by adding one column (an AOQ column) to the table used to construct an OC curve. Table 6-3 shows the information for the OC curve and the additional column for the AOQ curve. The average outgoing quality in percent nonconforming is determined by the formula AOQ = $(100p_0)(P_a)$. This formula does not account for the discarded nonconforming units; however, it is close enough for practical purposes and is simpler to use.

Note that to present a more readable graph, the AOQ scale is much larger than

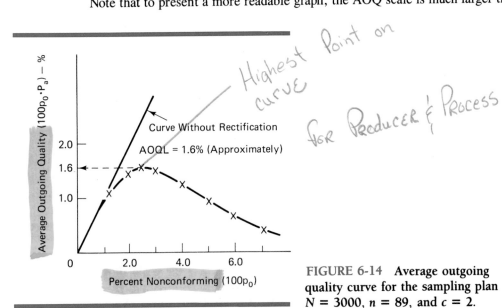

FIGURE 6-14 Average outgoing quality curve for the sampling plan N = 3000, n = 89, and c = 2.

TABLE 6-3   Average Outgoing Quality (AOQ) for the Sampling Plan $N = 3000$, $n = 89$, and $c = 2$

PROCESS QUALITY 100 p_0	SAMPLE SIZE, n	np_0	PROBABILITY OF ACCEPTANCE, P_a	AOQ, $100P_0 \cdot P_A$
1.0	89	0.9	0.938	0.938
2.0	89	1.8	0.731	1.462
3.0	89	2.7	0.494	1.482
4.0	89	3.6	0.302	1.208
5.0	89	4.5	0.174	0.870
6.0	89	5.3	0.106	0.636
7.0	89	6.2	0.055	0.385
2.5[a]	89	2.2	0.623	1.558

[a] Additional point where curve changes direction.

the incoming process quality scale. The curve is constructed by plotting the percent nonconforming ($100p_0$) with its corresponding AOQ value.

The average outgoing quality is the quality that leaves the inspection operation. It is assumed that any rejected lots have been rectified or sorted and returned with 100% good product. When rectification does not occur, the AOQ is the same as the incoming quality, and this condition is represented by the straight line in Figure 6-14.

Analysis of the curve shows that when the incoming quality is 2.0% noncon- forming, the average outgoing quality is 1.46% nonconforming, and when the incoming quality is 6.0% nonconforming, the average outgoing quality is 0.64% nonconforming. Therefore, because rejected lots are rectified, the average outgoing quality is always better than the incoming quality. In fact, there is a limit which is given the name average outgoing quality limit (AOQL). Thus, for this sampling plan, as the percent nonconforming of the incoming quality changes, the average outgoing quality never exceeds the limit of approximately 1.6% nonconforming.

A better understanding of the concept of acceptance sampling can be obtained from an example. Suppose that over a period of time 15 lots of 3000 each are shipped by the producer to the consumer. The lots are 2% nonconforming and a sampling plan of $n = 89$ and $c = 2$ is used to determine acceptance. Figure 6-15 shows this information by a solid line. The OC curve for this sampling plan (Figure 6-3) shows that the probability of acceptance for a 2% nonconforming lot is 0.731. Thus, 11 lots ($15 \times 0.731 = 10.97$) are accepted by the consumer, as indicated by the wavy line. Four lots are rejected by the sampling plan and returned to the pro- ducer for rectification, as shown by the dashed line. These four lots receive 100% inspection and are returned to the consumer with 0% nonconforming, as shown by a dashed line.

A summary of what the consumer actually receives is shown at the bottom of the figure. Two percent, or 240, of the four rectified lots are discarded by the producer, which gives 11,760 rather than 12,000. The calculations show that the

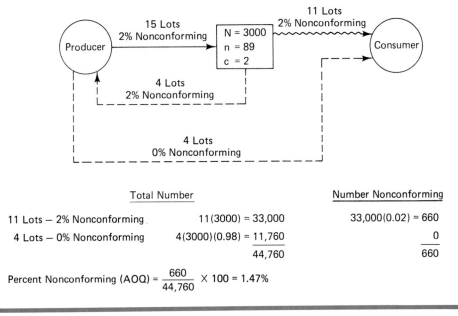

	Total Number	Number Nonconforming
11 Lots — 2% Nonconforming	11(3000) = 33,000	33,000(0.02) = 660
4 Lots — 0% Nonconforming	4(3000)(0.98) = 11,760	0
	44,760	660

Percent Nonconforming (AOQ) = $\dfrac{660}{44,760}$ × 100 = 1.47%

FIGURE 6-15　How acceptance sampling works.

consumer actually receives 1.47% nonconforming, whereas the producer's quality is 2% nonconforming.

It should be emphasized that the acceptance sampling system works only when rejected lots are returned to the producer and rectified. The AQL for this particular sampling plan at α = 0.05 is 0.9%; therefore, the producer at 2% nonconforming is not achieving desired quality level.

The AOQ curve, in conjunction with the OC curve, provides two powerful tools for describing and analyzing acceptance sampling plans.

Average Sample Number

The average sample number (ASN) is a comparison of the average amount inspected per lot by the consumer for single, double, and multiple sampling. Figure 6-16 shows the comparison for the three different but equally effective sampling plan types. In single sampling the ASN is constant and equal to the sample size, n. For double sampling the process is somewhat more complicated because a second sample may or may not be taken.

The formula for double sampling is

$$ASN = n_1 + n_2(1 - P_I)$$

where P_I is the probability of a decision on the first sample. An example problem will illustrate the concept.

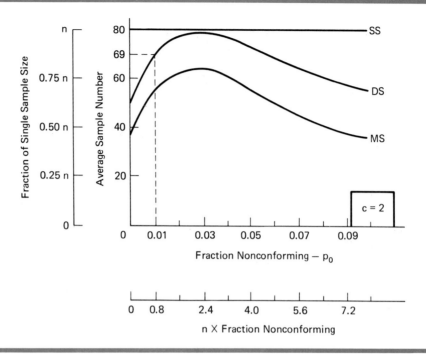

FIGURE 6-16   ASN curves for single, double, and multiple sampling.

EXAMPLE PROBLEM

Given the single sampling plan $n = 80$ and $c = 2$ and the equally effective double sampling plan $n_1 = 50$, $c_1 = 0$, $r_1 = 3$, $n_2 = 50$, $c_2 = 3$, and $r_2 = 4$, compare the ASN of the two by constructing their curves.

For single sampling the ASN is the straight line at $n = 80$. For double sampling the solution is

$$P_I = P_0 + P_{3 \text{ or more}}$$

Assume that $p_0 = 0.01$; then $np_0 = 50(0.01) = 0.5$. From Appendix C:

$$P_0 = 0.607$$

$$P_{3 \text{ or more}} = 1 - P_{2 \text{ or less}} = 1 - 0.986 = 0.014$$

$$\text{ASN} = n_1 + n_2(1 - P_0 - P_{3 \text{ or more}})$$

$$= 50 + 50(1 - 0.607 - 0.014)$$

$$= 69$$

Repeating for different values of p_0, the double sampling plan is plotted as shown in Figure 6-16.

The formula assumes that inspection continues even after the rejection number is reached. It is frequently the practice to discontinue inspection after the rejection number is reached on either the first or second sample. This practice is called curtailed inspection and the formula is much more complicated. Thus, the ASN curve for double sampling is somewhat lower than what actually occurs.

An analysis of the ASN curve for double sampling in Figure 6-16 shows that at a fraction nonconforming of 0.03, the single and double sampling plans have about the same amount of inspection. For fraction nonconforming less than 0.03, double sampling has less inspection because a decision to accept on the first sample is more likely. Similarly, for fraction nonconforming greater than 0.03, double sampling has less inspection because a decision to reject on the first sample is more likely and a second sample is not required. It should be noted that in most ASN curves the double sample curve does not get close to the single sample one.

Calculation of the ASN curve for multiple sampling is much more difficult than double sampling. The formula is

$$\text{ASN} = n_1 P_{\text{I}} + (n_1 + n_2)P_{\text{II}} + \cdots + (n_1 + n_2 + \cdots + n_k)P_k$$

where n_k is the sample size of the last level and P_k the probability of a decision at the last level. Determining the probabilities of a decision at each level is quite involved—more so than for the OC curve since the conditional probabilities must also be determined.

Figure 6-16 shows the ASN curve for an equivalent multiple sampling plan with seven levels. As expected, the average amount inspected is much less than single or double sampling.

The reader may have been curious concerning the two extra scales in Figure 6-16. Since we are comparing equivalent sampling plans, the double and multiple plans can be related to the single sampling plans where $c = 2$ and n is the equivalent single sample size by the additional scales. To use the horizontal scale, multiply the single sample size n by the fraction nonconforming. The ASN value is found from the vertical scale by multiplying the scale fraction with the single sample size.

Figure 6-17, which is taken from MIL-STD-105D (to be discussed), shows a number of ASN curve comparisons indexed by the acceptance number, c. These curves assume no curtailment of inspection and are approximate to the extent that they are based on the Poisson distribution, and that the sample sizes for double and multiple sampling are assumed to be $0.631n$ and $0.25n$, respectively. Therefore, these curves can be used to find the amount inspected per lot for different percent nonconforming without having to make the calculations. The arrow indicates the location of the AQL.

When inspection costs are great due to inspection time, equipment costs, or equipment availability, the ASN curves are a valuable tool for justifying double or multiple sampling.

Average Total Inspection

The average total inspection (ATI) is another technique for evaluating a sampling plan. ATI is the amount inspected by both the consumer and the producer. Like the

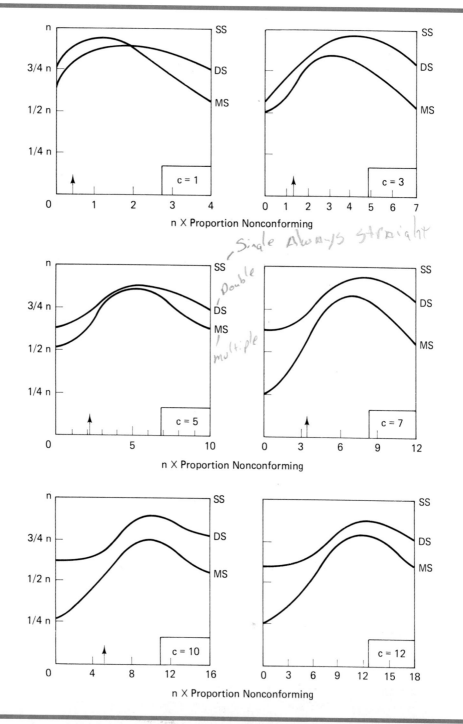

FIGURE 6-17   Typical ASN curves from MIL-STD-105D.

LOT-BY-LOT ACCEPTANCE SAMPLING BY ATTRIBUTES

ASN curve, it is a curve that provides information on the amount inspected and not on the effectiveness of the plan. For single sampling the formula is

$$ATI = n + (1 - P_a)(N - n)$$

It assumes that rectified lots will receive 100% inspection. If lots are submitted with zero percent nonconforming, the amount inspected is equal to n, and if lots are submitted that are 100% nonconforming, the amount inspected is equal to N. Since neither of these possibilities is likely to occur, then the amount inspected is a function of the probability of rejection $(1 - P_a)$. An example problem will illustrate the calculation.

EXAMPLE PROBLEM

Determine the ATI curve for the single sampling plan $N = 3000$, $n = 89$, and $c = 2$.

Assume that $p_0 = 0.02$. From the OC curve (Figure 6-3), $P_a = 0.731$.

$$ATI = n + (1 - P_a)(N - n)$$

$$= 89 + (1 - 0.731)(3000 - 89)$$

$$= 872$$

Repeat for other p_0 values until a smooth curve is obtained, as shown in Figure 6-18.

Examination of the curve shows that when the process quality is close to 0% nonconforming, the average total amount inspected is close to the sample size n. When process quality is very poor, at say 9% nonconforming, most all lots are rejected and the ATI curve becomes asymptotic to 3000. As the percent nonconforming increases, the amount inspected by the producer dominates the curve.

Double sampling and multiple sampling formulas for the ATI curves are more complicated. These ATI curves will be slightly below the one for single sampling. The amount below is a function of the ASN curve, which is the amount inspected by the consumer, and this amount is usually very small in relation to the ATI, which is dominated by the amount inspected by the producer. From a practical viewpoint, the ATI curves for double and multiple sampling are not necessary.

SAMPLING PLAN DESIGN

Sampling Plans for Stipulated Producer's Risk

When the producer's risk α and its corresponding acceptable quality level (AQL) are specified, a sampling plan or, more precisely, a family of sampling plans, can be determined. For a producer's risk, α, of say 0.05 and an AQL of 1.2%, the OC curves for a family of sampling plans as shown in Figure 6-19 are obtained. Each of the

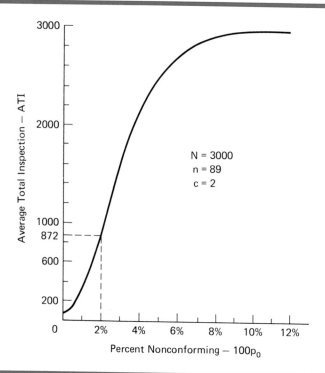

FIGURE 6-18   ATI curve for $N = 3000$, $n = 89$, $c = 2$.

plans passes through the point defined by $P_a = 0.95$ ($\alpha = 0.05$) and $p_{0.95} = 0.012$. Therefore, each of the plans will ensure that product 1.2% nonconforming will be rejected 5% of the time or, conversely, accepted 95% of the time.

The sampling plans are obtained by assuming a value for c and finding its corresponding np_0 value from Table C. Then knowing np_0 and p_0, the sample size n is obtained. In order to find the np_0 values using Table C, interpolation is required. To eliminate the interpolation operation, np_0 values for various α and β values are reproduced in Table 6-4. In this table, c is cumulative, which means that a c value of 2 represents 2 or less.

Calculations to obtain the three sampling plans of Figure 6-19 are as follows:

$$P_a = 0.95 \qquad p_{0.95} = 0.012$$

For $c = 1$, $np_{0.95} = 0.355$ (from Table 6-4) and

$$n = \frac{np_{0.95}}{p_{0.95}} = \frac{0.355}{0.012} = 29.6, \quad \text{or} \quad 30$$

For $c = 2$, $np_{0.95} = 0.818$ (from Table 6-4) and

$$n = \frac{np_{0.95}}{p_{0.95}} = \frac{0.818}{0.012} = 68.2, \quad \text{or} \quad 68$$

LOT-BY-LOT ACCEPTANCE SAMPLING BY ATTRIBUTES

TABLE 6-4   np Values for Corresponding c Values and Typical Producer's and Consumer's Risks

c	$P_a = 0.99$ ($\alpha = 0.01$)	$P_a = 0.95$ ($\alpha = 0.05$)	$P_a = 0.90$ ($\alpha = 0.10$)	$P_a = 0.10$ ($\beta = 0.10$)	$P_a = 0.05$ ($\beta = 0.05$)	$P_a = 0.01$ ($\beta = 0.01$)	RATIO OF $P_{0.10}/P_{0.95}$
0	0.010	0.051	0.105	2.303	2.996	4.605	44.890
1	0.149	0.355	0.532	3.890	4.744	6.638	10.946
2	0.436	0.818	1.102	5.322	6.296	8.406	6.509
3	0.823	1.366	1.745	6.681	7.754	10.045	4.890
4	1.279	1.970	2.433	7.994	9.154	11.605	4.057
5	1.785	2.613	3.152	9.275	10.513	13.108	3.549
6	2.330	3.286	3.895	10.532	11.842	14.571	3.206
7	2.906	3.981	4.656	11.771	13.148	16.000	2.957
8	3.507	4.695	5.432	12.995	14.434	17.403	2.768
9	4.130	5.426	6.221	14.206	15.705	18.783	2.618
10	4.771	6.169	7.021	15.407	16.962	20.145	2.497
11	5.428	6.924	7.829	16.598	18.208	21.490	2.397
12	6.099	7.690	8.646	17.782	19.442	22.821	2.312
13	6.782	8.464	9.470	18.958	20.668	24.139	2.240
14	7.477	9.246	10.300	20.128	21.886	25.446	2.177
15	8.181	10.035	11.135	21.292	23.098	26.743	2.122

Source: Extracted by permission from J. M. Cameron, "Tables for Constructing and for Computing the Operating Characteristics of Single-Sampling Plans," *Industry Quality Control,* 9, No. 1 (July 1952), 39.

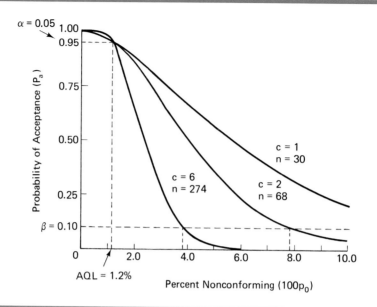

FIGURE 6-19   Single sampling plans for stipulated producer's risk and AQL.

For $c = 6$, $np_{0.95} = 3.286$ (from Table 6-4) and

$$n = \frac{np_{0.95}}{p_{0.95}} = \frac{3.286}{0.012} = 273.9, \quad \text{or} \quad 274$$

The sampling plans for $c = 1$, $c = 2$, and $c = 6$ were arbitrarily selected to illustrate the technique.

While all the plans provide the same protection for the producer, the consumer's risk, at say $\beta = 0.10$, is quite different. From Figure 6-19 for the plan $c = 1$, $n = 30$, product that is 13% nonconforming will be accepted 10% ($\beta = 0.10$) of the time; for the plan $c = 2$, $n = 68$, the product that is 7.8% nonconforming will be accepted 10% ($\beta = 0.10$) of the time; and for the plan $c = 6$, $n = 274$, product that is 3.8% nonconforming will be accepted 10% ($\beta = 0.10$) of the time. From the consumer's viewpoint the latter plan provides better protection; however, the sample size is greater, which increases the inspection cost. The selection of the appropriate plan to use is a matter of judgment, which usually involves the lot size. This selection would also include plans for $c = 0, 3, 4, 5, 7$, and so forth.

Sampling Plans for Stipulated Consumer's Risk

When the consumer's risk β and its corresponding limiting quality level (LQL) are specified, a family of sampling plans can be determined. For a consumer's risk, β, of say 0.10 and a LQL of 6.0%, the OC curves for a family of sampling plans as shown in Figure 6-20 are obtained. Each of the plans pass through the point defined

LOT-BY-LOT ACCEPTANCE SAMPLING BY ATTRIBUTES

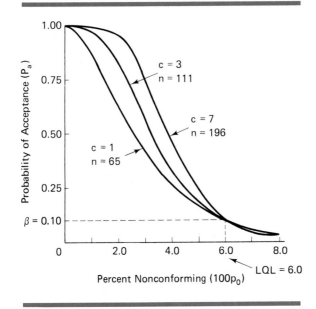

FIGURE 6-20 **Single sampling plans for stipulated consumer's risk and LQL.**

by $P_a = 0.10$ ($\beta = 0.10$) and $p_{0.10} = 0.060$. Therefore, each of the plans will ensure that product 6.0% nonconforming (unacceptable product) will be accepted 10% of the time.

The sampling plans are determined in the same manner as used for a stipulated producer's risk. Calculations are as follows:

$$P_a = 0.10 \qquad p_{0.10} = 0.060$$

For $c = 1$, $np_{0.10} = 3.890$ (from Table 6-4) and

$$n = \frac{np_{0.10}}{p_{0.10}} = \frac{3.890}{0.060} = 64.8, \quad \text{or} \quad 65$$

For $c = 3$, $np_{0.10} = 6.681$ (from Table 6-4) and

$$n = \frac{np_{0.10}}{p_{0.10}} = \frac{6.681}{0.060} = 111.4, \quad \text{or} \quad 111$$

For $c = 7$, $np_{0.10} = 11.771$ (from Table 6-4) and

$$n = \frac{np_{0.10}}{p_{0.10}} = \frac{11.771}{0.060} = 196.2, \quad \text{or} \quad 196$$

The sampling plans for $c = 1$, $c = 3$, and $c = 7$ were arbitrarily selected to illustrate the technique.

While all the plans provide the same protection for the consumer, the producer's risk, at say $\alpha = 0.05$, is quite different. From Figure 6-20 for the plan $c = 1$, $n = 65$, product that is 0.5% nonconforming will be rejected 5% ($\alpha = 0.05$) of the time; for the plan $c = 3$, $n = 111$, product that is 1.2% nonconforming will be rejected 5% ($\alpha = 0.05$) of the time; and for the plan $c = 7$, $n = 196$, product that is 2.0% nonconforming will be rejected 5% ($\alpha = 0.05$) of the time. From the producer's viewpoint the latter plan provides better protection; however, the sample size is greater, which increases the inspection costs. The selection of the appropriate plan is a matter of judgment, which usually involves the lot size. This selection would also include plans for $c = 0, 2, 4, 5, 6, 8$, and so forth.

Sampling Plans for Stipulated Producer's and Consumer's Risk

Sampling plans are also stipulated for both the consumer's risk and the producer's risk. It is difficult to obtain an OC curve that will satisfy both conditions. More than likely there will be four sampling plans that are close to meeting the consumer's and producer's stipulations. Figure 6-21 shows four plans that are close to meeting the stipulations of $\alpha = 0.05$, AQL = 0.9 and $\beta = 0.10$, LQL = 7.8. The OC curves of two plans meet the consumer's stipulation that product which is 7.8% nonconforming (LQL) will be accepted 10% ($\beta = 0.10$) of the time and comes close to the producer's stipulation. These two plans are shown by the dashed lines in Figure 6-21 and are $c = 1$, $n = 50$, and $c = 2$, $n = 68$. The two other plans exactly meet the producer's stipulation that product which is 0.9% nonconforming (AQL) will be rejected 5% ($\alpha = 0.05$) of the time. These two plans are shown by the solid lines and are $c = 1$, $n = 39$, and $c = 2$, $n = 91$.

In order to determine the plans, the first step is to find the ratio of $p_{0.10}/p_{0.95}$, which is

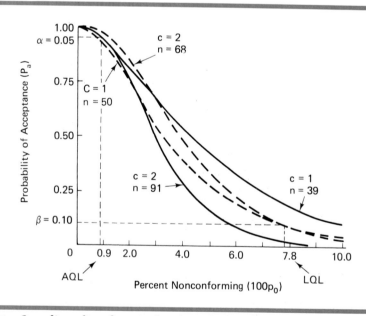

FIGURE 6-21   Sampling plans for stipulated producer's and consumer's risk.

LOT-BY-LOT ACCEPTANCE SAMPLING BY ATTRIBUTES

$$\frac{p_{0.10}}{p_{0.95}} = \frac{0.078}{0.009} = 8.667$$

From the ratio column of Table 6-4, the ratio of 8.667 falls between the row for $c = 1$ and the row for $c = 2$. Thus, plans that exactly meet the consumer's stipulation of LQL = 7.8% for $\beta = 0.10$ are:

For $c = 1$,

$$p_{0.10} = 0.078$$

$$np_{0.10} = 3.890 \qquad \text{(from Table 6-4)}$$

$$n = \frac{np_{0.10}}{p_{0.10}} = \frac{3.890}{0.078} = 49.9, \quad \text{or} \quad 50$$

For $c = 2$,

$$p_{0.10} = 0.078$$

$$np_{0.10} = 5.322 \qquad \text{(from Table 6-4)}$$

$$n = \frac{np_{0.10}}{p_{0.10}} = \frac{5.322}{0.078} = 68.2, \quad \text{or} \quad 68$$

Plans that exactly meet the producer's stipulation of AQL = 0.9% for $\alpha = 0.05$ are:

For $c = 1$,

$$p_{0.95} = 0.009$$

$$np_{0.95} = 0.355 \qquad \text{(from Table 6-4)}$$

$$n = \frac{np_{0.95}}{p_{0.95}} = \frac{0.355}{0.009} = 39.4, \quad \text{or} \quad 39$$

For $c = 2$,

$$p_{0.95} = 0.009$$

$$np_{0.95} = 0.818 \qquad \text{(from Table 6-4)}$$

$$n = \frac{np_{0.95}}{p_{0.95}} = \frac{0.818}{0.009} = 90.8, \quad \text{or} \quad 91$$

Which of the four plans to select is based on one of four additional criteria. The first additional criterion is the stipulation that the plan with the lowest sample size be selected. The plan with the lowest sample size is one of the two with the lowest acceptance number. Thus, for the example problem, only the two plans for $c = 1$ are calculated, and $c = 1$, $n = 39$ is the sampling plan selected. A second additional criterion is the stipulation that the plan with the greatest sample size be selected. The plan with the greatest sample size is one of two with the largest acceptance number. Thus, for the example problem, only the two plans for $c = 2$ are calculated; and $c = 2$, $n = 91$ is the sampling plan selected.

A third additional criterion is the stipulation that the plan exactly meet the consumer's stipulation and comes as close as possible to the producer's stipulation. The two plans that exactly meet the consumer's stipulation are $c = 1$, $n = 50$ and $c = 2$, $n = 68$. Calculations to determine which plan is closest to the producer's stipulation of AQL = 0.9%, $\alpha = 0.05$, are

For $c = 1$, $n = 50$,

$$p_{0.95} = \frac{np_{0.95}}{n} = \frac{0.355}{50} = 0.007$$

For $c = 2$, $n = 68$,

$$p_{0.95} = \frac{np_{0.95}}{n} = \frac{0.818}{68} = 0.012$$

Since $p_{0.95} = 0.007$ is closest to the stipulated value of 0.009, the plan of $c = 1$, $n = 50$ is selected.

The fourth additional criterion for the selection of one of the four sampling plans is the stipulation that the plan exactly meet the producer's stipulation and comes as close as possible to the consumer's stipulation. The two plans that are applicable are $c = 1$, $n = 39$ and $c = 2$, $n = 91$. Calculations to determine which is the closest to the consumer's stipulation of LQL = 7.8%, $\beta = 0.10$ are:

For $c = 1$, $n = 39$,

$$p_{0.10} = \frac{np_{0.10}}{n} = \frac{3.890}{39} = 0.100$$

For $c = 2$, $n = 91$,

$$p_{0.10} = \frac{np_{0.10}}{n} = \frac{5.322}{91} = 0.058$$

Since $p_{0.10} = 0.058$ is closest to the stipulated value of 0.078, the plan of $c = 2$, $n = 91$ is selected.

Some Comments

The previous discussions have concerned single sampling plans. Double and multiple sampling plan design, although more difficult, would follow similar techniques.

In the previous discussion a producer's risk of 0.05 and a consumer's risk of 0.10 were used to illustrate the technique. The producer's risk is usually set at 0.05, but can be as small as 0.01 or as high as 0.15. And the consumer's risk is usually set at 0.10, but can be as low as 0.01 or as high as 0.20.

Sampling plans can also be specified by the average outgoing quality limit (AOQL). If an AOQL of 1.5% for an incoming quality of, say, 2.0% is stipulated, the probability of acceptance is

$$AOQL = 100 p_0 \cdot P_a$$

$$1.5 = 2.0 P_a$$

$$P_a = 0.75$$

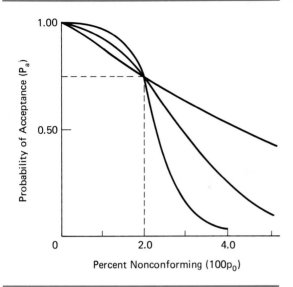

FIGURE 6-22   **AOQL sampling plans.**

Figure 6-22 shows a family of OC curves for various sampling plans which satisfy the AOQL criteria.

To design a sampling plan, some initial stipulations are necessary by the producer, consumer, or both. These stipulations are decisions based on historical data, experimentation, or engineering judgment. In some cases the stipulations are negotiated as part of the purchasing contract.

The task of designing a sampling plan system is a tedious one. Fortunately, sampling plan systems are available. One such system that is almost universally used for the acceptance of product is MIL-STD-105D. This system is an AQL, or producer's risk system. Another system, Dodge-Romig, uses the LQL or consumer's risk and AOQL methods for determining the sampling plan.

MIL-STD-105D AND ANSI/ASQC Z1.4-1981

Introduction

An acceptance sampling plan for lot-by-lot inspection by attributes for use by the government was first devised in 1942 by a group of engineers at Bell Telephone Laboratories. It was designated JAN-STD-105. Since that time, there have been four revisions, the last one occurring in 1963. The last revision was accomplished by a team of American, British, and Canadian personnel and is, therefore, a common standard for the three countries. In 1973, it was adopted by the International Organization for Standardization and designated International Standard ISO/DIS-2859. While MIL-STD-105D was developed for government procurement, it has become the standard for attribute inspection for industry.

Modifications to MIL-STD-105D were made in 1981 by the American Society for Quality Control (ASQC) under the designation ANSI/ASQC Z1.4-1981. All tables and procedures remain unchanged. There are, however, three basic changes:

1. Nonconformity and nonconforming unit are substituted for the words defect and defective.

2. The switching rule that used a limit number for one of the reduced inspection criteria is eliminated.

3. Additional tables for AOQL, LQL, ASN, and OC curves are added. These tables reflect scheme performance, which is the combination of switching among normal, tightened, and reduced sampling plans.

The first two changes are included in the material that follows, but the third is not.

The standard is applicable, but not limited, to attribute inspection of the following: (1) end items, (2) components and raw materials, (3) operations, (4) materials in process, (5) supplies in storage, (6) maintenance operations, (7) data or records, and (8) administrative procedures. Sampling plans of this standard are intended to be used for a continuing series of lots, but plans may be designed for isolated lots by consulting the OC curve to determine the plan with the desired protection.

The standard provides for three types of sampling: single, double, and multiple. For each type of sampling plan, provision is made for normal, tightened, or reduced inspection. Tightened inspection is used when the producer's recent quality history has deteriorated. Acceptance requirements under tightened inspection are more stringent than under normal inspection. Reduced inspection is used when the producer's recent quality history has been exceptionally good. Figure 6-23 illustrates the differences among the OC curves for normal (N), tightened (T), and reduced (R) inspection.

The number inspected under reduced inspection is less than under normal inspection. The decision as to the type of plan to use (single, double, or multiple) is left to the responsible authority (consumer) but should be based on information given earlier in the chapter. Normal inspection is used at the start of inspection with changes to tightened or reduced inspection being a function of the quality.

Nonconformities are classified as critical, major, or minor. These classifications are given in Chapter 5. Nonconforming units are also classified as critical, major, or minor. A critical nonconforming unit contains one or more critical nonconformities and may contain major or minor nonconformities. A major nonconforming unit contains one or more major nonconformities and may contain minor nonconformities. A minor nonconforming unit contains one or more minor nonconformities.

Product is submitted in homogeneous lots with the manner of presentation and identification designated or approved by the responsible authority (consumer). Samples are selected at random without regard to their quality. Rejected lots are resubmitted after all nonconforming units are removed or nonconformities corrected. The responsible authority will determine whether reinspection should include all types or

LOT-BY-LOT ACCEPTANCE SAMPLING BY ATTRIBUTES

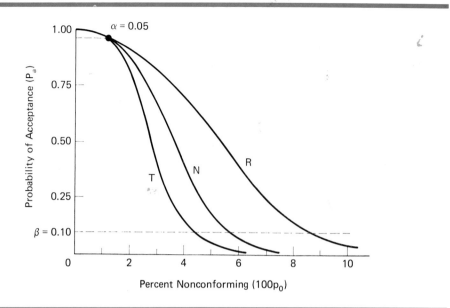

FIGURE 6-23   **Comparison of normal (N), tightened (T), and reduced (R) inspection.**

classes of nonconformities or for the particular types or classes of nonconformities that caused initial rejection.

Acceptable Quality Level

The acceptable quality level (AQL) is the most important part of the standard because the AQL and the sample-size code letter index the sampling plan. AQL is defined as the maximum percent nonconforming (or the maximum number of nonconformities per hundred units) that, for purposes of sampling inspection, can be considered satisfactory as a process average. The phrase "can be considered satisfactory" is interpreted as a producer's risk, α, equal to 0.05; actually, α varies from 0.01 to 0.10 in the standard.

When the standard is used for percent nonconforming plans, the AQLs range from 0.010% to 10.0%. For nonconformity-per-unit plans, there are additional AQLs so AQLs are possible from 0.010 nonconformities per 100 units to 1000 nonconformities per 100 units. The AQLs are in a geometric progression, each being approximately 1.585 times the preceding one.

The AQL is designated in the contract or by the responsible authority. Different AQLs may be designated for groups of nonconformities considered collectively or for individual nonconformities. Critical, major, and minor nonconformities or nonconforming units can have different AQLs, with lower values for critical ones and higher values for minor ones. AQLs are determined from (1) historical data; (2) empirical judgment; (3) engineering information, such as function, safety, interchangeable manufacturing, life testing, etc.; (4) experimentation by testing lots with various percent nonconforming or nonconformities per 100 units; (5) producer's capability; and (6) in some situations the consumer's requirements. AQL determination is a best-judgment decision. The standard helps to determine the AQL since only a finite number are available in the standard. It is a frequent practice to use AQL values of 0.10% or less for critical, 1.00% for major, and 2.5% for minor. The acceptance number for critical should be zero.

The AQL is a reference point on the OC curve. It does not imply that any percent nonconforming or nonconformities per 100 units is tolerable. The only way the producer can be guaranteed that a lot will be accepted is to have zero percent nonconforming or to have the number of nonconforming units less than or equal to the sampling plan acceptance number.

Sample Size

The sample size is determined by the lot size and the inspection level. The inspection level to be used for a particular requirement will be prescribed by the responsible authority. Three general inspection levels (I, II, and III) are given in Table 6-5. The different levels of inspection provide approximately the same protection to the producer, but different protections to the consumer. Inspection level II is the norm, with level I providing about one-half the amount of inspection and level III providing about twice the amount of inspection. Thus, level III gives a steeper OC curve and consequently more discrimination and increased inspection costs. Figure 6-24 illustrates the differences among the OC curves for inspection levels I, II, and III.

The decision on the inspection level is also a function of the type of product. For inexpensive items, for destructive testing, or for harmful testing, inspection level II should be considered. When subsequent production costs are high or when the items are complex and expensive, inspection level III may be applicable.

TABLE 6-5   Sample-Size Code Letters (Table I of MIL-STD-105D)

LOT OR BATCH SIZE	SPECIAL INSPECTION LEVELS				GENERAL INSPECTION LEVELS		
	S-1	S-2	S-3	S-4	I	II	III
2–8	A	A	A	A	A	A	B
9–15	A	A	A	A	A	B	C
16–25	A	A	B	B	B	C	D
26–50	A	B	B	C	C	D	E
51–90	B	B	C	C	C	E	F
91–150	B	B	C	D	D	F	G
151–280	B	C	D	E	E	G	H
281–500	B	C	D	E	F	H	J
501–1200	C	C	E	F	G	J	K
1201–3200	C	D	E	G	H	K	L
3201–10,000	C	D	F	G	J	L	M
10,001–35,000	C	D	F	H	K	M	N
35,001–150,000	D	E	G	J	L	N	P
150,001–500,000	D	E	G	J	M	P	Q
500,001 and over	D	E	H	K	N	Q	R

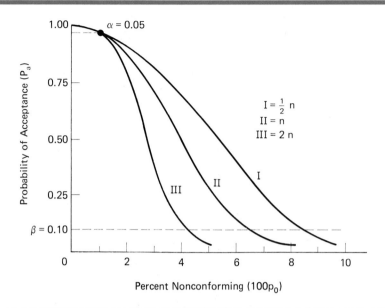

FIGURE 6-24   **Comparison of inspection levels I, II, and III.**

Four additional special levels (S-1, S-2, S-3, and S-4) are given in Table 6-5 and may be used where relatively small sample sizes are necessary and large sampling risks can or must be tolerated.

Table 6-5 does not immediately provide the sample size based on the lot size and inspection level but does give a sample-size code letter. The AQL and the sample-size code letter index the desired sampling plan.

Implementation

The steps required to use the plan are as follows:

1. Determine the lot size (usually the responsibility of materials management).
2. Determine the inspection level (usually level II—it can be changed if conditions warrant).
3. Enter table and find sample-size code letter.
4. Determine the AQL.
5. Determine the type of sampling plan (single, double, or multiple).
6. Enter the appropriate table to find the sampling plan.
7. Start with normal inspection and change to tightened or reduced based on switching rules.

Example problems for single, double, and multiple sampling plans are given in subsequent sections.

MIL-STD-105D AND ANSI/ASQC Z1.4-1981   239

Single Sampling Plans

The single sampling plans of the standard are given in Tables 6-6, 6-7, and 6-8 for normal, tightened, and reduced inspection, respectively. In order to use the tables, the AQL, lot size, inspection level, and type of sampling plan are needed. An example problem will illustrate the technique.

EXAMPLE PROBLEM

For a lot size of 2000, an AQL of 0.65%, and an inspection level of III, determine the single sampling plans for normal, tightened, and reduced inspection.

Normal. Using the lot size $N = 2000$ and inspection level III, the sample-size code letter L is obtained from Table 6-5. From Table 6-6 (Single Sampling Plans for Normal Inspection), the desired plan is obtained for code letter L and AQL 0.65%. It is $n = 200$, Ac = 3, Re = 4. Thus, from a lot of 2000, a random sample of 200 is inspected. If 3 or fewer nonconforming units are found, the lot is accepted; if 4 or more nonconforming units are found, the lot is rejected.

Tightened. The sample-size code letter, L, is the same as the one for normal inspection. From Table 6-7 (Single Sampling Plans for Tightened Inspection), the desired plan is obtained for code letter L and AQL 0.65%. It is $n = 200$, Ac = 2, Re = 3. Thus, from a lot of 2000, a random sample of 200 is inspected. If 2 or less nonconforming units are found, the lot is accepted; if 3 or more nonconforming units are found, the lot is rejected.

Reduced. The sample-size code letter, L, is the same as the one for normal inspection. From Table 6-8 (Single Sampling Plans for Reduced Inspection), the desired plan is obtained for code letter L and AQL 0.65%. It is $n = 80$, Ac = 1, Re = 4. Thus, from a lot of 2000, a random sample of 80 is inspected. If 1 or fewer nonconforming units are found, the lot is accepted; if 4 or more nonconforming units are found, the lot is rejected. If 2 or 3 nonconforming units are found, the lot is accepted, but the type of inspection changes from reduced to normal. A change to normal inspection is also required when a lot is rejected.

In comparing the three plans, notice that the acceptance requirements are more stringent for tightened than for normal inspection. In fact, a sample with 3 defectives is accepted under normal inspection but rejected under tightened inspection. The sample size for reduced inspection is approximately 40% of the sample size of normal or tightened inspection, which represents a considerable saving in sampling costs.

If a vertical arrow is encountered, the first sampling plan above or below the arrow is used. When this occurs, the sample-size code letter and the sample size change. For example, if a single sample tightened plan (Table 6-7) is indexed by an AQL of 4.0% and a code letter D, the code letter changes to F and the sample size

TABLE 6-6 Single Sampling Plans for Normal Inspection (Table II-A of MIL-STD-105D)

Acceptable Quality Levels (normal inspection)

Each cell below shows **Ac Re** (Acceptance number / Rejection number).

Sample size code letter	Sample size	0.010	0.015	0.025	0.040	0.065	0.10	0.15	0.25	0.40	0.65	1.0	1.5	2.5	4.0	6.5	10	15	25	40	65	100	150	250	400	650	1000
A	2	↓	↓	↓	↓	↓	↓	↓	↓	↓	↓	↓	↓	↓	↓	↓	↓	0 1	1 2	2 3	3 4	5 6	7 8	10 11	14 15	21 22	30 31
B	3	↓	↓	↓	↓	↓	↓	↓	↓	↓	↓	↓	↓	↓	↓	↓	0 1	1 2	2 3	3 4	5 6	7 8	10 11	14 15	21 22	30 31	44 45
C	5	↓	↓	↓	↓	↓	↓	↓	↓	↓	↓	↓	↓	↓	↓	0 1	1 2	2 3	3 4	5 6	7 8	10 11	14 15	21 22	30 31	44 45	↑
D	8	↓	↓	↓	↓	↓	↓	↓	↓	↓	↓	↓	↓	↓	0 1	1 2	2 3	3 4	5 6	7 8	10 11	14 15	21 22	30 31	44 45	↑	↑
E	13	↓	↓	↓	↓	↓	↓	↓	↓	↓	↓	↓	↓	0 1	1 2	2 3	3 4	5 6	7 8	10 11	14 15	21 22	30 31	44 45	↑	↑	↑
F	20	↓	↓	↓	↓	↓	↓	↓	↓	↓	↓	↓	0 1	1 2	2 3	3 4	5 6	7 8	10 11	14 15	21 22	30 31	44 45	↑	↑	↑	↑
G	32	↓	↓	↓	↓	↓	↓	↓	↓	↓	↓	0 1	1 2	2 3	3 4	5 6	7 8	10 11	14 15	21 22	30 31	44 45	↑	↑	↑	↑	↑
H	50	↓	↓	↓	↓	↓	↓	↓	↓	↓	0 1	1 2	2 3	3 4	5 6	7 8	10 11	14 15	21 22	30 31	44 45	↑	↑	↑	↑	↑	↑
J	80	↓	↓	↓	↓	↓	↓	↓	↓	0 1	1 2	2 3	3 4	5 6	7 8	10 11	14 15	21 22	30 31	44 45	↑	↑	↑	↑	↑	↑	↑
K	125	↓	↓	↓	↓	↓	↓	↓	0 1	1 2	2 3	3 4	5 6	7 8	10 11	14 15	21 22	30 31	44 45	↑	↑	↑	↑	↑	↑	↑	↑
L	200	↓	↓	↓	↓	↓	↓	0 1	1 2	2 3	3 4	5 6	7 8	10 11	14 15	21 22	30 31	44 45	↑	↑	↑	↑	↑	↑	↑	↑	↑
M	315	↓	↓	↓	↓	↓	0 1	1 2	2 3	3 4	5 6	7 8	10 11	14 15	21 22	30 31	44 45	↑	↑	↑	↑	↑	↑	↑	↑	↑	↑
N	500	↓	↓	↓	↓	0 1	1 2	2 3	3 4	5 6	7 8	10 11	14 15	21 22	30 31	44 45	↑	↑	↑	↑	↑	↑	↑	↑	↑	↑	↑
P	800	↓	↓	↓	0 1	1 2	2 3	3 4	5 6	7 8	10 11	14 15	21 22	30 31	44 45	↑	↑	↑	↑	↑	↑	↑	↑	↑	↑	↑	↑
Q	1250	↓	↓	0 1	1 2	2 3	3 4	5 6	7 8	10 11	14 15	21 22	30 31	44 45	↑	↑	↑	↑	↑	↑	↑	↑	↑	↑	↑	↑	↑
R	2000	↓	0 1	1 2	2 3	3 4	5 6	7 8	10 11	14 15	21 22	30 31	44 45	↑	↑	↑	↑	↑	↑	↑	↑	↑	↑	↑	↑	↑	↑

↓ = Use first sampling plan below arrow. If sample size equals, or exceeds, lot or batch size, do 100 percent inspection.

↑ = Use first sampling plan above arrow.

Ac = Acceptance number.

Re = Rejection number.

TABLE 6-7 Single Sampling Plans for Tightened Inspection (Table II-B of MIL-STD-105D)

(margin annotation, handwritten: "MORE critical")

Acceptable Quality Levels (tightened inspection)

Each data cell lists **Ac Re** (Ac = Acceptance number, Re = Rejection number). ↓ = use first sampling plan below arrow; ↑ = use first sampling plan above arrow.

Code letter	Sample size	0.010	0.015	0.025	0.040	0.065	0.10	0.15	0.25	0.40	0.65	1.0	1.5	2.5	4.0	6.5	10	15	25	40	65	100	150	250	400	650	1000
A	2	↓	↓	↓	↓	↓	↓	↓	↓	↓	↓	↓	↓	↓	↓	↓	↓	↓	0 1	1 2	2 3	3 4	5 6	8 9	12 13	18 19	27 28
B	3	↓	↓	↓	↓	↓	↓	↓	↓	↓	↓	↓	↓	↓	↓	↓	↓	0 1	1 2	2 3	3 4	5 6	8 9	12 13	18 19	27 28	41 42
C	5	↓	↓	↓	↓	↓	↓	↓	↓	↓	↓	↓	↓	↓	↓	↓	0 1	1 2	2 3	3 4	5 6	8 9	12 13	18 19	27 28	41 42	↑
D	8	↓	↓	↓	↓	↓	↓	↓	↓	↓	↓	↓	↓	↓	↓	0 1	1 2	2 3	3 4	5 6	8 9	12 13	18 19	27 28	41 42	↑	↑
E	13	↓	↓	↓	↓	↓	↓	↓	↓	↓	↓	↓	↓	↓	0 1	1 2	2 3	3 4	5 6	8 9	12 13	18 19	27 28	41 42	↑	↑	↑
F	20	↓	↓	↓	↓	↓	↓	↓	↓	↓	↓	↓	↓	0 1	1 2	2 3	3 4	5 6	8 9	12 13	18 19	27 28	41 42	↑	↑	↑	↑
G	32	↓	↓	↓	↓	↓	↓	↓	↓	↓	↓	↓	0 1	1 2	2 3	3 4	5 6	8 9	12 13	18 19	27 28	41 42	↑	↑	↑	↑	↑
H	50	↓	↓	↓	↓	↓	↓	↓	↓	↓	↓	0 1	1 2	2 3	3 4	5 6	8 9	12 13	18 19	27 28	41 42	↑	↑	↑	↑	↑	↑
J	80	↓	↓	↓	↓	↓	↓	↓	↓	↓	0 1	1 2	2 3	3 4	5 6	8 9	12 13	18 19	27 28	41 42	↑	↑	↑	↑	↑	↑	↑
K	125	↓	↓	↓	↓	↓	↓	↓	↓	0 1	1 2	2 3	3 4	5 6	8 9	12 13	18 19	27 28	41 42	↑	↑	↑	↑	↑	↑	↑	↑
L	200	↓	↓	↓	↓	↓	↓	↓	0 1	1 2	2 3	3 4	5 6	8 9	12 13	18 19	27 28	41 42	↑	↑	↑	↑	↑	↑	↑	↑	↑
M	315	↓	↓	↓	↓	↓	↓	0 1	1 2	2 3	3 4	5 6	8 9	12 13	18 19	27 28	41 42	↑	↑	↑	↑	↑	↑	↑	↑	↑	↑
N	500	↓	↓	↓	↓	↓	0 1	1 2	2 3	3 4	5 6	8 9	12 13	18 19	27 28	41 42	↑	↑	↑	↑	↑	↑	↑	↑	↑	↑	↑
P	800	↓	↓	↓	↓	0 1	1 2	2 3	3 4	5 6	8 9	12 13	18 19	27 28	41 42	↑	↑	↑	↑	↑	↑	↑	↑	↑	↑	↑	↑
Q	1250	↓	↓	↓	0 1	1 2	2 3	3 4	5 6	8 9	12 13	18 19	27 28	41 42	↑	↑	↑	↑	↑	↑	↑	↑	↑	↑	↑	↑	↑
R	2000	↓	↓	0 1	1 2	2 3	3 4	5 6	8 9	12 13	18 19	27 28	41 42	↑	↑	↑	↑	↑	↑	↑	↑	↑	↑	↑	↑	↑	↑
S	3150	↓	0 1	1 2	2 3	3 4	5 6	8 9	12 13	18 19	27 28	41 42	↑	↑	↑	↑	↑	↑	↑	↑	↑	↑	↑	↑	↑	↑	↑

↓ = Use first sampling plan below arrow. If sample size equals or exceeds lot or batch size, do 100 percent inspection.
↑ = Use first sampling plan above arrow.
Ac = Acceptance number.
Re = Rejection number.

TABLE 6-8 Single Sampling Plans for Reduced Inspection (Table II-C of MIL-STD-105D)

Acceptable Quality Levels (reduced inspection)†

Each cell below shows the pair "Ac Re" (Acceptance number, Rejection number); ↓ = use first sampling plan below arrow; ↑ = use first sampling plan above arrow.

Code	n	0.010	0.015	0.025	0.040	0.065	0.10	0.15	0.25	0.40	0.65	1.0	1.5	2.5	4.0	6.5	10	15	25	40	65	100	150	250	400	650	1000
A	2	↓	↓	↓	↓	↓	↓	↓	↓	↓	↓	↓	↓	↓	↓	↓	↓	0 1	1 2	2 3	3 4	5 6	7 8	10 11	14 15	21 22	30 31
B	2	↓	↓	↓	↓	↓	↓	↓	↓	↓	↓	↓	↓	↓	↓	↓	0 1	0 2	1 3	2 4	3 5	5 6	7 8	10 11	14 15	21 22	30 31
C	2	↓	↓	↓	↓	↓	↓	↓	↓	↓	↓	↓	↓	↓	↓	0 1	0 2	1 3	1 4	2 5	3 6	5 8	7 10	10 13	14 17	21 24	↑
D	3	↓	↓	↓	↓	↓	↓	↓	↓	↓	↓	↓	↓	↓	0 1	0 2	1 3	1 4	2 5	3 6	5 8	7 10	10 13	14 17	21 24	↑	↑
E	5	↓	↓	↓	↓	↓	↓	↓	↓	↓	↓	↓	↓	0 1	0 2	1 3	1 4	2 5	3 6	5 8	7 10	10 13	14 17	21 24	↑	↑	↑
F	8	↓	↓	↓	↓	↓	↓	↓	↓	↓	↓	↓	0 1	0 2	1 3	1 4	2 5	3 6	5 8	7 10	10 13	14 17	21 24	↑	↑	↑	↑
G	13	↓	↓	↓	↓	↓	↓	↓	↓	↓	↓	0 1	0 2	1 3	1 4	2 5	3 6	5 8	7 10	10 13	↑	↑	↑	↑	↑	↑	↑
H	20	↓	↓	↓	↓	↓	↓	↓	↓	↓	0 1	0 2	1 3	1 4	2 5	3 6	5 8	7 10	10 13	↑	↑	↑	↑	↑	↑	↑	↑
J	32	↓	↓	↓	↓	↓	↓	↓	↓	0 1	0 2	1 3	1 4	2 5	3 6	5 8	7 10	10 13	↑	↑	↑	↑	↑	↑	↑	↑	↑
K	50	↓	↓	↓	↓	↓	↓	↓	0 1	0 2	1 3	1 4	2 5	3 6	5 8	7 10	10 13	↑	↑	↑	↑	↑	↑	↑	↑	↑	↑
L	80	↓	↓	↓	↓	↓	↓	0 1	0 2	1 3	1 4	2 5	3 6	5 8	7 10	10 13	↑	↑	↑	↑	↑	↑	↑	↑	↑	↑	↑
M	125	↓	↓	↓	↓	↓	0 1	0 2	1 3	1 4	2 5	3 6	5 8	7 10	10 13	↑	↑	↑	↑	↑	↑	↑	↑	↑	↑	↑	↑
N	200	↓	↓	↓	↓	0 1	0 2	1 3	1 4	2 5	3 6	5 8	7 10	10 13	↑	↑	↑	↑	↑	↑	↑	↑	↑	↑	↑	↑	↑
P	315	↓	↓	↓	0 1	0 2	1 3	1 4	2 5	3 6	5 8	7 10	10 13	↑	↑	↑	↑	↑	↑	↑	↑	↑	↑	↑	↑	↑	↑
Q	500	↓	↓	0 1	0 2	1 3	1 4	2 5	3 6	5 8	7 10	10 13	↑	↑	↑	↑	↑	↑	↑	↑	↑	↑	↑	↑	↑	↑	↑
R	800	↓	0 1	0 2	1 3	1 4	2 5	3 6	5 8	7 10	10 13	↑	↑	↑	↑	↑	↑	↑	↑	↑	↑	↑	↑	↑	↑	↑	↑

↓ = Use first sampling plan below arrow. If sample size equals or exceeds lot or batch size, do 100 percent inspection.

↑ = Use first sampling plan above arrow.

Ac = Acceptance number.

Re = Rejection number.

† = If the acceptance number has been exceeded, but the rejection number has not been reached, accept the lot, but reinstate normal inspection (see 10.1.4).

changes from 8 to 20. If the vertical arrow points down, it means that the sample size is too small to make a decision; if the vertical arrow points up, it means that a decision can be made with a smaller sample size. In some cases the sample size will exceed the lot size and in those cases 100% inspection is required.

Double Sampling Plans

The double sampling plans of the standard are given in Tables 6-9, 6-10, and 6-11 for normal, tightened, and reduced inspection, respectively. Use of the tables is similar to the technique described under single sampling plans. An example problem will illustrate the technique.

EXAMPLE PROBLEM

non conforming   *Reduced*

For a lot size of 20,000, an AQL of 1.5%, and an inspection level of I, determine the double sampling plans for normal, tightened, and reduced inspection.

Normal. Using the lot size $N = 20{,}000$ and inspection level I, the sample-size code letter K is obtained from Table 6-5. From Table 6-9 (Double Sampling Plans for Normal Inspection), the desired plan is obtained for code letter K and AQL 1.5%. It is:

n	Ac	Re
80	2	5
80	6	7

Thus, from a lot of 20,000, a random sample of 80 is inspected. If 2 or fewer are nonconforming, the lot is accepted; if 5 or more are nonconforming, the lot is rejected. When 3 or 4 nonconforming units are found in the first sample, a second sample of 80 is inspected. If the total number of nonconforming units is 6 or fewer on both samples, the lot is accepted; if 7 or more, the lot is rejected.

Tightened. The sample-size code letter K is the same as the one for normal inspection. From Table 6-10 (Double Sampling Plans for Tightened Inspection), the desired plan is obtained for code letter K and AQL 1.5%. It is:

n	Ac	Re
80	1	4
80	4	5

Thus, from a lot of 20,000, a random sample of 80 is inspected. If 1 or fewer is nonconforming, the lot is accepted; if 4 or more are nonconforming, the lot is rejected. When 2 or 3 nonconforming units are found in the first sample, a

TABLE 6-9   Double Sampling Plans for Normal Inspection (Table III-A of MIL-STD-105D)

Acceptable Quality Levels (normal inspection). Each AQL cell shows "Ac Re".

Sample size code letter	Sample	Sample size	Cumulative sample size	0.010	0.015	0.025	0.040	0.065	0.10	0.15	0.25	0.40	0.65	1.0	1.5	2.5	4.0	6.5	10	15	25	40	65	100	150	250	400	650	1000
A				↓	↓	↓	↓	↓	↓	↓	↓	↓	↓	↓	↓	↓	↓	↓	↓	↓	↓	↓	↓	↓	↓	↓	↓	↓	↓
B	First	2	2	↓	↓	↓	↓	↓	↓	↓	↓	↓	↓	↓	↓	↓	↓	↓	*	0 2	0 3	1 4	2 5	3 7	5 9	7 11	11 16	17 22	25 31
B	Second	2	4	↓	↓	↓	↓	↓	↓	↓	↓	↓	↓	↓	↓	↓	↓	↓	*	1 2	3 4	4 5	6 7	8 9	12 13	18 19	26 27	37 38	56 57
C	First	3	3	↓	↓	↓	↓	↓	↓	↓	↓	↓	↓	↓	↓	↓	↓	*	0 2	0 3	1 4	2 5	3 7	5 9	7 11	11 16	17 22	25 31	↑
C	Second	3	6	↓	↓	↓	↓	↓	↓	↓	↓	↓	↓	↓	↓	↓	↓	*	1 2	3 4	4 5	6 7	8 9	12 13	18 19	26 27	37 38	56 57	↑
D	First	5	5	↓	↓	↓	↓	↓	↓	↓	↓	↓	↓	↓	↓	↓	*	0 2	0 3	1 4	2 5	3 7	5 9	7 11	11 16	17 22	25 31	↑	↑
D	Second	5	10	↓	↓	↓	↓	↓	↓	↓	↓	↓	↓	↓	↓	↓	*	1 2	3 4	4 5	6 7	8 9	12 13	18 19	26 27	37 38	56 57	↑	↑
E	First	8	8	↓	↓	↓	↓	↓	↓	↓	↓	↓	↓	↓	↓	*	0 2	0 3	1 4	2 5	3 7	5 9	7 11	11 16	17 22	25 31	↑	↑	↑
E	Second	8	16	↓	↓	↓	↓	↓	↓	↓	↓	↓	↓	↓	↓	*	1 2	3 4	4 5	6 7	8 9	12 13	18 19	26 27	37 38	56 57	↑	↑	↑
F	First	13	13	↓	↓	↓	↓	↓	↓	↓	↓	↓	↓	↓	*	0 2	0 3	1 4	2 5	3 7	5 9	7 11	11 16	17 22	25 31	↑	↑	↑	↑
F	Second	13	26	↓	↓	↓	↓	↓	↓	↓	↓	↓	↓	↓	*	1 2	3 4	4 5	6 7	8 9	12 13	18 19	26 27	37 38	56 57	↑	↑	↑	↑
G	First	20	20	↓	↓	↓	↓	↓	↓	↓	↓	↓	↓	*	0 2	0 3	1 4	2 5	3 7	5 9	7 11	11 16	17 22	25 31	↑	↑	↑	↑	↑
G	Second	20	40	↓	↓	↓	↓	↓	↓	↓	↓	↓	↓	*	1 2	3 4	4 5	6 7	8 9	12 13	18 19	26 27	37 38	56 57	↑	↑	↑	↑	↑
H	First	32	32	↓	↓	↓	↓	↓	↓	↓	↓	↓	*	0 2	0 3	1 4	2 5	3 7	5 9	7 11	11 16	17 22	25 31	↑	↑	↑	↑	↑	↑
H	Second	32	64	↓	↓	↓	↓	↓	↓	↓	↓	↓	*	1 2	3 4	4 5	6 7	8 9	12 13	18 19	26 27	37 38	56 57	↑	↑	↑	↑	↑	↑
J	First	50	50	↓	↓	↓	↓	↓	↓	↓	↓	*	0 2	0 3	1 4	2 5	3 7	5 9	7 11	11 16	17 22	25 31	↑	↑	↑	↑	↑	↑	↑
J	Second	50	100	↓	↓	↓	↓	↓	↓	↓	↓	*	1 2	3 4	4 5	6 7	8 9	12 13	18 19	26 27	37 38	56 57	↑	↑	↑	↑	↑	↑	↑
K	First	80	80	↓	↓	↓	↓	↓	↓	↓	*	0 2	0 3	1 4	2 5	3 7	5 9	7 11	11 16	17 22	25 31	↑	↑	↑	↑	↑	↑	↑	↑
K	Second	80	160	↓	↓	↓	↓	↓	↓	↓	*	1 2	3 4	4 5	6 7	8 9	12 13	18 19	26 27	37 38	56 57	↑	↑	↑	↑	↑	↑	↑	↑
L	First	125	125	↓	↓	↓	↓	↓	↓	*	0 2	0 3	1 4	2 5	3 7	5 9	7 11	11 16	17 22	25 31	↑	↑	↑	↑	↑	↑	↑	↑	↑
L	Second	125	250	↓	↓	↓	↓	↓	↓	*	1 2	3 4	4 5	6 7	8 9	12 13	18 19	26 27	37 38	56 57	↑	↑	↑	↑	↑	↑	↑	↑	↑
M	First	200	200	↓	↓	↓	↓	↓	*	0 2	0 3	1 4	2 5	3 7	5 9	7 11	11 16	17 22	25 31	↑	↑	↑	↑	↑	↑	↑	↑	↑	↑
M	Second	200	400	↓	↓	↓	↓	↓	*	1 2	3 4	4 5	6 7	8 9	12 13	18 19	26 27	37 38	56 57	↑	↑	↑	↑	↑	↑	↑	↑	↑	↑
N	First	315	315	↓	↓	↓	↓	*	0 2	0 3	1 4	2 5	3 7	5 9	7 11	11 16	17 22	25 31	↑	↑	↑	↑	↑	↑	↑	↑	↑	↑	↑
N	Second	315	630	↓	↓	↓	↓	*	1 2	3 4	4 5	6 7	8 9	12 13	18 19	26 27	37 38	56 57	↑	↑	↑	↑	↑	↑	↑	↑	↑	↑	↑
P	First	500	500	↓	↓	↓	*	0 2	0 3	1 4	2 5	3 7	5 9	7 11	11 16	17 22	25 31	↑	↑	↑	↑	↑	↑	↑	↑	↑	↑	↑	↑
P	Second	500	1000	↓	↓	↓	*	1 2	3 4	4 5	6 7	8 9	12 13	18 19	26 27	37 38	56 57	↑	↑	↑	↑	↑	↑	↑	↑	↑	↑	↑	↑
Q	First	800	800	↓	↓	*	0 2	0 3	1 4	2 5	3 7	5 9	7 11	11 16	17 22	25 31	↑	↑	↑	↑	↑	↑	↑	↑	↑	↑	↑	↑	↑
Q	Second	800	1600	↓	↓	*	1 2	3 4	4 5	6 7	8 9	12 13	18 19	26 27	37 38	56 57	↑	↑	↑	↑	↑	↑	↑	↑	↑	↑	↑	↑	↑
R	First	1250	1250	↓	*	0 2	0 3	1 4	2 5	3 7	5 9	7 11	11 16	17 22	25 31	↑	↑	↑	↑	↑	↑	↑	↑	↑	↑	↑	↑	↑	↑
R	Second	1250	2500	↓	*	1 2	3 4	4 5	6 7	8 9	12 13	18 19	26 27	37 38	56 57	↑	↑	↑	↑	↑	↑	↑	↑	↑	↑	↑	↑	↑	↑

↓ = Use first sampling plan below arrow. If sample size equals or exceeds lot or batch size, do 100 percent inspection.

↑ = Use first sampling plan above arrow.

Ac = Acceptance number.

Re = Rejection number.

* = Use corresponding single sample plan (or alternatively, use double sampling plan below, where available).

245

TABLE 6-10 Double Sampling Plans for Tightened Inspection (Table III-B of MIL-STD-105D)

Acceptable Quality Levels (tightened inspection)

Sample size code letter	Sample	Sample size	Cumulative sample size	0.010 Ac	0.010 Re	0.015 Ac	0.015 Re	0.025 Ac	0.025 Re	0.040 Ac	0.040 Re	0.065 Ac	0.065 Re	0.10 Ac	0.10 Re	0.15 Ac	0.15 Re	0.25 Ac	0.25 Re	0.40 Ac	0.40 Re	0.65 Ac	0.65 Re	1.0 Ac	1.0 Re	1.5 Ac	1.5 Re	2.5 Ac	2.5 Re	4.0 Ac	4.0 Re	6.5 Ac	6.5 Re	10 Ac	10 Re	15 Ac	15 Re	25 Ac	25 Re	40 Ac	40 Re	65 Ac	65 Re	100 Ac	100 Re	150 Ac	150 Re	250 Ac	250 Re	400 Ac	400 Re	650 Ac	650 Re	1000 Ac	1000 Re
A																																																					
B	First	2	2																																								0	2					2	5	3	7	9	14	14	20	20	23	23	24
	Second	2	4																																						1	2					6	7	11	12	23	24	34	35	52	52	53	
C	First	3	3																															0	2					2	5	3	7	6	10	9	14	15	20	23	24				
	Second	3	6																															1	2					6	7	11	12	15	16	23	24	34	35	52	53				
D	First	5	5																										0	2					2	5	3	7	6	10	9	14	15	20	23	24								
	Second	5	10																										1	2					6	7	11	12	15	16	23	24	34	35	52	53								
E	First	8	8																					0	2					2	5	3	7	6	10	9	14	15	20	23	24											
	Second	8	16																					1	2					6	7	11	12	15	16	23	24	34	35	52	53											
F	First	13	13																			0	2					2	5	3	7	6	10	9	14	16	23														
	Second	13	26																			1	2					6	7	11	12	15	16	23	24	23	24														
G	First	20	20																	0	2					2	5	3	7	6	10	9	14																	
	Second	20	40																	1	2					6	7	11	12	15	16	23	24																	
H	First	32	32															0	2					2	5	3	7	6	10	9	14																			
	Second	32	64															1	2					6	7	11	12	15	16	23	24																			
J	First	50	50													0	2					2	5	3	7	6	10	9	14																					
	Second	50	100													1	2					6	7	11	12	15	16	23	24																					
K	First	80	80											0	2					2	5	3	7	6	10	9	14																							
	Second	80	160											1	2					6	7	11	12	15	16	23	24																							
L	First	125	125									0	2					2	5	3	7	6	10	9	14																									
	Second	125	250									1	2					6	7	11	12	15	16	23	24																									
M	First	200	200							0	2					2	5	3	7	6	10	9	14																											
	Second	200	400							1	2					6	7	11	12	15	16	23	24																											
N	First	315	315					0	2					2	5	3	7	6	10	9	14																													
	Second	315	630					1	2					6	7	11	12	15	16	23	24																													
P	First	500	500			0	2					2	5	3	7	6	10	9	14																															
	Second	500	1000			1	2					6	7	11	12	15	16	23	24																															
Q	First	800	800	0	2					2	5	3	7	6	10	9	14																																		
	Second	800	1600	1	2					6	7	11	12	15	16	23	24																																		
R	First	1250	1250					2	5	3	7	6	10	9	14																																				
	Second	1250	2500					6	7	11	12	15	16	23	24																																				
S	First	2000	2000																																																
	Second	2000	4000																																																

⇩ Use first sampling plan below arrow. If sample size equals or exceeds lot or batch size, do 100 percent inspection.

⇧ Use first sampling plan above arrow

Ac = Acceptance number.

Re = Rejection number.

↓ Use corresponding single sampling plan (or alternatively, use double sampling plan below, where available)

* = Use corresponding single sampling plan (or alternatively, use double sampling plan below, where available)

246

TABLE 6-11 Double Sampling Plans for Reduced Inspection (Table III-C of MIL-STD-105D)

Acceptable Quality Levels (reduced inspection)†

Sample size code letter	Sample	Sample size	Cumulative sample size
A			
B			
C			
D	First	2	2
	Second	2	4
E	First	3	3
	Second	3	6
F	First	5	5
	Second	5	10
G	First	8	8
	Second	8	16
H	First	13	13
	Second	13	26
J	First	20	20
	Second	20	40
K	First	32	32
	Second	32	64
L	First	50	50
	Second	50	100
M	First	80	80
	Second	80	160
N	First	125	125
	Second	125	250
P	First	200	200
	Second	200	400
Q	First	315	315
	Second	315	630
R	First	500	500
	Second	500	1000

The body of the table lists the Acceptance (Ac) and Rejection (Re) numbers for each Acceptable Quality Level column: 0.010, 0.015, 0.025, 0.040, 0.065, 0.10, 0.15, 0.25, 0.40, 0.65, 1.0, 1.5, 2.5, 4.0, 6.5, 10, 15, 25, 40, 65, 100, 150, 250, 400, 650, 1000. Each AQL column is subdivided into Ac and Re sub-columns, with First and Second sample values given per code letter. Cells contain directional arrows (↑ = use first sampling plan above arrow; ↓ = use first sampling plan below arrow) and the symbol *. Representative paired acceptance/rejection values read from the diagonal include:

First/Second (Ac Re): 0 2 / 0 2; 0 3 / 1 4; 0 4 / 3 5; 1 5 / 4 6; 2 6 / 7 9; 3 8 / 8 12; 5 10 / 10 16; 5 12; 7 18; 11 22; 12 22; 11 26; 17 30.

Legend:

↓ = Use first sampling plan below arrow. If sample size equals or exceeds lot or batch size, do 100 percent inspection.

↑ = Use first sampling plan above arrow.

Ac = Acceptance number

Re = Rejection number

* = Use corresponding single sampling plan (or alternatively, use double sampling plan below, when available).

† = If, after the second sample, the acceptance number has been exceeded, but the rejection number has not been reached, accept the lot, but reinstate normal inspection (see 10.14).

247

second sample of 80 is inspected. If the total number of nonconforming units is 4 or fewer, the lot is accepted; if 5 or more, the lot is rejected.

Reduced. The sample-size code letter K is the same as the one for normal inspection. From Table 6-11 (Double Sampling Plans for Reduced Inspection), the desired plan is obtained for code letter K and AQL 1.5%. It is:

n	Ac	Re
32	0	4
32	3	6

Thus, from a lot of 20,000, a random sample of 32 is inspected. If 0 is nonconforming, the lot is accepted; if 4 or more nonconforming, the lot is rejected. When 1, 2 or 3 nonconforming units are found in the first sample, a second sample of 32 is inspected. If the total number of nonconforming units is 3 or fewer the lot is accepted; if the total number of nonconforming units is 4 or 5, the lot is accepted, but normal inspection is reinstated; and if the total number of nonconforming units is 6 or more, the lot is rejected and normal inspection is reinstated.

The same comparisons among normal, tightened, and reduced inspection that were given for single sampling plans are applicable to double sampling plans. A change in the sample-size code letter and the sample size as a result of a vertical arrow has the same interpretation for double sampling plans as for single sampling plans.

An asterisk, *, is used in the double sampling tables. In most cases where an asterisk is encountered, the corresponding single sampling plan is applicable because the relationship between the acceptance number and the sample size is unrealistic. In other cases the double sampling plan immediately below the asterisk is applicable, as illustrated in Table 6-9 for plans with code letter A and AQLs from 25 to 1000 nonconformities/100 units.

Multiple Sampling Plans

The multiple sampling plans of the standard provide for seven samples and are given in Tables 6-12, 6-13, and 6-14 for normal, tightened, and reduced inspection, respectively. Use of the tables is similar to the technique described under single and double sampling plans. Because of the similarity, a detailed explanation is not given.

EXAMPLE PROBLEM

For a lot size of 450, an AQL of 4.0%, and an inspection level of II, determine the multiple sampling plans for normal, tightened, and reduced inspection.

(Continued on page 255)

TABLE 6-12 Multiple Sampling Plans for Normal Inspection (Table IV-A of MIL-STD-105D)

Acceptable Quality Levels (normal inspection)

Legend

◇ = Use first sampling plan below arrow (refer to continuation of table on following page, when necessary). If sample size equals or exceeds lot or batch size, do 100 percent inspection.
◇ = Use first sampling plan above arrow.
Ac = Acceptance number.
Re = Rejection number.
* = Use corresponding single sampling plan (or alternatively, use multiple sampling plan below, where available).
‡ = Use corresponding double sampling plan (or alternatively, use multiple sampling plan below, where available).
# = Acceptance not permitted at this sample size.

Sample size code letters A, B and C: no sample sizes given (use arrows / single or double sampling plans per legend). AQL levels to the left of each code's numeric range use the "↓" (plan below) arrow; levels to the right use the "↑" (plan above) arrow. AQL columns 650 and 1000, and 0.010–0.25 (where not shown) carry arrows or the symbols * / ‡ per legend.

Sample size code letter D (sample size 2)

Sample	n	Σn	4.0 Ac Re	6.5 Ac Re	10 Ac Re	15 Ac Re	25 Ac Re	40 Ac Re	65 Ac Re	100 Ac Re	150 Ac Re	250 Ac Re	400 Ac Re
First	2	2	# 2	# 2	# 2	# 3	# 4	# 4	0 5	1 7	2 9	4 12	6 16
Second	2	4	# 2	0 3	0 3	0 3	1 5	1 6	3 8	4 10	7 14	11 19	17 27
Third	2	6	0 2	0 3	0 4	1 4	2 6	3 8	6 10	8 13	13 19	19 27	29 39
Fourth	2	8	0 3	1 4	1 5	2 5	3 7	5 10	8 13	12 17	19 25	27 34	40 49
Fifth	2	10	1 3	1 4	2 5	3 6	5 8	7 11	11 15	17 20	25 29	36 40	53 58
Sixth	2	12	1 3	2 4	3 6	5 7	7 9	10 12	14 17	21 23	31 33	45 47	66 68
Seventh	2	14	2 3	3 4	5 6	7 8	9 10	13 14	18 19	25 26	37 38	54 55	77 78

Sample size code letter E (sample size 3)

Sample	n	Σn	2.5 Ac Re	4.0 Ac Re	6.5 Ac Re	10 Ac Re	15 Ac Re	25 Ac Re	40 Ac Re	65 Ac Re	100 Ac Re	150 Ac Re	250 Ac Re
First	3	3	# 2	# 2	# 2	# 3	# 4	# 4	0 5	1 7	2 9	4 12	6 16
Second	3	6	# 2	0 3	0 3	0 3	1 5	1 6	3 8	4 10	7 14	11 19	17 27
Third	3	9	0 2	0 3	0 4	1 4	2 6	3 8	6 10	8 13	13 19	19 27	29 39
Fourth	3	12	0 3	1 4	1 5	2 5	3 7	5 10	8 13	12 17	19 25	27 34	40 49
Fifth	3	15	1 3	1 4	2 5	3 6	5 8	7 11	11 15	17 20	25 29	36 40	53 58
Sixth	3	18	1 3	2 4	3 6	5 7	7 9	10 12	14 17	21 23	31 33	45 47	66 68
Seventh	3	21	2 3	3 4	5 6	7 8	9 10	13 14	18 19	25 26	37 38	54 55	77 78

Sample size code letter F (sample size 5)

Sample	n	Σn	1.5 Ac Re	2.5 Ac Re	4.0 Ac Re	6.5 Ac Re	10 Ac Re	15 Ac Re	25 Ac Re	40 Ac Re	65 Ac Re	100 Ac Re	150 Ac Re
First	5	5	# 2	# 2	# 2	# 3	# 4	# 4	0 5	1 7	2 9	4 12	6 16
Second	5	10	# 2	0 3	0 3	0 3	1 5	1 6	3 8	4 10	7 14	11 19	17 27
Third	5	15	0 2	0 3	0 4	1 4	2 6	3 8	6 10	8 13	13 19	19 27	29 39
Fourth	5	20	0 3	1 4	1 5	2 5	3 7	5 10	8 13	12 17	19 25	27 34	40 49
Fifth	5	25	1 3	1 4	2 5	3 6	5 8	7 11	11 15	17 20	25 29	36 40	53 58
Sixth	5	30	1 3	2 4	3 6	5 7	7 9	10 12	14 17	21 23	31 33	45 47	66 68
Seventh	5	35	2 3	3 4	5 6	7 8	9 10	13 14	18 19	25 26	37 38	54 55	77 78

Sample size code letter G (sample size 8)

Sample	n	Σn	1.0 Ac Re	1.5 Ac Re	2.5 Ac Re	4.0 Ac Re	6.5 Ac Re	10 Ac Re	15 Ac Re	25 Ac Re	40 Ac Re	65 Ac Re	100 Ac Re
First	8	8	# 2	# 2	# 2	# 3	# 4	# 4	0 5	1 7	2 9	4 12	6 16
Second	8	16	# 2	0 3	0 3	0 3	1 5	1 6	3 8	4 10	7 14	11 19	17 27
Third	8	24	0 2	0 3	0 4	1 4	2 6	3 8	6 10	8 13	13 19	19 27	29 39
Fourth	8	32	0 3	1 4	1 5	2 5	3 7	5 10	8 13	12 17	19 25	27 34	40 49
Fifth	8	40	1 3	1 4	2 5	3 6	5 8	7 11	11 15	17 20	25 29	36 40	53 58
Sixth	8	48	1 3	2 4	3 6	5 7	7 9	10 12	14 17	21 23	31 33	45 47	66 68
Seventh	8	56	2 3	3 4	5 6	7 8	9 10	13 14	18 19	25 26	37 38	54 55	77 78

Sample size code letter H (sample size 13)

Sample	n	Σn	0.65 Ac Re	1.0 Ac Re	1.5 Ac Re	2.5 Ac Re	4.0 Ac Re	6.5 Ac Re	10 Ac Re	15 Ac Re	25 Ac Re	40 Ac Re	65 Ac Re
First	13	13	# 2	# 2	# 2	# 3	# 4	# 4	0 5	1 7	2 9	4 12	6 16
Second	13	26	# 2	0 3	0 3	0 3	1 5	1 6	3 8	4 10	7 14	11 19	17 27
Third	13	39	0 2	0 3	0 4	1 4	2 6	3 8	6 10	8 13	13 19	19 27	29 39
Fourth	13	52	0 3	1 4	1 5	2 5	3 7	5 10	8 13	12 17	19 25	27 34	40 49
Fifth	13	65	1 3	1 4	2 5	3 6	5 8	7 11	11 15	17 20	25 29	36 40	53 58
Sixth	13	78	1 3	2 4	3 6	5 7	7 9	10 12	14 17	21 23	31 33	45 47	66 68
Seventh	13	91	2 3	3 4	5 6	7 8	9 10	13 14	18 19	25 26	37 38	54 55	77 78

Sample size code letter J (sample size 20)

Sample	n	Σn	0.40 Ac Re	0.65 Ac Re	1.0 Ac Re	1.5 Ac Re	2.5 Ac Re	4.0 Ac Re	6.5 Ac Re	10 Ac Re	15 Ac Re	25 Ac Re	40 Ac Re
First	20	20	# 2	# 2	# 2	# 3	# 4	# 4	0 5	1 7	2 9	4 12	6 16
Second	20	40	# 2	0 3	0 3	0 3	1 5	1 6	3 8	4 10	7 14	11 19	17 27
Third	20	60	0 2	0 3	0 4	1 4	2 6	3 8	6 10	8 13	13 19	19 27	29 39
Fourth	20	80	0 3	1 4	1 5	2 5	3 7	5 10	8 13	12 17	19 25	27 34	40 49
Fifth	20	100	1 3	1 4	2 5	3 6	5 8	7 11	11 15	17 20	25 29	36 40	53 58
Sixth	20	120	1 3	2 4	3 6	5 7	7 9	10 12	14 17	21 23	31 33	45 47	66 68
Seventh	20	140	2 3	3 4	5 6	7 8	9 10	13 14	18 19	25 26	37 38	54 55	77 78

TABLE 6-12 (continued)

MIL-STD master table for normal inspection — multiple sampling plans. Acceptable Quality Levels (normal inspection), code letters K through R.

Sample size code letter	Sample	Sample size	Cumulative sample size
K	First	32	32
	Second	32	64
	Third	32	96
	Fourth	32	128
	Fifth	32	160
	Sixth	32	192
	Seventh	32	224
L	First	50	50
	Second	50	100
	Third	50	150
	Fourth	50	200
	Fifth	50	250
	Sixth	50	300
	Seventh	50	350
M	First	80	80
	Second	80	160
	Third	80	240
	Fourth	80	320
	Fifth	80	400
	Sixth	80	480
	Seventh	80	560
N	First	125	125
	Second	125	250
	Third	125	375
	Fourth	125	500
	Fifth	125	625
	Sixth	125	750
	Seventh	125	875
P	First	200	200
	Second	200	400
	Third	200	600
	Fourth	200	800
	Fifth	200	1000
	Sixth	200	1200
	Seventh	200	1400
Q	First	315	315
	Second	315	630
	Third	315	945
	Fourth	315	1260
	Fifth	315	1575
	Sixth	315	1890
	Seventh	315	2205
R	First	500	500
	Second	500	1000
	Third	500	1500
	Fourth	500	2000
	Fifth	500	2500
	Sixth	500	3000
	Seventh	500	3500

Representative acceptance/rejection (Ac/Re) number sets used in the body of the table (cumulative, First → Seventh):

AQL set	First Ac/Re	Second	Third	Fourth	Fifth	Sixth	Seventh
2.5	# / 4	1 / 6	3 / 8	5 / 10	7 / 11	10 / 12	13 / 14
4.0	0 / 5	3 / 8	6 / 10	8 / 13	11 / 15	14 / 17	18 / 19
6.5	1 / 7	4 / 10	8 / 13	12 / 17	17 / 20	21 / 23	25 / 26
10	2 / 9	7 / 14	13 / 19	19 / 25	25 / 29	31 / 33	37 / 38

↓ = Use first sampling plan below arrow. If sample size equals or exceeds lot or batch size, do 100 percent inspection.
↑ = Use first sampling plan above arrow (refer to preceding page, when necessary).
Ac = Acceptance number.
Re = Rejection number.
* = Use corresponding single sampling plan (or alternatively, use multiple sampling plan below, where available).
# = Acceptance not permitted at this sample size.

TABLE 6-13 Multiple Sampling Plans for Tightened Inspection (Table IV-B of MIL-STD-105D)

Acceptable Quality Levels (tightened inspection)

The AQL columns (each with an Ac and Re sub-column) are, left to right:
0.010, 0.015, 0.025, 0.040, 0.065, 0.10, 0.15, 0.25, 0.40, 0.65, 1.0, 1.5, 2.5, 4.0, 6.5, 10, 15, 25, 40, 65, 100, 150, 250, 400, 650, 1000.

Sample size code letters A, B, C: no sample size is tabulated; the cell at the highest AQL shows `*` and `‡‡` with arrows directing the user to a corresponding plan.

For code letters D–J the acceptance (Ac) / rejection (Re) numbers are given below. AQL columns to the left of the first numeric column in each block carry a "use first sampling plan below" arrow (and a `*`); columns to the right of the last numeric column carry `*` and `‡‡`.

Code letter D (Sample size 2 each)

Sample	Cumulative sample size	10 (Ac Re)	15 (Ac Re)	25 (Ac Re)	40 (Ac Re)	65 (Ac Re)	100 (Ac Re)	150 (Ac Re)	250 (Ac Re)	400 (Ac Re)
First	2	# 2	# 3	0 3	0 4	# 4	0 6	1 8	3 10	6 15
Second	4	# 2	0 3	0 4	1 6	1 6	3 9	6 12	10 17	16 25
Third	6	0 2	0 4	1 5	2 7	3 8	7 12	11 17	17 24	26 36
Fourth	8	0 3	1 5	2 6	3 8	6 9	10 15	16 22	24 31	37 46
Fifth	10	1 3	2 5	3 6	5 9	8 12	14 18	22 25	32 37	49 55
Sixth	12	1 3	3 5	4 7	7 9	11 14	18 20	27 29	40 43	61 64
Seventh	14	2 3	4 5	6 7	9 10	14 15	21 22	32 33	48 49	72 73

Code letter E (Sample size 3 each)

Sample	Cumulative sample size	6.5	10	15	25	40	65	100	150	250
First	3	# 2	# 3	0 3	0 4	# 4	0 6	1 8	3 10	6 15
Second	6	# 2	0 3	0 4	1 6	1 6	3 9	6 12	10 17	16 25
Third	9	0 2	0 4	1 5	2 7	3 8	7 12	11 17	17 24	26 36
Fourth	12	0 3	1 5	2 6	3 8	6 9	10 15	16 22	24 31	37 46
Fifth	15	1 3	2 5	3 6	5 9	8 12	14 18	22 25	32 37	49 55
Sixth	18	1 3	3 5	4 7	7 9	11 14	18 20	27 29	40 43	61 64
Seventh	21	2 3	4 5	6 7	9 10	14 15	21 22	32 33	48 49	72 73

Code letter F (Sample size 5 each)

Sample	Cumulative sample size	4.0	6.5	10	15	25	40	65	100	150
First	5	# 2	# 3	0 3	0 4	# 4	0 6	1 8	3 10	6 15
Second	10	# 2	0 3	0 4	1 6	1 6	3 9	6 12	10 17	16 25
Third	15	0 2	0 4	1 5	2 7	3 8	7 12	11 17	17 24	26 36
Fourth	20	0 3	1 5	2 6	3 8	6 9	10 15	16 22	24 31	37 46
Fifth	25	1 3	2 5	3 6	5 9	8 12	14 18	22 25	32 37	49 55
Sixth	30	1 3	3 5	4 7	7 9	11 14	18 20	27 29	40 43	61 64
Seventh	35	2 3	4 5	6 7	9 10	14 15	21 22	32 33	48 49	72 73

Code letter G (Sample size 8 each)

Sample	Cumulative sample size	2.5	4.0	6.5	10	15	25	40	65	100
First	8	# 2	# 3	0 3	0 4	# 4	0 6	1 8	3 10	6 15
Second	16	# 2	0 3	0 4	1 6	1 6	3 9	6 12	10 17	16 25
Third	24	0 2	0 4	1 5	2 7	3 8	7 12	11 17	17 24	26 36
Fourth	32	0 3	1 5	2 6	3 8	6 9	10 15	16 22	24 31	37 46
Fifth	40	1 3	2 5	3 6	5 9	8 12	14 18	22 25	32 37	49 55
Sixth	48	1 3	3 5	4 7	7 9	11 14	18 20	27 29	40 43	61 64
Seventh	56	2 3	4 5	6 7	9 10	14 15	21 22	32 33	48 49	72 73

Code letter H (Sample size 13 each)

Sample	Cumulative sample size	1.5	2.5	4.0	6.5	10	15	25	40	65
First	13	# 2	# 3	0 3	0 4	# 4	0 6	1 8	3 10	6 15
Second	26	# 2	0 3	0 4	1 6	1 6	3 9	6 12	10 17	16 25
Third	39	0 2	0 4	1 5	2 7	3 8	7 12	11 17	17 24	26 36
Fourth	52	0 3	1 5	2 6	3 8	6 9	10 15	16 22	24 31	37 46
Fifth	65	1 3	2 5	3 6	5 9	8 12	14 18	22 25	32 37	49 55
Sixth	78	1 3	3 5	4 7	7 9	11 14	18 20	27 29	40 43	61 64
Seventh	91	2 3	4 5	6 7	9 10	14 15	21 22	32 33	48 49	72 73

Code letter J (Sample size 20 each)

Sample	Cumulative sample size	1.0	1.5	2.5	4.0	6.5	10	15	25	40
First	20	# 2	# 3	0 3	0 4	# 4	0 6	1 8	3 10	6 15
Second	40	# 2	0 3	0 4	1 6	1 6	3 9	6 12	10 17	16 25
Third	60	0 2	0 4	1 5	2 7	3 8	7 12	11 17	17 24	26 36
Fourth	80	0 3	1 5	2 6	3 8	6 9	10 15	16 22	24 31	37 46
Fifth	100	1 3	2 5	3 6	5 9	8 12	14 18	22 25	32 37	49 55
Sixth	120	1 3	3 5	4 7	7 9	11 14	18 20	27 29	40 43	61 64
Seventh	140	2 3	4 5	6 7	9 10	14 15	21 22	32 33	48 49	72 73

Legend

↓ = Use first sampling plan below arrow (refer to continuation of table on following page, when necessary). If sample size equals or exceeds lot or batch size, do 100 percent inspection.
↑ = Use first sampling plan above arrow.
Ac = Acceptance number.
Re = Rejection number.
* = Use corresponding single sampling plan (or alternatively, use multiple sampling plan below, where available).
‡‡ = Use corresponding double sampling plan below (or alternatively, use multiple sampling plan below, where available).
# = Acceptance not permitted at this sample size.

251

TABLE 6-13 (continued)

Master table for multiple sampling — Acceptable Quality Levels (tightened inspection).

Sample size code letter	Sample	Sample size	Cumulative sample size
K	First	32	32
	Second	32	64
	Third	32	96
	Fourth	32	128
	Fifth	32	160
	Sixth	32	192
	Seventh	32	224
L	First	50	50
	Second	50	100
	Third	50	150
	Fourth	50	200
	Fifth	50	250
	Sixth	50	300
	Seventh	50	350
M	First	80	80
	Second	80	160
	Third	80	240
	Fourth	80	320
	Fifth	80	400
	Sixth	80	480
	Seventh	80	560
N	First	125	125
	Second	125	250
	Third	125	375
	Fourth	125	500
	Fifth	125	625
	Sixth	125	750
	Seventh	125	875
P	First	200	200
	Second	200	400
	Third	200	600
	Fourth	200	800
	Fifth	200	1000
	Sixth	200	1200
	Seventh	200	1400
Q	First	315	315
	Second	315	630
	Third	315	945
	Fourth	315	1260
	Fifth	315	1575
	Sixth	315	1890
	Seventh	315	2205
R	First	500	500
	Second	500	1000
	Third	500	1500
	Fourth	500	2000
	Fifth	500	2500
	Sixth	500	3000
	Seventh	500	3500
S	First	800	800
	Second	800	1600
	Third	800	2400
	Fourth	800	3200
	Fifth	800	4000
	Sixth	800	4800
	Seventh	800	5600

↓↑ = Use first sampling plan below arrow. If sample size equals or exceeds lot or batch size, do 100 percent inspection.

◇◆ = Use first sampling plan above arrow (refer to preceding page when necessary).

Ac = Acceptance number.

Re = Rejection number.

✳ = Use corresponding single sampling plan (or alternatively, use multiple sampling plan below, where available).

✦ = Acceptance not permitted at this sample size.

252

TABLE 6-14 Multiple Sampling Plans for Reduced Inspection (Table IV-C of MIL-STD-105D)

Acceptable Quality Levels (reduced inspection)†

Sample size code letter	Sample	Sample size	Cumulative sample size
A			
B			
C			
D			
E			
F	First	2	2
	Second	2	4
	Third	2	6
	Fourth	2	8
	Fifth	2	10
	Sixth	2	12
	Seventh	2	14
G	First	3	3
	Second	3	6
	Third	3	9
	Fourth	3	12
	Fifth	3	15
	Sixth	3	18
	Seventh	3	21
H	First	5	5
	Second	5	10
	Third	5	15
	Fourth	5	20
	Fifth	5	25
	Sixth	5	30
	Seventh	5	35
J	First	8	8
	Second	8	16
	Third	8	24
	Fourth	8	32
	Fifth	8	40
	Sixth	8	48
	Seventh	8	56
K	First	13	13
	Second	13	26
	Third	13	39
	Fourth	13	52
	Fifth	13	65
	Sixth	13	78
	Seventh	13	91

The body of the table carries the Acceptance (Ac) and Rejection (Re) numbers under the Acceptable Quality Level columns: 0.010, 0.015, 0.025, 0.040, 0.065, 0.10, 0.15, 0.25, 0.40, 0.65, 1.0, 1.5, 2.5, 4.0, 6.5, 10, 15, 25, 40, 65, 100, 150, 250, 400, 650, 1000 (each with Ac and Re sub-columns). Arrows and symbols direct the user to the appropriate plan.

Legend:

↓ = Use first sampling plan below arrow (refer to continuation of table on following page, when necessary). If sample size equals or exceeds lot or batch size, do 100 percent inspection.

↑ = Use first sampling plan above arrow.

Ac = Acceptance number.

Re = Rejection number.

* = Use corresponding single sampling plan (or alternatively, use multiple sampling plan below, where available).

‡ = Use corresponding double sampling plan (or alternatively, use multiple sampling plan below, where available).

= Acceptance not permitted at this sample size.

† = If, after the final sample, the acceptance number has been exceeded, but the rejection number has not been reached, accept the lot but reinstate normal inspection (see 10.1.4).

253

TABLE 6-14 (continued)

Acceptable Quality Levels (reduced inspection)[†]

Master table for multiple sampling — reduced inspection. Column headings (Acceptable Quality Levels) with Ac (acceptance number) and Re (rejection number) sub-columns:

0.010 · 0.015 · 0.025 · 0.040 · 0.065 · 0.10 · 0.15 · 0.25 · 0.40 · 0.65 · 1.0 · 1.5 · 2.5 · 4.0 · 6.5 · 10 · 15 · 25 · 40 · 65 · 100 · 150 · 250 · 400 · 650 · 1000

Sample size code letter	Sample	Sample size	Cumulative sample size
L	First	20	20
	Second	20	40
	Third	20	60
	Fourth	20	80
	Fifth	20	100
	Sixth	20	120
	Seventh	20	140
M	First	32	32
	Second	32	64
	Third	32	96
	Fourth	32	128
	Fifth	32	160
	Sixth	32	192
	Seventh	32	224
N	First	50	50
	Second	50	100
	Third	50	150
	Fourth	50	200
	Fifth	50	250
	Sixth	50	300
	Seventh	50	350
P	First	80	80
	Second	80	160
	Third	80	240
	Fourth	80	320
	Fifth	80	400
	Sixth	80	480
	Seventh	80	560
Q	First	125	125
	Second	125	250
	Third	125	375
	Fourth	125	500
	Fifth	125	625
	Sixth	125	750
	Seventh	125	875
R	First	200	200
	Second	200	400
	Third	200	600
	Fourth	200	800
	Fifth	200	1000
	Sixth	200	1200
	Seventh	200	1400

Note: The body of the table consists of Ac/Re numbers appearing on diagonals with directional arrows (↓ = use first sampling plan below arrow; ↑ = use first sampling plan above arrow) and left-pointing arrows for the higher AQL columns. The highest AQL column (6.5) for code letter L gives the largest numbered plan (Ac: 0, 3, 6, 8, 11, 14, 18 / Re: 6, 9, 12, 15, 17, 20, 22 over the seven cumulative samples).

◇ = Use first sampling plan below arrow. If sample size equals or exceeds lot or batch size, do 100 percent inspection.
△ = Use first sampling plan above arrow. (refer to preceding page when necessary).
Ac = Acceptance number.
Re = Rejection number.
‡ = Acceptance not permitted at this sample size.
† = If, after the final sample, the acceptance number has been exceeded, but the rejection number has not been reached, accept the lot, but reinstate normal inspection (see 10.1.4).

254

Sample-size code letter = H (from Table 6-5). Normal inspection (from Table 6-12):

n	Ac	Re
13	#	4
13	1	5
13	2	6
13	3	7
13	5	8
13	7	9
13	9	10

Tightened inspection (from Table 6-13):

n	Ac	Re
13	#	3
13	0	3
13	1	4
13	2	5
13	3	6
13	4	6
13	6	7

Reduced inspection (from Table 6-14):

n	Ac	Re
5	#	3
5	0	4
5	0	5
5	1	6
5	2	7
5	3	7
5	4	8

Two different symbols are used in the multiple sampling tables. The symbol # is used to indicate that acceptance is not permitted at this time because the sample size is too small. When the symbol ++ is encountered in the table, it indicates that the corresponding double sampling plan should be used. Or the multiple sampling plan immediately below can be used, where available.

Normal, Tightened, and Reduced Inspection

Unless otherwise directed by the responsible authority, inspection starts with the normal inspection condition. Normal, tightened, or reduced inspection will continue unchanged for each class of nonconformities or nonconforming units or until the switching procedures given below require a change.

Normal to tightened. When normal inspection is in effect, tightened inspection shall be instituted when 2 out of 5 consecutive lots or batches have been rejected on original inspection (i.e., ignoring resubmitted lots).

Tightened to normal. When tightened inspection is in effect, normal inspection shall be instituted when 5 consecutive lots or batches are accepted on original inspection.

Normal to reduced. When normal inspection is in effect, reduced inspection shall be instituted provided all four of the following conditions are satisfied.

1. The preceding 10 lots or batches have been on normal inspection and none of the lots has been rejected on original inspection.

2. The total number of nonconforming units (nonconformities) in the samples from the preceding 10 lots or batches is equal to or less than the applicable number given in Table 6-15. For example, if the total number inspected for the past 10 lots or batches is 600 and the AQL is 2.5%, the limit number is 7. Therefore, to qualify for reduced inspection, the number nonconforming in the 600 inspected must be equal to or less than 7. In some cases more than 10 lots or batches are necessary to obtain a sufficient number of sample units for a particular AQL, as indicated by the note of Table 6-15. This condition is optional in Z1.4.

3. Production is at a steady rate. In other words, no difficulties, such as machine breakdowns, material shortages, or labor problems, have occurred recently.

4. Reduced inspection is considered desirable by the responsible authority (consumer). The consumer must decide if the savings from fewer inspections warrants the additional record-keeping and inspector training expenses.

Reduced to normal. When reduced inspection is in effect, normal inspection shall be instituted provided any of the four conditions below are satisfied on original inspection.

1. A lot or batch is rejected.

2. When the sampling procedure terminates with neither acceptance nor rejection criteria having been met, the lot or batch is accepted, but normal inspection is reinstated starting with the next lot.

3. Production is irregular or delayed.

4. Other conditions, such as customer desire, warrant that normal inspection will be instituted.

In the event that 10 consecutive lots or batches remain on tightened inspection

TABLE 6-15 Limit Numbers for Reduced Inspection (Table VIII of MIL-STD-105D)

Number of sample units from last 10 lots or batches	Acceptable Quality Level																									
	0.010	0.015	0.025	0.040	0.065	0.10	0.15	0.25	0.40	0.65	1.0	1.5	2.5	4.0	6.5	10	15	25	40	65	100	150	250	400	650	1000
20-29	*	*	*	*	*	*	*	*	*	*	*	*	*	*	*	0	0	2	4	8	14	22	40	68	115	181
30-49	*	*	*	*	*	*	*	*	*	*	*	*	*	*	0	0	1	3	7	13	22	36	63	105	178	277
50-79	*	*	*	*	*	*	*	*	*	*	*	*	*	0	0	2	3	7	14	25	40	63	110	181	301	
80-129	*	*	*	*	*	*	*	*	*	*	*	*	0	0	2	4	7	14	24	42	68	105	181	297		
130-199	*	*	*	*	*	*	*	*	*	*	*	0	0	2	4	7	13	25	42	72	115	177	301	490		
200-319	*	*	*	*	*	*	*	*	*	*	0	0	2	4	8	14	22	40	68	115	181	277	471			
320-499	*	*	*	*	*	*	*	*	*	0	0	1	4	8	14	24	39	68	113	189						
500-799	*	*	*	*	*	*	*	*	0	0	2	3	7	14	25	40	63	110	181							
800-1249	*	*	*	*	*	*	*	0	0	2	4	7	14	24	42	68	105	181								
1250-1999	*	*	*	*	*	*	0	0	2	4	7	13	24	40	69	110	169									
2000-3149	*	*	*	*	*	0	0	2	4	8	14	22	40	68	115	181										
3150-4999	*	*	*	*	0	0	1	4	8	14	24	38	67	111	186											
5000-7999	*	*	*	0	0	2	3	7	14	25	40	63	110	181												
8000-12499	*	*	0	0	2	4	7	14	24	42	68	105	181													
12500-19999	*	0	0	2	4	7	13	24	40	69	110	169														
20000-31499	0	0	2	4	8	14	22	40	68	115	181															
31500-49999	0	1	4	8	14	24	38	67	111	186																
50000 & Over	2	3	7	14	25	40	63	110	181	301																

* Denotes that the number of sample units from the last ten lots or batches is not sufficient for reduced inspection for this AQL. In this instance more than ten lots or batches may be used for the calculation, provided that the lots or batches used are the most recent ones in sequence, that they have all been on normal inspection, and that none has been rejected while on original inspection.

257

(or such other number as may be designed by the responsible authority), inspection under the provisions of this document should be discontinued pending action to improve the quality of submitted material.

Supplementary Information

The standard includes operating characteristic curves for single sampling plans with normal inspection that indicate the percentage of lots or batches that may be expected to be accepted under the various sampling plans for a given process quality. OC curves for double and multiple sampling plans are not given in the standard but are matched as closely as practical.

Table V (not reproduced in this text) of the standard gives the average outgoing quality limit for single sampling plans with normal and tightened inspection.

Average sample-size curves for double and multiple sampling as a function of the equivalent single sample size are shown in Table IX and are reproduced in Figure 6-17. These show the average sample sizes that may be expected to occur under the various sampling plans for a given process quality.

MIL-STD-105D is designed for use where the units of product are produced in a continuing series of lots or batches. However, if a sampling plan is desirable for a lot or batch of an isolated nature, it should be chosen based on the limiting quality level (LQL) and consumer's risk. Tables (not reproduced in this text) for consumer's risks of 0.05 and 0.10 are included in the standard. Therefore, a sampling plan for isolated lots can be obtained that will come close to both the producer's and consumer's criteria.

COMPUTER PROGRAM

The computer program given in Figure 6-25 calculates the probability of acceptance (P_a) for the process quality as given by the fraction nonconforming (p) for an OC curve for single sampling. It is based on the calculated value of the Poisson probability formula rather than the table value. Therefore, it is more accurate because there are no rounding errors as occur with the table values. The reader may wish to check the P_a values with Table 6-2. If more plotted points are desired, the increment in statement 180 can be reduced to, say, 0.005.

PROBLEMS

1. A real estate firm evaluates incoming selling agreement forms using the single sampling plan $N = 1500$, $n = 110$, and $c = 3$. Construct the OC curve using about seven points.

2. A doctor's clinic evaluates incoming disposable cotton-tipped applicators using the single sampling plan $N = 8000$, $n = 62$, and $c = 1$. Construct the OC curve using about seven points.

```
10 REM                        OC  CURVE - SS PLAN
20 REM                           Based on Poisson
30 REM
40 REM          N = Sample Size
50 REM          P = Process Quality(Fraction Nonconforming)
60 REM          C = Acceptance Number
70 REM          PA = Probability of Acceptance
80 REM
90 PRINT "Enter the Sample Size." : INPUT N
100 LPRINT TAB(5); " n ="; N
110 PRINT "Enter the Acceptance Number." : INPUT K
120 LPRINT TAB(5); " c = "; K : LPRINT
130 P = 0
140 LPRINT TAB(5); " p "; TAB(15); " Pa "
150 P = P + .01
160 NP = N * p
170 Pa = 0
180        FOR C = K TO 0 STEP -1
190        CF = C
200        IF C < 1 THEN CF = 1
210        IF C < 3 THEN 260
220        CF = 2
230             FOR J = 3 TO C
240             CF = CF * J
250             NEXT J
260        PA = PA + NP ^ C / (CF * 2.71828 ^ NP)
270        NEXT C
280 LPRINT TAB(4);P; TAB(12);Pa
290 IF PA < .05 GOTO 310
300 GOTO 150
310 END
```

```
                    N = 89
                    c = 2


                    p          Pa
                   .01       .93878
                   .02       .735971
                   .03       .501003
                   .04       .309893
                   .05       .179281
                   .06       .0987847
                   .07       .0524594
                   .08       .0270673
```

FIGURE 6-25   Computer program in BASIC for the OC curve for a single sampling plan.

3. Determine the equation for the OC curve for the sampling plan $N = 10,000$, $n_1 = 200$, $c_1 = 2$, $r_1 = 6$, $n_2 = 350$, $c_2 = 6$, and $r_2 = 7$. Construct the curve using about five points.

4. Determine the equation for the OC curve for the following sampling plans:
   (a) $N = 500$, $n_1 = 50$, $c_1 = 0$, $r_1 = 3$, $n_2 = 70$, $c_2 = 2$, $r_2 = 3$
   (b) $N = 6000$, $n_1 = 80$, $c_1 = 2$, $r_1 = 4$, $n_2 = 160$, $c_2 = 5$, $r_2 = 6$
   (c) $N = 22,000$, $n_1 = 260$, $c_1 = 5$, $r_1 = 9$, $n_2 = 310$, $c_2 = 8$, $r_2 = 9$
   (d) $N = 10,000$, $n_1 = 300$, $c_1 = 4$, $n_2 = 300$, $c_2 = 8$
   (e) $N = 800$, $n_1 = 100$, $c_1 = 0$, $n_2 = 100$, $c_2 = 4$

5. For the sampling plan of Problem 1, determine the AOQ curve and the AOQL.

6. For the sampling plan of Problem 2, determine the AOQ curve and the AOQL.

7. A major USA automotive manufacturer is using a sampling plan of $n = 200$ and $c = 0$ for all lot sizes. Construct the OC and AOQ curves. Graphically determine the AQL value for $\alpha = 0.05$ and the AOQL value.

8. One of the leading computer firms uses a sampling plan of $n = 50$ and $c = 0$ regardless of lot sizes. Construct the OC and AOQ curves. Graphically determine the AQL value for $\alpha = 0.05$ and the AOQL value.

9. Construct the ASN curves for the single sampling plan $n = 200$, $c = 5$, and the equally effective double sampling $n_1 = 125$, $c_1 = 2$, $r_1 = 5$, $n_2 = 125$, $c_2 = 6$, $r_2 = 7$. Compare with Figure 6-17.

10. Construct the ASN curves for the single sampling plan $n = 80$, $c = 3$, and the equally effective double sampling plan $n_1 = 50$, $c_1 = 1$, $r_1 = 4$, $n_2 = 50$, $c_2 = 4$, $r_2 = 5$. Compare with Figure 6-17.

11. Construct the ATI curve for $N = 500$, $n = 80$, $c = 0$.

12. Construct the ATI curve for $N = 10,000$, $n = 315$, $c = 5$.

13. Determine the AOQ curve and the AOQL for the single sampling plan $N = 16,000$, $n = 280$, $c = 4$.

14. Using $c = 1$, $c = 5$, and $c = 8$, determine three sampling plans which ensure that product 0.8% nonconforming (good product) will be rejected 5.0% of the time.

15. For $c = 3$, $c = 6$, and $c = 12$, determine the sampling plans for AQL = 1.5% and $\alpha = 0.01$.

16. A bed-sheet supplier and a large motel system have decided to evaluate product in lots of 1000 using an AQL of 1.0% with a probability of rejection of 0.10. Determine sampling plans for $c = 0, 1, 2,$ and 4. How would you select the most appropriate plan?

17. For a consumer's risk of 0.10 and a LQL of 6.5%, determine the sampling plans for $c = 2, 6,$ and 14.

18. If product that is 8.3% nonconforming is accepted 5% of the time, determine three sampling plans which meet this criteria. Use $c = 0, 3,$ and 7.

19. A manufacturer of loudspeakers has decided that product 2% nonconforming will be accepted with a probability of 0.01. Determine single sampling plans for $c = 1, 3,$ and 5.

20. Construct the OC and AOQ curves for the $c = 3$ plan of Problem 19.

21. A single sampling plan is desired with a consumer's risk of 0.10 of accepting 3.0% nonconforming product and a producer's risk of 0.05 of rejecting 0.7% nonconforming product. Select the plan with the lowest sample size.

22. The producer's risk is defined by $\alpha = 0.05$ for 1.5% nonconforming product and the consumer's risk is defined by $\beta = 0.10$ for 4.6% nonconforming product. Select a sampling plan that exactly meets the producer's stipulation and comes as close as possible to the consumer's stipulation.

23. For the information of Problem 21, select the plan that exactly meets the consumer's stipulation and comes as close as possible to the producer's stipulation.

24. For the information of Problem 22, select the plan with the smallest sample size.

25. Give $p_{0.10} = 0.053$ and $p_{0.95} = 0.014$, determine the single sampling plan that exactly meets the consumer's stipulation and comes as close as possible to the producer's stipulation.

26. For the information of Problem 25, select the plan that meets the producer's stipulation and comes as close as possible to the consumer's stipulation.

27. If a single sampling plan is desired with an AOQL of 1.8% at an incoming quality of 2.6%, what is the common point on the OC curves for a family of sampling plans that meet the AOQL and $100p_0$ stipulation?

28. Using MIL-STD-105D/Z1.4, a General Services Administration inspector needs to determine the single sampling plans for the following information.

	INSPECTION LEVEL	INSPECTION	AQL	LOT SIZE
(a)	II	Tightened	1.5%	1,400
(b)	I	Normal	65	115
(c)	III	Reduced	0.40%	160,000
(d)	III	Normal	2.5%	27

29. Explain the meaning of the sampling plan determined in Problem 28(c) if (a) 6 nonconforming units are found in the sample, (b) if 8 nonconforming units are found, and (c) if 4 nonconforming units are found.

30. Using MIL-STD-105D a U.S. Navy inspector needs to determine the double sampling plans for the information below.

	INSPECTION LEVEL	INSPECTION	AQL	LOT SIZE
(a)	I	Normal	150	145
(b)	II	Reduced	0.15%	1,150
(c)	II	Tightened	2.5%	65
(d)	III	Reduced	15	8,050
(e)	III	Tightened	0.40%	24,000

31. Describe the double sampling plan of Problem 30(d).

32. Write the equations for OC curves for the double sampling plan of problem 30(e).

33. Using MIL-STD-105D/Z1.4, determine the multiple sampling plans for the following information.

	INSPECTION LEVEL	INSPECTION	AQL	LOT SIZE
(a)	III	Tightened	0.25%	70
(b)	I	Normal	0.25%	12,500
(c)	III	Reduced	1.5%	3,400

34. Inspection results for the last 8 lots using MIL-STD-105D/Z1.4 and the single sampling of $n = 225$, $c = 3$ are

I.	1 nonconforming unit		V.	3 nonconforming units	
II.	4 nonconforming units		VI.	0 nonconforming units	
III.	5 nonconforming units		VII.	2 nonconforming units	
IV.	1 nonconforming unit		VIII.	2 nonconforming units	

If normal inspection was used for lot I, what inspection should be used for lot IV?

35. Using the information from Problem 34, what was the status after lot V? Lot VII?

36. A U.S. Air Force inspector has recorded the following results using MIL-STD-105D/Z1.4 for a double sampling plan, code letter L, normal inspection, and AQL = 2.5%.

	n	np		n	np
I.	125	0	VI.	125	5
II.	125	2	VII.	125	1
III.	125	3	VIII.	125	2
IV.	250	10	IX.	125	3
V.	125	1	X.	125	4

If production is at a steady rate and reduced inspection is authorized, can a change from normal to reduced inspection be initiated?

37. If lot IX of Problem 36 has 9 nonconforming units rather than 3 nonconforming units, is a change from normal to reduced inspection warranted?

38. For a single sampling plan using MIL-STD-105D/Z1.4, code letter C, normal inspection, and AQL = 25 nonconformities/100 units, the number inspected and the count of nonconformities for the last 10 lots are:

	n	c		n	c
I.	5	0	VI.	5	3
II.	5	1	VII.	5	0
III.	5	2	VIII.	5	2
IV.	5	2	IX.	5	4
V.	5	1	X.	5	1

If production is at a steady rate and reduced inspection is authorized, can a change from normal to reduced inspection be initiated?

39. Test and, if necessary, rewrite the computer program for your computer.

40. Modify the computer program to output the answer for your graphical output device.

41. Write a computer program for:
(a) OC curve for multiple sampling
(b) AOQ curve
(c) ASN curve for double sampling
(d) ASN curve for multiple sampling
(e) ATI curve

7

ADDITIONAL ACCEPTANCE SAMPLING PLAN SYSTEMS

MIL-STD-105D/Z1.4 is the most common type of lot-by-lot acceptance sampling plan for attributes and is well suited for receiving inspection. There are, however, other types of acceptance sampling plans. It is the purpose of this chapter to discuss these other acceptance sampling plans with sufficient depth to provide the reader with an adequate background.

The chapter covers three different types of acceptance sampling plans: (1) lot-by-lot acceptance sampling for attributes, (2) continuous production acceptance sampling for attributes, and (3) acceptance sampling for variables.

LOT-BY-LOT ACCEPTANCE SAMPLING PLANS FOR ATTRIBUTES

MIL-STD-105D and ANSI/ASQC Z1.4-1981

A complete discussion of this system is given in Chapter 6. It is the most widely used acceptance sampling plan in the world.

Dodge-Romig Tables

In the 1920s H. F. Dodge and H. G. Romig developed a set of inspection tables for the lot-by-lot acceptance of product by sampling for attributes. These tables are based on two of the concepts discussed in Chapter 6, limiting quality level (LQL)[1] and average outgoing quality limit (AOQL). For each of these concepts there are tables for single and double sampling. No provision is made for multiple sampling.

The principal advantage of the Dodge–Romig tables is a minimum amount of inspection for a given inspection procedure. This advantage makes the tables desirable for in-house inspection.

1. *Limiting quality level* (LQL). These tables are based on the probability that a particular lot, which has a percent nonconforming equal to the LQL, will be accepted. This probability is the consumer's risk, β, and is equal to 0.10. LQL plans give assurance that individual lots of poor quality will rarely be accepted.

There are two sets of LQL tables: one set for single sampling and one set for double sampling. Each set has tables for LQL values of 0.5, 1.0, 2.0, 3.0, 4.0, 5.0, 7.0, and 10.0%, making a total of 16 tables. For explanatory purposes, Tables 7-1 and 7-2 are shown for single and double sampling, respectively, using LQL = 1.0%. Tables for other LQL values are not given.

To use the tables, an initial decision concerning single sampling or double sampling is required. This decision can be based on the information presented in Chapter 6. In addition, the LQL needs to be determined, which can be accomplished in a manner similar to that used for the AQL as described in Chapter 6. The type of sampling (single or double) and the limiting quality level (LQL) indicate the table to use.

Knowing the lot size and the process average, the acceptance sampling plan is easily obtained. For example, if the lot size, N, is 1500 and the process average is 0.25%, the required single sampling plan for LQL = 1.0% is found in Table 7-1. The answer is

$$N = 1500$$

$$n = 490$$

$$c = 2$$

The table also gives the average outgoing quality limit (AOQL) for each plan, which for this example is 0.21%.

In a similar manner, an acceptance sampling plan for double sampling can be obtained. For example, if $N = 4400$ and the process average is 0.15%, the required double sampling plan for LQL = 1.0% is found in Table 7-2. The answer is

$$N = 4400$$

$$n_1 = 275$$

$$c_1 = 0$$

$$n_2 = 565$$

$$c_2 = 4$$

[1] Dodge and Romig used the term "lot tolerance percent defective" (LTPD). In this text, "limiting quality level" (LQL) has been substituted, since it is the appropriate present-day term.

TABLE 7-1 Dodge–Romig Single Sampling Lot Inspection Table, Based on Limiting Quality Level[a]

LQL = 1.0%

LOT SIZE	PROCESS AVERAGE (%)																	
	0–0.010			0.011–0.10			0.11–0.20			0.21–0.30			0.31–0.40			0.41–0.50		
	n	c	AOQL (%)	n	c	AOQL (%)	n	c	AOQL (%)	n	c	AOQL (%)	n	c	AOQL (%)	n	c	AOQL (%)
1–120	All	0	0	All	0	0	All	0	0	All	0	0	All	0	0	All	0	0
121–150	120	0	0.06	120	0	0.06	120	0	0.06	120	0	0.06	120	0	0.06	120	0	0.06
151–200	140	0	0.08	140	0	0.08	140	0	0.08	140	0	0.08	140	0	0.08	140	0	0.08
201–300	165	0	0.10	165	0	0.10	165	0	0.10	165	0	0.10	165	0	0.10	165	0	0.10
301–400	175	0	0.12	175	0	0.12	175	0	0.12	175	0	0.12	175	0	0.12	175	0	0.12
401–500	180	0	0.13	180	0	0.13	180	0	0.13	180	0	0.13	180	0	0.13	180	0	0.13
501–600	190	0	0.13	190	0	0.13	190	0	0.13	190	0	0.13	190	0	0.13	305	1	0.14
601–800	200	0	0.14	200	0	0.14	200	0	0.14	330	1	0.15	330	1	0.15	330	1	0.15
801–1,000	205	0	0.14	205	0	0.14	205	0	0.14	335	1	0.17	335	1	0.17	335	1	0.17
1,001–2,000	220	0	0.15	220	0	0.15	360	1	0.19	490	2	0.21	490	2	0.21	610	3	0.22
2,001–3,000	220	0	0.15	375	1	0.20	505	2	0.23	630	3	0.24	745	4	0.26	870	5	0.26
3,001–4,000	225	0	0.15	380	1	0.20	510	2	0.24	645	3	0.25	880	5	0.28	1,000	6	0.29
4,001–5,000	225	0	0.16	380	1	0.20	520	2	0.24	770	4	0.28	895	5	0.29	1,120	7	0.31
5,001–7,000	230	0	0.16	385	1	0.21	655	3	0.27	780	4	0.29	1,020	6	0.32	1,260	8	0.34
7,001–10,000	230	0	0.16	520	2	0.25	660	3	0.28	910	5	0.32	1,150	7	0.34	1,500	10	0.37
10,001–20,000	390	1	0.21	525	2	0.26	785	4	0.31	1,040	6	0.35	1,400	9	0.39	1,980	14	0.43
20,001–50,000	390	1	0.21	530	2	0.26	920	5	0.34	1,300	8	0.39	1,890	13	0.44	2,570	19	0.48
50,001–100,000	390	1	0.21	670	3	0.29	1,040	6	0.36	1,420	9	0.41	2,120	15	0.47	3,150	23	0.50

[a] n, size of sample; entry of "All" indicates that each piece in lot is to be inspected. c, acceptance number. AOQL, average outgoing quality limit.

265

TABLE 7-2 Dodge–Romig Double Sampling Lot Inspection Table, Based on Limiting Quality Level[a]
LQL = 1.0%

	PROCESS AVERAGE (%)																	
	0–0.010						0.011–0.10						0.11–0.20					
	TRIAL 1		TRIAL 2			AOQL	TRIAL 1		TRIAL 2			AOQL	TRIAL 1		TRIAL 2			AOQL
LOT SIZE	n_1	c_1	n_2	n_1+n_2	c_2	(%)	n_1	c_1	n_2	n_1+n_2	c_2	(%)	n_1	c_1	n_2	n_1+n_2	c_2	(%)
1–120	All	0	—	—	—	0	All	0	—	—	—	0	All	0	—	—	—	0
121–150	120	0	—	—	—	0.06	120	0	—	—	—	0.06	120	0	—	—	—	0.06
151–200	140	0	—	—	—	0.08	140	0	—	—	—	0.08	140	0	—	—	—	0.08
201–260	165	0	—	—	—	0.10	165	0	—	—	—	0.10	165	0	—	—	—	0.10
261–300	180	0	75	255	1	0.10	180	0	75	255	1	0.10	180	0	75	255	1	0.10
301–400	200	0	90	290	1	0.12	200	0	90	290	1	0.12	200	0	90	290	1	0.12
401–500	215	0	100	315	1	0.14	215	0	100	315	1	0.14	215	0	100	315	1	0.14
501–600	225	0	115	340	1	0.15	225	0	115	340	1	0.15	225	0	115	340	1	0.15
601–800	235	0	125	360	1	0.16	235	0	125	360	1	0.16	235	0	125	360	1	0.16
801–1,000	245	0	135	380	1	0.17	245	0	135	380	1	0.17	245	0	250	495	2	0.19
1,001–2,000	265	0	155	420	1	0.18	265	0	155	420	1	0.18	265	0	285	550	2	0.21
2,001–3,000	270	0	160	430	1	0.19	270	0	300	570	2	0.22	270	0	420	690	3	0.25
3,001–4,000	275	0	160	435	1	0.19	275	0	305	580	2	0.22	275	0	435	710	3	0.25
4,001–5,000	275	0	165	440	1	0.19	275	0	310	585	2	0.23	275	0	565	840	4	0.28
5,001–7,000	275	0	170	445	1	0.20	275	0	315	590	2	0.23	275	0	580	855	4	0.29
7,001–10,000	280	0	320	600	1	0.24	280	0	460	740	3	0.26	280	0	590	870	4	0.30
10,001–20,000	280	0	325	605	1	0.24	280	0	465	745	3	0.27	450	1	700	1,150	6	0.33
20,001–50,000	280	0	325	605	1	0.25	280	0	605	885	4	0.30	450	1	830	1,280	7	0.36
50,001–100,000	280	0	325	605	1	0.25	280	0	605	885	4	0.30	450	1	960	1,410	8	0.38

TABLE 7-2 (Continued)

	PROCESS AVERAGE (%)																	
	0.21–0.30						0.31–0.40						0.41–0.50					
	TRIAL 1		TRIAL 2			AOQL	TRIAL 1		TRIAL 2			AOQL	TRIAL 1		TRIAL 2			AOQL
LOT SIZE	n_1	c_1	n_2	$n_1 + n_2$	c_2	(%)	n_1	c_1	n_2	$n_1 + n_2$	c_2	(%)	n_1	c_1	n_2	$n_1 + n_2$	c_2	(%)
1–120	All	0	—	—	—	0	All	0	—	—	—	0	All	0	—	—	—	0
121–150	120	0	—	—	—	0.06	120	0	—	—	—	0.06	120	0	—	—	—	0.06
151–200	140	0	—	—	—	0.08	140	0	—	—	—	0.08	140	0	—	—	—	0.08
201–260	165	0	—	—	—	0.10	165	0	—	—	—	0.10	165	0	—	—	—	0.10
261–300	180	0	75	255	1	0.10	180	0	75	255	1	0.10	180	0	75	255	1	0.10
301–400	200	0	90	290	1	0.12	200	0	90	290	1	0.12	200	0	90	290	1	0.12
401–500	215	0	100	315	1	0.14	215	0	100	315	1	0.14	215	0	100	315	1	0.14
501–600	225	0	115	340	1	0.15	225	0	115	340	1	0.15	225	0	205	430	2	0.16
601–800	235	0	230	465	2	0.18	235	0	230	465	2	0.18	235	0	230	465	2	0.18
801–1,000	245	0	250	495	2	0.19	245	0	250	495	2	0.19	245	0	250	495	2	0.19
1,001–2,000	265	0	405	670	3	0.23	265	0	515	780	4	0.24	265	0	515	780	4	0.24
2,001–3,000	270	0	545	815	4	0.26	430	1	620	1,050	6	0.28	430	1	830	1,260	8	0.30
3,001–4,000	435	1	645	1,080	6	0.29	435	1	865	1,300	8	0.30	580	2	940	1,520	10	0.33
4,001–5,000	440	1	660	1,100	6	0.30	440	1	1,000	1,440	9	0.33	585	2	1,075	1,660	11	0.35
5,001–7,000	445	1	785	1,230	7	0.33	590	2	990	1,580	10	0.36	730	3	1,190	1,920	13	0.38
7,001–10,000	450	1	920	1,370	8	0.35	600	2	1,240	1,840	12	0.39	870	4	1,540	2,410	17	0.41
10,001–20,000	605	2	1,035	1,640	10	0.39	745	3	1,485	2,230	15	0.43	1,150	6	1,990	3,140	23	0.44
20,001–50,000	605	2	1,295	1,900	12	0.42	885	4	1,845	2,730	19	0.47	1,280	7	2,600	3,880	29	0.52
50,001–100,000	605	2	1,545	2,150	14	0.44	885	4	2,085	2,970	21	0.49	1,410	8	3,280	4,690	36	0.55

[a] n_1, size of first sample; n_2 = size of second sample; entry of "All" indicates that each piece in lot is to be inspected. c_1, acceptance number for first sample; c_2 = acceptance number for first and second samples combined. AOQL, average outgoing quality limit.

267

The table also gives the AOQL for each double sampling plan, which for this example is 0.28%.

An analysis of the LQL tables shows the following:

a. As the lot size increases, the relative sample size decreases. Thus, for a process average of 0.25%, a lot size of 1000 has a sample size of 335, whereas a lot size of 4000 has a sample size of 645. The lot size increased by a factor of 4 while the sample size increased by a factor of about 2. Therefore, inspection costs are more economical with large lot sizes.

b. The tables extend until the process average is one-half of the LQL. Provision for additional process averages is unnecessary, since 100% inspection becomes more economical than sampling inspection when the process average exceeds one-half of the LQL.

c. As the process average increases, a corresponding increase occurs in the amount inspected. Therefore, an improvement in the process average results in fewer inspections and a lower sampling inspection cost.

2. *Average outgoing quality limit* (AOQL). Sampling plans for the AOQL concept were developed as a practical need in certain manufacturing situations. When the lot quantity is specified, as is the case with customer lots (homogeneous), the LQL concept is applicable; however, when the inspected lot is a convenient subdivision of a flow of product for materials-handling purposes (nonhomogeneous), the AOQL concept is applicable. AOQL plans limit the amount of poor outgoing quality on an average basis, but give no assurance on individual lots. Tables for the AOQL have one set for single sampling and one set for double sampling. Each set has tables for AOQL values of 0.1, 0.25, 0.5, 0.75, 1.0, 1.5, 2.0, 2.5, 3.0, 4.0, 5.0, 7.0, and 10.0%, making a total of 26 tables. For explanatory purposes, tables of single and double sampling are shown in Tables 7-3 and 7-4, respectively, using an AOQL = 3.0%. Tables for other AOQL values are not given.

In addition to determining whether single or double sampling is to be used, the AOQL is required. This can be accomplished using the same techniques as those used for finding the AQL, which was described in Chapter 6. The type of sampling (single or double) and the AOQL indicate the table to use.

Knowing the lot size and the process average, the acceptance sampling plan can be obtained. For example, if the lot size, N, is 1500 and the process average is 1.60%, then the required single sampling plan for an AOQL = 3.0% is found in Table 7-3. The answer is

$$N = 1500$$

$$n_1 = 65$$

$$c_1 = 3$$

The corresponding LQL for this plan is 10.2%.

In a similar manner an acceptance sampling plan for double sampling can be obtained. For example, if the lot size, N, is 6000 and the process average is 0.50%,

TABLE 7-3 Dodge–Romig Single Sampling Lot Inspection Table, Based on Average Outgoing Quality Limit[a]

AOQL = 3.0%

| | PROCESS AVERAGE (%) | | | | | | | | | | | | | | | | | |
| | 0–0.06 | | | 0.07–0.60 | | | 0.61–1.20 | | | 1.21–1.80 | | | 1.81–2.40 | | | 2.41–3.00 | | |
LOT SIZE	n	c	LQL (%)	n	c	LQL (%)	n	c	LQL (%)	n	c	LQL (%)	n	c	LQL (%)	n	c	LQL (%)
1–10	All	0	—	All	0	—	All	0	—	All	0	—	All	0	—	All	0	—
11–50	10	0	19.0	10	0	19.0	10	0	19.0	10	0	19.0	10	0	19.0	10	0	19.0
51–100	11	0	18.0	11	0	18.0	11	0	18.0	11	0	18.0	11	0	18.0	22	1	16.4
101–200	12	0	17.0	12	0	17.0	12	0	17.0	25	1	15.1	25	1	15.1	25	1	15.1
201–300	12	0	17.0	12	0	17.0	26	1	14.6	26	1	14.6	26	1	14.6	40	2	12.8
301–400	12	0	17.1	27	1	17.1	26	1	14.7	26	1	14.7	41	2	12.7	41	2	12.7
401–500	12	0	17.2	27	1	14.1	27	1	14.1	42	2	12.4	42	2	12.4	42	2	12.4
501–600	12	0	17.3	27	1	14.2	27	1	14.2	42	2	12.4	42	2	12.4	60	3	10.8
601–800	12	0	17.3	27	1	14.2	27	1	14.2	43	2	12.1	60	3	10.9	60	3	10.9
801–1,000	12	0	17.4	27	1	14.2	44	2	11.8	44	2	11.8	60	3	11.0	80	4	9.8
1,001–2,000	12	0	17.5	28	1	13.8	45	2	11.7	65	3	10.2	80	4	9.8	100	5	9.1
2,001–3,000	12	0	17.5	28	1	13.8	45	2	11.7	65	3	10.2	100	5	9.1	140	7	8.2
3,001–4,000	12	0	17.5	28	1	13.8	65	3	10.3	85	4	9.5	125	6	8.4	165	8	7.8
4,001–5,000	28	1	13.8	28	1	13.8	65	3	10.3	85	4	9.5	125	6	8.4	210	10	7.4
5,001–7,000	28	1	13.8	45	2	11.8	65	3	10.3	105	5	8.8	145	7	8.1	235	11	7.1
7,001–10,000	28	1	13.9	46	2	11.6	65	3	10.3	105	5	8.8	170	8	7.6	280	13	6.8
10,001–20,000	28	1	13.9	46	2	11.7	85	4	9.5	125	6	8.4	215	10	7.2	380	17	6.2
20,001–50,000	28	1	13.9	65	3	10.3	105	5	8.8	170	8	7.6	310	14	6.5	560	24	5.7
50,001–100,000	28	1	13.9	65	3	10.3	125	6	8.4	215	10	7.2	385	17	6.2	690	29	5.4

[a] n, size of sample; entry of "All" indicates that each piece in lot is to be inspected. c, acceptance number for sample. LQL, limiting quality level corresponding to a consumer's risk (β) = 0.10.

269

TABLE 7-4 Dodge–Romig Double Sampling Lot Inspection Table, Based on Average Outgoing Quality Limit[a]

AOQL = 3.0%

	PROCESS AVERAGE (%)																						
	0–0.06						0.07–0.60						0.61–1.20					
	TRIAL 1		TRIAL 2				TRIAL 1		TRIAL 2				TRIAL 1		TRIAL 2			
LOT SIZE	n_1	c_1	n_2	n_1+n_2	c_2	LQL (%)	n_1	c_1	n_2	n_1+n_2	c_2	LQL (%)	n_1	c_1	n_2	n_1+n_2	c_2	LQL (%)
---	---	---	---	---	---	---	---	---	---	---	---	---	---	---	---	---	---	---
1–10	All	0	—	—	—	—	All	0	—	—	—	—	All	0	—	—	—	—
11–50	10	0	—	—	—	19.0	10	0	—	—	—	19.0	10	0	—	—	—	19.0
51–100	16	0	9	25	1	16.4	16	0	9	25	1	16.4	16	0	9	25	1	16.4
101–200	17	0	9	26	1	16.0	17	0	9	26	1	16.0	17	0	9	26	1	16.0
201–300	18	0	10	28	1	15.5	18	0	10	28	1	15.5	21	0	23	44	2	13.3
301–400	18	0	11	29	1	15.2	21	0	24	45	2	13.2	23	0	37	60	3	12.0
401–500	18	0	11	29	1	15.2	21	0	25	46	2	13.0	24	0	36	60	3	11.7
501–600	18	0	12	30	1	15.0	21	0	25	46	2	13.0	24	0	41	65	3	11.5
601–800	21	0	25	46	2	13.0	21	0	25	46	2	13.0	24	0	41	65	3	11.5
801–1,000	21	0	26	47	2	12.8	21	0	26	47	2	12.8	25	0	40	65	3	11.4
1,001–2,000	22	0	26	48	2	12.6	22	0	26	48	2	12.6	27	0	58	85	4	10.3
2,001–3,000	22	0	26	48	2	12.6	25	0	40	65	3	11.4	28	0	62	90	4	10.0
3,001–4,000	23	0	26	49	2	12.4	25	0	45	70	3	11.0	29	0	76	105	5	9.6
4,001–5,000	23	0	26	49	2	12.4	26	0	44	70	3	11.0	30	0	75	105	5	9.5
5,001–7,000	23	0	27	50	2	12.2	26	0	44	70	3	11.0	30	0	80	110	5	9.4
7,001–10,000	23	0	27	50	2	12.2	27	0	43	70	3	11.0	30	0	80	110	5	9.4
10,001–20,000	23	0	27	50	2	12.2	27	0	43	70	3	11.0	31	0	94	125	6	9.2
20,001–50,000	23	0	27	50	2	12.2	28	0	67	95	4	9.7	55	1	120	175	8	8.0
50,001–100,000	23	0	27	50	2	12.2	31	0	84	115	5	9.0	60	1	140	200	9	7.6

[a] n_1, size of sample; n_2, size of second sample; entry of "All" indicates that each piece in lot is to be inspected. c_1, acceptance number for sample; c_2, acceptance number for first and second samples combined. LQL, limiting quality level corresponding to a consumer's risk (β) = 0.10.

270

TABLE 7-4 (continued)

PROCESS AVERAGE (%)

	1.21–1.80						1.81–2.40						2.41–3.00					
	TRIAL 1		TRIAL 2			LQL	TRIAL 1		TRIAL 2			LQL	TRIAL 1		TRIAL 2			LQL
LOT SIZE	n_1	c_1	n_2	n_1+n_2	c_2	(%)	n_1	c_1	n_2	n_1+n_2	c_2	(%)	n_1	c_1	n_2	n_1+n_2	c_2	(%)
1–10	All	0	—	—	—	—	All	0	—	—	—	—	All	0	—	—	—	—
11–50	10	0	—	—	—	19.0	10	0	—	—	—	19.0	10	0	—	—	—	19.0
51–100	17	0	17	34	2	15.8	17	0	17	34	2	15.8	17	0	17	34	2	15.8
101–200	20	0	21	41	2	13.7	22	0	33	55	3	12.4	22	0	33	55	3	12.4
201–300	23	0	37	60	3	12.0	23	0	37	60	3	12.0	24	0	51	75	4	11.1
301–400	23	0	37	60	3	12.0	25	0	55	80	4	10.8	42	1	63	105	6	10.4
401–500	24	0	36	60	3	11.7	25	0	55	80	4	10.8	46	1	79	125	7	9.7
501–600	26	0	54	80	4	10.7	46	1	69	115	6	9.7	48	1	97	145	8	9.2
601–800	26	0	54	80	4	10.7	49	1	81	130	7	9.4	50	1	115	165	9	8.9
801–1,000	27	0	58	85	4	10.3	49	1	86	135	7	9.2	70	2	120	190	10	8.4
1,001–2,000	49	1	76	125	6	9.1	50	1	150	200	10	8.0	100	3	180	280	14	7.5
2,001–3,000	50	1	95	145	7	8.7	80	2	165	245	12	7.6	130	4	260	390	19	6.9
3,001–4,000	55	1	110	165	8	8.5	105	3	200	305	14	7.0	155	5	330	485	23	6.5
4,001–5,000	60	1	135	195	9	7.8	110	3	225	335	15	6.7	215	7	390	605	27	6.0
5,001–7,000	60	1	165	225	10	7.3	110	3	250	360	16	6.6	270	9	505	775	34	5.7
7,001–10,000	85	2	160	245	11	7.2	115	3	290	405	18	6.5	285	9	680	965	41	5.4
10,001–20,000	85	2	180	265	12	7.2	140	4	315	455	20	6.3	315	10	805	1,120	47	5.3
20,001–50,000	85	2	205	290	13	7.0	170	5	420	590	26	6.0	390	13	940	1,330	56	5.2
50,001–100,000	90	2	245	335	15	6.8	200	6	505	705	30	5.7	445	15	1,105	1,550	65	5.1

then the required double sampling plan for an AOQL = 3.0% is found in Table 7-4 and is

$$N = 6000$$
$$n_1 = 26$$
$$c_1 = 0$$
$$n_2 = 44$$
$$c_2 = 3$$

The table also gives the LQL for each double sampling plan which, in this case, is 11.0%.

An analysis of the AOQL tables shows the following:
a. As the lot size increases, the relative sample size decreases.
b. Plans are not given for process averages which exceed the AOQL, since sampling is uneconomical when the average incoming quality is poorer than the specified AOQL.
c. The lower the process average, the smaller the sample size, resulting in lower inspection cost.

3. *Additional comments on Dodge–Romig tables.* The process average, $100\bar{p}$, is obtained by the same techniques used for the p chart. Using the first 25 lots, the average percent nonconforming is obtained. For double sampling, only the first sample is included in the computation. Any lot percent nonconforming, which exceeds the limit of $100\bar{p} + 3\sqrt{100\bar{p}(1 - 100\bar{p})/n}$ is discarded (if it has an assignable cause) and a new process average calculated. However, until it is possible to obtain a process average by the technique above, the largest possible process average should be used. Thus, the last column in the tables is used until $100\bar{p}$ can be determined.

The Dodge–Romig tables do not make provision for the type of nonconformity, although different LQL or AOQL values can be used—lower ones for critical nonconformities and higher ones for minor nonconformities. No provision is made for tightened or reduced inspection, although different LQL or AOQL values can also be used. Nonconformities/100 units rather than percent nonconforming can be used for the process average. Thus, a process average of 2.00% nonconforming is the same as two nonconformities/100 units.

Chain Sampling Inspection Plan[2]

A special type of lot-by-lot acceptance sampling plan for attributes was developed by H. F. Dodge. The plan was designated "Chain Sampling Plan ChSP-1." It is applicable to quality characteristics which involve destructive or costly tests.

When tests are destructive or costly, sampling plans with a small sample size are used as a matter of practical necessity. Plans with sample sizes of 5, 10, 15, etc., usually have acceptance numbers of zero ($c = 0$).

---

[2] For more information, see H. F. Dodge, "Chain Sampling Inspection Plan," *Industrial Quality Control,* 11, No. 4 (January 1955), 10–13.

Single sampling plans for $c = 0$ have an undesirable feature, which is the poor shape of the OC curve at the producer's risk, α. Figure 7-1 shows the general shape of single sampling plans for $c = 0$ and $c = 1$ or more. The comparison shows the desirability (from a producer's viewpoint) of plans with acceptance numbers equal to 1 or more.

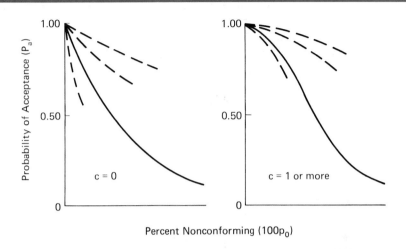

FIGURE 7-1 General shape of OC curves for single sampling plans. [Reproduced by permission from H. F. Dodge, "Chain Sampling Inspection Plan," *Industrial Quality Control,* 11, No. 4 (January 1955), 10–13.]

Chain sampling plans make use of the cumulative results of several preceding samples. The procedure is shown in Figure 7-2 and is as follows:

1. For each lot, select a sample of size n and test each for conformance to specifications.

2. If the sample has 0 nonconforming units accept the lot; if the sample has 2 or

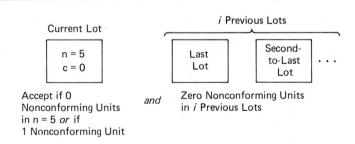

FIGURE 7-2 Chain sampling diagram.

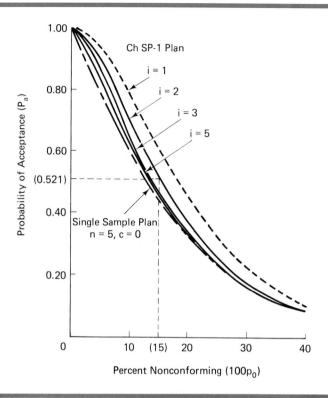

FIGURE 7-3 OC curves for ChSP-1 plans with values 1, 2, 3, 5, and for single sampling plan $n = 5$, $c = 0$.

more nonconforming units, reject the lot; and if the sample has 1 nonconforming unit, it may be accepted provided that there is 0 nonconforming units in the previous i samples of size n.

Thus, for a chain sampling plan given by $n = 5$, $i = 3$, the lot would be accepted (1) by 0 nonconforming units in the sample of 5, or (2) by 1 nonconforming unit in the sample of 5 and 0 nonconforming units in the previous 3 (i) samples of size 5 (n).

The value of i, the number of previous samples, is determined by analysis of the operating characteristic (OC) curves for a given sample size. Figure 7-3 shows the OC curve for the single sample plan $n = 5$, $c = 0$, and the OC curves for ChSP-1 plans for $i = 1$, 2, 3, and 5. The OC curves for the ChSP-1 plans are obtained from the general formula

$$P_a = P_0 + P_1[P_0]^i$$

An example will illustrate the technique. For the ChSP-1 plan $n = 5$, $c = 0$, $i = 2$, the calculations for an assumed value of $p_0 = 0.15$ are

$$P_0 = \frac{n!}{d!(n-d)!}p_0^d q_0^{n-d} = q_0^n = (0.85)^5 = 0.444$$

$$P_1 = \frac{n!}{d!(n-d)!}p_0^d q_0^{n-d} = np_0 q_0^{n-d} = 5(0.15)(0.85)^{5-1} = 0.392$$

$$P_a = P_0 + P_1[P_0]^i = 0.444 + (0392)(0.444)^2 = 0.521$$

The point $P_a = 0.521$ is shown in Figure 7-3. The binomial is used as an approximation for the hypergeometric.

The curve for $i = 1$ is shown dashed, since it is not a preferred choice. In practice i values of from 3 to 5 will be the most used, since their OC curves approximate the single sampling plan OC curve. Where the percent nonconforming is small, the ChSP-1 plans increase the probability that a sample with one nonconforming unit will be accepted. This provides for the occasional nonconforming unit that is expected every now and then.

For appropriate use of the chain sampling technique, the following conditions should be met:

1. The lot should be one of a continuing series of product that is sampled in substantially the order of its production.

2. The consumer can normally expect the lots to be essentially the same quality.

3. The consumer has confidence in the producer not occassionally sending an unacceptable lot that would have the optimum chance of acceptance.

4. The quality characteristic is one that involves destructive or costly tests, thereby dictating a small sample size.

Provision for an occasional nonconformity is satisfactory for major or minor classifications but not for critical.

Sequential Sampling

Sequential sampling is similar to multiple sampling except sequential sampling can theoretically continue indefinitely. In practice the plan is truncated after the number inspected is equal to three times the number inspected by a corresponding single sampling plan. Sequential sampling, which is used for costly or destructive tests, usually has a subgroup size of 1, thereby making it an item-by-item plan.

Item-by-item sequential sampling is based on the concept of the sequential probability ratio test (SPRT), which was developed by Wald.[3] Figure 7-4 illustrates the sampling plan technique. The "stepped" line shows the number nonconforming for the total number inspected and is updated with the inspection results of each item. If the cumulative results equal or are greater than the upper line, the lot is re-

[3] For more information, see Abraham Wald, *Sequential Analysis* (New York: John Wiley & Sons, Inc., 1947).

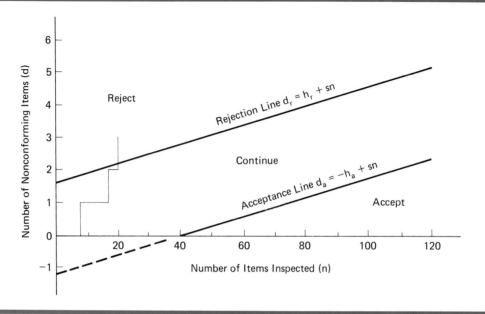

FIGURE 7-4   Graphical presentation of an item-by-item sequential plan.

jected. If the cumulative results equal or are less than the lower line, the lot is accepted. If neither decision is possible, another item is inspected. Thus, if the 20th sample is found to be nonconforming, the cumulative number of nonconforming units will be three. Since three exceeds the rejection line for 20 inspections, the lot is rejected.

The sequential sampling plan is defined by the producer's risk α, and its process quality, p_α, and by the consumer's risk, β, and its process quality, p_β. Using these requirements, the equations (slope intercept form) can be determined for the acceptance line and rejection line using the following formulas:

$$h_a = \log\left(\frac{1-\alpha}{\beta}\right)\bigg/\left[\log\left(\frac{p_\beta}{p_\alpha}\right) + \log\left(\frac{1-p_\alpha}{1-p_\beta}\right)\right]$$

$$h_r = \log\left(\frac{1-\beta}{\alpha}\right)\bigg/\left[\log\left(\frac{p_\beta}{p_\alpha}\right) + \log\left(\frac{1-p_\alpha}{1-p_\beta}\right)\right]$$

$$s = \log\left(\frac{1-p_\alpha}{1-p_\beta}\right)\bigg/\left[\log\left(\frac{p_\beta}{p_\alpha}\right) + \log\left(\frac{1-p_\alpha}{1-p_\beta}\right)\right]$$

$$d_a = -h_a + sn$$

$$d_r = h_r + sn$$

where s = slope of the lines
   h_r = intercept for the rejection line
   h_a = intercept for acceptance line

p_β = fraction nonconforming for the consumer's risk
p_α = fraction nonconforming for the producer's risk
β = consumer's risk
α = producer's risk
d_a = number of nonconforming units for acceptance
d_r = number of nonconforming units for rejection
n = number of units inspected

Thus, the equations for the sequential plan, which is defined by $\alpha = 0.05$, $p_\alpha = 0.01$, $\beta = 0.10$, and $p_\beta = 0.06$, is obtained by the following calculations:

$$h_a = \log\left(\frac{1-\alpha}{\beta}\right)\bigg/\left[\log\left(\frac{p_\beta}{p_\alpha}\right) + \log\left(\frac{1-p_\alpha}{1-p_\beta}\right)\right]$$

$$= \log\left(\frac{1-0.05}{0.10}\right)\bigg/\left[\log\left(\frac{0.06}{0.01}\right) + \log\left(\frac{0.99}{0.94}\right)\right]$$

$$= 1.22$$

$$h_r = \log\left(\frac{1-\beta}{\alpha}\right)\bigg/\left[\log\left(\frac{p_\beta}{p_\alpha}\right) + \log\left(\frac{1-p_\alpha}{1-p_\beta}\right)\right]$$

$$= \log\left(\frac{1-0.10}{0.05}\right)\bigg/\left[\log\left(\frac{0.06}{0.01}\right) + \log\left(\frac{0.99}{0.94}\right)\right]$$

$$= 1.57$$

$$s = \log\left(\frac{1-p_\alpha}{1-p_\beta}\right)\bigg/\left[\log\left(\frac{p_\beta}{p_\alpha}\right) + \log\left(\frac{1-p_\alpha}{1-p_\beta}\right)\right]$$

$$= \log\left(\frac{1-0.01}{1-0.06}\right)\bigg/\left[\log\left(\frac{0.06}{0.01}\right) + \log\left(\frac{0.99}{0.94}\right)\right]$$

$$= 0.03$$

Substituting the values of $h_a = 1.22$, $h_r = 1.57$, and $s = 0.03$ into the formulas for d_a and d_r, we obtain the following equations:

$$d_a = -1.22 + 0.03n$$

$$d_r = 1.57 + 0.03n$$

The above equations are the same as those used for the acceptance and rejection lines of Figure 7-4.

While the graphical presentation of Figure 7-4 can be used as the sampling plan, it is usually more convenient to use the tabular form. This is easily accomplished by substituting values of n into the equations for the acceptance and rejection lines and calculating d_a and d_r. For example, the calculations for $n = 17$ are:

$$d_a = -1.22 + 0.03n \qquad d_r = 1.57 + 0.03n$$

$$= -1.22 + 0.03(17) \qquad = 1.57 + 0.03(17)$$

$$= -0.71 \qquad\qquad = 2.08$$

Since number of nonconforming units (d_a and d_r) are whole numbers, the rejection number is the next whole number above d_r and the acceptance number is the next whole number below d_a. Thus, $n = 17$, $d_a = 0$, and $d_r = 3$. Table 7-5 illustrates the sampling plan for the first 113 samples.

TABLE 7-5   Unit-by-Unit Sequential Sampling Plan $\alpha = 0.05$, $p_\alpha = 0.01$, $\beta = 0.10$, and $p_\beta = 0.06$

NUMBER OF UNITS INSPECTED, n	ACCEPTANCE NUMBER, d_a	REJECTION NUMBER, d_r
1	a	b
2–15	a	2
16–40	a	3
41–47	0	3
48–73	0	4
74–80	1	4
81–106	1	5
107–113	2	5

[a] Acceptance not possible.
[b] Rejection not possible.

It is sometimes preferable to take the sample in groups rather than singly. This is accomplished by using multiples of the desired sample size. Therefore, if the sample size is 5, the acceptance and rejection numbers are determined for n values of 5, 10, 15, ...

Sequential sampling is used to reduce the number inspected for items that require costly or destructive testing. It is also applicable for any situation since the average amount inspected will be less than for multiple sampling.

Skip-Lot Sampling

Skip-lot sampling was devised by H. F. Dodge in 1955.[4] It is a single sampling plan for minimizing inspection costs when there is a continuing supply of lots of raw material, component parts, subassemblies, and finished parts from the same source. It is particularly applicable to chemical and physical characteristics that require laboratory analyses.

The skip-lot sampling plan designated SkSP-1 is based on the AOQL. However, the AOQL refers to units rather than lots, as discussed in Chapter 6. Thus, an AOQL of 1% means that on the average the plan will accept no more than 1% of the lots that are nonconforming for the characteristic under consideration.

The SkSP-1 plan begins with the inspection of every lot. When a prescribed

[4] H. F. Dodge, "Skip-Lot Sampling Plans," *Industrial Quality Control,* 11, No. 5 (February 1955), 3–5.

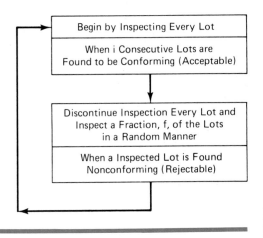

FIGURE 7-5   Procedure for SkSP-1 plans.

number of lots have been accepted, a sampling of lots occurs. Figure 7-5 describes the SkSP-1 in a flow-chart format. When a lot is rejected while in the sampling mode, the plan reverts to inspecting every lot.

The plan is a modification of a continuous sampling plan, CSP-1, which is described later in the chapter. The primary difference is that SkSP-1 refers to lots and CSP-1 refers to units. Table 7-6 is used for both plans to provide a family of i and f values for each AOQL value. Thus, for an AOQL of 1.22% any of the following i and f values could be used:

f	i
$\frac{1}{2}$	23
$\frac{1}{3}$	38
$\frac{1}{4}$	49
$\frac{1}{5}$	58
⋮	⋮
$\frac{1}{200}$	255

In general, the f values used will be those at the top of the table—$\frac{1}{2}$ to $\frac{1}{5}$.

The best way to select lots to be inspected, while in the sampling mode, is to use a known probability sampling method. Thus, if $f = \frac{1}{2}$, then a head on the flip of a coin would decide if the lot is inspected; if $f = \frac{1}{3}$, a 1 or 2 on the roll of a six-sided die would determine if the lot is inspected; or if $f = \frac{1}{4}$, a spade on a draw from a deck of cards would determine if the lot is inspected.

The plans assume that nonconforming (rejected) lots will be rectified. If this does not occur, then the i value has to be increased by 1.

TABLE 7-6 Values of i for CSP-1 plans

f	AOQL (%)															
	0.018	0.033	0.046	0.074	0.113	0.143	0.198	0.33	0.53	0.79	1.22	1.90	2.90	4.94	7.12	11.46
$\frac{1}{2}$	1,540	840	600	375	245	194	140	84	53	36	23	15	10	6	5	3
$\frac{1}{3}$	2,550	1,390	1,000	620	405	321	232	140	87	59	38	25	16	10	7	5
$\frac{1}{4}$	3,340	1,820	1,310	810	530	420	303	182	113	76	49	32	21	13	9	6
$\frac{1}{5}$	3,960	2,160	1,550	965	630	498	360	217	135	91	58	38	25	15	11	7
$\frac{1}{7}$	4,950	2,700	1,940	1,205	790	623	450	270	168	113	73	47	31	18	13	8
$\frac{1}{10}$	6,050	3,300	2,370	1,470	965	762	550	335	207	138	89	57	38	22	16	10
$\frac{1}{15}$	7,390	4,030	2,890	1,800	1,180	930	672	410	255	170	108	70	46	27	19	12
$\frac{1}{25}$	9,110	4,970	3,570	2,215	1,450	1,147	828	500	315	210	134	86	57	33	23	14
$\frac{1}{50}$	11,730	6,400	4,590	2,855	1,870	1,477	1,067	640	400	270	175	110	72	42	29	18
$\frac{1}{100}$	14,320	7,810	5,600	3,485	2,305	1,820	1,302	790	500	330	215	135	89	52	36	22
$\frac{1}{200}$	17,420	9,500	6,810	4,235	2,760	2,178	1,583	950	590	400	255	165	106	62	43	26

ANSI/ASQC S1-1987[5]

The purpose of this standard is to provide procedures to reduce the inspection effort when the supplier's quality is superior. It is a skip-lot scheme used in conjunction with the attribute lot-by-lot plans given in MIL-STD-105D/Z1.4; it is not to be confused with Dodge's skip-lot scheme described in the previous section. This sampling plan is an alternate to the reduced inspection of MIL-STD-105D/Z1.4, which permits smaller sample sizes than normal inspection.

In order to use the plan, the supplier shall

1. Have a documented system for controlling product quality and design changes.

2. Have instituted a system that is capable of detecting and correcting changes that might adversely affect quality.

3. Not have experienced an organization change that might adversely affect quality.

In addition, the product shall

1. Be of stable design, which means that there have been no substantive design changes that might adversely affect the quality.

2. Have been manufactured on a continuous basis for at least 6 months unless the supplier and responsible authority agree to a longer period. The responsible authority is the purchaser or a delegated inspection agency.

3. Have been on normal and reduced inspection at the general inspection levels I, II, or III of the MIL-STD-105D/Z1.4 during this qualification period.

4. Have maintained a quality level at or less than the AQL for at least 6 months unless the supplier and responsible authority agree to a longer period.

5. Meet the following requirements in Table 7-7 and Table 7-8.
    a. The previous 10 or more consecutive lots have been accepted.
    b. The minimum cumulative sample size in Table 7-7 for the last 10 or more consecutive lots have been met.
    c. The acceptance numbers in Table 7-8 for the last two lots have been met.

When double or multiple sampling are used, only the results of the first sample are counted.

The example problem on page 284 will illustrate the use of Tables 7-7 and 7-8.

---

[5] This section is extracted from ANSI/ASQC S1-1987 by permission of the American Society for Quality Control.

TABLE 7-7 Minimum Cumulative Sample Size to Initiate Skip-Lot Inspection—Table I of ANSI/ASQC S1–1987

NONCONFORMITIES OR NONCONFORMING ITEMS	AQL (PERCENT NONCONFORMING OR NONCONFORMITIES PER HUNDRED UNITS)												
	0.1	0.15	0.25	0.40	0.65	1.0	1.5	2.5	4.0	6.5	10.0	15.0	25.0
0	2600	1740	1040	650	400	260	174	104	65	40	26	17	10
1	4250	2840	1700	1070	654	425	284	170	107	65	43	28	17
2	5740	3830	2300	1440	883	574	383	230	144	88	57	38	23
3	7140	4760	2860	1790	1098	714	476	286	179	110	71	48	29
4	8490	5660	3400	2120	1306	849	566	340	212	131	85	57	34
5	9800	6530	3920	2450	1508	980	653	392	245	151	98	65	39
6	11090	7390	4440	2770	1706	1109	739	444	277	171	111	74	44
7	12360	8240	4940	3090	1902	1236	824	494	309	190	124	82	49
8	13610	9070	5440	3400	2094	1361	907	544	340	209	136	91	54
9	14850	9900	5940	3710	2285	1485	990	594	371	229	149	99	59
10	16080	10720	6430	4020	2474	1608	1072	643	402	247	161	107	64
11	17290	11530	6920	4320	2660	1729	1153	692	432	266	173	115	69
12	18500	12330	7400	4630	2846	1850	1233	740	463	285	185	123	74
13	19700	13130	7880	4930	3031	1970	1313	788	493	303	197	131	79
14	20890	13930	8360	5220	3214	2089	1393	836	522	321	209	139	84
15	22080	14720	8830	5520	3397	2208	1472	883	552	340	221	147	88
16	23260	15500	9300	5820	3578	2326	1550	930	582	358	233	155	93
17	24430	16290	9770	6110	3758	2443	1629	977	611	376	244	163	98
18	25600	17070	10240	6400	3938	2560	1707	1024	640	394	256	171	102
19	26760	17840	10700	6690	4117	2676	1784	1070	669	412	268	178	107
20	27930	18620	11170	6980	4297	2793	1862	1117	698	430	279	186	112
Each additional	1170	780	470	290	180	117	78	47	29	18	12	8	5

TABLE 7-8 Acceptance Numbers to Initiate or Continue Skip-Lot Inspection (Individual Lot Criterion)—Table II of ANSI/ASQC SI—1987

SAMPLE SIZE	AQL (PERCENT NONCONFORMING OR NONCONFORMITIES PER HUNDRED UNITS)												
	0.1	0.15	0.25	0.4	0.65	1.0	1.5	2.5	4.0	6.5	10.0	15.0	25.0
2	-	-	-	-	-	-	-	-	-	-	0	0	1
3	-	-	-	-	-	-	-	-	-	0	0	1	1
5	-	-	-	-	-	-	-	-	0	0	1	1	2
8	-	-	-	-	-	-	-	0	0	1	1	2	3
13	-	-	-	-	-	-	0	0	1	1	2	3	5
20	-	-	-	-	-	0	0	1	1	2	3	5	7
32	-	-	-	-	0	0	1	1	2	3	5	7	11
50	-	-	-	0	0	1	1	2	3	5	7	11	17
80	-	-	0	0	1	1	2	3	5	7	11	17	-
125	-	0	0	1	1	2	3	5	7	11	17	-	-
200	0	0	1	1	2	3	5	7	11	17	-	-	-
315	0	1	1	2	3	5	7	11	17	-	-	-	-
500	1	1	2	3	5	7	11	17	-	-	-	-	-
800	1	2	3	5	7	11	17	-	-	-	-	-	-
1250	2	3	5	7	11	17	-	-	-	-	-	-	-
2000	3	5	7	11	17	-	-	-	-	-	-	-	-

A manufacturer of $3\frac{1}{2}$-in. computer disks meets the supplier requirements and the first four product requirements. In addition, the responsible authority established an AQL of 0.25. From 12 consecutive lots, all of which were accepted, a total of 6000 units were inspected. Nine nonconforming items were found in the 12 lots, and in the last two lots with a sample size of 500, there were one and zero nonconforming items, respectively.

Twelve lots were used because the requirements were not met on the tenth or eleventh lots. The requirements of Table 7-7 are met because the minimum cumulative sample size for nine nonconforming items is 5940, which is less than the 6000 inspected. Also, the requirements of Table 7-8 are met because for a sample size of 500, the allowable number of nonconforming items is two, and the last two lots had one and zero, respectively. Therefore, the product qualifies for skip-lot inspection.

Percent nonconforming applies only to AQL values of 10.0 or less in tables. All AQL values are applicable to nonconformities per hundred units. Table 7-7 can be extended beyond 20 by adding the value in the last row for each additional nonconforming item. Thus, for an AQL of 1.5 and 24 nonconforming items, the minimum cumulative sample size is 2174 [1862 + 4(78)].

There are three basic states to the standard. State 1 is the lot-by-lot inspection activity. When the supplier and product qualify for skip-lot inspection as described before, the scheme switches to state 2, which is the skip-lot state. State 3 is a temporary state in which skip-lot inspection can be interrupted while requalification occurs under less stringent procedures. While in state 2 or 3, disqualification can occur, in which case the program switches to state 1. Figure 7-6 shows the three states. Mul-

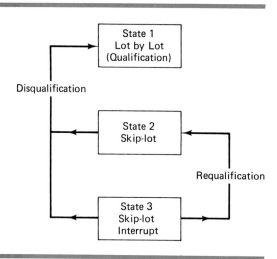

FIGURE 7-6 **Diagram of the three states.**

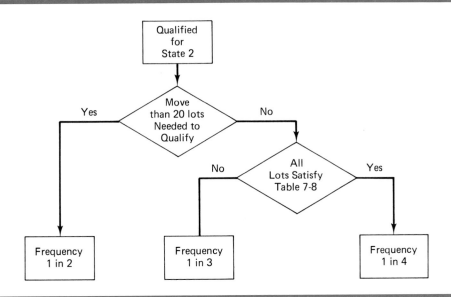

FIGURE 7-7   Diagram of the initial frequency.

tiple sampling is not allowed during states 2 and 3 and it is strongly recommended that an acceptance number of zero ($c = 0$) not be used during states 2 and 3.

Skip-lot inspection (state 2) provides for four possible frequencies: 1 lot inspected in 2 submitted, 1 lot inspected in 3 submitted, 1 lot inspected in 4 submitted, and 1 lot inspected in 5 submitted. The first three frequencies are applicable for the initial skip-lot inspection frequency. Figure 7-7 shows the decision diagram for the initial frequency. It is based on the inspection results during State 1. If more than 20 lots are needed to qualify, then the frequency is 1 out of 2, which is the worst-case situation. If 20 or fewer lots are needed to qualify but some of the lots do not satisfy Table 7-8, the frequency is 1 out of 3. However, if all of the 20 or fewer lots satisfy Table 7-8, the frequency is 1 out of 4.

EXAMPLE PROBLEM

Determine the initial frequency of the previous example problem, the qualifying state (state 1). The initial frequency will be 1 in 4 because Table 7-7 was met in 20 or fewer lots, and all lots met Table 7-8.

The frequency of inspection can be shifted to the next lower frequency by meeting the following conditions:

1. Preceding 10 or more inspected lots accepted
2. Cumulation results satisfy Table 7-7

3. Each of last two lots satisfy Table 7-8

4. Approval of the responsible authority

The first three conditions are identical to item 5 of the product qualification requirements. If a supplier's initial frequency is 1 out of every 3, it could be reduced to 1 out of every 4, which would be a substantial savings. If double sampling is used, only the first sample is counted.

EXAMPLE PROBLEM

After an initial frequency of 1 in 4, under a scheme with an AQL of 0.65, the next 10 lots inspected are accepted with a cumulative sample size of 1625 units and a total of five nonconforming units. If the inspection results of each of the last two lots are one nonconforming unit for sample sizes of 125 and 200, is a shift to the next lower frequency possible?

Since the requirements of Table 7-7 and Table 7-8 are met, a shift to a frequency of 1 in 5 is authorized, provided the responsible authority approves.

State 3, the skip-lot interrupt state occurs whenever the last inspected lot does not meet the requirements of Table 7-8. When this situation occurs, the inspection is on a lot-by-lot basis. If four consecutive lots are accepted and the last two meet the requirements of Table 7-8, skip-lot inspection is reinstated. However, the frequency is increased to the next higher level unless the previous level was 1 out of 2. Thus, if the previous frequency was 1 out of 4, the next higher is 1 out of 3.

The product shall be disqualified for skip-lot inspection and lot-by-lot resumed when any of the following criteria are met:

1. A lot is rejected during state 3.

2. Requalification is not achieved within 10 lots.

3. There is no production activity during a period specified by the supplier and responsible authority (if no period is agreed to, it is 2 months).

4. The supplier significantly deviates from the supplier qualifications or product qualifications.

5. The responsible authority decides to return to the lot-by-lot inspection of MIL-STD-105D/Z1.4.

Skip-lot inspection should be used when it is more cost-effective than reduced inspection under MIL-STD-105D/Z1.4. Just-in-time procurement activities increase inspection costs because of smaller lot sizes; therefore, reduced inspection or skip-lot inspection is an attractive alternate to normal inspection. One feature of skip-lot is the fact that its OC curves closely approximate the corresponding normal plans.

ACCEPTANCE SAMPLING PLANS
FOR CONTINUOUS PRODUCTION

Introduction

Acceptance sampling plans that have been discussed in this chapter and in Chapter 6 were lot-by-lot plans. Many manufacturing operations do not create lots as a normal part of the production process, since they are produced by a continuous process on a conveyor or other straight-line system. In such cases acceptance sampling plans for continuous production are required.

Plans for continuous production consist of alternating sequences of sampling inspection and screening (100%) inspection. These plans usually begin with 100% inspection, and if a stated number of units (clearance number, i) are free of nonconformities, sampling inspection is instituted. Sampling continues until a specific number of nonconforming units are found, at which time 100% inspection is reinstated.

Sampling plans for continuous production are applicable to attribute, nondestructive inspection of moving product. The inspection must be of such a nature that it is relatively easy and rapid so that no "bottlenecks" occur because of the inspection activity. In addition, the process must be capable of manufacturing homogeneous product. Production personnel usually handle the 100% inspection and quality personnel the sampling. Critical, major, and minor classifications in a unit will have different AOQL and i values, but usually the same f value.

The concept of sampling for continuous production was first devised by H. F. Dodge in 1943, with a sampling plan that has been commonly referred to as CSP-1. This plan and two additional plans, CSP-2 and CSP-3, are categorized as single-level plans. In 1955 the theory of multilevel continuous plans was presented by G. Licherman and H. Soloman. Multilevel plans provide for reduced levels of sampling inspection when the quality continues to be superior.[6] Much of this early work was incorporated into MIL-STD-1235 (ORD), which was superseded by MIL-STD-1235A (MU) on June 28, 1974. The designation for the standard was changed to MIL-STD-1235B when the U. S. Navy adopted the plan on December 10, 1981.

CSP-1[7] Plans

This plan begins by 100% inspection (screening) of the product in the order of production until a certain number of successive units are free of nonconformities. When that number is obtained, 100% inspection is discontinued and sampling inspection begun. The sample is a fraction of the flow of the product and is selected in such a manner as to minimize any bias. If a nonconformity occurs, sampling inspection is discontinued and 100% inspection begins. Figure 7-8 shows the procedure for CSP-1 plans. The clearance number i is the number of defect-free units in 100% in-

---

[6] G. Licherman and H. Soloman, "Multi-level Continuous Sampling Plans," *Annals of Mathematical Statistics,* 26 (December 1955), 686–704.

[7] H. F. Dodge, "A Sampling Inspection Plan for Continuous Production," *Annals of Mathematical Statistics,* 14 (September 1943), 264–279.

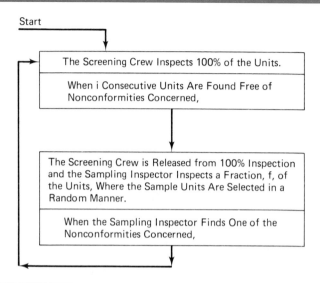

Start

The Screening Crew Inspects 100% of the Units.

When i Consecutive Units Are Found Free of Nonconformities Concerned,

The Screening Crew is Released from 100% Inspection and the Sampling Inspector Inspects a Fraction, f, of the Units, Where the Sample Units Are Selected in a Random Manner.

When the Sampling Inspector Finds One of the Nonconformities Concerned,

FIGURE 7-8   **Procedure for CSP-1 and CSP-F plans.**

spection, and the sampling frequency f is the ratio of units inspected to the total units passing an inspection station during periods of sampling inspection. Thus, an f value of $\frac{1}{20}$ means that 1 sampling inspection is made for every 20 units of product.

CSP-1 plans are indexed by an average outgoing quality limit (AOQL). For a particular AOQL, there are different combinations of i and f which are given in Table 7-6. Thus, one plan for an AOQL of 0.79 is $i = 59$ and $f = \frac{1}{3}$. This plan specifies that sampling inspection of 1 out of every 3 products is instigated after 59 consecutive products are free of nonconformities. Sampling continues until a nonconformity is found, at which time screening inspection is reinstated. Some other plans for an AOQL of 0.79 are:

$$i = 113 \qquad f = \tfrac{1}{7}$$
$$= 270 \qquad = \tfrac{1}{50}$$

Analysis of the table shows that as the f value decreases, the i value increases.

The choice of i and f values for a particular AOQL are based on practical considerations. As f gets smaller, the protection from spotty quality decreases, especially for values less than $\frac{1}{50}$. Another practical consideration is the amount of production per shift; as the amount increases, the value of f can decrease. Also, the value of f can be influenced by the sampling inspector's work load.

CSP-2 Plans

Continuous sampling inspection plan designated CSP-2 is a modification of CSP-1. Plan CSP-1 requires a return to 100% inspection wherever a nonconformity is found during the sampling inspection. CSP-2, however, does not require a return to 100%

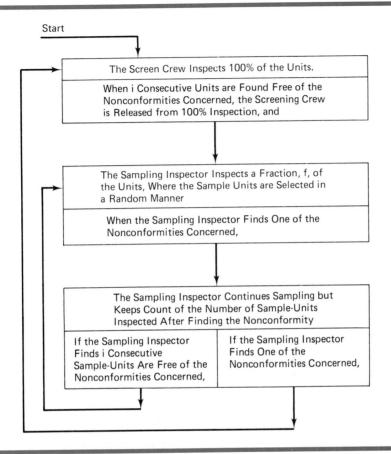

Start

The Screen Crew Inspects 100% of the Units.

When i Consecutive Units are Found Free of the Nonconformities Concerned, the Screening Crew is Released from 100% Inspection, and

The Sampling Inspector Inspects a Fraction, f, of the Units, Where the Sample Units are Selected in a Random Manner

When the Sampling Inspector Finds One of the Nonconformities Concerned,

The Sampling Inspector Continues Sampling but Keeps Count of the Number of Sample-Units Inspected After Finding the Nonconformity

If the Sampling Inspector Finds i Consecutive Sample-Units Are Free of the Nonconformities Concerned,

If the Sampling Inspector Finds One of the Nonconformities Concerned,

FIGURE 7-9   Procedure for CSP-2 plans.

inspection unless a second nonconformity is found in the next i or fewer sample units.[8] Figure 7-9 gives the procedure for CSP-2 plans.

The purpose of CSP-2 plans is to provide protection against the occurrence of an isolated nonconformity that would initiate a return to 100% inspection.

Plans are indexed by a specific AOQL which provides for different combinations of i and f, as shown in Table 7-9 on page 290. Thus, $i = 35, f = \frac{1}{5}$ and $i = 59$, $f = \frac{1}{15}$ are two of many plans for an AOQL of 2.90.

For the latter plan, $i = 59$ and $f = \frac{1}{15}$, sampling inspection of 1 out of every 15 continues after one nonconformity is found. If a second nonconformity is found in the next 59 sample units, 100% inspection is invoked. If a second nonconformity does not occur, sampling continues without the conditional stipulation.

[8] H. F. Dodge and M. N. Torrey, "Additional Continuous Sampling Inspection Plans," *Industrial Quality Control*, 7, No. 5 (March 1951), 7–12.

TABLE 7-9 Values of *i* for CSP-2 Plans

f	AOQL (%)							
	0.53	0.79	1.22	1.90	2.90	4.94	7.12	11.46
$\frac{1}{2}$	80	54	35	23	15	9	7	4
$\frac{1}{3}$	128	86	55	36	24	14	10	7
$\frac{1}{4}$	162	109	70	45	30	18	12	8
$\frac{1}{5}$	190	127	81	52	35	20	14	9
$\frac{1}{7}$	230	155	99	64	42	25	17	11
$\frac{1}{10}$	275	185	118	76	50	29	20	13
$\frac{1}{15}$	330	220	140	90	59	35	24	15
$\frac{1}{25}$	395	265	170	109	71	42	29	18
$\frac{1}{50}$	490	330	210	134	88	52	36	22

MIL-STD-1235B

The standard is composed of five different continuous sampling plans. Inspection is by attributes for nonconformities or nonconforming units using the three classes of severity: critical, major, and minor.

Continuous sampling plans are designed based on the average outgoing quality limit (AOQL). In order to be comparable with MIL-STD-105D/Z1.4 and other standards, the plans are also indexed by the acceptable quality level (AQL). The AQL is merely an index to the plans and has no other meaning.

The standard has a special provision for critical nonconformities. Only two plans, CSP-1 and CSP-F, can be used for critical nonconformities. Even in these cases the responsible authority (consumer) can require 100% inspection at all times.

In each of the five sampling plans, provision is made for the discontinuation of inspection. The consumer can suspend product acceptance when the product quality is such that 100% inspection continues beyond a prescribed number of units, *s*. In other words, if sampling inspection does not occur within *s* units, the product quality is below standard and product acceptance can be suspended. The table for *s* values is not reproduced in the text.

Sampling plans are designated by code letters. Table 7-10 provides a range of permissible code letters based on the number of units in the production interval (usually an 8-h shift). Factors that influence the selection of the code letter are inspection time per unit of product, production rate, and proximity to other inspection stations. When idle inspection time is a significant consideration, a plan with a higher sampling frequency and lower clearance number is usually preferred.

CSP-1 and CSP-2 plans. Both of Dodge's plans, CSP-1 and CSP-2, are incorporated into the standard, except the form of the plan is different. It includes sample-size code letters and AQL's as shown in Table 7-12 for the CSP-T plan.

CSP-F plans. CSP-F is a single-level continuous sampling procedure that provides for alternating sequences of 100% inspection and sampling inspection. The proce-

TABLE 7-10   Sampling-Frequency Code Letters

NUMBER OF UNITS IN PRODUCTION INTERVAL	PERMISSIBLE CODE LETTERS
2–8	A, B
9–25	A–C
26–90	A–D
91–500	A–E
501–1,200	A–F
1,201–3,200	A–G
3,201–10,000	A–H
10,001–35,000	A–I
35,001–150,000	A–J
150,001–up	A–K

dure is the same as the CSP-1 plan, which is shown in Figure 7-8. CSP-F plans are indexed by the AOQL and also by the amount of product manufactured in a production interval. This allows smaller clearance numbers to be used, which permits CSP-F plans to be applied for short-production-run situations or to be applied where the inspection operation is time-consuming.

There are 12 tables for the CSP-F plans; each table represents a different AOQL value. Table 7-11 is an example of the table for AOQL = 0.33%. Tables for other AOQL values are not included in the book. The i values in the last row of the table are the same as those given for the CSP-1 plan with an AOQL = 0.33%.

TABLE 7-11   Values of i for CSP-F Plans (AQL,[a] 0.25%; AOQL, 0.33%) [Table 3-A-8 of MIL-STD-1235B].

SAMPLE-FREQUENCY CODE LETTER	A	B	C	D	E	F	G
f	$\frac{1}{2}$	$\frac{1}{3}$	$\frac{1}{4}$	$\frac{1}{5}$	$\frac{1}{7}$	$\frac{1}{10}$	$\frac{1}{15}$
N							
1–500	70	99	114	123	133	140	146
501–1,000	77	116	140	155	174	188	200
1,001–2,000	81	127	158	181	211	236	258
2,001–3,000	82	132	166	192	228	261	291
3,001–4,000	83	134	170	198	237	276	312
4,001–5,000	83	135	173	201	244	286	327
5,001–6,000	84	136	174	204	248	293	338
6,001–7,000	84	137	176	206	251	298	346
7,001–8,000	84	137	177	207	254	302	353
8,001–9,000	84	138	177	209	256	305	358
9,001–10,000	84	138	178	209	257	308	362
10,001–11,000	84	138	178	210	259	310	366
11,001–12,000	84	139	179	211	260	312	369
12,001–15,000	84	139	180	212	262	316	376
15,001–20,000	84	140	181	214	265	320	384
20,001 and over	84	140	182	217	270	335	410

[a] AQLs are provided as indices to simplify use of this table but have no other meaning relative to the plans.

An example problem will illustrate the procedure. An AOQL value of 0.33%, an f value of $\frac{1}{4}$, and a lot size of 7500 gives an answer of $i = 177$ from Table 7-11.

CSP-T plans. CSP-T is a multilevel continuous sampling procedure that provides for alternate sequences of 100% inspection and sampling inspection. It differs from the previous inspection plans in that it provides for a reduced sampling frequency upon demonstration of superior product quality. Figure 7-10 shows the CSP-T pro-

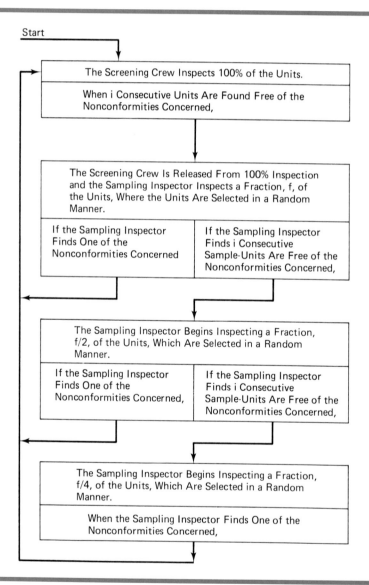

FIGURE 7-10 Procedure for CSP-T plans.

292   ADDITIONAL ACCEPTANCE SAMPLING PLAN SYSTEMS

TABLE 7-12   Values of i for CSP-T plans [Table 5-A of MIL-STD-1235B (MU)]

SAMPLING- FREQUENCY CODE LETTER	f	AQL[a] (%)							
		0.40	0.65	1.0	1.5	2.5	4.0	6.5	10.0
A	$\frac{1}{2}$	87	58	38	25	16	10	7	5
B	$\frac{1}{3}$	116	78	51	33	22	13	9	6
C	$\frac{1}{4}$	139	93	61	39	26	15	11	7
D	$\frac{1}{5}$	158	106	69	44	29	17	12	8
E	$\frac{1}{7}$	189	127	82	53	35	21	14/	9
F	$\frac{1}{10}$	224	150	97	63	41	24	17	11
G	$\frac{1}{15}$	226	179	116	74	49	29	20	13
H	$\frac{1}{25}$	324	217	141	90	59	35	24	15
I	$\frac{1}{50}$	409	274	177	114	75	44	30	19
J, K	$\frac{1}{100}$	499	335	217	139	91	53	37	23
		0.53	0.79	1.22	1.90	2.90	4.94	7.12	11.46
					AOQL (%)				

[a] AQLs are provided as indices to simplify use of this table but have no other meaning relative to the plans.

cedure. Table 7-12 gives the values of i and f for a specified AOQL. Note that the AOQL values are at the bottom of the table.

An example problem will illustrate the use of the procedure. For an AOQL value of 2.90% and an f value of $\frac{1}{7}$, the corresponding i value from Table 7-12 is 35. Screening inspection (100%) continues until 35 units are found free of nonconformities, and then sampling inspection with a frequency of $\frac{1}{7}$ commences. If no nonconformities are found in the next 35 sample units, the sample frequency is changed to $f/2$ or $\frac{1}{14}$. Sampling continues with this new frequency of $\frac{1}{14}$ until 35 sample units are found free of nonconformities, at which point the sampling frequency is further reduced. This last reduction is changed to $f/4$ or $\frac{1}{28}$, and sampling continues at this rate until production of the item is completed. Of course, any time a nonconformity is found, 100% inspection is reinstated and the procedure starts over again.

While CSP-T plans reduce the amount inspected as a result of superior quality, they create inspection personnel allocation problems. For example, with an f value of $\frac{1}{4}$, there will need to be 16 people for 100% inspection, 4 people at the first level, 2 people at the second level, and 1 person at the last level.

CSP-V plans. The fifth plan in MIL-STD-1235B is a single-level continuous sampling procedure. A return to 100% inspection is required whenever a nonconformity is discovered during the inspection of the first i sample units. Once the initial i sample units have passed and a nonconformity occurs, a return to 100% inspection is required; however, the clearance number, i, is reduced by $\frac{2}{3}$. Thus, if the original i value is 39 the clearance number, i, is reduced to 13. This type of plan can be beneficially applied in those situations where there is no advantage to reducing the sampling frequency, f. The situation occurs when inspection personnel cannot be assigned to other duties.

Figure 7-11 shows the CSP-V procedure. This plan simplifies the inspection personnel allocation problem. In addition, it will minimize the amount inspected when, and if, a nonconformity occurs.

ACCEPTANCE SAMPLING PLANS FOR VARIABLES

Introduction

While attribute sampling plans are the most common type of acceptance sampling, there are situations where variable sampling is required. Variable sampling plans are based on the sample statistics of average and standard deviation and the type of frequency distribution.

Advantages and disadvantages. Variable sampling has the principal advantage that the sample size is considerably less than with attribute sampling. In addition, variable sampling provides a better basis for improving quality and gives more information for decision making.

One of the disadvantages of variable sampling is that only one characteristic can be evaluated; a separate plan is required for each quality characteristic. Variable sampling usually involves greater administrative, clerical, and equipment costs. Furthermore, the distribution of the population has to be known or estimated.

Types of sampling plans. There are two types of variable plans—percent nonconforming and process parameter. Variable plans for percent nonconforming are designed to determine the proportion of product that is outside specifications. Of the variable plans for percent nonconforming, two will be discussed in this section. These are the Shainin lot plot and MIL-STD-414/Z1.9.

Variable plans for process parameter are designed to control the average and standard deviation of the distribution of the product to specified levels. Plans of this type are acceptance control chart, sequential sampling for variables, and hypothesis testing. Because of the limited application of these plans, they are briefly discussed at the end of this chapter.

Shainin Lot Plot Plan

The Shainin lot plot plan is a variable sampling plan used in many industries. It was developed by Dorian Shainin while he was Chief Inspector at Hamilton Standard Division of United Aircraft Corporation.[9] The plan uses a plotted frequency distribution to evaluate a sample for decisions concerning acceptance or rejection of a lot. The most significant feature of the plan is the fact that it is applicable to both normal and nonnormal frequency distributions. Another feature is its simplicity. It is a practical plan for in-house inspection as well as receiving inspection.

---

[9] Dorian Shainin, "The Hamilton Standard Lot Plot Method of Acceptance Sampling by Variables," *Industrial Quality Control,* 7, No. 1 (July 1950), 15–34.

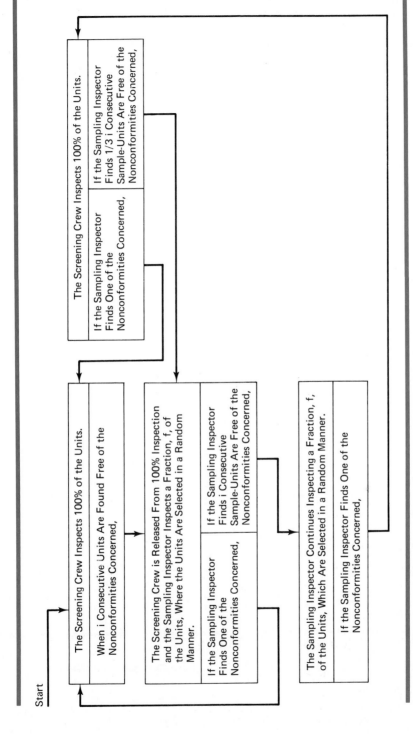

FIGURE 7-11 Procedure for CSP-V plans.

TABLE 7-13   Random Sample of 10 Subgroups of 5 Each for a Total of 50 (Data for the width of a brass plate, in millimeters)

	1	2	3	4	5	6	7	8	9	10
	96.7	97.0	98.0	97.8	97.5	98.5	98.3	98.2	97.9	97.4
	97.7	98.3	99.0	97.2	96.7	97.1	97.7	97.9	97.7	96.5
	98.4	97.2	98.3	97.6	98.1	96.8	97.6	97.8	97.8	96.9
	97.4	97.2	97.5	98.0	97.1	97.6	98.8	98.1	97.1	97.3
	97.0	97.8	97.7	97.4	96.9	98.2	98.0	98.8	98.3	98.4
Avg.	97.4	97.5	98.1	97.6	97.3	97.6	98.1	98.2	97.8	97.3
Range	1.7	1.3	0.8	1.4	1.7	1.2	1.0	1.2	1.2	1.9

Lot plot method. The method[10] for obtaining the lot plots is as follows:

1. A random sample of 10 subgroups of 5 each for a total of 50 items, is obtained from the lot. Table 7-13 shows the inspection results.

2. The average, $\overline{X}$, and range, R, are calculated for each subgroup and are shown in Table 7-13.

3. A histogram is constructed using the techniques described in Chapter 2. The Shainin plan states that the number of cells should be between 7 and 16, which is somewhat larger than the guidelines given previously. The histogram with an interval of 0.3 and 9 cells is shown in Figure 7-12.

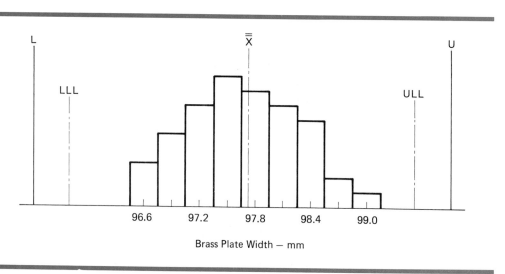

FIGURE 7-12   Lot plot histogram showing lot limits and specifications.

[10] The method has been modified to utilize modern calculation techniques and prior information given in the book.

4. The average of the averages, $\overline{\overline{X}}$, and the average of the ranges, $\overline{R}$, are

$$\overline{\overline{X}} = \frac{\Sigma \overline{X}}{g} = \frac{976.8}{10} = 97.7 \qquad \overline{R} = \frac{\Sigma R}{g} = \frac{13.7}{10} = 1.4$$

5. Using these values, the upper lot limit and lower lot limit are calculated as follows:

$$\text{ULL} = \overline{\overline{X}} + \frac{3\overline{R}}{d_2} \qquad\qquad \text{LLL} = \overline{\overline{X}} - \frac{3\overline{R}}{d_2}$$

$$= 97.7 + \frac{(3)(1.4)}{2.326} \qquad\qquad = 97.7 - \frac{(3)(1.4)}{2.326}$$

$$= 99.5 \qquad\qquad\qquad = 95.8$$

These values are shown in Figure 7-12.

Lot plot evaluation. Once the lot plot and the lot limits are obtained, the decision concerning acceptance or rejection is made. This decision is based on a comparison of the lot plot with 11 different types of lot plots which are shown in Figure 7-13.

The first four types are applicable to lot plots which are approximately normally distributed. In the type 1 situation, the lot plot is well within specification limits, and the lot is accepted without the need to calculate the lot limits. If the lot limits are within the specifications, as illustrated by type 2, the lot is accepted. When the lot limits are outside the specifications as shown by types 3 and 4, the percentage of product beyond specifications is obtained and a review board determines the final disposition of the stock. In some cases an attribute plan is employed to determine the lot acceptability when one or two values are beyond the lot limits.

The other types of lot plots are used for nonnormal distributions. For example, type 5 is skewed; types 6 and 9 indicate that the lot was screened or sorted; types 7 and 10 illustrate the bimodal condition; and type 11 is for stray values. The example problem, as shown by Figure 7-12, illustrates the type 5 lot plot and the lot would be accepted. Special techniques are specified for analyzing the nonnormal lot plots.

Comments

1. Once learned, the lot plot procedure is relatively simple and has resulted in improved quality and lower inspection costs.
2. Lot plots are returned to the producer, and this action will cause a subsequent improvement in quality.
3. Inspectors can accept lots; however, disposition of unsatisfactory lots is left to a material-review board.
4. Many users of the lot plot method have modified the Shainin method for their own situation.
5. The major criticism of the plan is that the shape of the lot plot does not always give an accurate indication of the true distribution. Shainin states that the lot

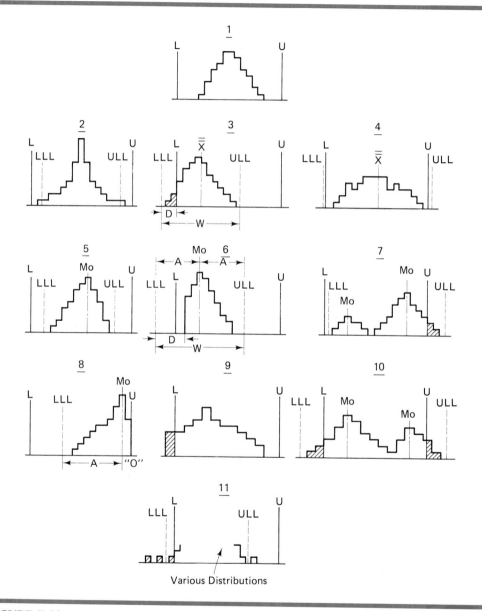

FIGURE 7-13 Eleven typical types of lot plots. [Reproduced by permission from Dorian Shainin, "The Hamilton Standard Lot Plot Method," *Industrial Quality Control,* 7, No. 1 (July 1950), 17.]

plot is close enough to have no practical effect on the final decision or if there are any errors, they are in a safe direction.

6. For additional information, the reader is referred to the published articles.[11]

MIL-STD-414 and ANSI/ASQC Z1.9-1980

MIL-STD-414 is a lot-by-lot acceptance sampling plan by variables. Modifications to MIL-STD-414 were made in 1980 by the American Society for Quality Control so that it would be more closely matched to MIL-STD-105D/Z1.4. These modifications have been included in this book.

The standard is indexed by numerical values of the AQL that range from 0.10 to 10.0%. Provision is made for normal, tightened, and reduced inspection. Sample sizes are a function of the lot size and the inspection level. The standard assumes a normally distributed random variable. Since MIL-STD-414/Z1.9 is 100 pages long, only a portion of the tables and the procedures will be given.

The standard makes provision for nine different procedures that can be used to evaluate a lot for acceptance or rejection. Figure 7-14 shows the composition of the standard. If the variability (σ) of the process is known and stable, the variability known plan is the most economical. When the variability is unknown, the standard deviation method or the range method is used. Since range method requires a larger sample size the standard deviation method is recommended. There are two types of specifications—single and double. Two alternative procedures, Forms 1 and 2, are available and will lead to the same acceptance–rejection decision. While Form 1 is somewhat easier, it is only applicable to single specification situations. Therefore, Form 2 is the preferred procedure.

MIL-STD-414 is divided into four sections. Section A contains a general description, sample-size code letters, and OC curves for the sampling plans. Procedure and examples for the unknown variability—standard deviation method are given in

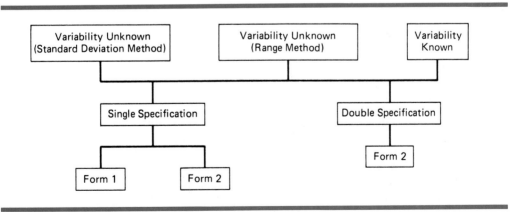

FIGURE 7-14 Composition of MIL-STD-414/Z1.9.

[11] Dorian Shainin, "Recent Lot Plot Experiences Around the Country," *Industrial Quality Control,* 8, No. 5 (March 1952), 22.

TABLE 7-14   Sample-Size Code Letters
(Table A-2 of MIL-STD-414/Z1.9)

LOT SIZE		SPECIAL		GENERAL		
		S3	S4	I	II	III
2 to	8	B	B	B	B	C
9 to	15	B	B	B	B	D
16 to	25	B	B	B	C	E
26 to	50	B	B	C	D	F
51 to	90	B	B	D	E	G
91 to	150	B	C	E	F	H
151 to	280	B	D	F	G	I
281 to	400	C	E	G	H	J
401 to	500	C	E	G	I	J
501 to	1,200	D	F	H	J	K
1,201 to	3,200	E	G	I	K	L
3,201 to	10,000	F	H	J	L	M
10,001 to	35,000	G	I	K	M	N
35,001 to	150,000	H	J	L	N	P
150,001 to	500,000	H	K	M	P	P
500,001 and over		H	K	N	P	P

Section B; procedures and examples for unknown variability—range method are given in Section C; and procedures and examples for known variability are given in Section D.

The sample size for all the methods is designated by code letters. These code letters are based on the lot size and the inspection level as shown in Table 7-14. There are five inspection levels: Special Levels S3, S4, and General Levels I, II, and III. The special levels are used when small sample sizes are necessary and large risks can and must be tolerated. An analysis of the general inspection levels is similar to MIL-STD-105D/Z1.4. Unless otherwise specified, inspection level II will be used. Inspection level III gives a steeper OC curve and therefore reduced consumer's risk. When greater consumer's risks can be tolerated, inspection level I can be used.

An example problem for unknown variability—standard deviation method, single specification, and Form 2 is used to demonstrate the procedure.

EXAMPLE PROBLEM

The minimum temperature of operation for a certain device is specified as 180°C. A lot of 40 items is submitted for inspection where inspection level II, normal inspection, and AQL = 1.0% are the criteria.

From Table 7-14 the code letter is D, which gives a sample $n = 5$ (from Table 7-15). The temperatures for the five samples are 197°, 188°, 184°, 205°, and 201°C.

$$\bar{X} = \frac{\Sigma X}{n} = \frac{197 + 188 + 184 + 205 + 201}{5} = 195°C$$

$$s = \sqrt{\frac{\Sigma X^2 - \frac{(\Sigma X)^2}{n}}{n - 1}} = \sqrt{\frac{190,435 - 190,125}{5 - 1}} = 8.80$$

Lower-quality index:

$$Q_L = \frac{\bar{X} - L}{s} = \frac{195 - 180}{8.80} = 1.70$$

Estimate of lot percent nonconforming below L: p_L

From Table 7-16, $p_L = 0.66\%$

Maximum allowable percent nonconforming: M

From Table 7-15, $M = 3.32\%$

The lot meets acceptance criterion if $p_L \leqq M$:

Since $0.66\% < 3.32\%$, accept lot

The example problem pertained to a lower specification. If the single specification had pertained to an upper specification, U, the method would have been the same except Q_U would have been calculated using the formula

$$Q_U = \frac{U - \bar{X}}{s}$$

The estimate of the percent nonconforming above U, p_U, is obtained from Table 7-16 and compared to M for the acceptance–rejection decision.

If the problem involves an upper and lower specification, then both p_U and p_L are calculated and compared to M.

EXAMPLE PROBLEM

Assuming that there is also an upper specification of 209°C for the previous example problem, determine the status of the lot.

Upper-quality index:

$$Q_U = \frac{U - \bar{X}}{s} = \frac{195 - 209}{8.80} = 1.59 \qquad \text{(say 1.60)}$$

Estimate of lot percent nonconforming above $U = p_U$

From Table 7-16, $p_U = 2.03\%$

The lot meets acceptance criteria if $p_L + p_U \leq M$

Since $(0.66 + 2.03)\% \leq 3.32\%$, accept lot

TABLE 7-15 Master Table for Normal and Tightened Inspection for Plans Based on Variability Unknown, Standard Deviation Method, (Double Specification Limit and Form 2–Single Specification Limit)—Table 13-3 of MIL-STD-414/Z1.9

SAMPLE SIZE CODE LETTER	SAMPLE SIZE	ACCEPTABLE QUALITY LEVELS (NORMAL INSPECTION)											
		T	.10	.15	.25	.40	.65	1.00	1.50	2.50	4.00	6.50	10.00
		M	M	M	M	M	M	M	M	M	M	M	M
B	3	↓	↓	↓	↓	↓	↓	↓	↓	7.59	18.86	26.94	33.69
C	4							1.53	5.50	10.92	16.45	22.86	29.45
D	5	↓	↓	↓	↓	↓	1.33	3.32	5.83	9.80	14.39	20.19	26.56
E	7				0.422	1.06	2.14	3.55	5.35	8.40	12.20	17.35	23.29
F	10			0.349	0.716	1.30	2.17	3.26	4.77	7.29	10.54	15.17	20.74
G	15	0.186	0.312	0.503	0.818	1.31	2.11	3.05	4.31	6.56	9.46	13.71	18.94
H	20	0.228	0.365	0.544	0.846	1.29	2.05	2.95	4.09	6.17	8.92	12.99	18.03
I	25	0.250	0.388	0.551	0.877	1.29	2.00	2.86	3.97	5.97	8.63	12.57	17.51
J	35	0.264	0.388	0.535	0.847	1.23	1.87	2.68	3.70	5.57	8.10	11.87	16.65
K	50	0.250	0.363	0.503	0.789	1.17	1.71	2.49	3.45	5.20	7.61	11.23	15.87
L	75	0.228	0.330	0.467	0.720	1.07	1.60	2.29	3.20	4.87	7.15	10.63	15.13
M	100	0.220	0.317	0.447	0.689	1.02	1.53	2.20	3.07	4.69	6.91	10.32	14.75
N	150	0.203	0.293	0.413	0.638	0.949	1.43	2.05	2.89	4.43	6.57	9.88	14.20
P	200	0.204	0.294	0.414	0.637	0.945	1.42	2.04	2.87	4.40	6.53	9.81	14.12
		.10	.15	.25	.40	.65	1.00	1.50	2.50	4.00	6.50	10.00	10.00
		Acceptance Quality Levels (tightened inspection)											

All AQL values are in percent nonconforming. T denotes plan used exclusively on tightened inspection and provides symbol for identification of appropriate OC curve. Use first sampling plan below arrow; that is, both sample size as well as M value. When sample size equals or exceeds lot size, every item in the lot must be inspected.

TABLE 7-16 Table for Estimating the Lot Percent Nonconforming (p_L or p_U) Using Standard Deviation Method (Values in percent) (Table B-5 of MIL-STD-414/Z1.9[a])

Q_U OR Q_L	5	10	20	30	40	50	100	200
				SAMPLE SIZE				
0	50.00	50.00	50.00	50.00	50.00	50.00	50.00	50.00
0.10	46.44	46.16	46.08	46.05	46.04	46.04	46.03	46.02
0.20	42.90	42.35	42.19	42.15	42.13	42.11	42.09	42.08
0.30	39.37	38.60	38.37	38.31	38.28	38.27	38.24	38.22
0.40	35.88	34.93	34.65	34.58	34.54	34.53	34.49	34.47
0.50	32.44	31.37	31.06	30.98	30.95	30.93	30.89	30.87
0.60	29.05	27.94	27.63	27.55	27.52	27.50	27.46	27.44
0.70	25.74	24.67	24.38	24.31	24.28	24.26	24.23	24.21
0.80	22.51	21.57	21.33	21.27	21.25	21.23	21.21	21.20
0.90	19.38	18.67	18.50	18.46	18.44	18.43	18.42	18.41
1.00	16.36	15.97	15.89	15.88	15.87	15.87	15.87	15.87
1.10	13.48	13.50	13.52	13.53	13.54	13.54	13.55	13.56
1.20	10.76	11.24	11.38	11.42	11.44	11.46	11.48	11.49
1.30	8.21	9.22	9.48	9.55	9.58	9.60	9.64	9.66
1.40	5.88	7.44	7.80	7.90	7.94	7.97	8.02	8.05
1.50	3.80	5.87	6.34	6.46	6.52	6.55	6.62	6.65
1.60	2.03	4.54	5.09	5.23	5.30	5.33	5.41	5.44
1.70	0.66	3.41	4.02	4.18	4.25	4.30	4.38	4.42
1.80	0.00	2.49	3.13	3.30	3.38	3.43	3.51	3.55
1.90	0.00	1.75	2.40	2.57	2.65	2.70	2.79	2.83
2.00	0.00	1.17	1.81	1.98	2.06	2.10	2.19	2.23
2.10	0.00	0.74	1.34	1.50	1.58	1.62	1.71	1.75
2.20	0.00	0.437	0.968	1.120	1.192	1.233	1.314	1.352
2.30	0.00	0.233	0.685	0.823	0.888	0.927	1.001	1.037
2.40	0.00	0.109	0.473	0.594	0.653	0.687	0.755	0.787
2.50	0.00	0.041	0.317	0.421	0.473	0.503	0.563	0.592
2.60	0.00	0.011	0.207	0.293	0.337	0.363	0.415	0.441
2.70	0.00	0.001	0.130	0.200	0.236	0.258	0.302	0.325
2.80	0.00	0.000	0.079	0.133	0.162	0.181	0.218	0.237
2.90	0.00	0.000	0.046	0.087	0.110	0.125	0.155	0.171
3.00	0.00	0.000	0.025	0.055	0.073	0.084	0.109	0.122

[a] The actual Table B-5 of MIL-STD-414/Z1.9 contains more sample sizes and about 10 times as many values for Q_U or Q_L.

The formula for the quantity index, Q, is very similar to the formula for the Z value which is given in Chapter 2. Table 7-16 is based on Q and the sample size, whereas Table A in the Appendix is based on the Z value and the infinite situation. The value of p is the estimate of the percent nonconforming, which is above or below the specification limit as shown in Figure 7-15. As long as p_L, p_U, or $p_L + p_U$ is less than the maximum allowable percent nonconforming, M (for a particular AQL and n), the lot is accepted.

Normal and tightened inspection use the same table. The AQL values for normal inspection are indexed from the top of the table, and for tightened inspection

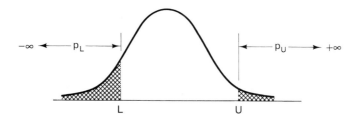

FIGURE 7-15   **Percent nonconforming below and above specifications.**

they are indexed from the bottom of the table. Switching rules are the same as MIL-STD-105D/Z1.4.

MIL-STD-414/Z1.9 contains a special procedure for application of mixed variable–attribute sampling plans. If the lot does not meet the acceptability criterion of the variable plan, an attribute single sampling plan, with tightened inspection and the same AQL, is obtained from MIL-STD-105D/Z1.4. A lot can be accepted by either of the plans in sequence but must be rejected by both the variable and the attribute plans.

Other Acceptance Sampling Plans for Variables

There are three other types of acceptance sampling plans by variables that are occasionally used. These types of variable plans are concerned with the average quality or the variability in the quality of the product and not with the percent nonconforming. They may be used for sampling bulk material that is shipped in bags, drums, tank cars, and so on. A brief discussion of each is given in this section.

Acceptance control charts provide a technique for rejecting or accepting a lot using the sample average. Acceptance control limits and the sample size are established from the known standard deviation, specification limits, AQL, and values of the consumer and producer risks. The use of a control chart allows personnel to observe quality trends.[12]

Sequential sampling by variables can be used when the quality characteristic is normally distributed and when the standard deviation is known. The technique for this sampling plan is similar to the sequential plan by attributes that was discussed previously. However, the variable plan plots the cumulative sum, ΣX, while the attribute plan plots the number of nonconforming units, d. Sequential sampling can result in reduced sampling inspection.[13]

A third type of sampling by variables is referred to as *hypothesis testing*. There

[12] For more information, see R. A. Freund, "Acceptance Control Charts," *Industrial Quality Control*, October 1957, 13–23.

[13] For more information, see A. J. Duncan, *Quality Control and Industrial Statistics* (Homewood, Ill.: Richard D. Irwin, Inc., 1987) pp. 346–360.

are a number of different tests to evaluate the sample average or sample deviation for acceptance or rejection decisions.[14]

COMPUTER PROGRAM

The computer program given in Figure 7-16 computes the OC curve for Dodge's chain sampling plan. It is structured so that values of the sample size, n, and the number of previous lots, i, can be changed to achieve the optimum sampling plan without leaving the program. If more plotted points are desired, the increment in statement 220 can be reduced to, say, 0.01.

```
10 REM                    OC CURVE-CHAIN SAMPLING
20 REM                        Based on Binomial
30 REM
40 REM                N = Sample Size (n)
50 REM                P = Proportion Nonconforming (p)
60 REM                I = Number of Previous Lots (i)
70 REM               PA = Probability  of Acceptance (pa)
80 REM
90 LPRINT "Enter the Sample Size or Enter 0 to stop program."
100 INPUT N
110 IF N = 0 GOTO 250
120 LPRINT TAB(5); " n = "; N
130 LPRINT "Enter Number of Previous Lots.": INPUT I
140 LPRINT TAB(5); " i="; I: PRINT
150 P = .01
160 LPRINT TAB(5); " p"; TAB(15); "Pa": GOTO 180
170 P = P + .04
180 Q = 1 - P
190 PO = Q ^ N
200 P1 = N * P * Q ^ (N - 1)
210 PA = PO + P1 * PO ^ I
220 LPRINT TAB(4); P; TAB(12); PA
230 IF PA < .1 GOTO 90
240 GOTO 170
250 END
```

```
n = 8
i = 5

 p         Pa
.01      .972627
.05      .699318
.09      .478809
.13      .329706
.17      .225443
.21      .151737
.25      .100116
.29      .0645756
```

FIGURE 7-16   Computer program in BASIC for the OC curves for chain sampling.

[14] For more information, see J. M. Juran, ed., *Quality Control Handbook,* 4th ed. (New York: McGraw-Hill Book Company, 1988), Sec. 23, pp. 60–81.

1. Using the Dodge–Romig tables the quality manager of a telephone manufacturer wants to determine the double sampling plan for minor nonconformities for an AOQL $= 3.0\%$ when the process average is 0.80% and the lot size is 2500. What is the LQL?

2. What would be the sampling plan of Problem 1 if the lot is a new product and the process average is unknown?

3. An insurance company is using the Dodge–Romig tables for LQL to determine a single sampling plan for a LQL $= 1.0\%$ when the process average is 0.35% and $N = 600$. What is the AOQL?

4. If the insurance company cited in Problem 3 has initiated a new form and the process average is not available, what plan is recommended?

5. If the process average is 0.19% nonconforming, what double sampling plan is recommended using the Dodge–Romig LQL tables? LQL is 1.0% and the lot size is 8000. What is the AOQL?

6. For the information in Problem 5, give the three equations needed to calculate the OC curve.

7. Determine the probability of acceptance of product that is 0.5% nonconforming using the sampling plan for Problem 3.

8. Determine the OC curve for a ChSP-1 where $n = 4$, $c = 0$, and $i = 3$. Use five points to determine the curve.

9. A chain sampling plan, ChSP-1, is being used for the inspection of lots of 250 pieces. Six samples are inspected. If none are nonconforming, the lot is accepted; if one nonconforming unit is found, the lot is accepted if the three previous lot samples were free of nonconforming units. Determine the probability of acceptance of a lot that is 3% nonconforming.

10. A unit sequential sampling plan is defined by $p_\alpha = 0.08$, $\alpha = 0.05$, $p_\beta = 0.18$, and $\beta = 0.10$. Determine the equations for the acceptance and rejection line and draw the graphical plan.

11. For a unit sequential sampling plan that is defined by $\alpha = 0.08$, $p_\alpha = 0.05$, $\beta = 0.15$, and $p_\beta = 0.12$, determine the equations for the acceptance and rejection line. Using these equations establish a table of the rejection number, acceptance number, and number of units inspected. The table can be stopped when the rejection number equals 6.

12. A food distribution warehouse is evaluating Dodge's SkSP-1 using an AOQL of 1.90%. Determine the i values for $f = \frac{1}{2}, \frac{1}{3}$, and $\frac{1}{4}$.

13. For SkSP-1 determine the i values for $f = \frac{1}{2}, \frac{1}{3}$, and $\frac{1}{4}$ using an AOQL of 0.79%.

14. A hospital supplier of disposable thermometers meets the supplier's first four product requirements and is wondering if they meet Table 7-7 and 7-8 of ANSI/ASQC S1-1987 for an AQL of 0.25. The sample size and nonconforming items for the first 10 consecutive lots are as follows:

LOT	SAMPLE SIZE	NUMBER NONCONFORMING	LOT	SAMPLE SIZE	NUMBER NONCONFORMING
1	315	0	6	315	0
2	315	2	7	315	0
3	315	0	8	315	0
4	315	0	9	315	1
5	315	1	10	315	0

15. The next 14 consecutive lots of Problem 14 are as follows:

LOT	SAMPLE SIZE	NUMBER NONCONFORMING	LOT	SAMPLE SIZE	NUMBER NONCONFORMING
11	315	1	18	315	1
12	315	0	19	315	2
13	315	0	20	315	1
14	315	0	21	315	0
15	315	0	22	315	1
16	315	0	23	315	0
17	315	0	24	315	0

Describe what happens in terms of states 1, 2, and 3. Be sure to specify the initial frequency and any changes. Note that the MIL-STD-105D/Z1.4 sampling plan for single sample normal is $n = 315$ and $c = 2$.

16. A manufacturer of capacitors is wondering if they meet Table 7-7 and Table 7-8 requirements and why. Data are as follows: AQL of 0.65%; 20 consecutive lots accepted with a total sample size of 2650; 11 nonconforming units; and the last lots have one nonconforming unit each with a sample size of 200.

17. If the product meets Table 7-7 and Table 7-8 requirements for the conditions in Problem 16, describe the initial sampling frequency (a) if all 20 lots meet the individual lot criteria, and (b) if one of the 20 lots does not meet the individual lot criteria.

18. What state occurs if lot 25 of Problem 17 has three nonconforming units?

19. A microwave manufacturer wants to evaluate three sampling plans for an AOQL = 0.143% using CSP-1. Determine the i values for $f = \frac{1}{2}, \frac{1}{4}$, and $\frac{1}{10}$.

20. For Dodge's CSP-2 plan, determine the value of i for an AOQL value of 4.94% and a frequency of 20%.

21. A computer-paper manufacturer is using MIL-STD-1235B with an AOQL of 1.22%. Determine the value of i for CSP-T with a sampling frequency of $\frac{1}{15}$. What is the sampling frequency for the second and third levels?

22. For CSP-1, determine the value of i for an AOQL = 0.198% and a frequency of $\frac{1}{4}$.

23. Determine the i value for a CSP-F plan with an AOQL of 0.33%, a lot size of 3000, and a frequency of $\frac{1}{5}$. What is the code letter?

24. If the original i value for a CSP-V plan is 150, what is the value once the initial 150 units have passed and a nonconformity occurs?

25. Using the Shainin lot plot, compute the lot limits and draw the lot plot. The hardness inspection results of 50 sample units using Rockwell-C are as follows:

SUBGROUP	DATA	AVERAGE
1	50, 49, 53, 49, 56	51.4
2	52, 50, 47, 50, 51	50.0
3	49, 49, 53, 51, 48	50.0
4	49, 52, 50, 52, 51	50.8
5	51, 53, 51, 52, 53	52.6
6	54, 50, 54, 53, 52	52.2
7	53, 51, 52, 47, 50	50.6
8	46, 55, 54, 52, 52	51.8
9	49, 53, 51, 51, 50	50.8
10	51, 48, 55, 51, 52	51.4

What type of lot plot does the distribution above represent? If the specifications are from 41 to 60, is the lot accepted or rejected?

26. The diameter of a $\frac{3}{8}$-in. thread has specifications of 9.78 mm and 9.65 mm. Sample results from 50 random inspections are given below. Determine the lot limits and draw the lot plot. What type of lot plot does the distribution below represent?

SUBGROUP	DATA	AVERAGE
1	9.77, 9.76, 9.75, 9.76, 9.76	9.760
2	9.73, 9.74, 9.77, 9.74, 9.77	9.750
3	9.73, 9.77, 9.76, 9.77, 9.75	9.756
4	9.78, 9.77, 9.77, 9.76, 9.78	9.772
5	9.72, 9.78, 9.77, 9.78, 9.74	9.758
6	9.75, 9.77, 9.76, 9.77, 9.77	9.764
7	9.78, 9.76, 9.77, 9.76, 9.78	9.770
8	9.77, 9.77, 9.77, 9.78, 9.78	9.774
9	9.78, 9.77, 9.76, 9.76, 9.77	9.768
10	9.75, 9.78, 9.77, 9.78, 9.76	9.768

27. A lot of 480 items is submitted for inspection with an inspection level of II. Determine the sample-size code letter and the sample size for inspection by variables using MIL-STD-414/Z1.9.

28. Assuming normal inspection, MIL-STD-414/Z1.9, variability unknown-standard deviation method, code letter D, AQL = 2.50%, and a single lower specification of 200 g, determine whether the lot is accepted or rejected using Form 2. The inspection results of the 5 samples are: 204, 211, 199, 209, and 208 g.

29. If the lower specification of Problem 28 is 200.5 g, what is the acceptance–rejection decision?

30. For tightened inspection, MIL-STD-414/Z1.9, variability unknown-standard deviation method, code letter F, AQL = 0.65%, and an upper single specification of 4.15 mm, determine whether the lot is accepted or rejected. Use Form 2. The results of the 10 sample inspections are 3.90, 3.70, 3.40, 4.20, 3.60, 3.50, 3.70, 3.60, 3.80, and 3.80 mm.

31. If Problem 30 has normal inspection, what is the decision?

32. If Problem 28 has tightened inspection, what is the decision?

33. If Problem 28 also has an upper specification of 212 g, what is the decision?

34. If Problem 30 also has a lower specification of 3.25 mm, what is the decision?

35. Test and, if necessary, rewrite the computer program for your computer.

36. Modify the computer program to output the OC curve for your graphical output device.

37. Write a computer program for:
    (a) Sequential sampling by attributes
    (b) CSP-1

8

RELIABILITY

FUNDAMENTAL ASPECTS

Definition

Simply stated, reliability is quality over the long run. Quality is the condition of the product during manufacturing or immediately afterward, whereas reliability is the ability of the product to perform its intended function over a period of time. A product that "works" for a long period of time is a reliable one. Since all units of a product will fail at different times, reliability is a probability.

A more precise definition is: *Reliability is the probability that a product will perform its intended function satisfactorily for a prescribed life under certain stated environmental conditions*. From the definition, there are four factors associated with reliability: (1) numerical value, (2) intended function, (3) life, and (4) environmental conditions.

The numerical value is the probability that failure[1] of the product will not oc-

---

[1] The word *failure* is used in this chapter in its limited technical sense and refers to the testing activity rather than usage.

cur during a particular time. Thus, a value of 0.93 would represent the probability that 93 of 100 products would function after a prescribed period of time and 7 products would fail before the prescribed period of time. Particular probability distributions can be used to describe the failure rate of units of product.

The second factor concerns the intended function of the product. Products are designed for particular applications and are expected to be able to perform those applications. For example, an electric hoist is expected to lift a certain design load; it is not expected to lift a load that exceeds the design specification. The screwdriver is designed to turn screws, not open paint cans.

The third factor in the definition of reliability is the intended life of the product; in other words, how long the product is expected to last. Thus, the life of automobile tires is specified by different values, such as 36 months or 48,000 km, depending on the construction of the tire. Product life is specified as a function of usage, time, or both.

The last factor in the definition involves the environmental conditions. A product that is designed to function indoors, such as an upholstered chair, cannot be expected to function reliably outdoors in the sun, wind, and precipitation. Environmental conditions also include the storage and transportation aspects of the product. These aspects may be more severe than actual use.

Achieving Reliability

Emphasis. Increased emphasis is being given to product reliability. One of the reasons for this emphasis is due to the Consumer Protection Act of 1972, which is discussed in Chapter 10. Another reason is the fact that products are more complicated. At one time the washing machine was a simple device that agitated the clothes in a hot, soapy solution. Today, a washing machine has different agitating speeds, different rinse speeds, different cycle times, different water temperatures, different water levels, and provisions to dispense a number of washing ingredients at precise times in the cycle. An additional reason for the increased emphasis on reliability is due to automation; people are, in many cases, not able to manually operate the product if an automated component fails.

System reliability. As products become more complex (have more components), the chance of failure increases. The method of arranging the components affects the reliability of the entire system. Components can be arranged in series, parallel, or a combination. Figure 8-1 illustrates the various arrangements.

When components are arranged in series, the reliability of the system is the product of the individual components. Thus, for the series arrangement of Figure 8-1a, the multiplicative theorem is applicable and the series reliability, R_s, is calculated as follows:

$$R_s = (R_A)(R_B)(R_C)$$
$$= (0.95)(0.75)(0.99)$$
$$= 0.71$$

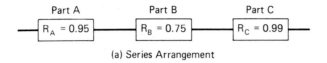

(a) Series Arrangement

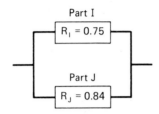

(b) Parallel Arrangement

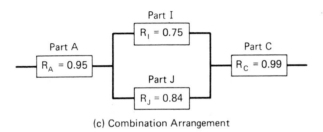

(c) Combination Arrangement

FIGURE 8-1   **Methods of arranging components.**

As components are added to the series, the system reliability decreases. Also, the system reliability is always less than its lowest value.

When components are arranged in series, the failure of any component causes failure of the system. This is not the case when the components are arranged in parallel. When a component fails, the product continues to function using another component until all parallel components have failed. Thus, for the parallel arrangement in Figure 8-1b, the parallel reliability, R_p, is calculated as follows:

$$R_p = 1 - (1 - R_I)(1 - R_J)$$

$$= 1 - (1 - 0.75)(1 - 0.84)$$

$$= 0.96$$

As the number of components in parallel increases, the reliability increases. The reliability for a parallel arrangement of components is greater than the reliability of the individual components.

Most complexed products are a combination of series and parallel arrangements of components. This is illustrated in Figure 8-1c, wherein part B is replaced by the parallel components, part I and part J. The reliability of the combination, R_c, is calculated as follows:

$$R_c = (R_a)(R_{I,J})(R_C)$$
$$= (0.95)(0.96)(0.99)$$
$$= 0.90$$

Product reliability depends on its design, manufacture, transportation, and maintenance.

Design. The most important aspect of reliability is the design. It should be as simple as possible. As previously pointed out, the greater the number of components, the greater the chance of product failure. If a system has 50 components in series, and each component has a reliability of 0.95, the system reliability is

$$R_s = R^n = 0.95^{50} = 0.08$$

Although this example is not realistic, it does support the fact that the fewer the components, the greater the reliability.

Another way of achieving reliability is to have a backup or redundant component. When the primary component fails, another component is activated. This concept was illustrated by the parallel arrangement of components. It is frequently cheaper to have inexpensive redundant components to achieve a particular reliability than to have a single expensive component.

Reliability can also be achieved by overdesign. The use of large factors of safety can increase the reliability of a product. For example, a 1-in. rope may be substituted for a $\frac{1}{2}$-in. rope even though the $\frac{1}{2}$-in. rope would have been sufficient.

When the failure of a product can lead to a fatality or substantial financial loss, a fail-safe type of device should be used. Thus, disabling extremity injuries from power-press operations are minimized by the use of a clutch. The clutch must be engaged for the ram and die to descend. If there is a malfunction of the clutch-activation system, the press will fail to operate.

The maintenance of the system is an important factor in reliability. Products that are easy to maintain will likely receive better maintenance. In some situations it may be more practical to eliminate the need for maintenance. For example, oil-impregnated bearings do not need lubrication for the life of the product.

Environmental conditions such as dust, temperature, moisture, and vibration can be the cause of failure. The designer must protect the product from these conditions. Heat shields, rubber vibration mounts, and filters are used to increase the reliability under adverse environmental conditions.

There is a definite relationship between investment in reliability (cost) and reliability. After a certain point, there is only a slight improvement in reliability for a large increase in product cost. For example, assume that a $50 component has a reliability of 0.75. If the cost is increased to $100, the reliability becomes 0.90; if the cost is increased to $150, the reliability becomes 0.94; and if the cost is increased to $200, the reliability becomes 0.96. As can be seen by this hypothetical example, there is a diminishing reliability return for the investment dollar.

Manufacturing. The manufacturing process is the second most important aspect of reliability. Basic quality control techniques that have been described in earlier chapters will minimize the risk of product failure. Emphasis should be placed on those components which are least reliable.

Manufacturing personnel can take action to ensure that the equipment used is right for the job and investigate new equipment as it becomes available. In addition, they can experiment with process conditions to determine which conditions produce the most reliable product.

Transportation. The third aspect of reliability is the transportation of the product to the customer. No matter how well conceived the design or how carefully manufactured, the actual performance of the product by the customer is the final evaluation. The reliability of the product at the point of use can be greatly affected by the type of handling the product receives in transit. Good packaging techniques and shipment evaluation are essential.

Maintenance. While designers try to eliminate the need for customer maintenance, there are many situations where it is not practical or possible. In such cases, the customer should be given ample warning. For example, a warning light or buzzer when a component needs a lubricant. Maintenance should be simple and easy to perform.

STATISTICAL ASPECTS

Distributions Applicable to Reliability

Types of continuous probability distributions used in reliability studies are exponential, normal, and Weilbull.[2] Their frequency distributions as a function of time are given in Figure 8-2a.

Reliability Curves

Reliability curves for the exponential, normal, and Weilbull distributions as a function of time are given in Figure 8-2b. The formulas for these distributions are also given in the figure. For the exponential and Weilbull curves the formulas are $R_t = e^{-t/\theta}$ and $R_t = e^{\alpha t}$, respectively. The formula for the normal distribution is

$$R_t = 1.0 - \int_0^t f(t)\, dt$$

which requires integration. However, Table A in the Appendix can be used to find the area under the curve, which is the $\int_0^t f(t)\, dt$.

Failure-Rate Curve

Failure-rate is important in describing the life-history curve of a product. The failure-rate curves and formulas for the exponential, normal, and Weibull as a function of time are shown in Figure 8-2c.

---

[2] A fourth type, the gamma distribution, is not given because of its limited application. Also, the discrete probability distributions, geometric and negative binomial, are not given for the same reason.

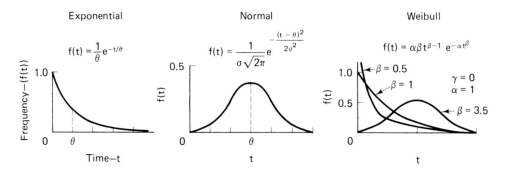

a) Frequency Distribution as a Function of Time

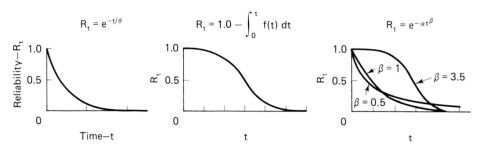

b) Reliability as a Function of Time

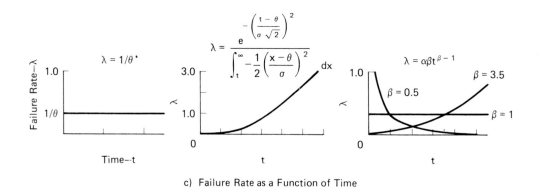

c) Failure Rate as a Function of Time

FIGURE 8-2 **Probability distributions, failure-rate curves, and reliability curves as a function of time.**

Failure rate can be estimated from test data by use of the formula

$$\lambda_{estimated} = \frac{\text{number of item failures}}{\text{sum of test times or cycles}}$$

For example, nine items are tested, with the following results at the end of 22 test hours:

Four items failed after 4, 12, 15, and 21, respectively. Five items were still operating at the end of 22 h.

$$\lambda = \frac{4}{4 + 12 + 15 + 21 + 5(22)} = 0.025$$

For the exponential distribution and for the Weibull distribution when β, the shape parameter, equals 1, there is a constant failure rate. When the failure rate is constant, the relationship between mean life and failure rate is as follows:[3]

$$\lambda = \frac{1}{\theta} \quad \text{(for constant failure rate)}$$

where λ = failure rate, which is the probability that a unit will fail in a stated unit of time or cycles

θ = mean life or mean time to failure (MTTF)

For the example problem, the mean life θ would be determined by

$$\theta = \frac{1}{\lambda} = \frac{1}{0.025} = 40 \text{ h}$$

Life-History Curve

Figure 8-3 shows a typical life-history curve of a complex product for an infinite number of items. The curve, sometimes referred to as the "bathtub" curve, is a comparison of failure rate with time. It has three distinct phases: debugging phase,

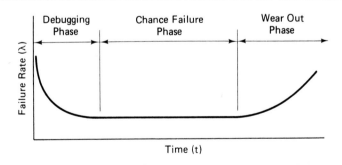

FIGURE 8-3 **Typical life history of a complexed product for an infinite number of items.**

[3] Failure rate is also equal to $f(t)/R_t$.

chance failure phase, and the wear-out phase. The probability distributions shown in Figure 8-2c are used to describe these phases.

The *debugging phase,* which is also called the burn-in or infant-mortality phase, is characterized by marginal and short-life parts that cause a rapid decrease in the failure rate. While the shape of the curve varies somewhat due to the type of product, the Weibull distribution with shaping parameters less than 1, $\beta < 1$, is used to describe the occurrence of failures. The debugging phase may be part of the testing activity prior to shipment for some products. For other products, this phase is usually covered by the warranty period. In either case, it is a significant quality cost.

The *chance failure phase* is shown in the figure as a horizontal line, thereby making the failure rate constant. Failures occur in a random manner due to the constant failure rate. The assumption of a constant failure rate is valid for most products; however, some products may have a failure rate that increases with time. In fact, a few products show a slight decrease, which means that the product is actually improving over time. The exponential distribution and the Weibull distribution with shape parameter equal to 1 are used to describe this phase of the life history. When the curve increases or decreases, a Weibull shape parameter greater or less than 1 can be used. Reliability studies and sampling plans are, for the most part, concerned with the chance failure phase. The lower the failure rate the better the product.

The third phase is the *wear-out phase,* which is depicted by a sharp rise in the failure rate. Usually the normal distribution is the one that best describes the wear-out phase. However, the Weibull distribution with shape parameters greater or less than 3.5 can be used depending on the type of wear-out distribution.

The curve shown in Figure 8-3 is the type of failure pattern exhibited by most products; however, there will be some products that deviate from this curve. It is important to know the type of failure pattern so that known probability distributions can be used for analysis and prediction of product reliability. Test results from samples are used to determine the appropriate probability distribution.

OC Curve Construction

The operating characteristic (OC) curve is constructed in a manner similar to that given in Chapter 6. However, the fraction nonconforming, p_0, is replaced by the mean life θ. The shape of the OC curve as shown in Figure 8-4 is different than those of Chapter 6. If lots are submitted with a mean life of 5000 h, the probability of acceptance is 0.697 using the sampling plan described by the OC curve of Figure 8-4.

An example problem for a constant failure rate will be used to illustrate the construction. A lot-by-lot acceptance sampling plan with replacement is as follows. Select a sample of 16 units from a lot and test each item for 600 h. If 2 or less items fail, accept the lot; if 3 or more items fail, reject the lot. In symbols, the plan is $n = 16$, $T = 600$ h, $c = 2$, and $r = 3$. When an item fails, it is replaced by another one from the lot. The first step in the construction of the curve is to assume values for the mean life θ. These values are converted to the failure rate, λ, as shown in the second column of Table 8-1. The expected average number of failures is obtained by multiplying nT by the failure rate as shown in the third column of the table. This constant is equal to 9600 h $[nT = (16)(600)]$ for this sampling plan.

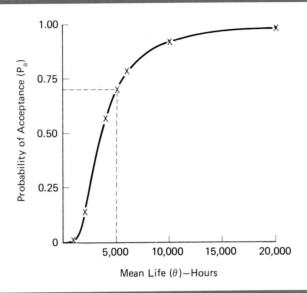

FIGURE 8-4　OC curve for the sampling plan $n = 16$, $T = 600$ h, $c = 2$, $r = 3$.

TABLE 8-1　Calculations for the OC Curve for the
Sampling Plan $n = 16$, $T = 600$ h, $c = 2$, and $r = 3$

MEAN LIFE, θ	FAILURE RATE, $\lambda = 1/\theta$	EXPECTED AVERAGE NUMBER OF FAILURES, $nT\lambda$	P_a $c = 2$
20,000	0.00005	0.48	0.983[a]
10,000	0.0001	0.96	0.927[a]
5,000	0.0002	1.92	0.698[a]
2,000	0.0005	4.80	0.142
1,000	0.0010	9.60	0.004
4,000	0.00025	2.40	0.570
6,000	0.00017	1.60	0.783

[a] By interpolation.

This value $nT\lambda$ performs the same function as the value of np_0, which was previously used for the construction of an OC curve. Values for the probability of acceptance of the lot are found in Table C of the Appendix for $c = 2$. Typical calculations are as follows: Assume that $\theta = 2000$:

$$\lambda = \frac{1}{\theta} = \frac{1}{2000} = 0.0005$$

$$nT\lambda = (16)(600)(0.0005) = 4.80$$

From Table C of the Appendix for $nT\lambda = 4.80$ and $c = 2$,

$$P_a = 0.142$$

Additional calculations for other assumed values of θ are shown in Table 8-1.

Since this OC curve assumes a constant failure rate, the exponential distribution is applicable. The Poisson distribution is used to construct the OC curve since it approximates the exponential.

Because of the constant failure rate, there are other sampling plans that will have the same OC curve. Some of these are:

$$n = 4, \qquad T = 2400 \text{ h}, \qquad c = 2$$

$$n = 8, \qquad T = 1200 \text{ h}, \qquad c = 2$$

$$n = 24, \qquad T = 450 \text{ h}, \qquad c = 2$$

Any combination of n and T values that give 9600 with $c = 2$ will have the same OC curve.

OC curves for reliability sampling plans are also plotted as a function of θ/θ_0, which is the actual mean life/acceptable mean life. When the OC curve is constructed in this manner, all OC curves for life tests with or without replacement have one point in common. This point is the producer's risk α and $\theta/\theta_0 = 1.0$.

LIFE AND RELIABILITY TESTING PLANS

Types of Tests

Since reliability testing requires the use of the product and sometimes its destruction, the type of test and the amount of testing is usually an economic decision. Testing is normally done on the end product; however, components and parts can be tested if they are presenting problems. Since testing is usually done in the laboratory, every effort should be made to simulate the real environment under controlled conditions.

Life tests are of three types, as described next.

Failure-terminated. These life-test sample plans are terminated when a pre-assigned number of failures occur to the sample. Acceptance criteria for the lot are based on the accumulated item test times when the test is terminated.

Time-terminated. This type of life-test sampling plan is terminated when the sample obtains a predetermined test time. Acceptance criteria for the lot are based on the number of failures in the sample during the test time.

Sequential. A third type of life-testing plan is a sequential life-test sampling plan whereby neither the number of failures nor the time required to reach a decision are fixed in advance. Instead, decisions depend on the accumulated results of the life test. The sequential life-test plans have the advantage that the expected test time and the expected number of failures required to reach a decision as to lot acceptability are less than the failure-terminated or the time-terminated type.

Testing may be conducted with replacement of a failed unit or without replacement. *With replacement* occurs when a failure is replaced with another unit. Test time continues to be accumulated with the new sample unit. This situation is possible when there is a constant failure rate and the replaced unit has an equal chance of failure. The *without-replacement* situation occurs when the failure is not replaced.

Tests are based on one or more of the following characteristics:

1. *Mean life*—the average life of the product.
2. *Failure rate*—the percentage of failures per unit time or number of cycles.
3. *Hazard rate*—the instantaneous failure rate at a specified time. This varies with age except in the special case of a constant failure rate wherein the failure rate and hazard rate are the same. The Weibull distribution is applicable and the hazard rate increases with age if the shape parameter β is greater than 1 and decreases with age if the shape parameter is less than 1.
4. *Reliable life*—the life beyond which some specified portion of the items in the lot will survive. The Weibull distribution and the normal distribution as they pertain to the wear-out phase are applicable.

Table 8-2 gives a summary of some of the life-testing and reliability plans. The time-terminated tests in terms of mean-life criteria are the most common plans.

Handbook H108

Quality Control and Reliability Handbook H108 gives sampling procedures and tables for life and reliability testing. Sampling plans in the handbook are based on the exponential distribution. The handbook provides for the three different types of tests: failure-terminated, time-terminated, and sequential. For each of these types of tests, provision is made for the two situations: with replacement of failed units during the test, or without replacement. Essentially, the plans are based on the mean-life criterion, although failure rate is used in one part of the handbook.

Since the handbook is over 70 pages long, only one of the plans will be illustrated. This plan is a time-terminated, with-replacement, mean-life plan, which is the most common plan. There are three methods of obtaining this plan. Example problems will be used to illustrate the methods.

1. *Stipulated producer's risk, consumer's risk, and sample size.* Determine the time-terminated, with-replacement, mean-life sampling plan, where the producer's risk, α, of rejecting lots with mean life $\theta_0 = 900$ h is 0.05 and the customer's risk, β, of accepting lots with mean life $\theta_1 = 300$ h is 0.10. The ratio θ_1/θ_0 is

$$\frac{\theta_1}{\theta_0} = \frac{300}{900} = 0.333$$

TABLE 8-2 Summary of Some Life-Testing and Reliability Plans

DOCUMENT	BASIC DISTRIBUTION AND TYPE OF PLAN	PLANS IN TERMS OF:				TYPE OF TEST		
		MEAN LIFE	HAZARD RATE	RELIABLE LIFE	FAILURE RATE (FR)	FAILURE-TERMINATED	TIME-TERMINATED	SEQUENTIAL
H 108[a]	Exponential, lot by lot	X			X	X	X	X
MIL-STD-690B[b]	Exponential, lot by lot				X		X	
MIL-STD-781C[c]	Exponential sampling scheme	X					X	X
TR-3[d]	Weibull, lot by lot	X					X	
TR-4[e]	Weibull, lot by lot		X				X	
TR-6[f]	Weibull, lot by lot			X			X	
TR-7[g]	Weibull, lot by lot, converts MIL-STD-105D	X	X	X			X	

[a] "H108, Sampling Procedures and Tables for Life and Reliability Testing (Based on Exponential Distribution)," U.S. Department of Defense, Quality Control and Reliability Handbook, Government Printing Office, Washington, D.C., 1960.
[b] "MIL-STD-690B, Failure Rate Sampling Plans and Procedures," U.S. Department of Defense, Military Standard, Government Printing Office, Washington, D.C., 1968.
[c] "MIL-STD-781C, Reliability Tests: Exponential Distribution," U.S. Department of Defense, Military Standard, Government Printing Office, Washington, D.C., 1977.
[d] "TR-3, Sampling Procedures and Tables for Life and Reliability Testing Based on the Weibull Distribution (Mean Life Criterion)," U.S. Department of Defense, Quality Control and Reliability Technical Report, Government Printing Office, Washington, D.C., 1961.
[e] "TR-4, Sampling Procedures and Tables for Life and Reliability Testing Based on the Weibull Distribution (Hazard Rate Criterion)," U.S. Department of Defense, Quality Control and Reliability Technical Report, Government Printing Office, Washington, D.C., 1962.
[f] "TR-6, Sampling Procedures and Tables for Life and Reliability Testing Based on the Weibull Distribution (Reliable Life Criterion)," U.S. Department of Defense, Quality Control and Reliability Technical Report, Government Printing Office, Washington, D.C., 1963.
[g] "TR-7, Factors and Procedures for Applying MIL-STD-105D Sampling Plans to Life and Reliability Testing," U.S. Department of Defense, Quality Control and Reliability Technical Report, Government Printing Office, Washington, D.C., 1965.

Source: Reproduced by permission from J. M. Juran ed., Quality Control Handbook (New York: McGraw-Hill Book Company, 1988), Sec. 25, p. 80.

From Table 8-3 for $\alpha = 0.05$, $\beta = 0.10$ and $\theta_1/\theta_0 = 0.333$, the code letter B-8 is obtained. Since the calculated ratio will rarely equal the one in the table, the next large one is used.

For each code letter, A, B, C, D, and E there is a table to determine the rejection number and the value of the ratio T/θ_0, where T is the test time. Table 8-4 on page 324 gives the value for code letter B. Thus, for code B-8, the rejection number r is 8. The value of T/θ_0 is a function of the sample size.

TABLE 8-3   Life-Test Sampling Plan Code Designation[a] (Table 2A-1 of H108)

$\alpha = 0.01$ $\beta = 0.01$		$\alpha = 0.05$ $\beta = 0.10$		$\alpha = 0.10$ $\beta = 0.10$		$\alpha = 0.25$ $\beta = 0.10$		$\alpha = 0.50$ $\beta = 0.10$	
CODE	θ_1/θ_0	CODE	θ_1/θ_0	CODE	θ_1/θ_0	CODE	θ_1/θ_0	CODE	θ_1/θ_0
A–1	0.004	B–1	0.022	C–1	0.046	D–1	0.125	E–1	0.301
A–2	0.038	B–2	0.091	C–2	0.137	D–2	0.247	E–2	0.432
A–3	0.082	B–3	0.154	C–3	0.207	D–3	0.325	E–3	0.502
A–4	0.123	B–4	0.205	C–4	0.261	D–4	0.379	E–4	0.550
A–5	0.160	B–5	0.246	C–5	0.304	D–5	0.421	E–5	0.584
A–6	0.193	B–6	0.282	C–6	0.340	D–6	0.455	E–6	0.611
A–7	0.221	B–7	0.312	C–7	0.370	D–7	0.483	E–7	0.633
A–8	0.247	B–8	0.338	C–8	0.396	D–8	0.506	E–8	0.652
A–9	0.270	B–9	0.361	C–9	0.418	D–9	0.526	E–9	0.667
A–10	0.291	B–10	0.382	C–10	0.438	D–10	0.544	E–10	0.681
A–11	0.371	B–11	0.459	C–11	0.512	D–11	0.608	E–11	0.729
A–12	0.428	B–12	0.512	C–12	0.561	D–12	0.650	E–12	0.759
A–13	0.470	B–13	0.550	C–13	0.597	D–13	0.680	E–13	0.781
A–14	0.504	B–14	0.581	C–14	0.624	D–14	0.703	E–14	0.798
A–15	0.554	B–15	0.625	C–15	0.666	D–15	0.737	E–15	0.821
A–16	0.591	B–16	0.658	C–16	0.695	D–16	0.761	E–16	0.838
A–17	0.653	B–17	0.711	C–17	0.743	D–17	0.800	E–17	0.865
A–18	0.692	B–18	0.745	C–18	0.774	D–18	0.824	E–18	0.882

[a] Producer's risk α, is the probability of rejecting lots with mean life θ_0; consumer's risk, β, is the probability of accepting lots with mean life θ_1.

The sample size is selected from one of the multiples of the rejection number: $2r$, $3r$, $4r$, $5r$, $6r$, $7r$, $8r$, $9r$, $10r$, and $20r$. For the life-test plans, the sample size depends on the relative cost of placing large numbers of units of product on test and on the expected length of time the life tests must continue in order to determine acceptability of the lots. Increasing the sample size will, on one hand, cut the average time required to determine acceptability but on the other hand will increase the cost due to placing more units of product on test. For this example problem, the multiple $3r$ is selected, which gives a sample size $n = 3(8) = 24$. The corresponding value of $T/\theta_0 = 0.166$, which gives a test time T of

$$T = 0.166(\theta_0)$$

$$= 0.166(900)$$

$$= 149.4 \quad \text{or} \quad 149 \text{ h}$$

TABLE 8-4　Values of T/θ_0 for $\alpha = 0.05$—Time-Terminated, with Replacement Code Letter B
[Table 2C-2(b) of H108]

CODE	r		2r	3r	4r	5r	6r	7r	8r	9r	10r	20r
							SAMPLE SIZE					
B–1	1		0.026	0.017	0.013	0.010	0.009	0.007	0.006	0.006	0.005	0.003
B–2	2		0.089	0.059	0.044	0.036	0.030	0.025	0.022	0.020	0.018	0.009
B–3	3		0.136	0.091	0.068	0.055	0.045	0.039	0.034	0.030	0.027	0.014
B–4	4		0.171	0.114	0.085	0.068	0.057	0.049	0.043	0.038	0.034	0.017
B–5	5		0.197	0.131	0.099	0.079	0.066	0.056	0.049	0.044	0.039	0.020
B–6	6		0.218	0.145	0.109	0.087	0.073	0.062	0.054	0.048	0.044	0.022
B–7	7		0.235	0.156	0.117	0.094	0.078	0.067	0.059	0.052	0.047	0.023
B–8	8		0.249	0.166	0.124	0.100	0.083	0.071	0.062	0.055	0.050	0.025
B–9	9		0.261	0.174	0.130	0.104	0.087	0.075	0.065	0.058	0.052	0.026
B–10	10		0.271	0.181	0.136	0.109	0.090	0.078	0.068	0.060	0.054	0.027
B–11	15		0.308	0.205	0.154	0.123	0.103	0.088	0.077	0.068	0.062	0.031
B–12	20		0.331	0.221	0.166	0.133	0.110	0.095	0.083	0.074	0.066	0.033
B–13	25		0.348	0.232	0.174	0.139	0.116	0.099	0.087	0.077	0.070	0.035
B–14	30		0.360	0.240	0.180	0.144	0.120	0.103	0.090	0.080	0.072	0.036
B–15	40		0.377	0.252	0.189	0.151	0.126	0.108	0.094	0.084	0.075	0.038
B–16	50		0.390	0.260	0.195	0.156	0.130	0.111	0.097	0.087	0.078	0.039
B–17	75		0.409	0.273	0.204	0.164	0.136	0.117	0.102	0.091	0.082	0.041
B–18	100		0.421	0.280	0.210	0.168	0.140	0.120	0.105	0.093	0.084	0.042

A sample of 24 items is selected from a lot and all are tested simultaneously. If the eighth failure occurs before the termination time of 149 h, the lot is rejected; if the eighth failure still has not occurred after 149 test hours, the lot is accepted.

2. *Stipulated producer's risk, rejection number, and sample size.* Determine the time-terminated, with replacement, mean-life sampling plan where the producer's risk of rejecting lots with mean life $\theta_0 = 1200$ h is 0.05, the rejection number is 5, and the sample size is 10, or $2r$. The same set of tables is used for this method as for the previous one. Table 8-4 is the table for the code letter B designation as well as for $\alpha = 0.05$. Thus, using Table 8-4, the value for $T/\theta_0 = 0.197$ and the value for T is

$$T = 0.197(\theta_0)$$

$$= 0.197(1200)$$

$$= 236.4 \quad \text{or} \quad 236 \text{ h}$$

A sample of 10 items is selected from a lot and all are tested simultaneously. If the fifth failure occurs before the termination time of 236 h, the lot is rejected; if the fifth failure still has not occurred after 236 h, the lot is accepted.

3. *Stipulated producer's risk, consumer's risk, and test time.* Determine the time-terminated, with-replacement, mean-life sampling plan which is not to exceed 500 h and which will accept a lot with mean life of 10,000 h (θ_0) at least 90% of the time ($\alpha = 0.10$) but will reject a lot with mean life of 2000 h (θ_1) about 95% of the time ($\beta = 0.05$). The first step is to calculate the two ratios, θ_1/θ_0 and T/θ_0.

$$\frac{\theta_1}{\theta_0} = \frac{2000}{10,000} = \frac{1}{5}$$

$$\frac{T}{\theta_0} = \frac{500}{10,000} = \frac{1}{20}$$

Using the value of θ_1/θ_0, T/θ_0, α, and β, the values of r and n are obtained from Table 8-5 and are $n = 34$ and $r = 4$.

The sampling plan is to select a sample of 34 items from a lot. If the fourth failure occurs before the termination time of 500 h, the lot is rejected; if the fourth failure still has not occurred after 500 h, the lot is accepted.

When using this technique the tables provided for values of $\alpha = 0.01$, 0.05, 0.10, and 0.25; $\beta = 0.01$, 0.05, 0.10, and 0.25; $\theta_1/\theta_0 = \frac{2}{3}, \frac{1}{2}, \frac{1}{3}, \frac{1}{5}, \frac{1}{10}$; and $T\theta_0 = \frac{1}{3}, \frac{1}{5}, \frac{1}{10}$, and $\frac{1}{20}$.

The method to use for obtaining the desired life-test sampling plan is determined by the available information.

TABLE 8-5 Sampling Plans for Specified α, β, θ_1/θ_0, and T/θ_0 (Table 2C-4 of H108)

θ_1/θ_0	r	T/θ_0 1/3 n	1/5 n	1/10 n	1/20 n	r	T/θ_0 1/3 n	1/5 n	1/10 n	1/20 n
		$\alpha=0.01$		$\beta=0.01$			$\alpha=0.05$		$\beta=0.01$	
2/3	136	331	551	1103	2207	95	238	397	795	1591
1/2	46	95	158	317	634	33	72	120	241	483
1/3	19	31	51	103	206	13	25	38	76	153
1/5	9	10	17	35	70	7	9	16	32	65
1/10	5	4	6	12	25	4	4	6	13	27
		$\alpha=0.01$		$\beta=0.05$			$\alpha=0.05$		$\beta=0.05$	
2/3	101	237	395	790	1581	67	162	270	541	1082
1/2	35	68	113	227	454	23	47	78	157	314
1/3	15	22	37	74	149	10	16	27	54	108
1/5	8	8	14	29	58	5	6	10	19	39
1/10	4	3	4	8	16	3	3	4	8	16
		$\alpha=0.01$		$\beta=0.10$			$\alpha=0.05$		$\beta=0.10$	
2/3	83	189	316	632	1265	55	130	216	433	867
1/2	30	56	93	187	374	19	37	62	124	248
1/3	13	18	30	60	121	8	11	19	39	79
1/5	7	7	11	23	46	4	4	7	13	27
1/10	4	2	4	8	16	3	3	4	8	16
		$\alpha=0.01$		$\beta=0.25$			$\alpha=0.05$		$\beta=0.25$	
2/3	60	130	217	434	869	35	77	129	258	517
1/2	22	37	62	125	251	13	23	38	76	153
1/3	10	12	20	41	82	6	7	13	26	52
1/5	5	4	7	13	25	3	3	4	8	16
1/10	3	2	2	4	8	2	1	2	3	7
		$\alpha=0.10$		$\beta=0.01$			$\alpha=0.25$		$\beta=0.01$	
2/3	77	197	329	659	1319	52	140	234	469	939
1/2	26	59	98	197	394	17	42	70	140	281
1/3	11	21	35	70	140	7	15	25	50	101
1/5	5	7	12	24	48	3	5	8	17	34
1/10	3	3	5	11	22	2	2	4	9	19
		$\alpha=0.10$		$\beta=0.05$			$\alpha=0.25$		$\beta=0.05$	
2/3	52	128	214	429	859	32	84	140	280	560
1/2	18	38	64	128	256	11	25	43	86	172
1/3	8	13	23	46	93	5	10	16	33	67
1/5	4	5	8	17	34	2	3	5	10	19
1/10	2	2	3	5	10	2	2	4	9	19
		$\alpha=0.10$		$\beta=0.10$			$\alpha=0.25$		$\beta=0.10$	
2/3	41	99	165	330	660	23	58	98	196	392
1/2	15	30	51	102	205	8	17	29	59	119
1/3	6	9	15	31	63	4	7	12	25	50
1/5	3	4	6	11	22	2	3	4	9	19
1/10	2	2	2	5	10	1	1	2	3	5
		$\alpha=0.10$		$\beta=0.25$			$\alpha=0.25$		$\beta=0.25$	
2/3	25	56	94	188	376	12	28	47	95	190
1/2	9	16	27	54	108	5	10	16	33	67
1/3	4	5	8	17	34	2	2	4	9	19
1/5	3	3	5	11	22	1	1	2	3	6
1/10	2	1	2	5	10	1	1	1	2	5

PROBLEMS

1. A system has four components, A, B, C, and D, with reliability values of 0.98, 0.89, 0.94, and 0.95, respectively. If the components are in series, what is the system reliability?

2. If component B of Problem 1 is changed to three parallel components and each has the same reliability, what is the system reliability now?

3. A system is composed of five components in series and each has a reliability of 0.96. If the system can be changed to three components in series, what is the change in the reliability?

4. Determine the failure rate for a 150-h test of 9 items where 3 items failed at 5, 76, and 135 h. What is the mean life?

5. If the mean life is 52 h, what is the failure rate?

6. Construct the OC curve for a sampling plan specified as $n = 24$, $T = 149$, and $r = 8$.

7. Construct the OC curve for a sampling plan specified as $n = 10$, $T = 236$, and $r = 5$.

8. Determine the time-terminated, with-replacement, mean-life sampling plan where the producer's risk of rejecting lots with mean life of 800 h is 0.05 and the consumer's risk of accepting lots with mean life $\theta_1 = 220$ is 0.10. The sample size is 30.

9. Determine the time-terminated, with-replacement sampling plan that has the following specifications: $T = 160$, $\theta_1 = 400$, $\beta = 0.10$, $\theta_0 = 800$, $\alpha = 0.05$.

10. Determine the time-terminated, with-replacement sampling plan where the producer's risk of rejecting lots with mean life $\theta_0 = 900$ h is 0.05, the rejection number is 3, and the sample size is 9.

11. Find a replacement life-test sampling plan of 300 h that will accept a lot with mean life of 3000 h 95% of the time but will reject a lot with mean life of 1000 h 90% of the time.

12. If the probability of accepting a lot with a mean life of 1100 cycles is 0.95 and the probability of rejecting a lot with mean life of 625 cycles is 0.90, what is the sampling plan for a sample size of 60?

13. Find a life-test, time-terminated sampling plan with replacement that will accept a lot with a mean life of 900 h with probability of 0.95 ($\alpha = 0.05$). The test is to be stopped after the occurrence of the second failure and 12 units of product are to be placed on test.

9

QUALITY COSTS

INTRODUCTION

In the preceding chapters, various quality control techniques were emphasized. However, in the final analysis the value of quality control must be based on its ability to contribute to profits. In our profit-oriented society, decisions are between alternatives and the effect each alternative will have on the expense and income of the business entity.

The efficiency of any business is measured in terms of dollars. Therefore, as with costs of maintenance, production, design, inspection, sales, and other activities, the cost of poor quality must be known. This cost is no different than other costs. It can be programmed, budgeted, measured, and analyzed to attain the objectives of better quality and customer satisfaction at less cost. A reduction in quality costs leads to increased profit.

Quality costs cross department lines by involving all activities of the company—marketing, purchasing, design, manufacturing, and service, to name a few.

This chapter is extracted from *Guide for Reducing Quality Costs, 2 Ed.,* 1987 and *Principles of Quality Costs,* 1986, by the Quality Cost Committee, with the permission of the American Society for Quality Control.

Some costs such as inspector salaries and rework are readily identifiable; other costs such as prevention costs associated with marketing, design, and purchasing are more difficult to identify and allocate. There are failure costs associated with lost sales and customer goodwill, which may be impossible to measure and must be estimated.

Quality costs are defined as those costs associated with the nonachievement of product or service quality as defined by the requirements established by the company and its contracts with customers and society. Simply stated it is the cost of poor products or services.

MANAGEMENT TECHNIQUE

Quality costs are used by management in its pursuit of quality improvement, customer satisfaction, market share, and profit enhancement. When quality costs are too great, it is a sign of management ineffectiveness, which can affect the company's competitive position. A quality cost program provides warning against oncoming, dangerous financial situations.

A quality cost program quantifies the magnitude of the quality problem in the language that management knows best—dollars. The cost of poor quality can exceed 20% of the sales dollar in manufacturing companies and 35% of the sales dollar in service companies. In addition, the program may show quality problem areas that were not known to exist.

Quality costs identify opportunities for quality improvement and establish funding priorities by means of Pareto analysis. This analysis allows the quality improvement program to concentrate on the vital few quality problem areas. Once corrective action has been completed, the quality costs will measure the effectiveness of that action in terms of dollars.

A quality cost program lends credence to the entire quality-management program. Arguments for quality improvement are stronger when the quality costs show a need. The program also provides cost justification for corrective action. All costs associated with poor quality and its correction are integrated into one system in order to enhance the quality management function. Quality improvement is synonymous with a reduction in the cost of poor quality. Every dollar of quality cost saved has a positive effect on profits.

There is a direct relationship between price leadership and quality leadership. You can't have one without the other.

One of the principal advantages of the program is the identification of hidden and buried costs that are not part of operations. Quality costs in marketing, purchasing, and design are brought to the forefront by the system. When senior management has all the facts on hidden and buried costs, they demand a quality cost program.

A quality cost program is a comprehensive system and should not be perceived as merely a "fire-fighting" technique. For example, one response to a customer's problem could be to increase inspection. Although this action might eliminate the problem, the quality costs would increase. Real quality improvement occurs when the root cause of the problem is found.

QUALITY COST CATEGORIES AND ELEMENTS

For the convenience of future reference and use, detailed quality costs are identified in numerical sequence. Not every element is applicable to all organizations. It is up to the reader to determine applicability in each case. The list is not meant to contain every element of quality cost applicable to every organization. It is intended to give a general idea of what types of elements are contained within each cost category to help in deciding individual classifications. If a significant cost exists that fits any part of the general description of the quality cost element, it should be used. Subelements are identified; however, detailed descriptions are not included.

1.0 Preventive Cost Category

The experience gained from the identification and elimination of specific causes of failure cost are utilized to prevent the recurrence of the same or similar failures in other products or services. Prevention is achieved by examining the total of such experience and developing specific activities for incorporation into the basic management system that will make it difficult or impossible for the same errors or failures to occur again. The prevention costs of quality have been defined to include the cost of all activities specifically designed for this purpose. Each activity may involve personnel from one or many departments. No attempt is made to define appropriate departments, since each company is organized differently.

1.1 Marketing/customer/user. Costs are incurred in the accumulation and continued evaluation of customer and user quality needs and perceptions (including feedback on reliability and performance) affecting users' satisfaction with the company's product or service. Subelements are: marketing research, customer and user-perception surveys or clinics, and contract and document review.

1.2 Product/service/design development. Costs are incurred to translate customer and user needs into reliable quality standards and requirements and manage the quality of new product or service developments prior to the release of authorized documentation for initial production. These costs are normally planned and budgeted and are applied to major design changes as well. Subelements are: design quality progress reviews, design support activities, product design qualification tests, service design qualification, and field trials.

1.3 Purchasing. Costs are incurred to assure conformance to requirements of supplier parts, materials, or processes and to minimize the impact of supplier nonconformances on the quality of delivered product or services. This area involves activities prior to and after finalization of purchase order commitments. Subelements are: supplier reviews, supplier rating, purchase order technical data reviews, and supplier quality planning.

1.4 Operations (manufacturing or service). Costs are incurred in assuring the capability and readiness of operations to meet quality standards and requirements;

quality control planning for all production activities; and the quality education of operating personnel. Subelements are: operations process validation, operations quality planning, design and development of quality measurement and control equipment, operations support quality planning, and operator quality education.

1.5 Quality administration. Costs are incurred in the overall administration of the quality management function. Subelements are: administrative salaries, administrative expenses, quality program planning, quality performance reporting, quality education, quality improvement, and quality audits.

1.6 Other prevention costs. These costs represent all other expenses of the quality system (planning, implementing, and maintaining), such as rent, travel, and telephone.

2.0 Appraisal Cost Category

The first responsibility of a quality management system is assurance of the acceptability of product or service as delivered to customers. This is the responsibility for evaluating a product or service at sequential stages, from design to first delivery and throughout the production process, to determine its acceptability for continuation in the production or life cycle. The frequency and spacing of these evaluations are based on a trade-off between the cost benefits of early discovery of defects and the cost of the evaluations (inspections and tests) themselves. Unless perfect control can be achieved, some appraisal cost will always exist. A company would never want the customer to be the only inspector. In line with this, the appraisal costs of quality have been defined to include all costs incurred in the planned conduct of product or service appraisals to determine compliance to requirements.

2.1 Purchasing appraisal costs. Purchasing appraisal costs can generally be considered to be the costs incurred for the inspection and/or test of purchased supplies or service to determine acceptability for use. These activities can be performed as part of a receiving inspection function or as a source inspection at the supplier's facility. Subelements are: receiving or incoming inspections and tests, measurement equipment, qualification of supplier product, and source inspection and control programs.

2.2 Operations (manufacturing or service) appraisal costs. Operations appraisal costs can generally be considered to be the costs incurred for the inspections, tests, or audits required to determine and assure the acceptability of product or service to continue into each discrete step in the operations plan from start of production to delivery. In each case where material losses are an integral part of the appraisal operation, such as machine setup pieces or destructive testing, the cost of the losses is to be included. Subelements are: planned operations, inspections, tests, audits, setup inspections and tests, special tests (manufacturing), process control measurements, laboratory support, measurement (inspection and test) equipment, and outside endorsements and certifications.

2.3 External appraisal costs. External appraisal costs will be incurred any time there is need for field setup or installation and checkout prior to official acceptance by the customer and also when there is need for field trials of new products or services. Subelements are: field performance evaluations, special product evaluations, and evaluations of field stock and spare parts.

2.4 Review of test and inspection data. Costs are incurred for regularly reviewing inspection and test data prior to release of the product for shipment, such as to determine whether product requirements have been met.

2.5 Miscellaneous quality evaluations. This area involves the cost of all support area quality evaluations (audits) to assure continued ability to supply acceptable support to the production process. Examples of areas included are mail rooms, storerooms, and packaging and shipping.

3.0 Internal Failure Cost Category

Whenever quality appraisals are performed, there exists the possibility for discovery of a failure to meet requirements. When this happens, unscheduled and possibly unbudgeted expenses are automatically incurred. When a complete lot of metal parts, for example, is rejected for being oversize, the possibility for rework must first be evaluated. Then the cost of rework may be compared to the cost of scrapping the parts and completely replacing them. Finally, a disposition is made and the action is carried out. The total cost of this evaluation, disposition, and subsequent action is an integral part of internal failure costs.

In attempting to cover all possibilities for failure to meet requirements within the internal product or service life cycle, failure costs have been defined to include basically all costs required to evaluate, dispose of, and either correct or replace nonconforming products or services prior to delivery to the customer and also to correct or replace incorrect or incomplete product or service description (documentation). In general, this includes all the material and labor expenses that are lost or wasted due to nonconforming or otherwise unacceptable work affecting the quality of end products or service. Corrective action that is directed toward elimination of the problem in the future may be classified as prevention.

3.1 Product or service design failure costs (internal). Design failure costs can generally be considered to be the unplanned costs that are incurred because of inherent design inadequacies in released documentation for production operations. They do not include billable costs associated with customer-directed changes (product improvements) or major redesign efforts (product upgrading) that are part of a company-sponsored marketing plan. Subelements are: design corrective action, rework due to design changes, scrap due to design changes, and production liaison costs.

3.2 Purchasing failure costs. Costs are incurred due to purchased item rejects. Subelements are: purchased material reject disposition costs, purchased material replacement costs, supplier corrective action, rework of supplier rejects, and uncontrolled material losses.

3.3 Operations (product or service) failure costs. Operations failure costs almost always represent a significant portion of overall quality costs and can generally be viewed as the costs associated with nonconforming product or service discovered during the operations process. They are categorized into three distinct areas: material review and corrective action, rework or repair costs, and scrap costs. Subelements are: material review and corrective action costs, operations rework and repair costs, and internal failure labor losses.

4.0 External Failure Cost Category

This category includes all costs incurred due to defective, or suspected defective, product or service after delivery to the customer. These costs consist primarily of costs associated with the product or service not meeting customer or user requirements. The responsibility for these losses may lie in marketing or sales, design development, or operations. Determination of responsibility is not part of the quality cost system. It can come about only through investigation and analysis of external failure cost inputs.

4.1 Complaint investigations of customer or user service. This category includes the total cost of investigating, resolving, and responding to individual customer or user complaints or inquiries, including necessary field service.

4.2 Returned goods. This category includes the total cost of evaluating and repairing or replacing goods not meeting acceptance by the customer or user due to quality problems. It does not include repairs accomplished as part of a maintenance or modification contract.

4.3 Retrofit and recall costs. Retrofit and recall costs are those costs required to modify or update products or field service facilities to a new design change level, based on major redesign due to design deficiencies. This includes only that portion of retrofits that are due to quality problems.

4.4 Warranty claims. Warranty costs include the total cost of claims paid to the customer or user after acceptance to cover expenses, including repair costs such as removing defective hardware from a system or cleaning costs due to a food or chemical service accident. In cases where a price reduction is negotiated in lieu of a warranty, the value of this reduction should be counted.

4.5 Liability costs. Liability costs are company-paid costs due to liability claims, including the cost of product or service liability insurance.

4.6 Penalties. Penalties costs are costs of any penalties incurred because of less than full product or service performance achieved as required by contracts with customers, or government rules and regulations.

4.7 Consumer or user goodwill. This category involves costs incurred, over and above normal selling costs, to customers or users who are not completely satisfied with the quality of delivered product or service, such as cost incurred because customers' quality expectations are greater than the quality they receive.

4.8 Lost sales. Lost sales include value of contribution margin lost due to sales reduction because of quality problems.

4.9 Other external failure costs. This category includes all other external failure costs.

COLLECTION AND REPORTING

Design of the Collection System

The measurement of actual quality costs is essentially an accounting function. However, the development of the collection system requires the close interaction of the quality and accounting departments. Since accounting cost data are established by departmental cost codes, a significant amount of quality cost can be obtained from this source. In fact, the system should be designed using the company's present system and modifying it where appropriate.

Some quality cost data cross departmental lines, and it is these types of costs that are the most difficult to collect. Special forms may be required to report some quality costs. For example, scrap and rework costs may require analysis by quality control personnel to determine the cause and the departments responsible.

In some cases, estimates are used to allocate the proportion of an activity that must be charged to a particular quality cost element. For example, when the marketing department engages in research, it is necessary for the departmental supervisor to estimate the proportion of the activity that pertains to customer quality needs and should be charged as a quality cost. Work-sampling techniques can be a valuable tool for assisting the supervisor in making the estimate.

Insignificant costs of poor quality, such as a secretary retyping a letter, may be difficult to determine and may be overlooked. However, significant ones are frequently hidden or buried because the accounting system is not designed to handle them. Quality cost is a tool that can determine opportunities for quality improvement, justify the corrective action, and measure its effectiveness. Including insignificant activities is not essential to use the tool effectively. All significant activities or major elements, however, must be captured even if they are only estimated.

The comptroller's office must be directly involved in the design of the collection system. Only this office has the ability to effectively create a new system that will integrate quality costs into the existing accounting system. An ideal system would be one where the quality cost is the difference between actual cost and the cost if everyone did a 100% perfect job *or* the difference between actual revenues and revenues if there were no unhappy customers. This ideal is not necessary and would be impossible to obtain.

By having the comptroller directly involved, high exposure for quality costs is provided. Also, involvement leads to teamwork with quality, which will enhance the company's ability to achieve cost reduction.

Quality costs should be collected by product line, projects, departments, operators, nonconformity classification, and work centers. This manner of collection provides sufficient information for subsequent quality cost analysis. Procedures are developed to insure that the system functions correctly.

Quality Cost Bases

Quality costs by themselves present insufficient information for analysis. A base line is required that will relate quality costs to some aspect of the business that is sensitive to change. Typical bases are labor, cost, sales, and unit. When these bases are compared with quality costs, a valuable index is obtained.

Labor. Quality cost per hour of direct labor is a common index. Direct labor information is readily available, since it is used for other indexes. Automation affects the base over an extended period of time; therefore, the value of a labor base is limited to comparisons within a short period of time.

Sometimes direct labor dollars are used rather than direct labor hours. This technique eliminates the inflation factor, since dollars are divided by dollars.

Costs. Quality costs per dollar of manufacturing cost is another common index. Manufacturing cost is composed of direct labor, direct material, and overhead. Manufacturing cost information is readily available, since it is used for other indexes. Since there are three costs involved, this index is not significantly affected by material price fluctuations or by automation. Design cost, marketing cost, or purchasing cost might also be appropriate in some situations as a substitute for the manufacturing cost.

Sales. Quality cost per dollar of net sales is the most common type of index. This information is a valuable tool for higher management decision making. Since sales lag behind production and are frequently subject to seasonal variations, this index is sometimes a poor one for short-term analysis. It is also affected by changes in selling price and shifts in available markets. However, there may be no better common denominator than net sales for year-to-year planning and measurement in the eyes of senior management.

Unit. Quality cost per unit, such as number of boxes, kilograms of aluminum, or meters of cloth, is an excellent index where product lines are similar. However, where product lines are dissimilar, comparisons are difficult to make and interpret.

Since each of the various indexes has disadvantages, it is the normal practice to use three indexes. From experience, the most useful indexes are used to compare trends in quality costs. Figure 9-2b on page 339 shows three indexes.

For current, ongoing applications, various ratios can be used. These ratios will reflect management emphasis on areas that are undergoing quality improvement. Typical ratios that may be considered are:

Operations failure costs as a percent of production costs

Purchasing quality costs as a percent of materials costs

Design quality costs as a percent of design costs

There is no limit to the number of ratios that can be used. Since there is no perfect ratio, more than one ratio is recommended.

Quality Cost Report

The basic quality cost control instrument is the quality cost report, which is usually issued by the accounting department. An example of this type report is shown in Figure 9-1 on page 338. Provision is made to report the quality costs for the current month for each cost element as well as the current and prior year year-to-date values. Applicable indexes and ratios are shown at the bottom of the report.

By comparing current quality costs with historical ones, a certain amount of control can be exercised. It is also possible to establish a budget for each cost element. By comparing actual quality costs with budget costs, favorable and unfavorable variances can be determined.

ANALYSIS

Analysis techniques for quality costs are quite varied. The quality cost report provides the information for the most common techniques: trend analysis and Pareto analysis. The objective of these techniques is to determine opportunities for quality improvement.

Trend Analysis

Trend analysis involves simply comparing present cost levels to past levels. It is suggested that at least 1 year elapse before drawing any conclusions from the data. Trend analysis provides information for long-range planning. It also provides information for the instigation and assessment of quality improvement programs. Data for trend analysis come from the monthly quality cost report and the detailed transactions that make up the elements.

Trend analysis can be accomplished by cost category, by subcategory, by product, by measurement base, by plants within a corporation, by department, by work center, and by combinations thereof. The graphs of some of these are shown in Figure 9-2 on page 339. Time scales for the graphs may be by month, quarter, or year depending on the purpose of the analysis; therefore, these graphs are also referred to as a time series.

Figure 9-2a shows a graph of the four cost categories by quarter. It is the cumulative type wherein the second line from the bottom includes the prevention and the appraisal costs; the third line includes the internal failure, appraisal, and prevention costs; and the top line includes all four cost categories. Figure 9-2a shows that

COMPANY _____ FOR MONTH ENDING _____ PREPARED BY _____

Prevention Costs $ (000)	Current Month	Year-to-Date Current	Year-to-Date Prior Yr.
Marketing/Customer			
Product/Service Development			
Purchasing			
Operations			
Quality Administration			
Total			

Appraisal Costs $ (000)	Current Month	Year-to-Date Current	Year-to-Date Prior Yr.
Product/Service Development			
Purchasing			
Operations			
External Appraisal Costs			
Total			

Internal Failure Costs $ (000)	Current Month	Year-to-Date Current	Year-to-Date Prior Yr.
Product/Service Design			
Purchasing			
Operations (Subtotal)			
Material Review			
Rework			
Repair			
Reappraisal			
Extra Operations			
Scrap			
Total			

External Failure Costs $ (000)	Current Month	Year-to-Date Current	Year-to-Date Prior Yr.
Customer Complaints			
Returned Goods			
Retrofit Costs			
Warranty Claims			
Liability Costs			
Penalties			
Customer Goodwill			
Total			

Baseline Data $ (000)	Current Month	Year-to-Date Current	Year-to-Date Prior Yr.
Net Sales			
Direct Labor			
Manufacturing Costs			
Design Costs			

Quality Cost Ratios $ (000)	Current Month	Year-to-Date Current	Year-to-Date Prior Yr.
External Failure Cost/Net Sales			
Operations Failure Costs/Production Costs			
Operations Appraisal Costs/Production Costs			
Purchasing Quality Costs/Material Costs			
Design Quality Costs/Design Costs			

FIGURE 9-1   Quality cost summary report.

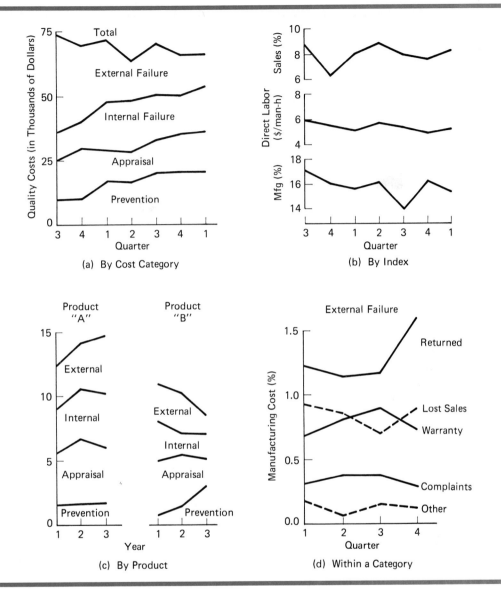

FIGURE 9-2 **Typical long-range trend analysis graphs.**

prevention and internal failure costs are increasing, appraisal costs remain unchanged, and external costs are decreasing.

Figure 9-2b shows the trend analysis for three different measurement bases.
The differences in the trends of the three bases point up the need for more than one
base. A decrease in the percent of net sales during the fourth quarter is due to a seasonal variation, while the variation in manufacturing costs for the third quarter is
due to excessive overtime costs during the quarter.

Figure 9-2c shows the trend analysis for two different products. The figure shows that the quality costs for product B are better than those for product A. In fact, product B is showing a nice improvement, whereas product A's costs are increasing. An increase in the prevention and appraisal costs will, it is hoped, improve the external and internal failure costs of product A. Comparisons between products and plants should be made with extreme caution.

A trend graph for the external failure category is shown in Figure 9-2d. Returned costs and lost sales costs have increased, while costs for the other subcategories have remained unchanged. In this figure the index is by manufacturing costs, and the time period is 6 months.

Figure 9-3 shows a short-run trend analysis chart for the assembly area. The ratio of rework costs to total assembly costs in percent is plotted by months. This ratio is compared to the quality measure, percent nonconforming. Both curves show a decrease, which supports the basic concept that quality improvement is synonymous with reduced costs.

Trend analysis is an effective tool provided it is recognized that some period-to-period fluctuations are chance variations. These variations are similar to those that occur on an $\bar{X}$ and R chart. The important factor to observe is the quality cost trend. It is also important to note that there may be a time lag between the occurrence of a cost and the actual reporting of that cost.

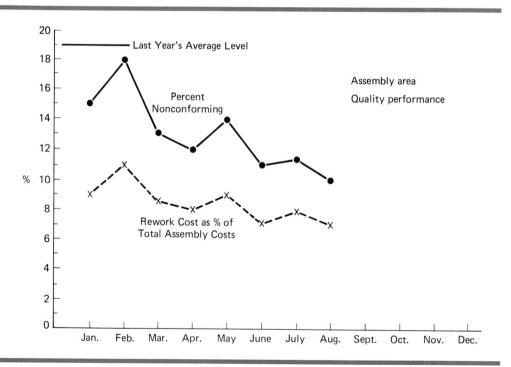

FIGURE 9-3   Typical short-run trend analysis graph.

Pareto Analysis

One of the most effective cost-analysis tools is the Pareto analysis. A typical Pareto diagram for internal failures is shown in Figure 9-4a on page 342. Items are located in descending order beginning with the largest one on the left. A Pareto diagram has a few items that represent a substantial amount of the total. These items are located on the left of the diagram and are referred to as the *vital few*. A Pareto diagram has many items that represent a small amount of the total. These items are located on the right and are referred to as the *trivial many*. Pareto diagrams can be established for quality costs by operator, by machine, by department, by product line, by nonconformity, by category, by element, and so forth.

Once the vital few are known, projects can be developed to reduce their quality costs. In other words, money is spent to reduce the vital few quality costs; little or no money is spent on the trivial many.

Figure 9-4b shows a Pareto diagram by department. This Pareto diagram is actually an analysis of one of the vital few elements (operations-scrap) in the Pareto diagram for the internal failure category in Figure 9-4a. Based on the diagram, department D would be an excellent candidate for a quality-improvement program.

OPTIMUM

In analyzing quality costs, management wants to know the optimum cost. This information is difficult to specify.

One technique is to make comparisons with other companies. More and more companies use net sales as an index, which makes comparison somewhat easier. Difficulties arise, however, because many companies keep their quality costs secret. Also, accounting systems treat the collection of quality costs differently. For example, overhead costs may or may not be included in a particular cost element. There are many variations in types of manufacturing and service organizations that cause quality cost to vary appreciably. Where complex, highly reliable products are involved, quality costs may be as high as 20% of sales; in industries that produce simple products with low tolerance requirements, quality costs of less than 2% of sales may be a realistic level.

Another technique is to optimize the individual categories. Failure costs are optimized when there are no identifiable and profitable projects for reducing them. Appraisal costs are also optimized when there are no identifiable and profitable projects for reducing them. Prevention costs are optimized when most of the dollar cost is used for improvement projects, when the prevention work itself has been analyzed for improvement, and when non-project prevention work is controlled by sound budgeting.

A third technique to determine the optimum is to analyze the relationships among the cost categories. Figure 9-5 on page 343 shows an economic model for quality costs. As the quality of conformance improves and approaches 100%, failure costs are reduced until they approach zero. In other words, if the product or service is perfect, there are no failure costs. To achieve a reduction in failure costs, it is necessary to increase appraisal and prevention costs. Combining the two curves gives

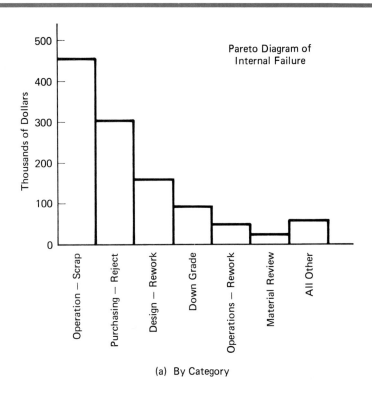

(a) By Category

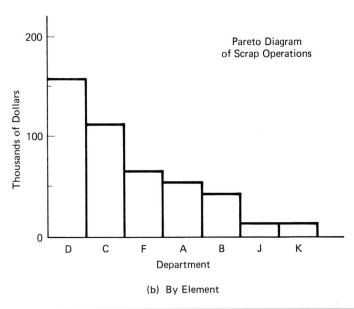

(b) By Element

FIGURE 9-4   **Pareto analysis.**

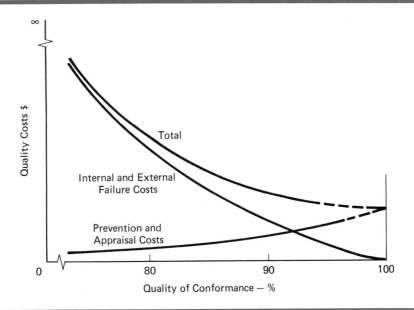

FIGURE 9-5 Optimum quality costs concept.

the total quality cost curve. The model shows that as quality increases, quality costs decrease; however, there is a school of thought that feels it is uneconomical to achieve 100% conformance. In this model, the upper two curves turn upward and their costs go to infinity rather than converge, as shown by the dashed lines. However, perfection is being economically achieved as the inspection process is automated and where the customer is willing to pay for perfect quality. Also, perfection is the goal where quality has a critical impact on safety, such as in the nuclear power field, or where lost sales can lead to bankruptcy. Therefore, this theoretical model appears to represent quality costs quite well.

Note that this model is for an entire system of quality costs. When analyzing an individual quality characteristic, it is possible to make the quality so good that it would be uneconomical.

QUALITY-IMPROVEMENT STRATEGY

The basic concept is that each failure has a root cause, causes are preventable, and prevention is cheaper. Based on this concept the following strategy is used:

1. Reduce failure costs by problem solving.
2. Invest in the "right" prevention activities.
3. Reduce appraisal costs where appropriate and in a statistically sound manner.
4. Continuously evaluate and redirect the prevention effort to gain further quality improvement.

Project Team

Once the problem area has been determined using the analysis techniques, a project team can be established. There are two types of problems: those that a department can correct with little or no outside help and those that require coordinated action from several functional areas in the organization.

Problems of the first type do not require an elaborate system. The project team could be composed of the operating supervisor, operator, quality engineer, maintenance supervisor, and any other responsible party. Usually the team has sufficient authority and resources to enact corrective action without approval of their superiors. Problems of this type usually account for about 15% of the total.

Unfortunately, about 85% of the quality problems cross departmental and functional area lines. Since these problems are usually more costly and more difficult to solve, a more elaborate and structured project team is established. Members of the team would most likely be composed of personnel from operations, quality, design, marketing, purchasing, and any other area of the entity. An operator and a senior manager could be a real asset as members of the team. The team receives written authority from the quality improvement council or a similar body. Resources are allocated and a schedule of activities is prepared. Periodic reports are given to the council.

Reducing Failure Costs

Most of the quality-improvement projects will be directed toward reducing failure costs. It is a fact that failures detected at the beginning of operations are less costly than failures detected at the end of operations or by the customer, and such failures are cheaper to correct. Therefore, external failures are frequently targeted for improvement because they can give the greatest return on investment.

The project team must concentrate on finding the root cause of the problem. In this regard, it may be necessary to trace the potential cause to purchasing, design, or marketing. Care must be exercised to ensure that the basic cause has been found rather than some pseudocause. Once the cause has been determined, the project team can concentrate on developing the corrective action to control or, preferably, eliminate the problem.

Follow-up activities are conducted to ensure that the corrective action was effective in solving the problem. The team should also review similar problems to determine if a similar solution might be effective. Finally, the quality cost saving is calculated, and a final report is presented to the quality improvement council.

Prevention of Quality Costs

Rather than solve problems that are costing money, it would be much better if problems could be prevented. Prevention activities are related to employee attitudes and to formal techniques to eliminate problems in the product cycle before they become costly.

Employee attitudes toward quality are determined by top management's commitment to quality and the involvement of both in the quality-improvement program. Suggestions for achieving this commitment and involvement are as follows:

1. Include both groups as members of project teams.
2. Establish a quality improvement council with the CEO as the chair and functional area managers as members.
3. Involve employees in the annual quality improvement program.
4. Provide a system whereby employees can present quality improvement ideas.
5. Communicate quality expectations to employees.

Formal techniques for preventing quality problems before they occur is a more desirable activity than problem solving. The following are some examples of these techniques:

1. New-product verification programs that require a comprehensive review before release for quantity production.
2. Design-review programs of new or changed designs that require involvement of appropriate functional areas at the beginning of the design process.
3. Supplier selection programs that concentrate on quality rather than price.
4. Reliability testing to prevent high field-failure costs.
5. Thorough training and testing of employees so that their jobs are done right the first time.

Effective management of prevention costs will provide the greatest quality improvement potential.

Reducing Appraisal Costs

As failure costs are reduced, the need for appraisal activities will, most likely, be reduced. Programs for cost improvement can have a significant impact on the total quality costs. Periodically, a project team should review the entire appraisal activity to determine its effectiveness.

Typical questions that the project team might investigate are these:

1. Is 100% inspection necessary?
2. Can inspection stations be combined, relocated, or eliminated?
3. Are inspection methods the most efficient?
4. Could the inspection and test activity be automated?
5. Could data be more efficiently collected, reported and analyzed using the computer?
6. Should statistical process control be used?

7. Should operating personnel be responsible for inspection?
8. Is appraisal being used as a substitute for prevention?

PROGRAM IMPLEMENTATION

The first step in the implementation of a quality cost program is to determine if the program can be beneficial to the company. A review and analysis of the cost data when made in sufficient detail will usually indicate that the costs are quite large. Before proceeding it is necessary to determine that top management is receptive to new ideas.

A presentation is prepared and given to top management to convince them of the need for the program. The presentation should describe the results to expect, the implementation plan, and the return on investment. Emphasis is placed on the company-wide aspects of quality costs and not just the operational aspects. It should be pointed out to management that they will need to take an active role in the program.

The program will have a greater chance of success if a single product line or department is used on a trial basis. Selection of the trial area should be strongly influenced by its potential to produce quick and significant results. A full-time leader who has the confidence of senior management will be needed. The steps of the trial program are: measurement of quality costs; determination of the appropriate indexes and ratios; establishment of trend-analysis charts; identification of improvement opportunities; assignment of project teams; and reporting of results.

All personnel who will be involved with the system are educated and trained. This initial training will be limited to those involved with the trial program and key members of each functional area. Education will concentrate on the purpose of quality costs: identification of opportunities for quality improvement, justification of corrective action, and measurement of results.

Concurrent with the progress of the trial program, the basic accounting procedures are revised to accommodate the quality cost system. Each cost element is described as well as how the data will be collected or estimated. Also, the methods of treating fringe benefits, overhead, and other accounting adjustments are determined. To ensure the integrity and acceptance of the data, the comptroller approves the procedures.

After the trial program is complete, the quality cost program is expanded to include the entire company. Because of better reporting, quality costs may actually increase while the system is in the development period. Data are collected onto appropriate spreadsheets by department, product, project, and so forth. Trend and Pareto analyses are conducted to determine opportunities for improvement. Projects are assigned and an ongoing system is in operation.

PROBLEMS

1. Construct a Pareto diagram for the analysis of internal failures for the following data:

TYPE OF COST	DOLLARS IN THOUSANDS
Purchasing—rejects (3.2)	205
Design—scrap (3.1)	120
Operations—rework (3.3)	355
Purchasing—rework (3.2)	25
All Other	65

2. Construct a Pareto diagram for the analysis of the external failure costs for a cellular telephone manufacturer using the following data:

TYPE OF COST	THOUSANDS OF DOLLARS
Customer complaints (4.1)	20
Returned goods (4.2)	30
Retrofit costs (4.3)	50
Warranty claims (4.4)	90
Liability costs (4.5)	10
Penalties (4.6)	5
Customer goodwill (4.7)	25

3. A building construction company needs a Pareto diagram for the analysis of the following design department quality costs:

ELEMENT	DOLLARS IN THOUSANDS
Progress reviews (1.2)	5
Support activities (1.2)	3
Qualification tests (1.2)	2
Corrective action (3.1)	15
Rework (3.1)	50
Scrap (3.1)	25
Liaison (3.1)	2

4. Construct a Pareto diagram for the analysis of the following purchasing department quality costs of a major airline:

ELEMENT	DOLLARS IN THOUSANDS
Supplier review (1.3)	10
Supplier rating (1.3)	5
Specification review (1.3)	2
Supplier quality planning (1.3)	5
Receiving inspection (2.1)	95
Measuring equipment (2.1)	60
Qualification of supplier product (2.1)	5
Source inspection (2.1)	15
Material reject (3.2)	120
Material replacement (3.2)	180
Supplier corrective action (3.2)	53
Rework of supplier (3.2)	5

5. Construct a trend-analysis graph for the four quality costs categories and the total. Quality cost data for a wheelbarrow manufacturer as a percent of net sales are as follows:

YEAR	PREVENTION	APPRAISAL	INTERNAL FAILURE	EXTERNAL FAILURE	TOTAL
1	0.2	2.6	3.7	4.7	11.2
2	0.6	2.5	3.3	3.6	10.0
3	1.2	2.8	4.0	1.8	9.8
4	1.2	1.7	3.4	1.2	7.5
5	1.0	1.3	1.8	0.9	5.0

6. For a homeowners' insurance company, prepare graph(s) and analyze the internal failure costs for the past 8 months using the labor index.

MONTH	COST	DIRECT LABOR (WORKER-HOURS)
June	$74,000	18,000
July	$69,000	16,600
Aug.	$71,000	17,300
Sept.	$74,000	17,800
Oct.	$72,000	17,600
Nov.	$74,000	17,500
Dec.	$73,000	16,800
Jan.	$81,000	18,200

7. Prepare graph(s) and analyze the appraisal costs of a leading bank for the past 8 months using the net sales index.

MONTH	COST	NET SALES IN THOUSANDS OF DOLLARS
Feb.	$45,000	$2,500
Mar.	$43,500	$2,290
April	$46,100	$2,560
May	$45,800	$2,540
June	$47,000	$2,470
July	$48,600	$2,550
Aug.	$49,900	$2,500
Sept.	$49,300	$2,580

8. For a hardware manufacturer, prepare graph(s) and analyze the internal failure costs for the past 6 months using the net sales index.

MONTH	COST	NET SALES IN THOUSANDS OF DOLLARS
Mar.	$45,300	755
April	$45,800	790
May	$46,100	840
June	$47,000	925
July	$48,600	1050
Aug.	$49,300	1232

9. For a microwave manufacturer, prepare and analyze the graph of the procurement appraisal costs as a percent of total purchased material costs using the data below:

MONTH	PROCUREMENT APPRAISAL COSTS IN THOUSANDS	PURCHASED MATERIAL COSTS IN THOUSANDS
June	8.5	102
July	7.9	127
Aug.	9.9	116
Sept.	7.2	115
Oct.	7.7	108
Nov.	6.2	112

10. Prepare a short-range trend chart of the operations appraisal cost/production cost ratio using the following data.

MONTH	OPERATION APPRAISAL COSTS IN THOUSANDS OF DOLLARS	PRODUCTION COSTS IN THOUSANDS
Jan.	10	100
Feb.	13	120
Mar.	9	115
April	11	145
May	9	125
June	8	95
July	8	105

What information does the chart give? Suggest additional information that could be valuable.

10

PRODUCT LIABILITY

INTRODUCTION

Consumers are initiating lawsuits in record numbers as a result of injury, death, and property damage from alleged faulty design or product workmanship. The number of lawsuits in this area has skyrocketed since the mid-1960s. Jury verdicts in favor of the injured party (plaintiff) have continued to rise in recent years. The size of the judgment or settlement has also increased significantly, which has caused an increase in product liability insurance. While the larger manufacturers have been able to absorb the judgment or settlement cost and pass it on to the consumer, smaller manufacturers have occasionally been forced into bankruptcy.

The development of strict liability in product liability law has made it easier for the plaintiff to obtain a favorable judgment. This implies that a manufacturer, retailer, or other member of the distributive chain is legally responsible to any customer who suffers an injury due to a defective product.

In spite of the perception created by product liability lawsuits, quality has been steadily improving. This difference is due to many reasons. There are more products

351

with more complicated designs and higher volume. Consumers are more quality-conscious and frequently do not know how to operate the product. Competition forces the marketing of products before they have been adequately tested. Indeed, exploding and unproven technology creates hazards that are not known prior to use.

History of Product Liability

Historical records indicate that in ancient times, the producers of grain were liable for the quality of their product. This liability was based on a sample, since it was physically impossible to inspect each and every grain. If the sample was of good quality, the entire shipment was considered to be good; if the sample was defective, the entire shipment was defective.[1]

By the fourteenth century, sampling inspection of textiles was commonplace. Seals and official stamps were used by producers, wholesalers, and government inspectors to attest to the quality of the goods. Sampling was used rather than 100% inspection because it was not economically feasible to inspect every yard of cloth. Economic damages were awarded to plaintiffs for defective products, and, in some cases, damages were awarded for injuries sustained as a result of defective products. Since manufactured products were of simple design, handcrafted, and relatively safe to use, lawsuits based on strict liability for injuries were infrequent.

By the middle of the eighteenth century, two concepts had developed that affected product liability litigation for about two centuries. *Caveat emptor* (let the buyer beware) is one of those concepts that resulted from Adam Smith's "invisible hand" theory of commercial regulation. This concept was part of the common law of England.

The other concept resulted from the case of *Winterbottom v. Wright*. In this case a defective wheel caused a coach to overturn, and the injured passenger sued the coach owner and the coach manufacturer. The court ruled that the coach owner was not liable because he was not aware that the wheel was defective. And the coach manufacturer was not liable because there was no contractual relationship between the injured party and the manufacturer. This decision brought about the legal concept of *privity of contract,* which required that the manufacturer and the injured party have a contractual relationship. Therefore, the manufacturer was liable to the wholesaler, the wholesaler to the retailer, and the retailer to the customer.

In cases involving food, drugs, firearms, explosives, and other ultrahazardous products, the privity of contract concept was turned aside because the harm done could be substantial. The *MacPherson v. Buick Motor Company* case of 1916 marked the beginning of the end of the privity of contract concept. In this case a defective wheel caused an injury and the court ruled that the manufacturer was liable, even in the absence of privity, since there was evidence of negligence in the assembly of the product.

Manufacturer's liability increased with the adoption of the warranty principle. There are two kinds of warranty—expressed and implied. An expressed warranty is

---

[1] In this chapter the terms defect and defective are appropriate, since they refer to usage rather than conformance.

part of the conditions of sale; the buyer purchases the product on the reasonable assumption that it is as stated by the seller. An implied warranty is implied by the law rather than the seller; the buyer purchases the product on the reasonable assumption that the product will be reliable and like the sample. Present law is such that an implied warranty is assumed for every sale by a merchant.

During the first half of the twentieth century the emphasis in product liability litigation changed from privity of contract to breach of warranty or to negligence. Negligence in the design or manufacture of the product was an effective argument for the plaintiff. However, since few manufacturers were knowingly derelict, proving negligence was difficult.

In 1965, the American Law Institute issued its Restatement of the Law of Torts Second, which is based on common law (legal decisions of cases called case law). The Restatement declared that if a product because of a defect becomes unreasonably dangerous and causes an injury, it is defectively made. A manufacturer who makes and sells that defective product has committed a fault. It is implied that he or she was negligent and, therefore, strictly liable to the injured party. This is the definition of strict liability.

On October 27, 1972, the Consumer Product Safety Act was passed. The purpose of this act is to prevent or minimize product-caused injury, illness, or death and to provide substantial civil or criminal penalties for safety violations. Details are given in the next section.

Consumer Product Safety Act

The Consumer Product Safety Act (CPSA) is a significant consumer safety law. It is a part of legislative law and augments the common law and case law of product liability.

The purposes of this act are:

1. To protect the public against unreasonable risks of injury associated with consumer products.
2. To assist consumers in evaluating the comparative safety of consumer products.
3. To develop uniform safety standards for consumer products and to minimize conflicting state and local regulations.
4. To promote research and investigation into the causes and prevention of product-related deaths, illnesses, and injuries.

Based on these purposes, it is evident that the intent of the CPSA is to prevent hazardous or defective products from reaching the customer.

A five-member commission, appointed by the President with the advice and consent of the Senate, administers this act as well as similar acts, such as the Refrigerator Safety Act and Flammable Fabrics Act. The commission is authorized to establish product safety standards relating to performance, composition, design, construction, finishing, labeling, or packaging of products. All consumer products used in and around a household, school, or for recreation are covered by the CPSA except for products administered by other agencies. Exempted products, which are covered by other agencies, include cars, boats, airplanes, food, drugs, cosmetics, tobacco, and poisons.

The commission is relying principally on the development of voluntary safety standards; however, conditions may warrant a mandatory standard. In extreme cases when a product presents an unreasonable risk of harm and when no feasible standard would adequately protect the public, the commission can declare the product a *banned hazardous product*.

The commission may file in a United States district court an action against an *imminently hazardous product* for condemnation and seizure. An imminently hazardous product is one that presents an imminent and unreasonable risk of death, serious illness, or severe personal injury. If the court declares that the product is imminently hazardous, public notice, recall, repair, replacement, or refund may be required.

A third category of hazard is a *substantial product hazard*. This category includes products that fail to comply with an applicable consumer product safety rule or contain a defect that could create a substantial risk of injury to the public. After notice and a hearing, the commission may determine that a substantial product hazard exists and order one or more of the following actions: (1) public notice of the defect, (2) mail notice to known purchasers, (3) repair of the product, (4) replacement of the product, and/or (5) refund of the purchase price.

Failure to comply with the act can invoke civil or criminal penalties. Any person who knowingly violates the rules is subject to a civil penalty not to exceed $2000 per violation. Any person who knowingly and willfully violates the rules after receiving notice of noncompliance can be fined not more than $50,000 or be imprisoned not more than one year, or both. Such criminal penalties can be imposed on officers of the corporation who knowingly violate the rules in addition to any penalties imposed on the corporation.[2]

The commission is required to maintain an injury information clearinghouse to collect, investigate, analyze, and disseminate injury data. It may conduct research and investigations on the safety of consumer products.

For purposes of implementing the act or rules, the commission can inspect manufacturing operations and appropriate records to ensure compliance.

Compliance with a consumer product safety rule does not relieve any person from liability under common law or state legislative law. However, compliance with an applicable federal standard can be an effective defense in a product liability lawsuit.

LEGAL ASPECTS

Product Liability Law

Two types of law are involved in product liability lawsuits: contracts and torts. A *contract* is an agreement between two or more parties that is enforceable in a court

[2] L. J. Lamatina, "The Consumer Product Safety Act," *Journal of Products Liability*, 4 (1981), 275–325.

of law. Warranties, either expressed or implied, are a part of the contract of sale of property at the time of sale. Lawsuits for a breach of warranty are based on contract law, since there is a contractual relationship between the parties.

A *tort* is a civil wrong committed by the invasion of any personal or private right that each person enjoys by virtue of federal and state laws. The personal or private right affected must be one that is determined by law rather than by contract. In addition to the tortious act, there must also be personal injury or property damage.

The majority of states have adopted the doctrine of strict liability in tort as set forth in the Restatement of the Law of Torts Second. This means that the injured person need only prove that a product was unreasonably dangerous to win his case. Proof that the manufacturer is negligent is not required. Contributory negligence, which means that the injured party acted in a careless and unreasonable manner while using the product, is no longer applicable.

Comparative negligence is becoming the most widely accepted defense to a products liability claim where the injured party was negligent in the use of the product. This concept apportions the award on the basis of the degree of negligence or fault of the parties. The adoption of this defense abolishes the assumption of the risk and diminishes, or completely bars, recovery by the injured party.[3]

Recent statutory enactments by some state legislatures declare that if a product does not injure a person within a period of 5, 10, 12 years, or within the useful life of the product from the date of manufacture, it is presumed to be free from defect unless the injured party can prove otherwise. The burden of proof that the product was defective lies with the injured party.[4]

It is apparent that product liability law, as with all laws, will vary somewhat from state to state. In all probability the lawsuit will be tried in the state where the injury occurred, which gives the plaintiff's attorney a decided advantage. The Consumer Product Safety Act is a federal law and therefore does not present the same problems of variance from state to state.

The Plaintiff

A lawsuit is a civil suit seeking money damages for injuries to either a person or his or her property or both. It is instigated by the injured party, called the plaintiff, and filed in a court of law as a claim against the responsible parties. The liability may arise as a result of a defect in design or manufacturing, improper service, breach of warranty, or negligence in marketing due to improper directions, warnings, or advertising.

Under the doctrine of strict liability the plaintiff must prove that: (1) the product was defective and unreasonably dangerous, (2) the defect was present when the product changed ownership, and (3) the defect caused the injury. Some of the facets of the case that are explored to prove that the product was defective and unreasonably dangerous are:

---

[3] W. P. Keeton, et al., *Prosser and Keeton on the Law of Torts,* 5th ed. (St. Paul, Minn.: West Publishing Co. 1984).

[4] R. K. Herrman, "An Overview of State Statutory Product Liability Law," *Trial Lawyer's Guide,* 7, No. 1 (1983).

1. The defective aspect of the product.
2. The design of similar and safer products, and the elimination of the danger.
3. The public's common knowledge of the product's danger.
4. The probability that an injury of this nature could occur assuming that reasonable care is exercised.
5. The adequacy of instructions and warnings.
6. The environment in which the product was used.

Investigation of these facets will usually provide some favorable or unfavorable arguments.

Proof that the product was defective at the time it changed ownership from the producer to the consumer is frequently difficult because the product may be entirely or partly destroyed by the accident. Expert testimony may be needed to ascertain when the defect occurred. This testimony will usually follow the line of reasoning that a microscopic flaw, which was present during the manufacturing operation, caused the product to fail at a future date.

Proof that the product caused the injury can also be difficult to determine if the product has been involved in an accident. One of the trends in product liability litigation is the requirement that the injured party need only show that the defect was the *proximate cause* of the injury. Proximate cause is a legal term that means that the defect need not be the sole cause of the injury but could be a contributing cause.

Before the lawsuit is brought to trial, the plaintiff is entitled to certain information by right of *discovery*. This information includes all records that pertain to the alleged defective product, such as product design, test and inspection results, customer complaints, and sales literature. The plaintiff is also entitled to take depositions of individuals involved with the case. A *deposition* is an oral questioning before a court reporter that permits both sides of the litigation to discover the important facts of the case.

The Defendant

While anyone along the trail of commerce (manufacturer, wholesaler, or retailer) can become a defendant in a lawsuit, it is usually the manufacturer who is held liable to the injured party. The manufacturer is the one with the "deepest pocket" or the one from which the largest award can be obtained.

In general, the defendant tries to prove that the product was not defective and not unreasonably dangerous. The same facets of the case, as those stated for the plaintiff, will be explored by the defendant to find favorable or unfavorable arguments.

The defendant tries to prove that there was no defect in the product at the time of manufacture which could have caused the accident. Test and inspection results and other records that can attest to the integrity, performance, and sales history of a particular product are valid arguments. The use of acceptance sampling plans based on government and industry standards help to build an effective defense.

A substantial portion of the trial is spent determining the cause of the accident. The defendant makes every effort to prove that the defect was not responsible for the injury. Proving that the plaintiff's bad judgment, his or her failure to properly maintain the product, or improper use of the product caused the injury are also persuasive arguments that a jury can readily understand. In this regard it may be possible to prove that the plaintiff used the product knowing it was defective. It is also possible that the accident was caused by a change or alteration of the product after it left the hands of the manufacturer.

As the Consumer Product Safety Commission develops product safety standards, it will be an effective defense to prove that the product complies with a federal product design standard.

Expert Witness

Expert witnesses are engaged by both sides of the litigation to prove their arguments. The defendant uses the services of expert technical witnesses within the manufacturing organization as well as outside or independent technical experts. While company experts are usually more knowledgeable about the product, the independent expert is considered to have less bias to his or her opinions.

The first requirement of an expert technical witness is his or her technical competency relative to the area of testimony. Technical competency can be substantiated by impressive credentials such as education, registration, and technical publications. In addition, the technical witness's personal character must be above reproach. Perhaps the most important requirement of an acceptable technical witness is the ability to communicate with the judge and jury. The technical expert must be able to explain and teach nontechnical people the technical aspects of the case. Testimony concerning science, product design, and quality control is given in a simple, truthful, and convincing manner. The objective is to convince the jury that the statements are true.

The technical expert and the lawyer will work together to develop an effective case. It is the duty of the expert to apprise the lawyer of the favorable and unfavorable technical aspects, and it is the duty of the lawyer to apprise the technical expert of the favorable and unfavorable legal aspects. While the lawyer has the primary responsibility for litigation strategy, it should be developed in cooperation with the technical expert.

The Outcome

After all the arguments are presented by the plaintiff and the defendant, the jury or judge returns a verdict. The verdict either absolves the defendant of any fault or requires that the defendant pay the plaintiff a stipulated amount of money.

If an unfavorable verdict is returned, the party can appeal to a higher court. The higher court, which is an odd number of judges, will review the earlier trial.

Written and oral arguments are presented by both sides and the court will uphold the decision, overturn the decision, or order a new trial of the entire lawsuit.

Before or during the trial a settlement may be negotiated between the parties. A settlement is a compromise between both sides to reach a middle ground. Since it is never possible to absolutely predict the outcome of a trial, the possibility of a settlement should be continually assessed.

If the defendant loses the case, the effect can be much greater than the loss of one lawsuit. The loss of a lawsuit increases the probability of future successful lawsuits against the same product.

Financial Loss

As a result of a lawsuit or to prevent future ones, there are a number of possible areas of financial loss. These areas include trial expenses, court judgments, bankruptcy, insurance premiums, and recalls.

Regardless of who wins the lawsuit, the defendant has certain legal expenses. These expenses include the attorney's fee, technical expert fees, investigation fees, and court costs if the verdict is unfavorable. In addition, at least one company representative will be present at all times during the trial, which indirectly adds to the expense.

The largest financial loss is the court judgment. When a judge or jury reaches a verdict for the plaintiff, the amount of the monetary award is also specified. Because the public believes that corporate enterprises have an almost unlimited amount of money, the awards have, in recent years, been particularly generous. Awards exceeding $2.0 million are not unusual. While monetary settlements have not been as large as the awards from a completed trial, they have been substantial. In the case of the larger enterprises, the financial loss imposed on the manufacturers is eventually passed on to the customer. However, smaller enterprises may have insufficient assets and/or liability insurance to cover the award and be forced into bankruptcy. This result is unfortunate, since it may affect adversely the competitive nature of a particular product or industry.

Another financial loss is due to the increase in insurance premiums that manufacturers pay for product liability. Product liability insurance has been too costly or impossible to obtain by many businesses in high-risk areas such as machine tools, industrial chemicals, medical devices, and auto parts.

Other financial considerations that may result directly or indirectly from a product liability lawsuit are:

1. Cost of recall, replacement, or repair of a product.
2. Cost of damage to a company's reputation and customer dissatisfaction.
3. Cost of a hold or delay in production due to a potential defect.
4. Cost of increased quality costs for prevention or appraisal.

In the long run, these financial losses may be more substantial than a $2.0 million judgment.

In the final analysis the manufacturer can absorb the cost, purchase insurance, prevent defective products, or some combination of all three. It is also important to recognize that much of the award goes to the lawyers.

Outlook for the Future

Product liability is continually changing. Many states have instituted remedies that prevent manufacturers from going out of business because of: (1) excessive court judgments, (2) exhorbitant insurance premiums, or (3) insurance cancellation. These remedies reduce the costs of product liability, which are passed on to the customer by both small and large manufacturers.

A bill, the Federal Product Liability Act, that has been proposed in the U.S. Congress would, if passed into law, supplant all existing state laws in the area of product liability. This law would virtually do away with strict liability claims. Instead, to recover on a claim under this act the plaintiff would have to prove that the product was unreasonably dangerous, that the product was the proximate cause of the injury, and that the product which caused the harm was manufactured by the defendant. Under this act, an unreasonably dangerous product is defined as having one or more of the following attributes: (1) a deficiency in construction, (2) a deficiency in design, (3) a failure to warn of potential danger, and (4) the product failed to conform to an expressed warranty. The law would have a 2-year statute of limitations in which a plaintiff could bring an action against a defendant. The time period for this statute of limitations begins from the point at which the plaintiff discovered or should have discovered the harm. The act, proposed in 1975, has yet to be passed, though the bill is still pending in Congress as of this writing.

It is noted that Europe does not have as serious a problem as the United States. Awards are made by judges, and lawyers have fixed costs rather than contingency fees.

PREVENTION[5]

The manufacturer of a consumer product must protect himself or herself against the risk of product liability litigation or at least reduce the risk to a level that will allow a reasonable profit and continued growth. To accomplish this protection, a product liability prevention program is required. While these programs will vary from corporation to corporation, certain common elements are essential for an effective program.

Organization

To have an effective product liability prevention program, an organizational structure must be established. This structure will be a function of the size of the company and the talents of available employees. The organizational structure must specify responsibilities and the necessary authority to achieve those responsibilities. Corporate

---

[5] This section is extracted by permission from W. H. Koch, *Products Liability Risk Control*, Technical Paper IQ75-538 (Dearborn, Mich.: Society of Manufacturing Engineers), pp. 5–12.

policies should reflect the prevention concepts that are covered in the remaining pages of this chapter.

A formal product safety committee should be established with either a safety engineer or an outside consultant. The function of the safety committee will be to review and coordinate the various safety activities. Members of the committee will be from legal, design, manufacturing, marketing, and quality, with the safety engineer as the chair. In addition, the safety engineer will: (1) maintain liaison with insurance companies and government regulators, (2) participate in injury cases, (3) maintain the education program, (4) conduct program audits, (5) act as a consultant to functional areas, and (6) keep informed of trends.

Education

Education is the cornerstone of an effective program. All employees should be made aware of the importance of product safety. An initial effort using available purchased materials, training sessions, and printed materials will educate personnel to the product liability prevention program. As new or transferred employees become part of the organization, they are exposed to the same educational effort.

Some form of continuing education is part of the plan of action. Information such as changes to state and national law, results of relevant lawsuits, and feedback on product audits is especially important to disseminate to employees.

New-Product Review

New products are more likely to be involved in product liability litigation than well-established products; therefore, a special review is required before the product can be released to manufacturing. The safety of the consumer is the paramount consideration in the review process, with function, cost, and sales appeal being of secondary importance. In other words, product safety is one of the design parameters.

Product safety design techniques should be adopted. Some of these techniques are: (1) failure-mode, effect, and criticality analysis, (2) fault-tree analysis, (3) fail-safe concepts, (4) Weibull and other test data analysis, (5) safety symbol for safety-oriented product characteristics, and (6) coded identification for traceability.

A written description of the product by the designer is the starting point for the review process. This description includes the intended use of the product, expected life, probable failure, limiting design parameters, service environment, development tests, and final acceptance criteria. The design and development of the product are thoroughly documented.

A product review team is established that has no preconceived notions about the product. The review team evaluates the product's compliance with present and foreseeable industry and government standards as well as applicable codes, laws, and regulations. Customer requirements and customer's known or anticipated end use of the item will also be reviewed. In addition, the team will review any past injury data of related products. These reviews are conducted at appropriate stages of the product life cycle.

It is frequently impossible to economically design a product with zero safety incident. In these situations the unsafe area is guarded or protected from injury exposure. Product defects can, in some situations, be designed to occur in such a manner that a disabling injury does not occur. If it is not possible or practical to design and/or guard against an injury exposure, then adequate warnings by word, color, or illustration should be permanently attached to the product.

Customer-oriented tests are performed to predict the misuse of the product. Designers test a product to determine if it performs as intended when correctly used. A customer-oriented test tries to determine what happens when the product is misused. Consideration is given to the wide variance in the physical and mental ability of *all* potential customers.

Since minor design and material changes to an existing product can cause disabling injury, the same type of review is necessary for any and all changes.

Initial Production Review

The new product review is usually based on hand-built prototypes. Therefore, a subsequent review is necessary on the first production items to determine if any defects are encountered that did not materialize in the prototypes. For an inherently hazardous product, a limited production run and controlled distribution is recommended. From this limited sample, meaningful information can be obtained from customers while the liability risk exposure is minimized.

The production review will evaluate the manufacturing plan to determine the adequacy of

1. Tooling and work-holding devices
2. Production machinery
3. Materials handling
4. Test equipment
5. Inspection system
6. Sampling plan
7. Packaging and shipping
8. Operating instructions
9. Safety warnings
10. Advanced service information for distributors and dealers

All personnel who are active in the initial production review process can informally evaluate the product design for safety. The more people evaluating a product for safety, the greater the likelihood that a potential liability exposure will be detected before the product is sold in the marketplace.

Periodic Production Audits

Most manufacturing organizations periodically perform production audits to verify or validate the effectiveness of the quality control system. These audits can be extended to evaluate the safety parameters. The audit should be performed on recently manufactured products, or products that have been through the distribution system, and on products that have been in customer use a substantial period of time. Inspection and testing of the product is based on a simulation of the customer's activities. Feedback of the results of the audit is sent to the product safety committee.

Control of Warranties, Advertisements, Agreements, and the Like

The product liability loss-prevention program must provide for a continual review of warranty, advertising literature, dealer agreements, catalogs, and technical publications. The review should include:

1. A check to determine that the terms and conditions of sale are limited to a statement of *merchantability,* which means that the product is of good material and workmanship. The use of such phrases as "safe" and "ensures the safety of the operator" are to be avoided. If the product is referred to as "safe" and a person is injured, he or she has established that the product was defective.

2. An analysis by legal counsel of all advertising copy, sales brochures, other promotional literature, and technical reports and presentations.

3. An examination of purchase orders to determine the acceptability of any special warranty provisions.

4. An analysis of dealer distributorships and franchise agreements to determine the handling of "defective" items. These agreements are allowed in court and can constitute an admission that the company manufactures "defective" products.

5. A check to determine that the words nonconformity and nonconforming unit have been used where appropriate.

Complaints and Claims

A complaint or a claim is a communication between the marketplace and the company concerning the performance of the product. This information serves to alert the manufacturer to the need for corrective action. A Pareto analysis of complaints can lead to a change in product design or manufacturing that will reduce the exposure to disabling injuries.

The investigation of bodily injury or property damage claims or product safety complaints should be acted upon quickly. Usually, the notice of a claim or complaint is given to a dealer, distributor, or employee. This initial notice is sent to the proper department for action. A qualified expert as well as the insurance company reviews the situation and determines:

1. The cause of the claim or complaint.
2. The nature and seriousness of the injury, if one has occurred.
3. The failure mode that caused the situation, if there was one.
4. The age of the defect and if it was present when the product was sold.
5. The negligence of the parties.

An early investigation can lead to quick settlement of reasonable claims or the preparation of defenses for those claims which may require litigation.

The complaint and claim procedure should make provision for notifying the appropriate departments, depending on the seriousness of the claim. It may even be necessary to implement the product-recall plan.

Records Retention

The defense of a product liability lawsuit necessitates the availability of design, production, and sales records. Particular types of records that should be retained are:

1. Product development and test records.
2. Results of process, product, and system inspections and audits.
3. Records of verbal and written communications with customers relative to requirements, product application, nonstandard materials, and claims.
4. Original design data.
5. Service-life data.
6. Acceptance and approvals by government agencies, customers, or independent testing companies.
7. Critical raw material acceptance records.

Records are maintained in such a manner that the material or product can be traced to a given shipment, operator, machine, time, and so on.

Records must be protected from loss by storage in fireproof cabinets and by having duplicate sets. The question of how long records should be retained is based on a number of considerations. Usually, records are maintained for the expected useful life of the product plus 18 years, in order to cover the time when an injured minor could bring a lawsuit upon reaching the legal age of 18. Other retention considerations are the inherent risk of the product, the need for records critical to the defense, and the method of storage.

Product-Recall Plan

Although the cost of recalling a product varies significantly with the type of product and the quantities involved, the costs are substantial and have forced more than one company into bankruptcy. An effective recall contingency plan helps to minimize the recall costs and the product liability risk.

Once notification of a defective product is received, the company must decide whether or not to recall all product suspected of having the defective condition. Consideration for this decision will be given to:

1. Determination of the maximum exposure to personal injury or property damage if the product is not recalled. This determination will be based on the pattern of defect, the quantity involved, the severity of the risk, and the cost of the recall.

2. The form of communication (radio, TV, newspaper, telephone, and registered letter) to use in contacting the users of the product.

3. Determining if the product will be repaired, or replaced, or if the customer will be reimbursed.

If the defective condition is classified as a substantial product hazard, the Consumer Product Safety Commission may order the manufacturer to take specific action. In such a case the decision is made for the manufacturer.

When a recall is required, it is extremely important to identify those units with the defective condition and correlate this identification with the applicable manufacturing records. This type of identification is referred to as *traceability*. The traceability of a product can have a decided influence on whether 100 or 10,000 units are recalled. For some products the expiration date is also important.

Subrogation

Part of a product liability prevention program involves the raw material, component parts, and subassembly suppliers. The same elements of evaluation and safety criteria that are applicable to the buyer are applicable to the supplier. A visit to the supplier's plant and an audit of his or her prevention program is a necessity. The supplier should also visit the buyer's plant to evaluate product safety exposure of the raw material, component part, or subassembly.

All communication between supplier and buyer concerning defective raw materials, component parts, and subassembly are made in writing. The buyer advises the supplier of all relevant product safety information, such as complaints, audits, warranties, and product reviews.

Risk Criteria

If a company manufactures a broad range of products, it usually has a range of potential product liability loss. Some products, for inherent reasons, pose a much greater risk than others; therefore, products are evaluated based on certain risk criteria. The degree of prevention control is then based on the degree of potential liability loss. This technique enables a company to exert its maximum preventive effort on those vital few products where it is most needed.

Standards

All prevention programs, especially those of large corporations, should make provision for employees to be involved in the development of design and manufacturing standards. Since manufacturers have the most to lose from stringent, unrealistic standards, their employees should be involved in professional groups that develop standards. In this connection the legal staff should be actively involved in the evolution of product liability law.

Audit

Periodic audits of the prevention programs are absolutely essential to determine whether or not the program is operating satisfactorily. These audits are for the most part system audits which operate in much the same manner as audits of the total quality control system. Periodic audits are useful tools for measuring progress and for providing feedback to improve the prevention program. The audits are scheduled and performed by internal company personnel or knowledgeable external people. Results of the audit are written and circulated within the company.

Customer Service

The customer service activity can have a great deal of influence on the effectiveness of the prevention program. By making friends rather than enemies the likelihood of a lawsuit is substantially reduced. Customer service should report observations on how the product is being used or misused and any near misses. Also, if a repair activity is involved, it must be subjected to the same requirements as the initial production.

Redress

Customers will usually accept failures if there is redress. It requires.

1. A warranty policy that responds to customer needs.
2. The availability of information concerning the redress procedure.
3. Prompt handling of complaints, returns, claims, and so forth.
4. Repair facilities that give prompt, skilled, and fair-priced service.

Companies can improve customer loyalty through an effective redress policy.

Resources are limited; therefore, the perfect product is in many cases an unattainable goal. In the long term, customers pay for the cost of regulation and lawsuits. Although product safety is a major concern of insurance companies, only a small percentage of people consider it to be the most important characteristic of a product.

In conclusion, it is appropriate to mention the old cliché, "An ounce of prevention is worth a pound of cure." An adequate prevention program can substantially reduce the risk of damaging litigation.

11

COMPUTERS
AND QUALITY CONTROL

INTRODUCTION

Computers play an essential role in the quality function. They perform very simple operations at fast speeds with an exceptionally high degree of accuracy. The computer must be programmed to execute these simple operations in the correct sequence in order to accomplish a given task. Computers can be programmed to perform complex calculations, to control a process or test, to analyze data, to write reports, and to recall information on command.

There are two classes of computers, digital and analog. Digital computers operate on numbers represented by sequences of digits. The analog computers operate on a continuous input of data such as voltage or angular displacement of a wheel.

Computers range from pocket size to desk size to huge multiprocessing computing centers. The large computers are capable of handling many jobs at the same time and of storing vast amounts of information. As the size of the computer increases, its cost and versatility increase.

Since the use of a computer is a costly proposition, it must be justified. The cost of preparing a program, using the computer, and implementing the results is substantial. This cost has to be less than the potential benefits, which include money or time saved, data created, improved accuracy, and greater control.

Quality control needs served by the computer are: (1) data collection, (2) data analysis and reporting, (3) statistical analysis, (4) process control, (5) test and inspection, and (6) system design.

DATA COLLECTION

Computers are well suited for the collection of data. Principal benefits are faster data transmission, fewer errors, and lower collection costs. Data are transmitted to the computer by paper or magnetic tape, optical character recognition, touch telephone, voice, keyboard, bar-code scan, and direct interface with the process.

The type and amount of data are the principal problems of data collection. Sources of data are process inspection stations, scrap and waste reports, product audits, testing laboratories, customer complaints, service information, process control, and incoming material inspection. From these sources a vast amount of data can be collected. The decision as to how much data to collect and analyze is based on the reports to be issued, the processes to be controlled, the records to be retained, and the nature of the quality improvement program.

A typical form for collecting data for an internal failure or deficiency is shown in Figure 11-1. In addition to the basic information concerning the internal failure or deficiency, a number of identifiers are used. Typical identifiers are part number, operator, foreman, data, vendor, product line, work center, and department. Identifiers are necessary for data analysis, report preparation, and record traceability. Once the disposition of the nonconforming material is determined, this particular report is routed to accounting, where the failure costs are assigned and the information is transmitted to the computer.

The collection, utilization, and dissemination of quality control information is best accomplished when the information is incorporated into a data-base management system. A data-base management system maintains relationships with other activities, such as inventory control, purchasing, accounting, and production control. The data base is essential for all the quality needs described in this chapter. Linkages are developed between the stored data records of the various activities in order to obtain additional information with a minimum of programming and to improve the storage utilization.

Sometimes information is stored in the computer in order for it to be transmitted efficiently to remote terminals. For example, the operating instructions, specifications, tools, inspection gages, and inspection requirements for a particular job are stored in the computer. This information is then provided to the employee at the same time the work assignment is given. One of the principal advantages of this type of system is the ability to quickly update or change the information. Another

DEFICIENCY REPORT

1. PART NUMBER | 2. ISSUE | SUF.

IDENTIFICATION

3. TELL | HUNT | 4. TELL OPER.# | 4A. RESP. OPER.# | 5. FOREMAN# | 6. DATE WRITTEN: MONTH | DAY | YEAR

7. PART NAME | 8. MATERIAL LOCATION | 9. DEF. OPN. | SUF. | 10. QTY. REJECTED

11. DEFICIENCY DESCRIPTION
USE STANDARD ABBREVIATIONS

12. SHOP ORDER NUMBER | 13. CLERK# | 14. DATE

15. DEPT.# | 16. SEC.-SH. | 17. DEFECT CODE | 18. LAST OPN. | SUF. | 19. COMPONENT S/N | 20. MODEL/S | 21. SERIAL NUMBER

22. VENDOR NAME | 23. VENDOR CODE | 24. WRITER # | REJECTED BY SIGNATURE

RESPONSIBILITY

27. DISPOSITION

25. DEPT. | 26. ACCOUNT

USE AS IS ☐ | RTV ☐

REWORK ☐ | SCRAP ☐

REPAIR ☐ | HOLD FOR—SORT ☐ | DISP. ☐

28. ROUTING

TO 1ST | TO 2ND | TO 3RD | TO 4TH | TO LAST

29. DETAILED DEFICIENCY DESCRIPTION

30. COMMENTS

OPERATOR'S SIGNATURE | FOREMAN'S SIGNATURE

31. DISPOSITION INSTRUCTIONS

32. MFG. SIGNATURE | 33. MFG. ENGR. SIGNATURE | 34. QA SIGNATURE

35. PROD. ENGR. SIGNATURE | 36. APPROVED | 37. APPROVED

38. CANCEL | REPLACE | 39. PREVIOUS DR | 40. PREVIOUS DISP. | 41. PREVIOUS QTY. | 42. UPDATE AUTHORITY—QA

43. REASON FOR UPDATE

FIGURE 11-1 Deficiency report. (Courtesy of Fiat-Allis Construction Machinery, Inc.)

advantage is the likelihood of fewer errors, since the operator is using current information rather than obsolete or hard-to-read instructions.

A computer has a limited amount of storage capacity; therefore, quality control data are periodically analyzed to determine what data to retain in the computer, what data to store by another method, and what data to destroy. Data can be stored on magnetic tape or a disk and reentered into the computer if needed. Product liability requirements determine the amount and type of data to destroy.

DATA ANALYSIS, REDUCTION, AND REPORTING

While some of the quality control information is merely stored in the computer for retrieval at a future time, most of the information is analyzed, reduced to a meaningful amount, and disseminated in the form of a report. These activities of analysis, reduction, and reporting are programmed to occur automatically as the data are collected or to occur on command by the computer operator.

Typical reports for scrap and rework as produced by a computer are shown in Figure 11-2. The weekly scrap and rework cost report of Figure 11-2a is a listing by part number of the information transmitted to the computer from the internal failure deficiency report. Identifiers reported for each transaction are a function of the report and the space available. For this report the identifiers are part number, operation code, and deficiency ticket number.

The basic data can be summarized in a number of different ways. Figure 11-2b shows a summary by failure code. Summaries are also compiled by operator, department, work center, defect, product line, part number, subassembly, vendor, and material.

A monthly Pareto analysis of the data by defect for Department 4 is shown in Figure 11-2c. This Pareto analysis is in tabular form; however, the computer could have been programmed to present the information in graphical form, as illustrated by the Pareto analysis in Chapter 10. Pareto analyses could also have been computed for operators, work centers, departments, part numbers, and so on.

The previous paragraphs have described the reports associated with scrap and rework. Reports for inspection results, product audits, service information, customer complaints, vendor evaluation, and laboratory testing are all similar. Information of a graphical nature, such as for a p chart can be programmed, displayed at a terminal, and reproduced as shown by Figure 11-3 on page 372. This particular p-chart program uses control limits based on an average subgroup size and then computes individual control limits based on the performance for that day. The chart is current as of January 24. Data for the rest of the month will be posted as it occurs.

Data can be analyzed as they are being accumulated rather than on a weekly or monthly basis. When this technique is practiced, decision rules can be employed in the program which will automatically signal the likelihood of a quality problem. In this manner, information concerning a potential problem is provided and corrective action taken prior to the issuance of the formal report.

```
SCRAP AND REWORK COST REPORT FOR THE WEEK ENDING  11/26

PART#   CODE   TICKET   QTY    MATERIAL   LABOR   OVERHEAD    TOTAL

1194     E     2387   40000     800.00     .00     24.80     824.80
1275     E     1980      15      31.50    2.28      5.59      39.37
1276     D     2021       7      11.76     .94      2.30      15.00
1276     E     2442      10      16.80    1.34      3.28      21.42

9020     D      608       1      30.79    6.01     14.72      51.52
9600     D     2411       3      48.03   19.00     46.55     113.38
9862     D     2424       1      23.73    4.92     12.05      40.70

     TOTAL              $13,627.35  2,103.65    5,153.98  21,307.41
```

(a) Scrap and Rework Report

```
RECAP OF FAILURE CODES SHOWING AMOUNT AND PERCENT OF TOTAL

          CODE EXPLANATION        AMOUNT        %

       A #OPERATION MISSED          5.36
       B #BROKEN PARTS               .00
       C #MISSING PARTS              .00
       D #IMPROPER MACHINING    11,882.72        56
       E #FOUNDRY OR PURCHASING  8,841.79        41
       F #MECHANICAL FAILURE         .00
       G #IMPROPER HANDLING       533.10          3
       H #OTHER                    44.44

                            $21,307.41         100
```

(b) Summary by Failure Code

```
          DEPARTMENT 4    MONTH OF OCTOBER

RANK    CODE    CODE DESCR.    $ SCRAP    $ RWK    TOTAL      %

01     D-T2     TURN           7,500     4,105    11,605    28.5
02     D-H1     HOB            5,810       681     6,491    16.0
03     D-G6     GRIND          4,152     1,363     5,515    13.8
04     D-D4     DRILL            793     3,178     3,971     9.8
05     D-L1     LAP              314     2,831     3,145     7.8
```

(c) Pareto Analysis

FIGURE 11-2 Typical scrap and rework reports: weekly cost report, weekly summary by failure code, Pareto analysis by nonconformity code and department.

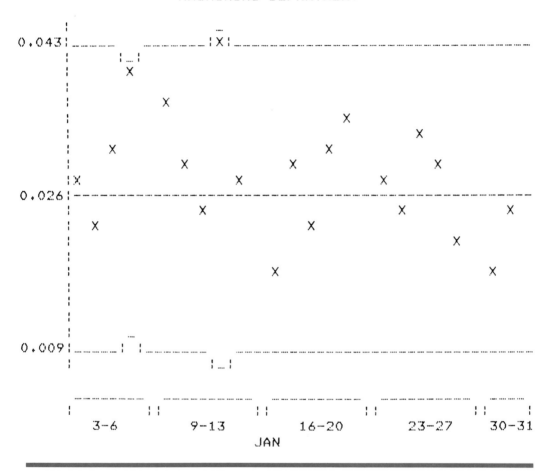

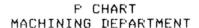

FIGURE 11-3 Computer-generated *p* chart.

STATISTICAL ANALYSIS

The first and still an important use of the computer in quality control was for statistical analysis. Most of the statistical techniques discussed in this book can be easily programmed. Once programmed, considerable calculation time is saved, and the calculations are error-free. A number of computer programs written in BASIC were given earlier in the book.

Many statistical computer programs have been published in the *Journal of Quality Technology* and can easily be adapted to any computer or programming language. In addition, information on statistical analysis techniques has been published in *Applied Statistics*. Most of these programs have been incorporated into software packages.

The advantages of programmed statistical software packages are:

1. Time-consuming manual calculations are eliminated.
2. Timely and accurate analyses may be performed to diagnose one-time problems or maintain process control.
3. Many practitioners with limited knowledge in advanced statistics can perform their own statistical analyses.

Once a statistical package of computer programs is developed or purchased the quality engineer can specify a particular sequence of statistical calculations to use for a given set of conditions. The results of these calculations can provide conclusive evidence or suggest additional statistical calculations for the computer to perform. Many of these tests are too tedious to perform without the use of a computer.

PROCESS CONTROL

The first application of computers in process control was with numerically controlled (N/C) machines. Numerically controlled machines used punched paper to transmit instructions to the computer, which then controlled the sequence of operations. A more sophisticated type of process control measures and controls the process variables to maintain their values within acceptable control limits.

An automatic process control system is illustrated by the flow diagram of Figure 11-4. While the computer is a key part of automatic process control, it is not the only part. There are two major interfacing subsystems between the computer and the process.

One subsystem has a sensor that measures a process variable such as temperature, pressure, voltage, length, weight, moisture content, and so on, and sends an analog signal to the digital computer. However, the digital computer can only receive information in digital form, so the signal is converted by an analog-to-digital interface. The variable value in digit form is evaluated by the computer to determine if the value is within the prescribed limits. If such is the case, no further action is necessary; however, if the digital value is outside the limits, corrective action is required. A corrected digital value is sent to the digital-to-analog interface, which converts to an analog signal that is acceptable to an actuator mechanism, such as a valve. Then the actuator mechanism increases or decreases the variable.

The other subsystem is essentially an attribute type, which either determines if a contact is on/off or controls an on/off function. Through the contact input interface, the computer continuously scans the actual on/off status of switches, motors, pumps, and so on, and compares these to the desired contact status. The computer program controls the sequence of events performed during the process cycle. Operating instructions are initiated by specific process conditions or as a function of time

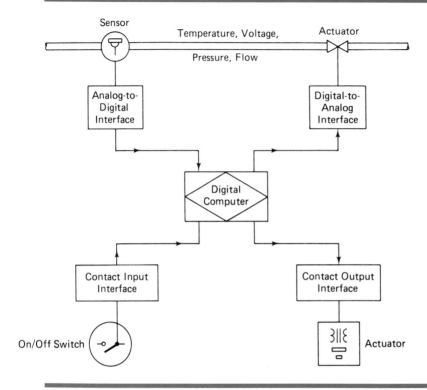

FIGURE 11-4   **Automatic process control system.**

and are sent to the contact output interface. This interface activates a solenoid, sounds an alarm, starts a pump, stops a conveyor, and so on.

The four interfaces in Figure 11-4 are capable of handling a number of signals at the same time. Also, the two subsystems can operate independently or in conjunction with each other. Since the computer operates in microseconds and the subsystems operate in milliseconds, a timing problem can occur unless the feedback loops are as tight as possible so that corrective action is immediate.[1] The benefits that are obtained from automatic process control are:

1. Constant product quality, owing to a reduction in process variation.
2. More uniform startup and shutdown, since the process can be monitored and controlled during these critical periods.
3. Increased productivity, because fewer people are needed to monitor the controls.
4. Safer operation for personnel and equipment, by either stopping the process or failing to start the process when an unsafe condition occurs.

[1] N. A. Poisson, "Interfaces for Process Control," *Textile Industries*, 134, No. 3 (March 1970), pp. 61–65.

One of the first automatic process-controlled installations occurred at Western Electric's North Carolina plant in 1960. The product variables were controlled by the computer using $\bar{X}$ and R control chart techniques. For example, the resistance value of deposited carbon resistors coming out of the furnace was controlled by the amount of methane in the furnace and by the speed through the furnace. Since the inspection and packaging operations were also under computer control, the entire production facility was completely automatic.[2]

AUTOMATIC TEST AND INSPECTION

If we consider test and inspection as a process in itself or a part of a manufacturing process, then automatic test and inspection is similar to the previous section on automatic process control. Computer-controlled test and inspection systems offer the following advantages: improved test quality, lower operating cost, better report preparation, improved accuracy, automatic calibration, and malfunction diagnostics. Their primary disadvantage is the high cost of the equipment.

Computer-controlled automatic inspection can be used for go/no-go inspection decisions or for sorting and classifying parts in selective assembly. Automatic inspection systems have the capacity and speed to be used on high-volume production lines.

Automatic test systems can be programmed to perform a complete quality audit of the product. Testing can be sequenced through the various product components and subassemblies. Parameters such as temperature, voltage, and force can be varied to simulate environmental and wear-out conditions. Reports are automatically prepared to reflect the performance of the product.

When automatic test and inspection is applied to automatic or semiautomatic produced product, the computer can generate the inspection instructions at the same time the product is manufactured.

SYSTEM DESIGN

Applications software adapted to the quality function is becoming more sophisticated and comprehensive. There are numerous packages that combine many of the quality functions described previously. Figure 11-5 illustrates a typical quality software package menu. Execution of the menu is by function key, cursor and entry key, or mouse. For example, one sequence of events creates a file, collects data, and analyzes it. These activities involve:

File creation

Data collection

Distribution analysis

[2] J. H. Boatwright, "Using a Computer for Quality Control of Automated Production," *Computers and Automation,* 13, No. 2 (February 1964), 10–17.

MAIN

1. File
2. Data
3. Cost Analysis
4. Graphics
5. Distribution
6. Variable Control Chart
7. Attribute Control Chart
8. Statistics
9. Acceptance Sampling
10. Exit to DOS
A1. Reliability

DISTRIBUTION

1. Histogram
2. Probability Plot
3. Pareto
4. Process Capability

PARETO

1. Frequency
2. Percent
3. Dollars
4. Cumulative

FIGURE 11-5 **Quality software menu.**

All these activities involve submenus. Thus for the distribution menu, there is a submenu of Histogram, Probability Plots, Pareto, and Process Capability. If the Pareto menu is selected, there is another menu to determine the type or types of Pareto diagrams.

These packages are user-friendly with help provision and tutorials. Package software is much cheaper than custom software. It usually has the benefit of proven usage and technical support. Each March *Quality Progress* publishes an updated directory of applications software particular to the quality function.

The integration of the various quality functions with other activities requires an extremely sophisticated system design. Components of a total system are available in:

CADD: Computer-aided Drafting and Design

CAM: Computer-aided Manufacturing

CAPP: Computer-aided Process Planning

CIM: Computer-integrated Manufacturing

DBM: Data-based Management

Integration of these components into a total system will occur during this decade.

When the computer is used effectively, it becomes a powerful tool to aid in the improvement of quality. However, the computer is not a device that can correct a poorly designed system. In other words, the use of a computer in quality is as effective as the people who create the total quality system.

12

QUALITY IMPROVEMENT TECHNIQUES

INTRODUCTION

Many quality-improvement techniques have been discussed in the preceding chapters. Those techniques are included in summary form in this chapter. However, the principal thrust of the chapter is to describe additional techniques. The basic techniques described are: Pareto diagram, matrix analysis, Grier diagram, time series, cause-and-effect diagram, histogram, process capability, control chart, precontrol, scatter diagram, run chart, and process flowchart.

PARETO DIAGRAM

Alfredo Pareto (1848–1923) conducted extensive studies of the distribution of wealth in Europe. He found that there were a few people with a lot of money, and many people with little money. This unequal distribution of wealth became an integral part of economic theory. Dr. Joseph Juran recognized this concept as a univer-

377

sal that could be applied to many fields. He coined the phrases *vital few* and *trivial many*.

A Pareto diagram is a graph that ranks data classifications in descending order from left to right, as shown in Figure 12-1. In this case, the data classifications are types of field failure. Other possible data classifications are problems, causes, types of nonconformities, and so forth. The vital few are on the left, and the trivial many are on the right. It is sometimes necessary to combine some of the trivial many into one classification called *other* and labeled *O* in the figure. When the other category is used, it is always on the far right. The vertical scale is dollars, frequency, or percent. Pareto diagrams can be distinguished from histograms by the fact that the horizontal scale of a Pareto is categorical, whereas the scale for the histogram is numerical.

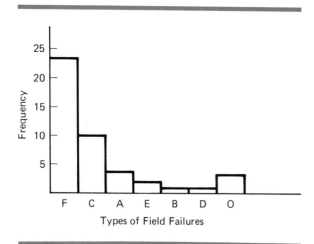

FIGURE 12-1   **Pareto diagram.**

Sometimes a Pareto diagram has a cumulative line, as shown in Figure 12-2. This line represents the sum of the data as they are added together from left to right. Two scales are used: The one on the left is either frequency or dollars, and the one on the right is percent.

Pareto diagrams are used to identify the most important problems. Usually, 80% of the total results from 20% of the items. This fact is shown in Figure 12-2, where the F and C types of field failures account for almost 80% of the total. Actually, the most important items could be identified by listing the items in descending order. However, the graph has the advantage of providing a visual impact of those vital few characteristics that need attention. Resources are then directed to take the necessary corrective action. Examples of the vital few are:

A few customers account for the majority of sales.

A few products, processes, or quality characteristics account for the bulk of the scrap or rework cost.

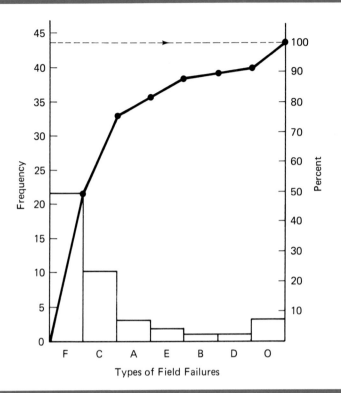

FIGURE 12-2　**Cumulative line.**

A few nonconformities account for the majority of customer complaints.
A few vendors account for the majority of rejected parts.
A few problems account for the bulk of the process downtime.
A few products account for the majority of the profit.
A few items account for the bulk of the inventory cost.

Construction of a Pareto diagram is very simple. There are six steps:

1. Determine the method of classifying the data: by problem, cause, type of non-conformity, and so forth.
2. Decide if dollars (best) or frequency is to be used to rank the characteristics.
3. Collect data for an appropriate time interval.
4. Summarize the data and rank order categories from largest to smallest.
5. Compute the cumulative percentage if it is to be used.
6. Construct the diagram and find the vital few.

The cumulative percentage scale, when used, must match with the dollar or frequency scale such that 100% is at the same height as the total dollars or frequency. See the arrow in Figure 12-2.

It is noted that a quality improvement of the vital few, of say 50%, is a much greater return on investment than a 50% improvement of the trivial many. Also, experience has shown that it is easier to make a 50% improvement in the vital few.

The use of a Pareto diagram is a never-ending process. For example, let's assume that F is the target for correction in the improvement program. A project team is assigned to investigate and make improvements. The next time a Pareto analysis is made, another field failure, say C, becomes the target for correction, and the improvement process continues until field failures become an insignificant quality problem.

The Pareto diagram is a powerful quality-improvement tool. It is applicable to problem identification and the measurement of progress.

MATRIX ANALYSIS

Matrix analysis is a simple, but effective, technique to compare groups of categories such as operators, salespeople, machines, and suppliers. All the elements in each category must be performing the same activity. Actually, matrix analysis is a two-dimensional Pareto.

Table 12-1 illustrates the technique for income tax preparers. Analysis of the columns shows that the preparer with the fewest nonconformities is D, followed by A. Once the best preparers are determined, it is usually not too difficult to discover their "knack" and impart this wisdom to the poorer preparers.

Analysis of the rows shows those nonconformities that are causing all preparers difficulty. In this case, nonconformity type 5 requires some type of corrective action, such as retraining. Nonconformity type 3 is a problem for preparer B; however, the other preparers are not having any difficulty.

TABLE 12-1   **Matrix of Errors by Income Tax Preparers.**

TYPES OF NONCONFORMITY	PREPARER						
	A	B	C	D	E	F	TOTAL
1	0	0	1	0	2	1	4
2	1	0	0	0	1	0	2
3	0	16	1	0	2	0	19
4	0	0	0	0	1	0	1
5	2	1	3	1	4	2	13
:	:	:	:	:	:	:	:
15	0	0	0	0	3	0	3
Totals	6	20	8	3	36	7	80

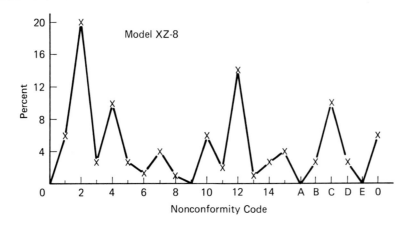

FIGURE 12-3   Nonconformity code signature.

Another adaptation of the Pareto concept was developed by Ted Grier, National Service Manager for Casio. He needed a technique to compare nonconformities in different models of similar products. To accomplish this need, a nonconformity code signature was developed, as shown in Figure 12-3.

In order to use the technique, a substantial number of the nonconformity codes in the product group must be the same. The nonconformity codes numbered 1 to 15 would be common to all the models, and the nonconformity codes A to E would be unique to the particular model. The nonconformity codes are located on the x-axis, and the percent of failure is located on the y-axis. The total percentage is 100%. Each product model has its own graph.

The y-axis can be reduced or expanded by the computer within the same physical bounds of the screen and printout. In other words, for one model, the scale might be 26%, and for another, the scale might be 21%. Each image is consistently proportioned, and, thus, the human-handwriting-like accentuations give maximum visibility. This feature enhances the usefulness of the graphs for some applications.

Data are collected in the same manner as a Pareto. In this case, the data represent the reason for the returned product. Care must be exercised to ensure that the data are representative of the product so that no bias exists. For example, only returns from, say, the first 3 months or last 3 months of the warranty period are included. In fact, different nonconformity code signatures could be constructed from different data for the same product model. Data are summarized periodically, say every month.

Experience has shown that there is little change in the diagram after 25 returned units. Once the nonconformity code signatures of the six product models are complete, they can be analyzed for any unusual situations. For example, nonconformity code 7 concerns the power supply. During one period, one of the models (XZ-8) showed an unusual low return percentage for nonconformity code 7, whereas the other five models had percentages similar to earlier periods. Further investigation showed a change in battery supplier for that model.

The nonconformity code signature is also used to trigger corrective action investigation. For example, whenever a nonconformity code exceeds 20% of the returned units, quality engineers are required to determine the possible cause of the condition and initiate corrective action.

By summarizing the data from each model, a defect code signature for the entire group can be constructed. This action provides information to compare each model against the group totals to determine if there are any significant variations. If desirable, the summarized data can also be graphed in the traditional Pareto diagram form.

The nonconformity code signature can also be modified to show trends by including three or more periods on one diagram. This technique is shown in Figure 12-4. The figure shows that returns due to nonconformity code 10 are declining, which indicates a quality improvement.

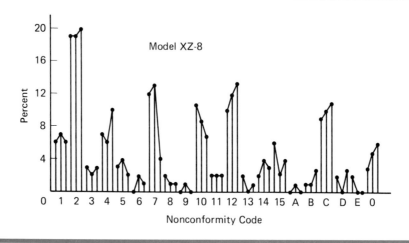

FIGURE 12-4   Nonconformity code signature for past three months.

This modification to the Pareto diagram is another tool to assist in the identification of quality problems. The Grier diagram is applicable where there are many similar models in a product group. Calculators, watches, vehicle tires, furniture, and appliances are a few of the possibilities.

TIME SERIES

A time series is a very simple technique to show the change in some factor over time. Figure 12-5 illustrates this type of graph. The horizontal scale is established with a time unit such as quarters and years. The vertical scale is the factor under consideration, which, in this case, is percent nonconforming. As can be seen by the figure, the quality of product A is remaining constant, whereas the quality of product B is showing continuous improvement. These graphs are excellent for showing trends and monitoring progress.

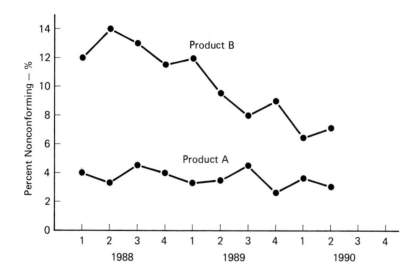

FIGURE 12-5 Time series graph for percent nonconforming.

CAUSE-AND-EFFECT DIAGRAM

A cause-and-effect (CE) diagram is a picture composed of lines and symbols designed to represent a meaningful relationship between an effect and its causes. It was developed by Dr. Kaoru Ishikawa in 1943 and is sometimes referred to as an Ishikawa diagram.

CE diagrams are used to investigate either a "bad" effect and to take action to correct the causes or a "good" effect and to learn those causes responsible. For every effect, there are likely to be numerous causes. Figure 12-6 illustrates a CE diagram

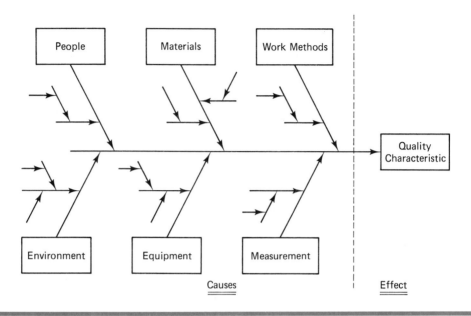

FIGURE 12-6   Cause-and-effect diagram.

with the effect on the right and causes on the left. The effect is the quality character-istic that needs improvement. Causes are usually broken down into the major causes of work methods, materials, measurement, people, and the environment. Manage-ment and maintenance are also sometimes used for the major cause. Each major cause is further subdivided into numerous minor causes. For example, under work methods, we might have training, knowledge, ability, physical characteristics, and so forth. CE diagrams (frequently called "fish-bone diagrams" because of their shape) are the means of picturing all these major and minor causes.

The first step in the construction of a CE diagram is for the project team to identify the effect or quality problem. It is placed on the right side of a large piece of paper by the team leader. Next, the major causes are identified and placed on the di-agram.

Determining all the minor causes requires brainstorming by the project team. Brainstorming is an idea-generating technique that is well-suited to the CE diagram. It uses the creative thinking capacity of the team.

Attention to a few essentials will provide a more accurate and usable result:

1. Participation by every member of the team is facilitated by each member taking a turn giving one idea at a time. If a member cannot think of a minor cause,

he or she passes for that round. Another idea may occur at a later round. By following this procedure, one or two individuals do not dominate the brainstorming session.

2. Quantity of ideas, rather than quality, is encouraged. One person's idea will trigger someone else's idea, and a chain reaction occurs. Frequently, a trivial or "dumb" idea will lead to the best solution.

3. Criticism of an idea is not allowed. There should be a freewheeling exchange of information that liberates the imagination. All ideas are placed on the diagram. Evaluation of ideas occurs at a later time.

4. Visibility of the diagram is a primary factor of participation. In order to have space for all the minor causes, a 2-ft by 3-ft piece of paper is recommended. It should be taped to a wall for maximum visibility.

5. Create a solution-oriented atmosphere and not a gripe session. Focus on solving a problem rather than discussing how it began. The team leader should ask questions using the why, what, where, when, who, and how techniques.

6. Let the ideas incubate for a period of time (at least overnight), and then have another brainstorming session. Provide team members with a copy of the ideas after the first session. When no more ideas are generated, the brainstorming activity is terminated.

Once the CE diagram is complete, it must be evaluated to determine the most likely causes. This activity is accomplished in a separate session. The procedure is to have each person vote on the minor causes. Team members may vote on more than one cause. Those causes with the most votes are circled, and the four or five most likely causes of the effect are determined.

Solutions are developed to correct the causes and improve the process. Criteria for judging the possible solutions include cost, feasibility, resistance to change, consequences, training, and so forth. Once the solutions have been agreed to by the team, testing and implementation follow.

Diagrams are posted in key locations to stimulate continued reference as similar or new problems arise. The diagrams are revised as solutions are found and improvements are made.

The cause-and-effect diagram has nearly unlimited application in research, manufacturing, marketing, office operations, and so forth. One of its strongest assets is the participation and contribution of everyone involved in the brainstorming process. The diagrams are useful in

1. *Analyzing* actual conditions for the purpose of product or service quality improvement, more efficient use of resources, and reduced costs.

2. *Elimination* of conditions causing nonconforming product and customer complaints.

3. *Standardization* of existing and proposed operations.

4. *Education and training* of personnel in decision-making and corrective-action activities.

The previous paragraphs have described the *cause-enumeration* type of cause-and-effect (CE) diagram which is the most common type. There are two other types of CE diagrams that are similar to the cause enumeration. They are the dispersion-analysis and process-analysis types. The only difference between the three methods is the organization and arrangement.

The *dispersion-analysis* type of CE diagram looks just like the cause-enumeration type when both are complete. The difference is in the approach to constructing it. For this type, each major branch is filled in completely before starting work on any of the other branches. Also, the objective is to analyze the causes of dispersion or variability.

The *process-analysis* type of CE diagram is the third type, and it does look different from the other two. In order to construct this diagram, it is necessary to write each step of the production process. This is often referred to as a *flow diagram*. Steps in the production process become the *major causes*, as shown in Figure 12-7. Minor causes are then connected to the major ones. This CE diagram is for elements within an operation. Other possibilities are operations within a process, an assembly process, a continuous chemical process, and so forth. The advantage of this type of CE diagram is the ease of construction and its simplicity, since it follows the production sequence.

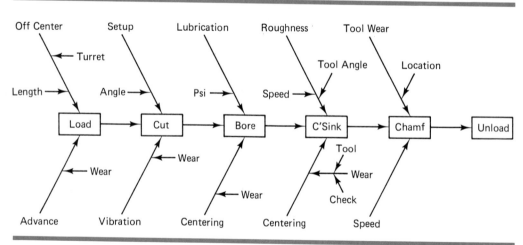

FIGURE 12-7 **Process analysis CE diagram.**

CHECK SHEETS

The main purpose of check sheets is to ensure that the data are collected carefully and accurately. They should be presented in such a form that the data can be quickly and easily used and analyzed. The form of the check sheet is individualized for each situation. Figure 12-8 shows a check sheet for paint nonconformities. Figure 12-9 in page 388 shows a maintenance check sheet for the swimming pool of a major motel chain. Checks are made on a daily and weekly basis, and some checks, such as temperature, are measured. This type of check sheet insures that a check or test is made.

CHECK SHEET

Product: Bicycle—32 **Date:** Jan. 21
Stage: Final Inspection **ID:** Paint
Number Inspected: 2217 **Inspector/Operator:** Jane Doe

Nonconformity Type	Check	Total
Blister	𝍸 𝍸 𝍸 𝍸 |	21
Light spray	𝍸 𝍸 𝍸 𝍸 𝍸 𝍸 𝍸 |||	38
Drips	𝍸 𝍸 𝍸 𝍸 ||	22
Overspray	𝍸 𝍸 |	11
Splatter	𝍸 |||	8
Runs	𝍸 𝍸 𝍸 𝍸 𝍸 𝍸 𝍸 𝍸 𝍸 ||	47
Others	𝍸	5
	Total	152
Number Nonconforming	𝍸 |||	113

FIGURE 12-8 **Check sheet for paint nonconformities.**

HISTOGRAM

Histograms are discussed in Chapter 2. They describe the variation in the process as illustrated by Figure 12-10. The histogram graphically shows the process capability and the relationship to the specifications and the nominal. It also suggests the shape of the population and indicates if there are any gaps in the data.

D = Daily A = As Needed								

Hot Tub

		Mon.	Tues.	Wed.	Th.	Fri.	Sat.	Sun.
Chemical Test (Add if Needed) ph/chlorine	(D)	7.4						
Temperature	(D)	81°						
Add Water (If Needed)	(D)							
Clean Deck Around Hot Tub	(D)	✓						

Pool

Chemical Test (Add if Needed)	(D)	7.6						
Add Water (If Needed)	(D)	300 gals.						
Check Temperature	(D)	78°						
Vacuum Pool (If Needed)	(A)							
Filter Backwash (20 lb.)	(A)	✓						
Lint Filter	(D)	✓						
Sweep and Hose Off Deck	(D)	✓						

General Cleaning

Vacuum Carpets	(D)	✓						
Vacuum and Sweep Building B	(D)	✓						
Clean Tables	(D)	✓						
Sweep and Mop Wooden Deck	(D)	✓						
Clean Outside Deck, Bring in Chairs	(D)	✓						
Take Out Trash	(D)	✓						
Empty Building B Trash Cans	(D)	✓						
Wash Windows	(D)	✓						

Bathrooms

Scrub Sinks, Toilets, and Showers	(D)	✓						
Sweep and Mop Floors	(D)	✓						
Empty Trash and Check Lockers	(D)	✓						
Cover Hot Tub (At End of the Night)	(D)	✓						
Check Pool Filters—Be Sure It's On	(D)	✓						

List any and all deviations from this work schedule on the reverse side, date it, and initial it.

FIGURE 12-9   Check sheet for swimming pool.

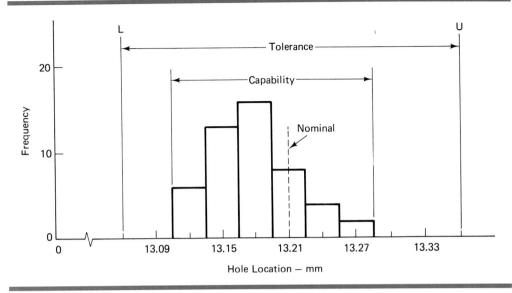

FIGURE 12-10   **Histogram for hole location.**

CONTROL CHARTS

Control charts are discussed in Chapters 3 and 5. A control chart, illustrating quality improvement, is shown in Figure 12-11. Control charts are an outstanding technique for problem solving and the resulting quality improvement.

Quality improvement occurs in two situations. When a control chart is first introduced, the process usually is unstable. As assignable causes for out-of-control conditions are identified and corrective action taken, the process becomes stable, with a resulting quality improvement.

The second situation concerns the testing or evaluation of ideas. Control charts are excellent decision makers because the pattern of the plotted points will determine if the idea is a good one, poor one, or has no effect on the process. If the idea is a good one, the pattern of plotted points of the $\bar{X}$ chart will converge on the central line, X_0. In other words, the pattern will get closer to perfection, which is the central line. For the R chart and the attribute charts, the pattern will tend toward zero, which is perfection. These improvement patterns are illustrated in Figure 12-11. If the idea is a poor one, an opposite pattern will occur. Where the pattern of plotted points does not change, then the idea has no effect on the process.

While the control charts are excellent for problem solving by improving the quality, they have limitations when used to monitor or maintain a process. The pre-control technique is much better at monitoring.

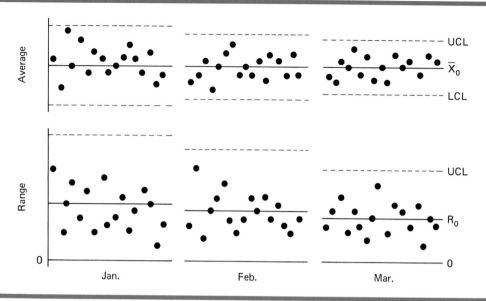

FIGURE 12-11 $\bar{X}$ and R charts, showing quality improvement.

PROCESS CAPABILITY

Management has the responsibility of ensuring that the process is capable of meeting the specifications. Capability is described in Chapter 3 and is reiterated in this chapter to emphasize its importance. A process may be stable and predictable, as shown by the control charts, but be producing waste. A measure of the process capability called the capability index and symbolized by C_p is a necessary complement to a variables control chart. A minimum C_p value of 1.33 is recognized as a de facto standard. It is also necessary to determine if the process is centered on the target or nominal value, and the symbol C_{pk} is used to measure the centering. A minimum value of 1.00 is recommended for C_{pk}.

When the C_p value is 1.33 or greater, then operating personnel have the responsibility of keeping the process centered, stable, and predictable.

PRECONTROL

Control charts for variables, notably the $\bar{X}$ and R charts, are excellent for problem solving. They do, however, have certain disadvantages when used by operating personnel to monitor a process after a project team has improved the process:

> On short runs, the process is often completed before the operators have time to calculate the limits.

> Operators may not have time or ability to make the necessary calculations.

Frequently, operators are confused about specifications and control limits. This fact is especially true when a process is out of control but waste is not being produced.

Precontrol corrects these disadvantages as well as offering some advantages of its own.

The first step in the process is to be sure that the process capability is less than the specifications. Therefore, a capability index, C_p, of 1.00 or more, preferably more, is required. It is management's responsibility to assure that the process is capable of meeting the specifications. Next, precontrol (PC) lines are established to divide the tolerance into five zones as shown in Figure 12-12a. These PC lines are located halfway between the nominal value and the outside limits of the tolerance as given by U for upper specifications and L for lower specifications. The center zone is one-half the print tolerance and is called the green area. On each side are the yellow zones, and each amounts to one-fourth of the total tolerance. Outside the specifications are the red zones. The colors make the procedure simple to understand and apply.

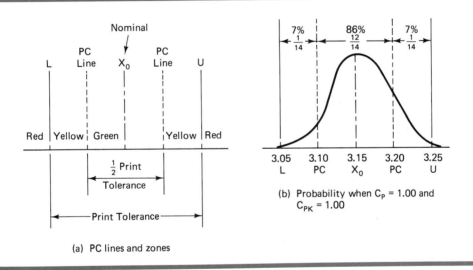

(a) PC lines and zones

(b) Probability when C_p = 1.00 and C_{PK} = 1.00

FIGURE 12-12   Precontrol lines.

For a specification of 3.15 ± 0.10 mm, the calculations are:

1. Divide tolerance by 4: $0.20/4 = 0.05$
2. Add value to lower specification, 3.05:

$$PC = 3.05 + 0.05 = 3.10$$

3. Subtract value from upper specification, 3.25:

$$PC = 3.25 - 0.05 = 3.20$$

Thus, the two PC lines are located at 3.10 and 3.20 mm. These values are shown in (b).

The statistical foundation of precontrol is shown in Figure 12-12b. First, the process capability is equal to the specifications and is centered as indicated by $C_p = 1.00$ and $C_{pk} = 1.00$. For a normal distribution, 86% of the parts (12 out of 14) will fall between the PC lines, which is the green zone, and 7 percent of the parts (1 out of 14) will fall between the PC line and the specifications, which are the two yellow zones. As the capability index increases, the chance of a part falling in the yellow zone decreases. Also, with a large capability index ($C_p = 1.33$ is considered a de facto standard), distributions that depart from normal are easily accommodated.

The precontrol procedure has two stages: start up and run. These stages are shown in Figure 12-13. One part is checked, and the results can fall in one of the three color zones. If the part is outside specifications (red zone), the process is stopped and reset. If the part is between the PC lines and the specifications (yellow zone), a second part is tested; if the second part is in the yellow zone, the process is stopped and reset. If the part falls between the PC lines (green zone), additional parts are tested until five consecutive parts are in the green zone. Operators become quite adept at "nudging" the setting when a reset is required.

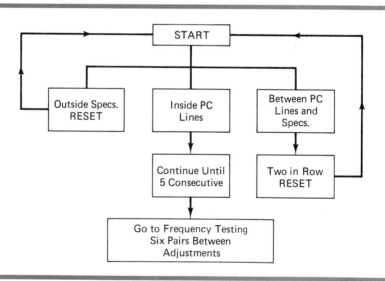

FIGURE 12-13   Precontrol procedure.

Once there are five consecutive parts in the green zone, the run, or frequency testing, stage commences. Frequency testing is the evaluation of pairs of parts. The frequency rule is to sample six pairs between adjustments, and Table 12-2 gives the time between measurements for various adjustment frequencies. As can be seen by the table, there is a linear relationship between the two variables. Thus, if, on the average, an adjustment is made every 6 h, the time between measurement of pairs is

TABLE 12-2 Frequency of Measuring

TIME BETWEEN ADJUSTMENTS, HOURS	TIME BETWEEN MEASUREMENT, MINUTES
1	10
2	20
3	30
4	40
⋮	⋮

60 mins. The time between adjustments is determined by the operator and supervisor based on historical information.

Figure 12-14 shows the decision rules for the measured pairs (designated A, B) for the different color zone possibilities:

1. Where a part falls in the red zone, the process is shut down, reset, and the procedure returned to the start-up stage.

2. Where an A, B pair falls in opposite yellow zones, the process is shut down and help is requested, since this may require a more sophisticated adjustment.

3. Where an A, B pair falls in the same yellow zone, the process is adjusted and the procedure returned to the start-up stage.

4. Where one or both A and B fall in the green zone, the process continues to run.

Decision	Red	Yellow	Green	Yellow	Red	Probability
Stop, Go to Start-up	A					nil
					A	nil
Stop, Get Help		A		B		$1/14 * 1/14 = 1/196$
		B		A		$1/14 * 1/14 = 1/196$
Adjust, Go to Start-up		A, B				$1/14 * 1/14 = 1/196$
				A, B		$1/14 * 1/14 = 1/196$
Continue			A, B			$12/14 * 12/14 = 144/196$
		A	B			$1/14 * 12/14 = 12/196$
		B	A			$1/14 * 12/14 = 12/196$
			A	B		$12/14 * 1/14 = 12/196$
			B	A		$12/14 * 1/14 = 12/196$
	L	PC	X_o PC		U	Total $= 196/196$

↑
Target

FIGURE 12-14 Run decision and probability.

On the right side of the figure is the probability that a particular A, B pair will occur.

Precontrol is made even easier to use by painting the measuring instrument in green, yellow, and red at the appropriate places. In this way, the operator knows when to go, apply caution, or stop.

Precontrol can also be used for attributes. Appropriately colored "go/no-go" gages that designate the precontrol lines are issued to the operator along with the usual gages for the upper and lower specifications. Precontrol is also used for visual characteristics by assigning visual standards for the PC lines.

The advantages of precontrol are as follows:

1. It is applicable to short production runs as well as long production runs.
2. No recording, calculating, or plotting of data is involved. A precontrol chart can be used if the consumer desires statistical evidence of process control (see Figure 12-15).
3. It is applicable to start up so the process is centered on the target.
4. It works directly with the tolerance rather than easily misunderstood control limits.
5. It is applicable to attributes.
6. It is simple to understand, so training is very easy.

While the precontrol technique has a lot of advantages, we must remember that it is only a control technique. Control charts are used for problem solving, since they have the ability to improve the process by correcting assignable causes and testing improvement ideas. Also, the control chart is more appropriate for process capability and detecting process shifts.

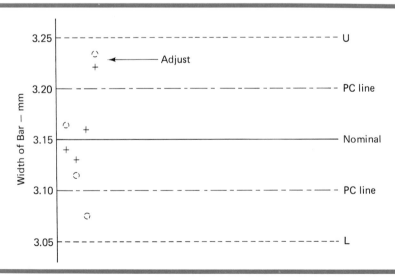

FIGURE 12-15 Precontrol chart.

In summary, operator precontrol means better management and operator understanding, operator responsibility for quality, reduced rejects, reduced adjustments, reduced operator frustration, and a subsequent increase in morale. These benefits have been realized for many different types of processes.

SCATTER DIAGRAM

The simplest way to determine if a cause-and-effect relationship exists is to plot a scatter diagram. Figure 12-16 shows the relationship between automotive speed and gas mileage. The figure shows that as speed increases, gas mileage decreases. Automotive speed is plotted on the x-axis and is the independent variable. The independent variable is usually controllable. Gas mileage is on the y-axis and is the dependent, or response, variable. Other examples of relationship are as follows:

  Cutting speed and tool life
  Moisture content and thread elongation
  Temperature and lipstick hardness
  Striking pressure and electrical current
  Temperature and percent foam in soft drinks
  Yield and concentration
  Breakdowns and equipment age

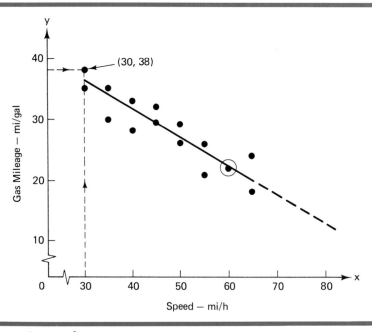

FIGURE 12-16   Scatter diagram.

TABLE 12-3   Data on Automotive Speed vs. Gas Mileage

SAMPLE NUMBER	SPEED (MI/H)	MILEAGE (MI/GAL)	SAMPLE NUMBER	SPEED (MI/H)	MILEAGE (MI/GAL)
1	30	38	9	50	26
2	30	35	10	50	29
3	35	35	11	55	32
4	35	30	12	55	21
5	40	33	13	60	22
6	40	28	14	60	22
7	45	32	15	65	18
8	45	29	16	65	24

There are a few simple steps in constructing a scatter diagram. Data are collected as ordered pairs (x, y). The automotive speed (cause) is controlled and the gas mileage (effect) is measured. Table 12-3 shows resulting x, y paired data.

The horizontal and vertical scales are constructed with the higher values on the right for the x-axis and on the top for the y-axis. After the scales are labeled, the data are plotted. Using dotted lines, the technique of plotting sample number 1 (30, 38) is illustrated in Figure 12-16. The x value is 30, and the y value is 38. Sample numbers 2 through 16 are plotted, and the scatter diagram is complete. If two points are identical, concentric circles can be used, as illustrated at 60 mi/h.

Once the scatter diagram is complete, the relationship or correlation between the two variables can be evaluated. Figure 12-17 shows different patterns and their interpretation. At (a), we have a positive correlation between the two variables because as x increases, y increases. At (b), there is a negative correlation between the two variables because as x increases, y decreases. At (c), there is no correlation, and this pattern is sometimes referred to as a shotgun pattern.

The patterns described in (a), (b), and (c) are easy to understand; however, those described in (d), (e), and (f) are more difficult. At (d), there may or may not be a relationship between the two variables. There appears to be a negative relationship between x and y, but it is not too strong. Further statistical analysis is needed to evaluate this pattern. At (e), we have stratified the data to represent different causes for the same effect. Some examples are gas mileage with the wind versus against the wind, two different suppliers of material, and two different machines. One cause is plotted with a small solid circle, and the other cause is plotted with an open triangle. When the data are separated, we see that there is a strong correlation. At (f), we have a curvilinear relationship rather than a linear one.

When all the plotted points fall on a straight line, we have a perfect correlation. Because of variations in the experiment and measurement error, this perfect situation will rarely occur.

It is sometimes desirable to fit a straight line to the data in order to write a prediction equation. For example, we may wish to estimate the gas mileage at 75 mi/h. A line can be placed on the scatter diagram by sight or mathematically using least squares analysis. In either approach, the idea is to make the deviation of the points on each side of the line equal. Where the line is extended beyond the data, a dashed line is used because there are no data in that area.

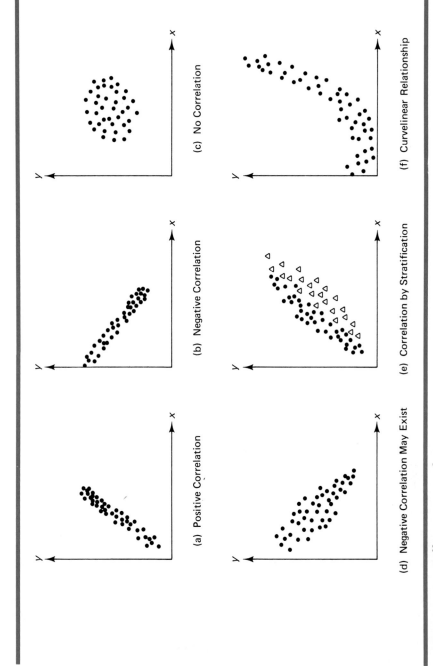

FIGURE 12-17 Different scatter diagram patterns.

RUN CHART

Run charts are discussed in Chapters 3 and 5. They are a very simple technique to analyze the process in the development stage or, for that matter, when other charting techniques are not applicable. The important point is to draw a picture of the process and let it "talk" to you. A picture is worth a thousand words, provided you are listening.

FLOWCHARTS

For many products and services, it may be useful to construct a flowchart. These charts show the flow of the product or service as it moves through the various processing stations. The chart makes it easy to visualize the entire system, identify potential trouble spots, and locate control activities.

Standardized symbols are used, as shown in Table 12-4. Figure 12-18 shows a flowchart for a grill casting of an outdoor grill.

DESIGN OF EXPERIMENTS

Design of experiments requires a different level of mathematical ability than the previously described techniques. It is, however, the only way that complex systems can be analyzed. A multivariate approach is used because the cost to change one variable at a time is usually prohibitive. Studies are run under laboratory, pilot plant, and manufacturing conditions. The short-term cost to make these studies is substantial; however, in the long run, they will give the optimum process and product parameters. Recent evidence indicates that management is increasing its use of this technique. Additional information on this subject is beyond the scope of this book.

PROBLEMS

1. Construct a Pareto diagram for replacement parts for an electric stove. Six-months' data are: oven door, 193; timer, 53; front burners, 460; rear burners, 290; burner control, 135; drawer rollers, 46; other, 84; and oven regulators, 265.

2. A project team is studying the downtime cost of a soft-drink bottling line. Data analysis in thousands of dollars for a 3-month period are: back pressure regulator, 30; adjust feed worm, 15; jam copper head, 6; lost cooling, 52; valve replacement, 8; and other, 5.

3. Approximately two-thirds of all automobile accidents are due to improper driving. Construct a Pareto diagram without the cumulative line for the data: improper turn, 3.6%; driving too fast for conditions, 28.1%; following too closely, 8.1%; right-of-way violations, 30.1%; driving left of center, 3.3%; improper overtaking, 3.2%; and other, 23.6%.

TABLE 12-4 Flowchart Symbols

SYMBOL	NAME	DESCRIPTION
◯	Operation	Type a letter; drill a hole
⇒	Transportation	Move material
☐	Inspection	Examine a document; read a gage
◻	Delay	Papers to be filed; waiting for elevator
▽	Storage	Record in file cabinet; finished product in warehouse

Symbol | Description

◯   Unload Trailer or Hand Truck

⇒   To Storage

▽   Stores

⇒   To Machine or Hand Truck

◻   Machine

◯   Null

◯   Place on Hand Truck

⇒   To Paint

◯   Hang on Line

◯   Clean — Paint — Bake

☐   Inspect Paint

◯   Unload — Stack on Hand Truck

⇒   To Packaging

◯   Unload — Package Grills in Canteen

⇒   To Assembly by Conveyor

FIGURE 12-18 Flow chart for grills.

4. A major record-of-the-month club collected data on the reasons for returned shipments during a quarter. Results are: wrong selection, 50,000; refused, 195,000; wrong address, 68,000; order canceled, 5000; and other, 15,000. Construct a Pareto diagram.

5. Paint nonconformities for a 1-month period for a riding lawn mower manufacturer are: blister, 212; light spray, 582; drips, 227; overspray, 109; splatter, 141; bad paint, 126; runs, 434; and other, 50. Construct a Pareto diagram.

6. Prepare and analyze the matrix for the assemblers of the transmission assembly section and their nonconforming manufacturing activities. Data are as shown in the table on page 401.

7. Four cloth-weaving looms are being compared by type of nonconformity. Prepare a matrix and analyze. Data are:

> Loom 24: broken string, 3; warp tension, 2; shuttle, 1; and jam, 3
>
> Loom 36: nonconforming splice, 2; shuttle, 8; warp tension, 8; broken string, 2; and jam, 1
>
> Loom 28: warp tension, 5; and jam, 2
>
> Loom 15: jam, 7; shuttle, 6; warp tension, 2; broken string, 7; and nonconforming splice, 4.

8. Prepare a Grier diagram for the model XYZ automotive tire. Data (first number is the code) on nonconformities are: 1—10, 2—5, 3—0, 4—9, 5—6, 6—0, 7—2, 8—0, 9—3, 10—1, A—6, B—1, C—3, and 0—5.

9. Prepare a time series graph for nonconformities per unit for hospital Medicare claims and analyze the results. Data are: 1986—0.20, 1987—0.15, 1988—0.16, and 1989—0.12.

10. Form a project team of six or seven people, elect a leader, and construct a cause-and-effect diagram for bad coffee from a 22-cup appliance used in the office.

11. Form a project team of six or seven people, elect a leader, and construct a CE diagram for:
    (a) Dispersion analysis type for a quality characteristic.
    (b) Process analysis type for a sequence of office activities on an insurance form.
    (c) Process analysis type for a sequence of production activities on a lathe: load 25 mm dia.—80 mm long rod, rough turn 12 mm dia.—40 mm long, UNF thread—12 mm dia., thread relief, finish turn 25 mm dia.—20 mm long, cut off, and unload.

12. Design a check sheet for the maintenance of a piece of equipment such as a gas furnace, laboratory scale, or typewriter.

13. What are the PC lines for a process that has a nominal of 32.0° and a tolerance of ±1.0°C?

LYNN	BRENT	MARY	KEN	DAVE	BILL
• Mushroomed hammer (1)	• Wrong tools (1)	• Leaky seals (4)	• Improper method (1)	• Loose fasteners (2)	• Leaky seals (2)
• Leaky seals (3)	• Leaky seals (3)	• Improper torque (5)	• Wrong tools (1)	• Mushroomed hammer (1)	• Defective lifting device (1)
• Wrong tools (4)	• Loose fasteners (1)	• Oil dry in hydraulic area (1)	• Oil dry in hydraulic area (2)	• Wrong tools (4)	• Loose fasteners (1)
• Loose fasteners (3)		• Improper method (2)	• Improper torque (1)	• Leaky seals (3)	
• Spliced air tool hose (1)		• Hoses and tubes uncapped (3)		• Improper method (3)	
• Improper method (5)		• Oil on floor (2)		• Hoses and tubes uncapped (1)	
• Open air line (1)		• Loose fasteners (4)		• Oil on floor (3)	
				• Improper torque (3)	

401

14. Determine the PC line for the concentricity of a shaft when the total indicator reading (TIR) tolerance is 0.06 mm and the target is 0. *Hint:* This problem is a one-sided tolerance; however, the green zone is still half the tolerance. Graph the results.

15. What is the probability of an A, B pair being green? Of an A, B pair having one yellow and one green?

16. By means of a scatter diagram, determine if a relationship exists between product temperatures and percent foam for a soft drink. Data are:

DAY	°F PRODUCT TEMPERATURE	% FOAM	DAY	°F PRODUCT TEMPERATURE	% FOAM
1	36	15	11	44	32
2	38	19	12	42	33
3	37	21	13	38	20
4	44	30	14	41	27
5	46	36	15	45	35
6	39	20	16	49	38
7	41	25	17	50	40
8	47	36	18	48	42
9	39	22	19	46	40
10	40	23	20	41	30

17. By means of a scatter diagram, determine if there is a relationship between hours of machine use and millimeters off the target. Data for 20 (x, y) pairs with hours of machine use as the x variable are (30, 1.10), (31, 1.21), (32, 1.00), (33, 1.21), (34, 1.25), (35, 1.23), (36, 1.24), (37, 1.28), (38, 1.30), (39, 1.30), (40, 1.38), (41, 1.35), (42, 1.38), (43, 1.38), (44, 1.40), (45, 1.42), (46, 1.45), (47, 1.45), (48, 1.50), and (49, 1.58). Draw a line for the data using eyesight only and estimate the number of millimeters off the target at 55 h.

18. Data on gas pressure (kg/cm²) and its volume (liters) are as follows: (0.5, 1.62), (1.5, 0.75), (2.0, 0.62), (3.0, 0.46), (2.5, 0.52), (1.0, 1.00), (0.8, 1.35), (1.2, 0.89), (2.8, 0.48), (3.2, 0.43), (1.8, 0.71), and (0.3, 1.80). Construct a scatter diagram and determine the relationship.

19. The following data (tensile strength, hardness) are for tensile strength (100 psi) and hardness (Rockwell E) of die-cast aluminum. Construct a scatter diagram and determine the relationship: (293, 53), (349, 70), (368, 40), (301, 55), (340, 78), (308, 64), (354, 71), (313, 53), (322, 82), (334, 67), (377, 70), (247, 56), (348, 86), (298, 60), (287, 72), (292, 51), (345, 88), (380, 95), (257, 51), (258, 75).

20. Data on the amount of water applied in inches and the yield of alfalfa in tons per acre are:

Water	12	18	24	30	36	42	48	60
Yield	5.3	5.7	6.3	7.2	8.2	8.7	8.4	8.2

Prepare a scatter diagram and analyze the results.

21. Construct a flowchart for the manufacture of a product or the providing of a service.

13

QUALITY IMPROVEMENT MANAGEMENT

─

INTRODUCTION

The importance of quality and the management of the quality function cannot be overlooked during the development and production of new products and the improvement of existing products. This chapter describes a framework for effective quality management.

AWARENESS

Management must be aware that the quality of the product or service must be improved. Awareness comes about when a company loses market shares or realizes that quality and productivity go hand in hand. Automation and other productivity enhancements will not help a corporation if it is unable to market its product or service because the quality is poor. The Japanese learned this fact from practical experience. Prior to World War II, they could sell their products only at ridiculously low prices

405

and even then it was difficult to secure repeat sales. Until recently, corporations have not recognized the importance of quality. But a new attitude has emerged—quality first among the equals of cost and service.

Quality and productivity are not mutually exclusive. Improvements in quality lead directly to increased productivity and other benefits. Table 13-1 illustrates this concept. As can be seen by the table, the improvement in quality results in a 5.6% improvement in productivity, capacity, and profit. Many quality-improvement projects are achieved with the same work force, same overhead, and no investment in new equipment.

TABLE 13-1   Gain in Productivity with Improved Quality

ITEM	BEFORE IMPROVEMENT 10% NONCONFORMING	AFTER IMPROVEMENT 5% NONCONFORMING
Relative total cost for 20 units	1.00	1.00
Conforming units	18	19
Relative cost for nonconforming units	0.10	0.05
Productivity increase		$\frac{1}{18}(100) = 5.6\%$
Capacity increase		$\frac{1}{18}(100) = 5.6\%$
Profit increase		$\frac{1}{18}(100) = 5.6\%$

Recent evidence suggests that more and more corporations are recognizing the importance and necessity of quality improvement if they are to survive worldwide competition. Quality improvement is not limited to the conformance of the product to specifications; it also involves the quality of the design of the product and the process. The prevention of product and process problems is a more desirable objective than taking corrective action after the product is manufactured.

Quality improvement is not something that will occur overnight. There are no quick remedies. It takes a long time to build the appropriate emphasis and techniques into the culture. Overemphasis on short-term results and profits must be set aside so long-term planning and constancy of purpose will prevail.

MANAGEMENT COMMITMENT

Upper management must recognize that the quality function is no more responsible for product quality than the finance function is responsible for profit and loss. Quality, like cost and service, is the responsibility of everyone in the corporation, especially the chief executive officer (CEO). When a commitment to quality is made, it becomes part of the corporation's business strategy and leads to enhanced profit and an improved competitive position.

To achieve never-ending quality improvement, the CEO must be directly involved in the organization and implementation of the quality improvement activity. The first step is a statement of overall company policy. A general statement is:

The Widget Company will develop and manufacture products that surpass the expectations of its customers.

Most companies have statements of two or three paragraphs.

In addition to the general policy statement, each functional area has its own policies. Examples are: the vice president for marketing will visit each customer twice per year *or* all new operating personnel will receive 30 hours of beginning training in statistical process control (SPC).

In order to build quality into the culture, a quality council is established to provide overall direction. The council is composed of the CEO, the senior managers of the functional areas, a coordinator, and perhaps a consultant. A coordinator is necessary to assume some of the added duties that a quality improvement activity requires. The individual selected for the coordinator's position should be a bright young person who has executive potential. That person will report to the CEO. The duties of the council are as follows:

1. Determine and continually monitor the cost of poor quality.
2. Create the total education and training plan.
3. Approve the quality measure for each functional area.
4. Approve the annual quality improvement program for each functional area and the entire company.
5. Determine those projects that have the greatest improvement potential.
6. Establish the project teams for new products as well as existing products and monitor the results.

Quality councils are also established at lower levels of the corporation. Their duties are similar but relate to that particular level in the organization. Initially these activities will require additional work by council members; however, in the long term their jobs will be easier with less hassle. These councils are the instrument for perpetuating the idea of never-ending quality improvement.

Once the quality-improvement program is well established, the agenda for committee meetings might be as follows:

1. The quality improvement process.
   a. How many employees have been educated?
   b. Are the teams functioning properly?
   c. What success stories do we have to share?
2. The cost of quality.
   a. Do we have the format in all operations?
   b. What are the trends?
   c. Where are the best improvement opportunities?
3. Conformance.
   a. Are we meeting our requirements?
   b. What actions are needed?

Eventually, say in 3 to 5 years, the quality council activities will become so ingrained in the culture of the organization that they become a regular part of the executive meetings. When this state is achieved, a separate quality council is no longer needed and quality becomes the first item on the executive meeting agenda.

DEFINING QUALITY

In order to manage the quality function effectively, it must be defined. In Chapter 1, quality was defined as meeting or exceeding the customer's expectations. And these expectations are used to determine the product requirements. However, quality has nine different dimensions. Table 13-2 shows these nine dimensions of quality with their meaning and explanation in terms of a slide projector.

TABLE 13-2 **The Dimensions of Quality**

DIMENSION	MEANING AND EXAMPLE
Performance	Primary product characteristics, such as the brightness of the picture
Features	Secondary characteristics, added features, such as remote control
Conformance	Meeting specifications or industry standards, workmanship
Reliability	Consistency of performance over time, average time for the unit to fail
Durability	Useful life, includes repair
Service	Resolution of problems and complaints, ease of repair
Response	Human-to-human interface, such as the courtesy of the dealer
Aesthetics	Sensory characteristics, such as exterior finish
Reputation	Past performance and other intangibles, such as being ranked first

These dimensions are somewhat independent; therefore, a product can be excellent in one dimension and average or poor in another. Very few, if any, products excel in all nine dimensions. For example, the Japanese were cited for high-quality cars in the 1970s based only on the dimensions of reliability, conformance, and aesthetics. Evidently, quality products can be determined by using a small number of the nine dimensions of quality.

Marketing has the responsibility of identifying the most important dimensions of quality. These dimensions are then translated into the requirements for the development of a new product or the improvement of an existing one.

MEASUREMENT OF QUALITY

Effective quality management requires a method of quality measurement. There are many methods, and each has its place in the organization.

There is nothing like money to get management's attention. The quality cost—or, more appropriately, the cost of not doing it right the first time—is a very significant measure. It has been estimated that this cost is more than 20% of sales in many companies. This cost represents an enormous opportunity for quality improvement, productivity increase, and profit enhancement. Quality costs are not limited to manufacturing. They are present in the other functional areas: accounting, marketing, product design, service, purchasing, and so forth. The comptroller will need to investigate thoroughly to find all the costs. Some examples are: incorrect color specification on an order, poorly designed component, basing the purchase of materials on price, inefficient routing of product, and incorrect cost-accounting figures.

Quality costs are separated into the categories of prevention, appraisal, internal failure, and external failure. The cost of poor quality is the most powerful tool for effectively managing the quality function. Chapter 9 discusses the quality cost categories and how they are used to identify opportunities for quality improvement.

Another measure of quality is percent nonconforming or count of nonconformities; this is discussed in Chapter 5. These statistical techniques directly measure the effect of quality improvement on an existing product. An overall measure such as percent nonconforming is necessary for the plant or the entire corporation. This measure can also effectively evaluate the CEO's performance. Each functional area and department within a functional area should have a measure that is displayed in some type of chart so it can be viewed by all personnel. These simple charts create quality awareness and measure the progress of quality improvement. A few companies have improved their performance to the point where a nonconformity per million chart is more appropriate than a count of nonconformity chart.

Quality can also be measured by comparing the specifications to the process capability. Dr. W. Edwards Deming has stated that we need to drive the specifications over the horizon. This statement is a figure of speech that actually means the process variability is so small around the target value and the specifications are so far away that they have the appearance of being out of sight. This concept is discussed in Chapter 3. Specifications are dynamic in that they are constantly getting smaller, which requires never-ending improvement in the process capability.

Conventional practice assumes that loss only occurs when the characteristic is outside the specifications. Dr. Genichi Taguchi states that loss to the customer and society occurs as soon as the characteristic deviates from the target value. Figure 13-1 on page 410 illustrates this concept. The target value and specifications are shown on the x scale and the loss in dollars is shown on the $f(x)$ scale. The more the characteristic deviates from the target value, the greater the loss. While the actual shape of the curve may be difficult to predict, the quadratic approximation shown in the figure frequently represents the economic loss function. Where the curve crosses the specifications, the cost of repairing or discarding the product is given in dollars at D. Using this value the equation for the curve can be determined. The concept (with a different shape curve) can be used for other situations, such as where the target value is the largest possible value or where the target value is zero. Taguchi has combined specifications, target value, minimum variation, and dollars into one package to measure quality.

All the measures of quality are needed for the quality-improvement program. They are each applied in different situations.

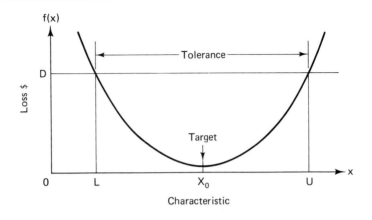

FIGURE 13-1 Taguchi's loss function.

EDUCATION AND TRAINING

The cost of education and training for all personnel is enormous and the time to achieve it is lengthy. The Japanese trained hundreds of thousands of managers and supervisors at all organization levels plus millions of nonsupervisors. As far as quality is concerned, this massive training program has made their managers, specialists, and workers the best trained on earth. This training took more than 10 years to achieve.

To a great extent education has been limited to the quality department. The entire company payroll must be educated in the new philosophy and the quality sciences as is appropriate to their positions. Top management will need a different education than operating personnel. While some education and training occurs concurrently, senior management will need to be first, followed by middle management and specialists, and, finally, by first-line supervisors and operating personnel.

Some education such as an attitude change, a rudimentary knowledge of statistical techniques, the quality-improvement sequence of events, and the concept of prevention is common to all levels. However, the educational needs of different functional areas, departments, and jobs will vary considerably. For example, purchasing personnel will need a knowledge of vendor survey, qualification, and rating; concept of price versus cost; number of suppliers; and statistical process control.

In addition to education related to quality, a rigorous program of retraining people in new skills to keep up with changes in materials, methods, product designs, and machinery is desirable. To a large extent, this retraining will be provided to the specialists within a company. For example, the product engineers of an appliance manufacturer must be aware of the impact of composite material technology on that company's products.

The education and training task is so formidable that the quality council may wish to establish a special task force to do the planning on a company-wide basis. The mission of this task force is to:

1. Identify the subject matter for each job category.
2. Identify possible sources of training materials and leaders.
3. Estimate the investment required in money, facilities, and personnel.
4. Recommend a program including trainees, leaders, and a time schedule.

Upper managers should become trainees in the program. Their training will be partly "by the book" and partly by the extent to which they participate in the management of the quality function.

ANNUAL QUALITY-IMPROVEMENT PROGRAM

The broad objectives for annual improvement programs should be to develop among all managers, specialists, and operating personnel:

1. A sense of responsibility for active participation in making improvements.
2. The skills needed to make improvements.
3. The habit of annual improvements so that each year the company's quality is significantly better than it was a year ago.

The program is developed from the departmental level with operating personnel involvement, through the functional areas, to the company-wide level.

Quality objectives must be stated in measurable terms, such as the following:

1. All billing clerks will receive training in error avoidance.
2. A preventive maintenance procedure will be developed and implemented for the milling department.
3. A project team will reduce field failures by 25%.
4. The wiring-harness assembly department will reduce nonconformities by 30%.

Operating personnel should be encouraged to set objectives or quality goals for themselves as indicated by item 4. Management should support these goals by training, projects, resources, and so forth.

Most likely there will be more quality objectives than can be accomplished with the available resources. Therefore, those that have the greatest opportunity for improvement will be used. Many objectives will require a project team. Some companies have well-structured annual quality-improvement programs. In companies that lack such structured programs, any improvements must come from the initiatives of middle managers and specialists. It takes a good deal of determination by these people to secure results, since they lack the legitimacy and support that comes from an official, structured program designed by the quality council.

PROJECT TEAMS

Project teams are used for both the development of new products and the improvement of existing products. The new product teams will be discussed first; however, many of the comments are equally applicable for existing product teams.

New products are developed from research and development or from unfulfilled needs determined by marketing. No matter what the source, it is important that there be early involvement of all appropriate personnel by placing them on project teams. Typical members will be from marketing, quality, materials management, service, finance, manufacturing, and, of course, product design. The project leader will most likely be from the product design area and is described as first among equals.

The basic idea is to build quality into the design at the beginning rather than fix it afterwards. Each of the team members has a role to play. For example, marketing will continue to assess the customer's requirements in regard to the design. Or manufacturing will provide advice about the ability of the process to meet a particular specification.

This approach to project development usually takes longer. It does, however, prevent problems from occurring rather than detecting them at a later time when the cost to correct the problem may be prohibitive.

The composition of project teams for existing projects will be a function of the desired improvement. Some teams might be composed of simply the operator, supervisor, and a member of the quality department. Other teams might be composed of representatives from many functional areas. Occasionally, it is desirable from a management commitment and involvement viewpoint to include the CEO or senior manager on a project team. This practice is a concrete illustration of leading by example. Each team should have the proper education in the basic statistical tools and in brainstorming.

The project team concept has an important by-product. It breaks down barriers between and within functional areas and departments.

PROBLEM-SOLVING METHOD

The project team achieves the optimal results when it operates within the framework of the problem-solving method. In the initial stages of a quality-improvement program, quick results are often obtained because the solutions are obvious or someone has a brilliant idea. However, in the long term, a systematic approach will yield the greatest benefits.

The problem-solving method (also called the scientific method) as applied to quality improvement has six steps:

1. Problem identification
2. Project team assignment
3. Problem analysis

4. Possible solutions

5. Evaluation

6. Remedial action

These steps are not totally independent; they are sometimes interrelated. In fact, some techniques such as the control chart can be effectively utilized in more than one step. Quality improvement is the goal, and the problem-solving process a framework to achieve that goal.

Problem identification is the first step. It answers the question, What are the quality problems? The answer leads to those problems that have the greatest potential for quality improvement.

Quality problems can be identified from a variety of inputs, such as the following:

Quality cost data.

Pareto analysis of repetitive external alarm signals (field failures, complaints, returns, and others).

Pareto analysis of repetitive internal alarm signals (scrap rework, sorting, and 100% test).

Proposals from key insiders (managers, supervisors, professionals, and union stewards).

Proposals from suggestions schemes.

Field study of users' needs.

Data on performance of products versus competitors (from users and from laboratory tests).

Comments of key people outside the company (customers, vendors, journalists, and critics).

Findings and comments of government regulators and independent laboratories.

Problem identification should not be a reaction to a negative situation but a constant searching for potential problems or opportunities to make significant quality improvement. This first step is the responsibility of the quality council.

Step 2 of the method is to form a project team. This step is also the responsibility of the quality council. The project team concept was discussed in the previous section.

In the problem-analysis step, the team mobilizes the necessary company resources to analyze the problem. All available information is collected for the project team. If this is not sufficient, then additional new information is obtained. Following are the common items of information:

Design information, such as specifications, drawings, function, bills of materials, costs, design reviews, field data, service, and maintainability.

Process information, such as routing, equipment, operators, raw materials, component parts, and supplies.

Statistical information, such as average, median, range, standard deviation, skewness, kurtosis, and frequency distribution.

Quality information, such as control charts, process capability, acceptance sampling, run charts, life testing, and operator and equipment matrix analysis.

Cause-and-effect diagrams.

Depending on the nature of the problem, more complex information, such as correlation, regression, analysis of variance, and design of experiments, may be necessary at later stages of the problem-solving method to obtain additional information.

Once all the information is available, the project team begins its search for possible solutions. With quality problems, more than one solution may be required to remedy a situation. Sometimes the solutions are quite evident from a cursory analysis of the data.

If the primary cause or causes are determined from the cause-and-effect approach, the solution might be determined quite easily. In this step, creativity plays the major role.

Evaluation or testing of the possible solutions is the fifth step. As mentioned, more than one solution is possible. Evaluation and/or testing determines which of the possible solutions have the greatest potential for success. Criteria for judging the possible solutions include such things as cost, feasibility, effect, resistance to change, consequences, and training. Solutions may be categorized into short range and long range.

It should be pointed out that one of the features of control charts is their ability to evaluate possible solutions. Whether the idea is good, poor, or has no effect is evident from the chart after 25 subgroups or, in some cases, fewer.

Remedial action, the last step, actually involves three activities. First, there is an approval process. While the project team usually has some authority to institute remedial action, more often than not the approval of the quality council or other appropriate authority is required. If such is the case, a written and/or oral report is given.

The project team is also responsible for the implementation and follow-up activities. These activities are usually included with the report that was presented for approval. If the follow-up activity does not achieve the necessary improvements, then some of the steps will need to be repeated.

While the problem-solving method is no guarantee of success, experience has indicated that an orderly approach will yield the highest probability of success. Problem solving concentrates on quality improvement rather than quality control.

PEOPLE

No resource is more valuable to an organization than its people. While the above expression is an old cliché, it is certainly a true one and very applicable to quality. Many companies view quality problems in terms of operating personnel. The frequent response is to develop motivation programs with goals and slogans. These programs result in an immediate "hype"; management actions (quality council) and deeds (project team success) rather than lip service will do more to motivate people than short-lived programs.

Consider the situation where an operator produces parts that have marginal quality. If management decides to sort or scrap the parts, then concrete evidence is given that management cares about quality. However, if the decision is to take a chance and ship the parts to the customer, then all the slogans and motivational programs will have little meaning or even be counterproductive.

Actually, management makes a serious mistake when it assumes that the quality problem is due to unconcerned operating personnel. Dr. Deming has estimated that only 15% of the quality problems of an organization are due to local faults (operators and first-line supervisors). The rest (85%) are due to the system (management).

Point 8 of Dr. Deming's 14 points is:

> Reduce fear throughout the organization by encouraging open, two-way, non-punitive communication. The economic loss resulting from fear to ask questions or report trouble is appalling.

He further states that quick results in quality improvement can be obtained by achieving this goal. Powerful economic results are obtainable within 2 or 3 years when the employment climate is changed.

Involving people in the quality-improvement program is an effective technique to improve the quality. Management commitment, annual quality improvement, education and training, project teams, and so forth, are all effective in utilizing the human resources of the organization.

The Japanese have had excellent success with their quality control circles. They can be used at all levels of an organization. However, the quality control circle approach is not a panacea. It is estimated that, at best, only 10% of the Japanese miracle in quality can be attributed to this approach. The reason for this low value is that the vital few (85%) quality problems are inherently due to the system (management). Quality control circles and other involvement programs have their greatest benefit in reducing fear and opening up the lines of communication.

Once the proper environment is established, a suggestion system can be developed that will provide another approach for quality improvement. In order to be effective, action by management is necessary on each suggestion. This action can be quite an increase in management's work load; however, it is the only way a suggestion system will provide the maximum benefits. A few CEOs answer each suggestion with a personal letter stating why or why not the suggestion was a good one and whether it will or will not be implemented. Monetary and/or recognition reward is also an essential part of a suggestion system, and the recognition part may be the most important.

Most suggestion systems require identification of a problem and a solution. Another approach is to provide a form whereby people need only state a problem. The appropriate functional area or department will develop the solution.

Typical problems are as follows:

1. This tool is not long enough for all the parts.
2. The sales department makes too many errors on their order entry forms.
3. We make a lot of changes in response to telephone calls, and many changes have to be redone.

Once people know that their problems will be heard and answered, communication is opened up, and the potential for quality improvement is enhanced.

DEMING'S 14 POINTS

A chapter on quality-improvement management would not be complete without listing Dr. Deming's 14 obligations of senior management. They are as follows:

1. Innovate and allocate resources to fulfill the long-term needs of the company and customer rather than short-term profitability.
2. Discard the old philosophy of accepting nonconforming products and services.
3. Eliminate dependence on mass inspection for quality control; instead, depend on process control, through statistical techniques.
4. Reduce the number of multiple-source suppliers. Price has no meaning without an integral consideration for quality. Encourage suppliers to use statistical process control.
5. Use statistical techniques to identify the two sources of waste—system (85%) and local faults (15%); strive to constantly reduce this waste.
6. Institute more thorough, better job-related training.
7. Provide supervision with knowledge of statistical methods; encourage use of these methods to identify which nonconformities should be investigated for solution.
8. Reduce fear throughout the organization by encouraging open, two-way, non-punitive communication. The economic loss resulting from fear to ask questions or report trouble is appalling.
9. Help reduce waste by encouraging design, research, and sales people to learn more about the problems of production.
10. Eliminate the use of goals and slogans to encourage productivity, unless training and management support is also provided.
11. Closely examine the impact of work standards. Do they consider quality or help anyone do a better job? They often act as an impediment to productivity improvement.
12. Institute rudimentary statistical training on a broad scale.

13. Institute a vigorous program for retraining people in new skills, to keep up with changes in materials, methods, product designs, and machinery.

14. Create a structure in top management that will push every day for continuous quality improvement.

Most of Dr. Deming's 14 points have been incorporated into the quality improvement material of this chapter.

FINAL COMMENTS

Management must know that quality is first among the equals of cost and service. In this regard, there is no economic level of quality or, if there is such a level, few, if any, companies have achieved it. The ultimate goal is prevention of quality problems rather than detection. Effective quality-improvement management is necessary for quality to become part of the company's business strategy.

The old attitudes toward quality are no longer acceptable. New products must be developed and existing products modified to meet the customer's requirements. Optimum process and product parameters need to be determined in order to achieve the smallest possible variation. The evidence shows that high-quality products increase productivity and provide the competitive advantage for company survival.

APPENDIX

TABLE A Areas Under the Normal Curve[a]

$\dfrac{X_i-\mu}{\sigma}$	0.09	0.08	0.07	0.06	0.05	0.04	0.03	0.02	0.01	0.00
−3.5	0.00017	0.00017	0.00018	0.00019	0.00019	0.00020	0.00021	0.00022	0.00022	0.00023
−3.4	0.00024	0.00025	0.00026	0.00027	0.00028	0.00029	0.00030	0.00031	0.00033	0.00034
−3.3	0.00035	0.00036	0.00038	0.00039	0.00040	0.00042	0.00043	0.00045	0.00047	0.00048
−3.2	0.00050	0.00052	0.00054	0.00056	0.00058	0.00060	0.00062	0.00064	0.00066	0.00069
−3.1	0.00071	0.00074	0.00076	0.00079	0.00082	0.00085	0.00087	0.00090	0.00094	0.00097
−3.0	0.00100	0.00104	0.00107	0.00111	0.00114	0.00118	0.00122	0.00126	0.00131	0.00135
−2.9	0.0014	0.0014	0.0015	0.0015	0.0016	0.0016	0.0017	0.0017	0.0018	0.0019
−2.8	0.0019	0.0020	0.0021	0.0021	0.0022	0.0023	0.0023	0.0024	0.0025	0.0026
−2.7	0.0026	0.0027	0.0028	0.0029	0.0030	0.0031	0.0032	0.0033	0.0034	0.0035
−2.6	0.0036	0.0037	0.0038	0.0039	0.0040	0.0041	0.0043	0.0044	0.0045	0.0047
−2.5	0.0048	0.0049	0.0051	0.0052	0.0054	0.0055	0.0057	0.0059	0.0060	0.0062
−2.4	0.0064	0.0066	0.0068	0.0069	0.0071	0.0073	0.0075	0.0078	0.0080	0.0082
−2.3	0.0084	0.0087	0.0089	0.0091	0.0094	0.0096	0.0099	0.0102	0.0104	0.0107
−2.2	0.0110	0.0113	0.0116	0.0119	0.0122	0.0125	0.0129	0.0132	0.0136	0.0139
−2.1	0.0143	0.0146	0.0150	0.0154	0.0158	0.0162	0.0166	0.0170	0.0174	0.0179
−2.0	0.0183	0.0188	0.0192	0.0197	0.0202	0.0207	0.0212	0.0217	0.0222	0.0228
−1.9	0.0233	0.0239	0.0244	0.0250	0.0256	0.0262	0.0268	0.0274	0.0281	0.0287
−1.8	0.0294	0.0301	0.0307	0.0314	0.0322	0.0329	0.0336	0.0344	0.0351	0.0359
−1.7	0.0367	0.0375	0.0384	0.0392	0.0401	0.0498	0.0418	0.0427	0.0436	0.0446
−1.6	0.0455	0.0465	0.0475	0.0485	0.0495	0.0505	0.0516	0.0526	0.0537	0.0548
−1.5	0.0559	0.0571	0.0582	0.0594	0.0606	0.0618	0.0630	0.0643	0.0655	0.0668
−1.4	0.0681	0.0694	0.0708	0.0721	0.0735	0.0749	0.0764	0.0778	0.0793	0.0808
−1.3	0.0823	0.0838	0.0853	0.0869	0.0885	0.0901	0.0918	0.0934	0.0951	0.0968
−1.2	0.0895	0.1003	0.1020	0.1038	0.1057	0.1075	0.1093	0.1112	0.1131	0.1151
−1.1	0.1170	0.1190	0.1210	0.1230	0.1251	0.1271	0.1292	0.1314	0.1335	0.1357
−1.0	0.1379	0.1401	0.1423	0.1446	0.1469	0.1492	0.1515	0.1539	0.1562	0.1587
−0.9	0.1611	0.1635	0.1660	0.1685	0.1711	0.1736	0.1762	0.1788	0.1814	0.1841
−0.8	0.1867	0.1894	0.1922	0.1949	0.1977	0.2005	0.2033	0.2061	0.2090	0.2119
−0.7	0.2148	0.2177	0.2207	0.2236	0.2266	0.2297	0.2327	0.2358	0.2389	0.2420
−0.6	0.2451	0.2483	0.2514	0.2546	0.2578	0.2611	0.2643	0.2676	0.2709	0.2743
−0.5	0.2776	0.2810	0.2843	0.2877	0.2912	0.2946	0.2981	0.3015	0.3050	0.3085
−0.4	0.3121	0.3156	0.3192	0.3228	0.3264	0.3300	0.3336	0.3372	0.3409	0.3446
−0.3	0.3483	0.3520	0.3557	0.3594	0.3632	0.3669	0.3707	0.3745	0.3783	0.3821
−0.2	0.3859	0.3897	0.3936	0.3974	0.4013	0.4052	0.4090	0.4129	0.4168	0.4207
−0.1	0.4247	0.4286	0.4325	0.4364	0.4404	0.4443	0.4483	0.4522	0.4562	0.4602
−0.0	0.4641	0.4681	0.4721	0.4761	0.4801	0.4840	0.4880	0.4920	0.4960	0.5000

[a] Proportion of total area under the curve that is under the portion of the curve from $-\infty$ to $(X_i - \mu)/\sigma$ (X_i represents any desired value of the variable X).

TABLE A (continued)

$\frac{X_i - \mu}{\sigma}$	0.00	0.01	0.02	0.03	0.04	0.05	0.06	0.07	0.08	0.09
+0.0	0.5000	0.5040	0.5080	0.5120	0.5160	0.5199	0.5239	0.5279	0.5319	0.5359
+0.1	0.5398	0.5438	0.5478	0.5517	0.5557	0.5596	0.5636	0.5675	0.5714	0.5753
+0.2	0.5793	0.5832	0.5871	0.5910	0.5948	0.5987	0.6026	0.6064	0.6103	0.6141
+0.3	0.6179	0.6217	0.6255	0.6293	0.6331	0.6368	0.6406	0.6443	0.6480	0.6517
+0.4	0.6554	0.6591	0.6628	0.6664	0.6700	0.6736	0.6772	0.6808	0.6844	0.6879
+0.5	0.6915	0.6950	0.6985	0.7019	0.7054	0.7088	0.7123	0.7157	0.7190	0.7224
+0.6	0.7257	0.7291	0.7324	0.7357	0.7389	0.7422	0.7454	0.7486	0.7517	0.7549
+0.7	0.7580	0.7611	0.7642	0.7673	0.7704	0.7734	0.7764	0.7794	0.7823	0.7852
+0.8	0.7881	0.7910	0.7939	0.7967	0.7995	0.8023	0.8051	0.8079	0.8106	0.8133
+0.9	0.8159	0.8186	0.8212	0.8238	0.8264	0.8289	0.8315	0.8340	0.8365	0.8389
+1.0	0.8413	0.8438	0.8461	0.8485	0.8508	0.8531	0.8554	0.8577	0.8599	0.8621
+1.1	0.8643	0.8665	0.8686	0.8708	0.8729	0.8749	0.8770	0.8790	0.8810	0.8830
+1.2	0.8849	0.8869	0.8888	0.8907	0.8925	0.8944	0.8962	0.8980	0.8997	0.9015
+1.3	0.9032	0.9049	0.9066	0.9082	0.9099	0.9115	0.9131	0.9147	0.9162	0.9177
+1.4	0.9192	0.9207	0.9222	0.9236	0.9251	0.9265	0.9279	0.9292	0.9306	0.9319
+1.5	0.9332	0.9345	0.9357	0.9370	0.9382	0.9394	0.9406	0.9418	0.9429	0.9441
+1.6	0.9452	0.9463	0.9474	0.9484	0.9495	0.9505	0.9515	0.9525	0.9535	0.9545
+1.7	0.9554	0.9564	0.9573	0.9582	0.9591	0.9599	0.9608	0.9616	0.9625	0.9633
+1.8	0.9641	0.9649	0.9656	0.9664	0.9671	0.9678	0.9686	0.9693	0.9699	0.9706
+1.9	0.9713	0.9719	0.9726	0.9732	0.9738	0.9744	0.9750	0.9756	0.9761	0.9767
+2.0	0.9773	0.9778	0.9783	0.9788	0.9793	0.9798	0.9803	0.9808	0.9812	0.9817
+2.1	0.9821	0.9826	0.9830	0.9834	0.9838	0.9842	0.9846	0.9850	0.9854	0.9857
+2.2	0.9861	0.9864	0.9868	0.9871	0.9875	0.9878	0.9881	0.9884	0.9887	0.9890
+2.3	0.9893	0.9896	0.9898	0.9901	0.9904	0.9906	0.9909	0.9911	0.9913	0.9916
+2.4	0.9918	0.9920	0.9922	0.9925	0.9927	0.9929	0.9931	0.9932	0.9934	0.9936
+2.5	0.9938	0.9940	0.9941	0.9943	0.9945	0.9946	0.9948	0.9949	0.9951	0.9952
+2.6	0.9953	0.9955	0.9956	0.9957	0.9959	0.9960	0.9961	0.9962	0.9963	0.9964
+2.7	0.9965	0.9966	0.9967	0.9968	0.9969	0.9970	0.9971	0.9972	0.9973	0.9974
+2.8	0.9974	0.9975	0.9976	0.9977	0.9977	0.9978	0.9979	0.9979	0.9980	0.9981
+2.9	0.9981	0.9982	0.9983	0.9983	0.9984	0.9984	0.9985	0.9985	0.9986	0.9986
+3.0	0.99865	0.99869	0.99874	0.99878	0.99882	0.99886	0.99889	0.99893	0.99896	0.99900
+3.1	0.99903	0.99906	0.99910	0.99913	0.99915	0.99918	0.99921	0.99924	0.99926	0.99929
+3.2	0.99931	0.99934	0.99936	0.99938	0.99940	0.99942	0.99944	0.99946	0.99948	0.99950
+3.3	0.99952	0.99953	0.99955	0.99957	0.99958	0.99960	0.99961	0.99962	0.99964	0.99965
+3.4	0.99966	0.99967	0.99969	0.99970	0.99971	0.99972	0.99973	0.99974	0.99975	0.99976
+3.5	0.99977	0.99978	0.99978	0.99979	0.99980	0.99981	0.99981	0.99982	0.99983	0.99983

TABLE B Factors for Computing Central Lines and 3σ Control Limits for $\bar{X}$, s, and R Charts

OBSERVATIONS IN SAMPLE, n	CHART FOR AVERAGES — FACTORS FOR CONTROL LIMITS			CHART FOR STANDARD DEVIATIONS — FACTOR FOR CENTRAL LINE	FACTORS FOR CONTROL LIMITS				CHART FOR RANGES — FACTOR FOR CENTRAL LINE	FACTORS FOR CONTROL LIMITS				
	A	A_2	A_3	c_4	B_3	B_4	B_5	B_6	d_2	d_3	D_1	D_2	D_3	D_4
2	2.121	1.880	2.659	0.7979	0	3.267	0	2.606	1.128	0.853	0	3.686	0	3.267
3	1.732	1.023	1.954	0.8862	0	2.568	0	2.276	1.693	0.888	0	4.358	0	2.574
4	1.500	0.729	1.628	0.9213	0	2.266	0	2.088	2.059	0.880	0	4.698	0	2.282
5	1.342	0.577	1.427	0.9400	0	2.089	0	1.964	2.326	0.864	0	4.918	0	2.114
6	1.225	0.483	1.287	0.9515	0.030	1.970	0.029	1.874	2.534	0.848	0	5.078	0	2.004
7	1.134	0.419	1.182	0.9594	0.118	1.882	0.113	1.806	2.704	0.833	0.204	5.204	0.076	1.924
8	1.061	0.373	1.099	0.9650	0.185	1.815	0.179	1.751	2.847	0.820	0.388	5.306	0.136	1.864
9	1.000	0.337	1.032	0.9693	0.239	1.761	0.232	1.707	2.970	0.808	0.547	5.393	0.184	1.816
10	0.949	0.308	0.975	0.9727	0.284	1.716	0.276	1.669	3.078	0.797	0.687	5.469	0.223	1.777
11	0.905	0.285	0.927	0.9754	0.321	1.679	0.313	1.637	3.173	0.787	0.811	5.535	0.256	1.744
12	0.866	0.266	0.886	0.9776	0.354	1.646	0.346	1.610	3.258	0.778	0.922	5.594	0.283	1.717
13	0.832	0.249	0.850	0.9794	0.382	1.618	0.374	1.585	3.336	0.770	1.025	5.647	0.307	1.693
14	0.802	0.235	0.817	0.9810	0.406	1.594	0.399	1.563	3.407	0.763	1.118	5.696	0.328	1.672
15	0.775	0.223	0.789	0.9823	0.428	1.572	0.421	1.544	3.472	0.756	1.203	5.741	0.347	1.653
16	0.750	0.212	0.763	0.9835	0.448	1.552	0.440	1.526	3.532	0.750	1.282	5.782	0.363	1.637
17	0.728	0.203	0.739	0.9845	0.466	1.534	0.458	1.511	3.588	0.744	1.356	5.820	0.378	1.622
18	0.707	0.194	0.718	0.9854	0.482	1.518	0.475	1.496	3.640	0.739	1.424	5.856	0.391	1.608
19	0.688	0.187	0.698	0.9862	0.497	1.503	0.490	1.483	3.689	0.734	1.487	5.891	0.403	1.597
20	0.671	0.180	0.680	0.9869	0.510	1.490	0.504	1.470	3.735	0.729	1.549	5.921	0.415	1.585

Copyright ASTM, 1916 Race Street, Philadelphia, PA, 19103. Reprinted with permission.

C = Non Conformaties

TABLE C   The Poisson Distribution $P(c) = (np_0^c/c!)e^{-np_0}$ (Cumulative Values Are in Parentheses)

c \ np_0	0.1		0.2		0.3		0.4		0.5	
0	0.905	(0.905)	0.819	(0.819)	0.741	(0.741)	0.670	(0.670)	0.607	(0.607)
1	0.091	(0.996)	0.164	(0.983)	0.222	(0.963)	0.268	(0.938)	0.303	(0.910)
2	0.004	(1.000)	0.016	(0.999)	0.033	(0.996)	0.054	(0.992)	0.076	(0.986)
3			0.010	(1.000)	0.004	(1.000)	0.007	(0.999)	0.013	(0.999)
4							0.001	(1.000)	0.001	(1.000)

c \ np_0	0.6		0.7		0.8		0.9		1.0	
0	0.549	(0.549)	0.497	(0.497)	0.449	(0.449)	0.406	(0.406)	0.368	(0.368)
1	0.329	(0.878)	0.349	(0.845)	0.359	(0.808)	0.366	(0.772)	0.368	(0.736)
2	0.099	(0.977)	0.122	(0.967)	0.144	(0.952)	0.166	(0.938)	0.184	(0.920)
3	0.020	(0.997)	0.028	(0.995)	0.039	(0.991)	0.049	(0.987)	0.061	(0.981)
4	0.003	(1.000)	0.005	(1.000)	0.008	(0.999)	0.011	(0.998)	0.016	(0.997)
5					0.001	(1.000)	0.002	(1.000)	0.003	(1.000)

c \ np_0	1.1		1.2		1.3		1.4		1.5	
0	0.333	(0.333)	0.301	(0.301)	0.273	(0.273)	0.247	(0.247)	0.223	(0.223)
1	0.366	(0.699)	0.361	(0.662)	0.354	(0.627)	0.345	(0.592)	0.335	(0.558)
2	0.201	(0.900)	0.217	(0.879)	0.230	(0.857)	0.242	(0.834)	0.251	(0.809)
3	0.074	(0.974)	0.087	(0.966)	0.100	(0.957)	0.113	(0.947)	0.126	(0.935)
4	0.021	(0.995)	0.026	(0.992)	0.032	(0.989)	0.039	(0.986)	0.047	(0.982)
5	0.004	(0.999)	0.007	(0.999)	0.009	(0.998)	0.011	(0.997)	0.014	(0.996)
6	0.001	(1.000)	0.001	(1.000)	0.002	(1.000)	0.003	(1.000)	0.004	(1.000)

c \ np_0	1.6		1.7		1.8		1.9		2.0	
0	0.202	(0.202)	0.183	(0.183)	0.165	(0.165)	0.150	(0.150)	0.135	(0.135)
1	0.323	(0.525)	0.311	(0.494)	0.298	(0.463)	0.284	(0.434)	0.271	(0.406)
2	0.258	(0.783)	0.264	(0.758)	0.268	(0.731)	0.270	(0.704)	0.271	(0.677)
3	0.138	(0.921)	0.149	(0.907)	0.161	(0.892)	0.171	(0.875)	0.180	(0.857)
4	0.055	(0.976)	0.064	(0.971)	0.072	(0.964)	0.081	(0.956)	0.090	(0.947)
5	0.018	(0.994)	0.022	(0.993)	0.026	(0.990)	0.031	(0.987)	0.036	(0.983)
6	0.005	(0.999)	0.006	(0.999)	0.008	(0.998)	0.010	(0.997)	0.012	(0.995)
7	0.001	(1.000)	0.001	(1.000)	0.002	(1.000)	0.003	(1.000)	0.004	(0.999)
8									0.001	(1.000)

TABLE C (*continued*)

c \ np_0	2.1		2.2		2.3		2.4		2.5	
0	0.123	(0.123)	0.111	(0.111)	0.100	(0.100)	0.091	(0.091)	0.082	(0.082)
1	0.257	(0.380)	0.244	(0.355)	0.231	(0.331)	0.218	(0.309)	0.205	(0.287)
2	0.270	(0.650)	0.268	(0.623)	0.265	(0.596)	0.261	(0.570)	0.256	(0.543)
3	0.189	(0.839)	0.197	(0.820)	0.203	(0.799)	0.209	(0.779)	0.214	(0.757)
4	0.099	(0.938)	0.108	(0.928)	0.117	(0.916)	0.125	(0.904)	0.134	(0.891)
5	0.042	(0.980)	0.048	(0.976)	0.054	(0.970)	0.060	(0.964)	0.067	(0.958)
6	0.015	(0.995)	0.017	(0.993)	0.021	(0.991)	0.024	(0.988)	0.028	(0.986)
7	0.004	(0.999)	0.005	(0.998)	0.007	(0.998)	0.008	(0.996)	0.010	(0.996)
8	0.001	(1.000)	0.002	(1.000)	0.002	(1.000)	0.003	(0.999)	0.003	(0.999)
9							0.001	(1.000)	0.001	(1.000)

c \ np_0	2.6		2.7		2.8		2.9		3.0	
0	0.074	(0.074)	0.067	(0.067)	0.061	(0.061)	0.055	(0.055)	0.050	(0.050)
1	0.193	(0.267)	0.182	(0.249)	0.170	(0.231)	0.160	(0.215)	0.149	(0.199)
2	0.251	(0.518)	0.245	(0.494)	0.238	(0.469)	0.231	(0.446)	0.224	(0.423)
3	0.218	(0.736)	0.221	(0.715)	0.223	(0.692)	0.224	(0.670)	0.224	(0.647)
4	0.141	(0.877)	0.149	(0.864)	0.156	(0.848)	0.162	(0.832)	0.168	(0.815)
5	0.074	(0.951)	0.080	(0.944)	0.087	(0.935)	0.094	(0.926)	0.101	(0.916)
6	0.032	(0.983)	0.036	(0.980)	0.041	(0.976)	0.045	(0.971)	0.050	(0.966)
7	0.012	(0.995)	0.014	(0.994)	0.016	(0.992)	0.019	(0.990)	0.022	(0.988)
8	0.004	(0.999)	0.005	(0.999)	0.006	(0.998)	0.007	(0.997)	0.008	(0.996)
9	0.001	(1.000)	0.001	(1.000)	0.002	(1.000)	0.002	(0.999)	0.003	(0.999)
10							0.001	(1.000)	0.001	(1.000)

c \ np_0	3.1		3.2		3.3		3.4		3.5	
0	0.045	(0.045)	0.041	(0.041)	0.037	(0.037)	0.033	(0.033)	0.030	(0.030)
1	0.140	(0.185)	0.130	(0.171)	0.122	(0.159)	0.113	(0.146)	0.106	(0.136)
2	0.216	(0.401)	0.209	(0.380)	0.201	(0.360)	0.193	(0.339)	0.185	(0.321)
3	0.224	(0.625)	0.223	(0.603)	0.222	(0.582)	0.219	(0.558)	0.216	(0.537)
4	0.173	(0.798)	0.178	(0.781)	0.182	(0.764)	0.186	(0.744)	0.189	(0.726)
5	0.107	(0.905)	0.114	(0.895)	0.120	(0.884)	0.126	(0.870)	0.132	(0.858)
6	0.056	(0.961)	0.061	(0.956)	0.066	(0.950)	0.071	(0.941)	0.077	(0.935)
7	0.025	(0.986)	0.028	(0.984)	0.031	(0.981)	0.035	(0.976)	0.038	(0.973)
8	0.010	(0.996)	0.011	(0.995)	0.012	(0.993)	0.015	(0.991)	0.017	(0.990)
9	0.003	(0.999)	0.004	(0.999)	0.005	(0.998)	0.006	(0.997)	0.007	(0.997)
10	0.001	(1.000)	0.001	(1.000)	0.002	(1.000)	0.002	(0.999)	0.002	(0.999)
11							0.001	(1.000)	0.001	(1.000)

TABLE C   (*continued*)

c	np_0 3.6		3.7		3.8		3.9		4.0	
0	0.027	(0.027)	0.025	(0.025)	0.022	(0.022)	0.020	(0.020)	0.018	(0.018)
1	0.098	(0.125)	0.091	(0.116)	0.085	(0.107)	0.079	(0.099)	0.073	(0.091)
2	0.177	(0.302)	0.169	(0.285)	0.161	(0.268)	0.154	(0.253)	0.147	(0.238)
3	0.213	(0.515)	0.209	(0.494)	0.205	(0.473)	0.200	(0.453)	0.195	(0.433)
4	0.191	(0.706)	0.193	(0.687)	0.194	(0.667)	0.195	(0.648)	0.195	(0.628)
5	0.138	(0.844)	0.143	(0.830)	0.148	(0.815)	0.152	(0.800)	0.157	(0.785)
6	0.083	(0.927)	0.088	(0.918)	0.094	(0.909)	0.099	(0.899)	0.104	(0.889)
7	0.042	(0.969)	0.047	(0.965)	0.051	(0.960)	0.055	(0.954)	0.060	(0.949)
8	0.019	(0.988)	0.022	(0.987)	0.024	(0.984)	0.027	(0.981)	0.030	(0.979)
9	0.008	(0.996)	0.009	(0.996)	0.010	(0.994)	0.012	(0.993)	0.013	(0.992)
10	0.003	(0.999)	0.003	(0.999)	0.004	(0.998)	0.004	(0.997)	0.005	(0.997)
11	0.001	(1.000)	0.001	(1.000)	0.001	(0.999)	0.002	(0.999)	0.002	(0.999)
12					0.001	(1.000)	0.001	(1.000)	0.001	(1.000)

c	np_0 4.1		4.2		4.3		4.4		4.5	
0	0.017	(0.017)	0.015	(0.015)	0.014	(0.014)	0.012	(0.012)	0.011	(0.011)
1	0.068	(0.085)	0.063	(0.078)	0.058	(0.072)	0.054	(0.066)	0.050	(0.061)
2	0.139	(0.224)	0.132	(0.210)	0.126	(0.198)	0.119	(0.185)	0.113	(0.174)
3	0.190	(0.414)	0.185	(0.395)	0.180	(0.378)	0.174	(0.359)	0.169	(0.343)
4	0.195	(0.609)	0.195	(0.590)	0.193	(0.571)	0.192	(0.551)	0.190	(0.533)
5	0.160	(0.769)	0.163	(0.753)	0.166	(0.737)	0.169	(0.720)	0.171	(0.704)
6	0.110	(0.879)	0.114	(0.867)	0.119	(0.856)	0.124	(0.844)	0.128	(0.832)
7	0.064	(0.943)	0.069	(0.936)	0.073	(0.929)	0.078	(0.922)	0.082	(0.914)
8	0.033	(0.976)	0.036	(0.972)	0.040	(0.969)	0.043	(0.965)	0.046	(0.960)
9	0.015	(0.991)	0.017	(0.989)	0.019	(0.988)	0.021	(0.986)	0.023	(0.983)
10	0.006	(0.997)	0.007	(0.996)	0.008	(0.996)	0.009	(0.995)	0.011	(0.994)
11	0.002	(0.999)	0.003	(0.999)	0.003	(0.999)	0.004	(0.999)	0.004	(0.998)
12	0.001	(1.000)	0.001	(1.000)	0.001	(1.000)	0.001	(1.000)	0.001	(0.999)
13									0.001	(1.000)

TABLE C   (*continued*)

c	np_0 4.6		4.7		4.8		4.9		5.0	
0	0.010	(0.010)	0.009	(0.009)	0.008	(0.008)	0.008	(0.008)	0.007	(0.007)
1	0.046	(0.056)	0.043	(0.052)	0.039	(0.047)	0.037	(0.045)	0.034	(0.041)
2	0.106	(0.162)	0.101	(0.153)	0.095	(0.142)	0.090	(0.135)	0.084	(0.125)
3	0.163	(0.325)	0.157	(0.310)	0.152	(0.294)	0.146	(0.281)	0.140	(0.265)
4	0.188	(0.513)	0.185	(0.495)	0.182	(0.476)	0.179	(0.460)	0.176	(0.441)
5	0.172	(0.685)	0.174	(0.669)	0.175	(0.651)	0.175	(0.635)	0.176	(0.617)
6	0.132	(0.817)	0.136	(0.805)	0.140	(0.791)	0.143	(0.778)	0.146	(0.763)
7	0.087	(0.904)	0.091	(0.896)	0.096	(0.887)	0.100	(0.878)	0.105	(0.868)
8	0.050	(0.954)	0.054	(0.950)	0.058	(0.945)	0.061	(0.939)	0.065	(0.933)
9	0.026	(0.980)	0.028	(0.978)	0.031	(0.976)	0.034	(0.973)	0.036	(0.969)
10	0.012	(0.992)	0.013	(0.991)	0.015	(0.991)	0.016	(0.989)	0.018	(0.987)
11	0.005	(0.997)	0.006	(0.997)	0.006	(0.997)	0.007	(0.996)	0.008	(0.995)
12	0.002	(0.999)	0.002	(0.999)	0.002	(0.999)	0.003	(0.999)	0.003	(0.998)
13	0.001	(1.000)	0.001	(1.000)	0.001	(1.000)	0.001	(1.000)	0.001	(0.999)
14									0.001	(1.000)

c	np_0 6.0		7.0		8.0		9.0		10.0	
0	0.002	(0.002)	0.001	(0.001)	0.000	(0.000)	0.000	(0.000)	0.000	(0.000)
1	0.015	(0.017)	0.006	(0.007)	0.003	(0.003)	0.001	(0.001)	0.000	(0.000)
2	0.045	(0.062)	0.022	(0.029)	0.011	(0.014)	0.005	(0.006)	0.002	(0.002)
3	0.089	(0.151)	0.052	(0.081)	0.029	(0.043)	0.015	(0.021)	0.007	(0.009)
4	0.134	(0.285)	0.091	(0.172)	0.057	(0.100)	0.034	(0.055)	0.019	(0.028)
5	0.161	(0.446)	0.128	(0.300)	0.092	(0.192)	0.061	(0.116)	0.038	(0.066)
6	0.161	(0.607)	0.149	(0.449)	0.122	(0.314)	0.091	(0.091)	0.063	(0.129)
7	0.138	(0.745)	0.149	(0.598)	0.140	(0.454)	0.117	(0.324)	0.090	(0.219)
8	0.103	(0.848)	0.131	(0.729)	0.140	(0.594)	0.132	(0.456)	0.113	(0.332)
9	0.069	(0.917)	0.102	(0.831)	0.124	(0.718)	0.132	(0.588)	0.125	(0.457)
10	0.041	(0.958)	0.071	(0.902)	0.099	(0.817)	0.119	(0.707)	0.125	(0.582)
11	0.023	(0.981)	0.045	(0.947)	0.072	(0.889)	0.097	(0.804)	0.114	(0.696)
12	0.011	(0.992)	0.026	(0.973)	0.048	(0.937)	0.073	(0.877)	0.095	(0.791)
13	0.005	(0.997)	0.014	(0.987)	0.030	(0.967)	0.050	(0.927)	0.073	(0.864)
14	0.002	(0.999)	0.007	(0.994)	0.017	(0.984)	0.032	(0.959)	0.052	(0.916)
15	0.001	(1.000)	0.003	(0.997)	0.009	(0.993)	0.019	(0.978)	0.035	(0.951)
16			0.002	(0.999)	0.004	(0.997)	0.011	(0.989)	0.022	(0.973)
17			0.001	(1.000)	0.002	(0.999)	0.006	(0.995)	0.013	(0.986)
18					0.001	(1.000)	0.003	(0.998)	0.007	(0.993)
19							0.001	(0.999)	0.004	(0.997)
20							0.001	(1.000)	0.002	(0.999)
21									0.001	(1.000)

TABLE C   (continued)

c	np₀ 11.0		12.0		13.0		14.0		15.0	
0	0.000	(0.000)	0.000	(0.000)	0.000	(0.000)	0.000	(0.000)	0.000	(0.000)
1	0.000	(0.000)	0.000	(0.000)	0.000	(0.000)	0.000	(0.000)	0.000	(0.000)
2	0.001	(0.001)	0.000	(0.000)	0.000	(0.000)	0.000	(0.000)	0.000	(0.000)
3	0.004	(0.005)	0.002	(0.002)	0.001	(0.001)	0.000	(0.000)	0.000	(0.000)
4	0.010	(0.015)	0.005	(0.007)	0.003	(0.004)	0.001	(0.001)	0.001	(0.001)
5	0.022	(0.037)	0.013	(0.020)	0.007	(0.011)	0.004	(0.005)	0.002	(0.003)
6	0.041	(0.078)	0.025	(0.045)	0.015	(0.026)	0.009	(0.014)	0.005	(0.008)
7	0.065	(0.143)	0.044	(0.089)	0.028	(0.054)	0.017	(0.031)	0.010	(0.018)
8	0.089	(0.232)	0.066	(0.155)	0.046	(0.100)	0.031	(0.062)	0.019	(0.037)
9	0.109	(0.341)	0.087	(0.242)	0.066	(0.166)	0.047	(0.109)	0.032	(0.069)
10	0.119	(0.460)	0.105	(0.347)	0.086	(0.252)	0.066	(0.175)	0.049	(0.118)
11	0.119	(0.579)	0.114	(0.461)	0.101	(0.353)	0.084	(0.259)	0.066	(0.184)
12	0.109	(0.688)	0.114	(0.575)	0.110	(0.463)	0.099	(0.358)	0.083	(0.267)
13	0.093	(0.781)	0.106	(0.681)	0.110	(0.573)	0.106	(0.464)	0.096	(0.363)
14	0.073	(0.854)	0.091	(0.772)	0.102	(0.675)	0.106	(0.570)	0.102	(0.465)
15	0.053	(0.907)	0.072	(0.844)	0.088	(0.763)	0.099	(0.669)	0.102	(0.567)
16	0.037	(0.944)	0.054	(0.898)	0.072	(0.835)	0.087	(0.756)	0.096	(0.663)
17	0.024	(0.968)	0.038	(0.936)	0.055	(0.890)	0.071	(0.827)	0.085	(0.748)
18	0.015	(0.983)	0.026	(0.962)	0.040	(0.930)	0.056	(0.883)	0.071	(0.819)
19	0.008	(0.991)	0.016	(0.978)	0.027	(0.957)	0.041	(0.924)	0.056	(0.875)
20	0.005	(0.996)	0.010	(0.988)	0.018	(0.975)	0.029	(0.953)	0.042	(0.917)
21	0.002	(0.998)	0.006	(0.994)	0.011	(0.986)	0.019	(0.972)	0.030	(0.947)
22	0.001	(0.999)	0.003	(0.997)	0.006	(0.992)	0.012	(0.984)	0.020	(0.967)
23	0.001	(1.000)	0.002	(0.999)	0.004	(0.996)	0.007	(0.991)	0.013	(0.980)
24			0.001	(1.000)	0.002	(0.998)	0.004	(0.995)	0.008	(0.988)
25					0.001	(0.999)	0.003	(0.998)	0.005	(0.993)
26					0.001	(1.000)	0.001	(0.999)	0.003	(0.996)
27							0.001	(1.000)	0.002	(0.998)
28									0.001	(0.999)
29									0.001	(1.000)

TABLE D Random Numbers

63271	59986	71744	51102	15141	80714	58683	93108
88547	09896	95436	79115	08303	01041	20030	63754
55957	57243	83865	09911	19761	66535	40102	26646
46276	87453	44790	67122	45573	84358	21625	16999
55363	07449	34835	15290	76616	67191	12777	21861
69393	92785	49902	58447	42048	30378	87618	26933
13186	29431	88190	04588	38733	81290	89541	70290
17726	28652	56836	78351	47327	18518	92222	55201
36520	64465	05550	30157	82242	29520	69753	72602
81628	36100	39254	56835	37636	02421	98063	89641
84649	48968	75215	75498	49539	74240	03466	49292
63291	11618	12613	75055	43915	26488	41116	64531
70502	53225	03655	05915	37140	57051	48393	91322
06426	24771	59935	49801	11081	66762	94477	02494
20711	55609	29430	70165	45406	78484	31699	52009
41990	70538	77191	25860	55204	73417	83920	69468
72452	36618	76298	26678	89334	33938	95567	29380
37042	40318	57099	10528	09925	89773	41335	96244
53766	52875	15987	46962	67342	77592	57651	95508
90585	58955	53122	16025	84299	53310	67380	84249
32001	96293	37203	64516	51530	37069	40261	61374
62606	64324	46354	72157	67248	20135	49804	09226
10078	28073	85389	50324	14500	15562	64165	06125
91561	46145	24177	15294	10061	98124	75732	08815
13091	98112	53959	79607	52244	63303	10413	63839
73864	83014	72457	22682	03033	61714	88173	90835
66668	25467	48894	51043	02365	91726	09365	63167
84745	41042	29493	01836	09044	51926	43630	63470
48068	26805	94595	47907	13357	38412	33318	26098
54310	96175	97594	88616	42035	38093	36745	56702
14877	33095	10924	58013	61439	21882	42059	24177
78295	23179	02771	43464	59061	71411	05697	67194
67524	02865	39593	54278	04237	92441	26602	63835
58268	57219	68124	73455	83236	08710	04284	55005
97158	28672	50685	01181	24262	19427	52106	34308
04230	16831	69085	30802	65559	09205	71829	06489
94879	56606	30401	02602	57658	70091	54986	41394
71446	15232	66715	26385	91518	70566	02888	79941
32886	05644	79316	09819	00813	88407	17461	73925
62048	33711	25290	21526	02223	75947	66466	06232

TABLE E   Commonly Used Conversion Factors

QUANTITY	CONVERSION	MULTIPLY BY	
Length	in. to m	2.54[a]	E−02
Area	in.^{2} to m^2	6.451 600	E−04
Volume	in.^{3} to m^3	1.638 706	E−05
	U.S. gallon to m^3	3.785 412	E−03
Mass	oz (avoir) to kg	2.834 952	E−02
Acceleration	ft/s^2 to m/s^2	3.048[a]	E−01
Force	poundal to N	1.382 550	E−01
Pressure, stress	poundal/ft^2 to Pa	1.488 164	E+00
	lb$_f$/in^2 to Pa	6.894 757	E+03
Energy, work	ft · lb$_f$ to J	1.355 818	E+00
Power	hp (550 ft · lb$_f$/s) to W	7.456 999	E+02

[a] Relationship is exact and needs no additional decimal points.

SELECTED BIBLIOGRAPHY

ASQC QUALITY COST COMMITTEE, *Guide for Reducing Quality Costs, 2d ed.*, Milwaukee, Wis.: American Society for Quality Control, Inc., 1987.

ASQC QUALITY COST COMMITTEE, *Principles of Quality Costs*, Milwaukee, Wis.: American Society for Quality Control, Inc., 1986.

ASQC STATISTICS DIVISION, *Glossary and Tables for Statistical Quality Control.* Milwaukee, Wis.: American Society for Quality Control, Inc., 1983.

CROSBY, PHILLIP B., *Quality Is Free.* New York: McGraw-Hill Book Company, 1979.

CROSBY, PHILLIP B., *Quality Without Tears.* New York: McGraw-Hill Book Company, 1984.

DEMING, W. EDWARDS, *Quality, Productivity, and Competitive Position.* Cambridge, Mass.: Massachusetts Institute of Technology, 1982.

DUNCAN, ACHESON J., *Quality Control and Industrial Statistics, 5th ed.*, Homewood, Ill.: Irwin, Inc., 1986.

GITLOW, H. S., AND S. J. GITLOW, *The Deming Guide to Quality and Competitive Position.* Englewood Cliffs, N.J.: Prentice Hall, Inc., 1987.

HENLEY, ERNEST J., AND HIROMITSU KUMAMOTO, *Reliability Engineering and Risk Assessment.* Englewood Cliffs, N.J.: Prentice Hall, Inc., 1981.

ISHIKAWA, K., *What is Total Quality Control?* Englewood Cliffs, N.J.: Prentice Hall, Inc., 1985.

JURAN, JOSEPH M. (ED.), *Quality Control Handbook*, 4th ed. New York: McGraw-Hill Book Company, 1988.

JURAN, JOSEPH M., AND FRANK M. GRYNA, JR., *Quality Planning and Analysis*, 2d ed. New York: McGraw-Hill Book Company, 1980.

SHAPIRO, SAMUEL S., The ASQC Basic References in Quality Control: Statistical Techniques, Edward J. Dudewicz, PhD., Editor, *Volume 3: How to Test Normality and Other Distributional Assumptions*. Milwaukee, Wis.: American Society for Quality Control, Inc., 1980.

TAGUCHI, G., *Introduction to Quality Engineering*. Tokyo: Asian Productivity Organization, 1986.

ANSWERS TO SELECTED PROBLEMS

Chapter 2

1. 0.86, 0.63, 0.15, 0.48

3. 66.4, 379.1, 5, 4.652, 6.2×10^2

5. Frequencies starting at 5.94 are 1, 2, 4, 8, 16, 24, 20, 17, 13, 3, 1, 1

9. (a) Relative frequencies starting at 5.94 (in %) are 0.9, 1.8, 3.6, 7.3, 14.5, 21.8, 18.2, 15.4, 11.8, 2.7, 0.9, 0.9

    (b) Cumulative frequencies starting at 5.945 are 1, 3, 7, 15, 31, 55, 75, 92, 105, 108, 109, 110

    (c) Relative cumulative frequencies starting at 5.945 (in %) are 0.9, 2.7, 6.4, 13.6, 28.2, 50.0, 68.2, 83.6, 95.4, 98.2, 99.1, 100.0

15. 116

17. 95

19. 3264

21. (a) 15; (b) 35.5

23. (a) 55, (b) none, (c) 14, 17

25. (a) 11; (b) 6; (c) 14; (d) 0.11

27. 0.004

29. 19.9

33. (b) Frequencies beginning at 0.55 are 1, 17, 29, 39, 42, 54, 74, 86, 100, 106, 110

37. (b) Relative frequencies beginning at 0.5 (in %) are 0.9, 14.5, 10.9, 9.1, 2.7, 10.9, 18.2, 10.9, 12.7, 5.4, 3.6

   (d) Cumulative relative frequencies beginning at 0.55 (in %) are 0.9, 15.4, 26.4, 35.4, 38.2, 49.1, 67.3, 78.2, 90.9, 96.4, 100.0

39. (b) -0.14, 3.11

41. Process is not capable—5 out of 65 above specification and 6 out of 65 below specification.

43. 0.0274, 0.0102, 0.9914

45. 0.606

47. (b) Normal

   (d) Not normal, but symmetrical

Chapter 3

1. $\bar{X}_0 = 20.40$; CLs = 20.56, 20.24; $R_0 = 0.34$; CLs = 0.68, 0

3. $\bar{X}_0 = 20.40$; CLs = 20.76, 20.04; $R_0 = 0.36$; CLs = 0.92, 0

5. $\bar{X}_0 = 2.08$; CLs = 2.42, 1.74; $R_0 = 0.47$; CLs = 1.08, 0

7. $\bar{X}_0 = 20.4$; CLs = 20.65, 20.15; $R_0 = 0.34$; CLs = 0.78, 0; Limits are wider

9. $\bar{X}_0 = 81.9$; CLs = 82.8, 81.0; $s_0 = 0.7$; CLs = 1.4, 0.0

13. 0.47% scrap, 2.27% rework, $\bar{X}_0 = 305.32$ mm, 6.43% rework

15. 0.27

17. $6\sigma = 160$

19. $6\sigma = 0.80$; 1.38

21. 0.82, change specifications or reduce σ

23. $C_{pk} = 0.82$; 0.41; 0; -0.41

25. $\bar{\bar{X}} = 4.58$; CLs = 4.78, 4.37; $\bar{R} = 0.20$; CLs = 0.52, 0

27. $Md_{Md} = 6.3$; CLs = 7.9, 4.7; $R_{Md} = 1.25$; CLs = 3.4, 0

29. CLs = 8.47, 6.71; CLs = 1.23, 0

31. $\bar{X}_0 = 25.0$; assume that $n = 4$, CLs = 25.15, 24.85

33. Histogram is symmetrical, while run chart slopes downward.

Chapter 4

1. 1.000, 0

3. 0.833

5. 0.50, 0.81

9. 0.57

11. 0.018

13. 0.989

15. 260

17. 3.13×10^{15}

19. 161,700

21. 25, 827, 165

23. 6.6×10^{15}

25. $C_r^n = C_{n-r}^n$

27. If $n = r$, then $C = 1$

29. 0.254, 0.510, 0.218, 0.18, P(4) is impossible

31. 0.087, 0.997

33. 0.0317

35. 0.246

37. Binomial $-$ 0.086; Poisson $=$ 0.076

39. 0.525

41. Binomial $-$ 0.384; Poisson $-$ 0.329; Poisson is poor estimator.

43. 0.084

Chapter 5

1. $p_0 = 0.0154$; CLs $= 0.0367, 0$

3. UCL $= .060$; LCL $= 0$

5. $p_0 = 0.0262$; CLs $= 0.0376, 0.0148$

7. $p_0 = 0.132$

9. $p_0 = 0.080$; CLs (1000) $= 0.106, 0.054$; CLs (1500) $= 0.101, 0.059$; CLs (2000) $= 0.098, 0.062$

11. $np_0 = 4.6$; CLs $= 11, 0$

13. $np_0 = 2.1$; CLs $= 6, 0$

15. $P_0 = .024$; CLs $= .047, .001$

19. $c_0 = 13.24$; CLs $= 24, 2$

21. CLs $= 0.255, 0.197$; Process is not stable

23. $\mu_0 = 0.38$; CLs $= 0.56, 0.20$

25. $D_0 = 8.6$; CLs $= 11.02, 6.18$; $D = 5.9$, out of control, exceptional good quality

Chapter 6

1. (p, P_a) pairs are (0.01, 0.972), (0.02, 0.819), (0.04, 0.359), (0.05, 0.208), (0.06, 0.110), (0.08, 0.025)

3. $(P_a)_I = P$ (2 or less)
$(P_a)_{II} = P(3)_I P$ (3 or less)$_{II}$ + $P(4)_I P$ (2 or less)$_{II}$ + $P(5)_I P$ (1 or less)$_{II}$
$(P_a)_{both} = (P_a)_I + (P_a)_{II}$

5. $(100p, AOQ)$ pairs are (1, 0.972), (2, 0.638), (4, 1.436), (5, 1.040), (6, 0.660), (8, 0.200); AOQL $\cong 1.7\%$

7. AQL $= 0.025\%$; AOQL $= 0.19\%$

9. (p, ASN) pairs are (0, 125), (0.01, 140), (0.02, 169), (0.03, 174), (0.04, 165), (0.05, 150), (0.06, 139)

11. (p, ATI) pairs are (0, 80), (0.00125, 120), (0.01, 311), (0.02, 415), (0.03, 462), (0.04, 483)

13. ($100p$, AOQ) pairs are (0.5, 0.493), (1.0, 0.848), (1.5, 0.885), (2.0, 0.694), (2.5, 0.430)

15. 3, 91; 6, 219; 12, 513

17. 2, 82; 6, 162; 14, 310

19. 1, 8; 3, 41; 5, 89

21. 3, 195

23. 4, 266

25. 5, 175

27. 0.69

29. (a) Ac but N in future
    (b) Re and N in future
    (c) Ac and R continues

33. (a) $n = 70$; $Ac = 0$, $Re = 1$
    (b) $n = 50$; (#, 2), (#, 2), (0, 2), (0, 3), (1, 3), (1, 3), (2, 3)

35. T, T

37. No

Chapter 7

1. 28, 0, 62, 4, LQL = 10.0%

3. 190, 0, AOQL = 0.13%

5. $n_1 = 280$, $c_1 = 0$, $n_2 = 590$, $c_2 = 4$, AOQL = 0.30%

7. $n = 190$, $c = 0$, AOQL = 0.13%

9. 0.923

11. $d_a = -1.91 + 0.080n$; $d_r = 2.48 + 0.080n$

13. 36, 59, 76

15. Start in State 1 ($f = 1/3$); Lot 11 go to State 2; Lot 19 go to State 3; Lot 23 back to State 2

17. $f = 1/4$; $f = 1/3$

19. 194, 420, 762

21. $i = 116$, 1/30, 1/60

23. $i = 192$, D

25. 6.88 cell units, -6.52 cell units, Type 1

27. I, 25

29. 10.76% > 9.80%, Re lot

31. $Q_u = 1.91$, Ac lot

33. Re lot

Chapter 8

1. 0.78

3. 0.06 difference

5. 0.019

7. (θ, P_a) pairs are (2000, 0.993), (1000, 0.909), (800, 0.832), (600, 0.642), (400, 0.301), (200, 0.009)

9. 80, 20, 160

11. 39, 8, 300

13. 12, 2, 94

Chapter 9

1. Cumulative %–46.1, 61.7, 88.3, 91.6, 100.0

3. Cumulative %–49.0, 73.5, 88.2, 93.1, 96.1, 98.0, 100.00

5. Graph shows total. Quality costs decreasing with time which is most likely due to the increase in prevention costs

7. Cost/Net Sales Index indicate that costs are a fairly constant % of net sales

9. Appraisal cost index is decreasing

Chapter 12

1. Cumulative %–30.1, 49.1, 66.5, 79.2, 88.0, 91.5, 94.5, 100.0

3. Cumulative %–30.1, 58.2, 66.3, 69.9, 73.2, 76.4, 100.0

5. Cumulative %–30.9, 54.0, 66.1, 77.4, 84.8, 91.5, 97.3, 100.0

7. Analyze loom 28 to discover why it does so well in most categories. Analyze loom 15 to discover why it performs poorly in all categories but warp tension

9. Overall nonconformities are decreasing

13. PC = 31.5, 32.5

15. 73.5%

INDEX

description of, 44–46
  relationship to mean and standard deviation,
    46–47
Normality tests:
  chi-square, 54
  histogram, 51–52
  kurtosis, 52
  probability plots, 52, 54
  skewness, 52
Normal probability distributions, 149–50

O

Operating characteristic curve (OC curve):
  consumer-producer relationship, 218–21
  double sampling plans, 210–13
  multiple sampling plans, 213
  properties of, 215–18
  for reliability, 318–20
  single sampling plans, 208–10
Optimum quality cost concept, 341, 343

P

Packing and shipping department, quality
  control, 9–10
Pareto analysis, 341, 342, 370, 376
Pareto diagram, 377–80
p chart, 159–72
Permutations, 138
Piece-to-piece variation, 66
Platykurtic curve, 28
Poisson probability distributions, 146–48
Polygon, frequency polygon, 27
Population, 42–43
Precontrol, 390–95
Probability:
  counting of events, 137–40
  definition of, 129–31
  theorems of, 131–37
Probability distributions:
  binomial, 142–46, 151
  hypergeometric, 140–41, 151, 153
  normal, 149–50
  poisson, 146–48
Probability plots, 52, 54
Problem-solving method, quality improvement,
  412–14
Process capability, 390
  control charts, 177–78
  procedure, 105–109
  tolerance and, 101–105
Product liability:
  history of, 352–53
  legal aspects, 353–59
  prevention of, 359–65
Product service department, quality control
  and, 10
Purchasing department, quality control, 6–7

Q

Quality:
  definition of, 1, 408
  management commitment to, 406–408
  measurement of, 408–409
  and productivity, 406
Quality assurance, quality control and, 10
Quality control:
  activities of, 2
  departments responsible for, 4–10
  historical view, 2–3
  statistical quality control, 2
Quality costs:
  appraisal costs, 332–33
  collection system, 335–37
  external failure costs, 334–35
  failure costs, 333–34, 346
  optimum quality cost concept, 341, 343
  Pareto analysis, 341, 342
  preventive costs, 331–32
  quality improvement strategies, 343–46
  team approach, 344
  trend analysis, 337–40
  use by management, 330
Quality improvement:
  annual program for, 411
  cause-and-effect diagram, 383–86
  check sheets, 387
  control charts, 389
  Deming's 14 points, 416–17
  design by experiments, 398
  flowcharts, 398, 399
  Grier diagram, 381–82
  histogram, 387
  matrix analysis, 380
  Pareto diagram, 377–80
  precontrol, 390–95
  problem-solving method, 412–14
  process capability, 390
  run charts, 398
  scatter diagram, 395–96
  team approach, 412
  time series, 383
Quality rating system, control charts, 188–89

R

Range, 36–37
Reject limits, charts with, 117–18
Relative frequency distribution, 18
Reliability:
  achieving reliability, aspects of, 312–15
  definition of, 311–12
  Handbook H108, 321–25
  life testing and reliability plans, 320–27
  statistical aspects, 315–20
Reliability curves, 315
  failure-rate curve, 315, 317
  life-history curve, 317–18